Pulp Fiction to Film Noir

ALSO BY WILLIAM HARE
AND FROM MCFARLAND

*L.A. Noir: Nine Dark Visions of the
City of Angels* (2004; paperback 2008)

Hitchcock and the Methods of Suspense (2007)

*Early Film Noir:
Greed, Lust and Murder Hollywood Style* (2003)

Pulp Fiction to Film Noir

The Great Depression and the Development of a Genre

WILLIAM HARE

McFarland & Company, Inc., Publishers
Jefferson, North Carolina, and London

LIBRARY OF CONGRESS CATALOGUING-IN-PUBLICATION DATA

Hare, William.
Pulp fiction to film noir : the Great Depression and
the development of a genre / William Hare.
p.   cm.

Includes bibliographical references and index.

ISBN 978-0-7864-6682-5
softcover : acid free paper ∞

1. Film noir — United States — History and criticism.
2. Noir fiction, American — History and criticism.
3. Detective and mystery stories — Film adaptations.
4. Film adaptations — History and criticism.   I. Title.
PN1995.9.F54H396 2012   791.43'6556 — dc23   2012022243

BRITISH LIBRARY CATALOGUING DATA ARE AVAILABLE

© 2012 William Hare. All rights reserved

*No part of this book may be reproduced or transmitted in any form
or by any means, electronic or mechanical, including photocopying
or recording, or by any information storage and retrieval system,
without permission in writing from the publisher.*

Front cover image: Humphrey Bogart as Sam Spade in
The Maltese Falcon, 1941 (Photofest);
cover design by David K. Landis (Shake It Loose Graphics)

Manufactured in the United States of America

*McFarland & Company, Inc., Publishers
Box 611, Jefferson, North Carolina 28640
www.mcfarlandpub.com*

Table of Contents

Acknowledgments — vii
Introduction — 1

One. Film Noir and the Great Depression — 5
Two. The Hammett Touch and a Huston Launching — 20
Three. Raymond Chandler and His Symphony of the Streets — 37
Four. Captain Joseph Shaw and the Flowering of Film Noir — 48
Five. Horace McCoy's Dance Marathon — 57
Six. Chandler's Blueprint for Mystery and His Career in Hollywood — 78
Seven. The Outsider and Film Noir — 103
Eight. Bogart's Dark Passage and Moorehead's Blockbuster Performance — 116
Nine. Berlin and Vienna, Film Noir Influences — 133
Ten. Siodmak's Phantom Femmes — 149
Eleven. Billy Wilder and Alcoholism Noir — 167
Twelve. Preminger's Noir Touch with *Fallen Angel* and Alice Faye — 180

Chapter Notes — 199
Bibliography — 202
Index — 205

Acknowledgments

I am indebted to the many film professionals who provided immeasurable assistance to me in the writing of this book. It is an impressive list of achievers who have displayed great knowledge and experience in the cinema field, combining thoroughness with love of the subject.

Lifelong San Franciscan Eddie Muller is a leading figure as a cinema historian with a decided penchant for film noir. His achievements prompted hard-hitting noir novelist James Ellroy to call Eddie "the czar of noir." He has furthered the cause of film noir as art by showcasing scores of works, including many that were sadly and unfairly neglected, not only in his hometown, where the genre holds high popularity standing, but in other leading U.S. cities as well. While residing in Seattle I saw many of the films that Eddie introduced with absorbing preludes at Seattle International Film Festival Theatre presentations.

In this work Muller provides important commentary in the link between the creation of film noir and the Great Depression. He believes that all too frequently, based on the awesome French presences of Albert Camus and Jean Paul Sartre, that the recognition and support of the Parisian intellectual community following World War II has resulted in an unfortunate de-emphasis in film historical circles on the importance of the Depression as a major force shaping the creation and development of film noir.

George McGhee contributed considerable knowledge and insight into the discussion of film noir through his assistance within this text. His friendship with leading lady Alice Faye gave him valuable insight which he shared in the making of the blonde star's role as Twentieth-Century–Fox's leading box-office performer. McGhee also provides valuable insight in a foreword in which he traces the roots of his own interest in film noir.

McGhee spent a significant portion of his professional life evaluating and selecting films for two important British television networks, BBC and Carlton. His expansive knowledge is now on display as a regular lecturer on the luxury cruise circuit with Cunard Lines.

I became initially acquainted with Steve Eifert when a mutual friend launched an Internet association with him. We shared a mutual interest in film noir. Steve operates the Back Alley Noir site, for which I began writing regularly. I was grateful to have Steve provide his views of film noir and how he became interested in the genre for my work. Meanwhile, he introduced me through the online circuit to a professional colleague at Ascent Media, where both work.

Eifert's colleague was Chris Shaw. His grandfather was one of the patriarchs of the film noir movement. This status occurred without Joseph Shaw becoming professionally associated with the film field. As publisher and editor of the hugely successful *Black Mask* detective magazine, it was Shaw who assisted his writers Dashiell Hammett and Raymond

Chandler to develop a new American detective story model. This model was exemplified in their *Black Mask* stories, in which their lead detectives (Sam Spade and Philip Marlowe, respectively) became legendary.

Hollywood reaped benefits from Hammett's novel *The Maltese Falcon*, featuring Sam Spade, and Chandler's *The Big Sleep* with Philip Marlowe. When the right actor was cast to play each author's favorite detective in the filmed versions of the above bestselling novels, Humphrey Bogart was en route to cinema immortality and film noir was born.

Since so little is known about the man who labored mightily behind the scenes to assist Hammett and Chandler to achieve worldwide status, it was absorbing to learn about him from his grandson Chris, who also reveals the impact that Joseph Shaw had on his family both inside and outside the artistic realm.

A knowledgeable and talented member of the community of film historians who also provided valuable assistance in this undertaking was Charles Tranberg. Tranberg's talents have been focused in the biography field. In addition to writing a well-received biography of Fred MacMurray (who won his film noir spurs starring opposite Barbara Stanwyck in the classic *Double Indemnity*), Tranberg also wrote one on the highly versatile character performer Agnes Moorehead.

Moorehead's most fascinating psychological film role could well have been her appearance as a most unique femme fatale in the Bogart-Bacall noir gem *Dark Passage*. What gave this role its stamp of uniqueness was that the traditional femme fatale role was turned on its head. Tranberg delivers trenchant commentary of Moorehead as a performer along with insights into her role in *Dark Passage*. Femmes fatales are traditionally women of such strong sexual appeal that they draw men into their web, sometimes to the point where the men are willing to kill for them. Tranberg presents the image of Moorehead in *Dark Passage* as the antidote to the appealing Lauren Bacall, in that she is overbearing, domineering, and thoroughly ruthless.

George Ulrich has (since 1999) operated the website alicefaye.com. It is devoted to perpetuating the memory of the glamorous blonde star who, during the thirties and forties, emerged as Twentieth-Century–Fox's most popular performer. Seattle native Ulrich graciously provided insight into the ingredients that resulted in making Alice Faye one of the most popularly acclaimed cinema performers of her era, both in the United States and globally.

Arthur Nicholson is owed a special measure of gratitude in that, during the final phase of his life, he combined pen and paper to write his thoughts about Alice Faye and her one journey into the realm of film noir in *Fallen Angel*, which was an excruciatingly painful process.

Nicholson, who was born, raised, and resided during his entire life in Hartlepool in Northeast England, in his final days wished to set the record straight regarding the controversies involving the filming of *Fallen Angel*. Shortly after completing that effort, Arthur, who for years was president of the organization he founded — the England-based Alice Faye Appreciation Society — died September 29, 2011. I was fortunate enough to have had one last conversation with Arthur by telephone less than a month before his death.

Robert Kendall, who for many years was my agent and frequent writing partner as well as a longstanding friend, died at his Seattle home on November 12, 2009. His attitude was philosophical as he told me shortly before his death that his life was without regrets and he had been blessed with many opportunities.

Those who knew him were aware that the largest part of him was his heart. Robert

Kendall possessed a generosity of spirit that made him an enduring figure to those privileged to know him. He possessed an indomitable will, refusing to give in to forces of despair or defeat.

Kendall came to Los Angeles initially after winning a talent contest called "Hollywood at Your Door" in Battle Creek, Michigan, the town where he spent most of his formative years. First prize was supposed to be a screen test, but when he arrived in Hollywood and visited the office of the contest sponsor he was told that the company was broke. In fact, the man he spoke with asked Kendall for a "loan."

When he returned to the Hollywood YMCA, where he had rented a room, his news worsened even more. Bob discovered that his suitcase had been stolen.

Given such tragic circumstances, some young Hollywood arrivals would have immediately returned home. Instead, the young man known to friends as "Robert the Resolute" considered the earlier setbacks learning experiences and went immediately to work. He found a room to rent in a lovely Hollywood hills home near Falcon Lair, the mansion once owned by Rudolph Valentino. Bob also got a job at a popular Hollywood drive-in frequented by the movie crowd.

One month later, Bob served a hamburger and coffee to prominent movie agent Christian Hofel. Hofel believed Bob was right for a role that Universal was having difficulty casting. Bob defied the odds by quickly landing a Hollywood job in the Universal Technicolor musical *Song of Scheherazade* starring Jean-Pierre Aumont and Yvonne De Carlo. Universal liked his work and signed Bob for its next major musical drama, *Casbah*, starring Tony Martin, Yvonne De Carlo, and Marta Toren.

I met Bob when we worked at the *Inglewood Daily News*. By then he had enhanced his acting credentials. He also taught for a time in the Los Angeles City School District. When he felt that minority students were being educationally shortchanged he wrote a bestselling novel that embodied his teaching experience in a thinly disguised fictional format and titled it *White Teacher in a Black School*. His effort spawned changes within the system. During that same period he lectured nationally and made many television and radio appearances. He also pursued his interest in international travel.

As a born and bred Los Angeles native fresh out of college, I found talking to Bob fascinating, hearing about his worldly travel and professional achievements in numerous interesting areas. I was the youngest sports editor in the L.A. area while Bob, who joined the paper a few months after me, was assigned to cover the Centinela Valley police beat. Although the paper already had an entertainment editor it was natural for Bob, given his film background, to contribute articles on the Hollywood entertainment front with so much happening locally in both the film and television industries.

I asked so many questions about Hollywood and revealed such an interest in the industry that, before long, Bob suggested that I try my hand at an article on the subject. When I replied that my journalistic background had been confined to sports writing and I would not know where to begin, he shrugged off my diffidence. I had no sooner gone back to my desk to work on my sports page than Bob had returned, telling me that he had lined up a visit for me at MGM. Before long there was a second MGM opportunity, and that was followed by visits to Warner Bros. and Disney.

Bob's confidence that I would find a niche in movie writing led to my eventual role of movie historian. On the way I ventured into the international historical field to write a book based on 3,500 years of Middle East history, *Struggle for the Holy Land: Arabs, Jews and the Emergence of Israel*. By then Bob was working as my agent. His spirited efforts resulted in my being interviewed on television on the BBC World Service in London. He also set up radio interviews on WOR in New York City, WGN in Chicago, and KOA in Denver.

His steady encouragement and unceasing optimism assisted me as I launched myself in the field of cinema history. Bob's background in the field was especially helpful in my early phases as he critiqued my work.

Bob was present at Alfred Hitchcock's final two major media press conferences, both in conjunction with his last film, *Family Plot*. The final press conference of the great director was a closed-circuit television presentation held simultaneously at NBC Studios in Burbank, the Plaza Hotel in New York City, the Registry Hotel in Dallas, and the Continental-Plaza Hotel in Chicago on March 23, 1976. With such a fitting background, I had Bob write the foreword for the book I did on the renowned director, *Hitchcock and the Methods of Suspense*.

Robert Kendall's buoyant confidence proved infectious. It enabled me to overcome early doubts and move forward. Lessons learned from Bob provide continuing benefits. Anyone with the chance to interact with him could not help but benefit from those experiences.

Introduction

Ask business people which factor they believe to be the essential component of success and the one-word response likely to dominate would be timing. If the timing is right, a product will almost sell itself. This is certainly true with motion pictures. When a subject resonates in the hearts and minds of movie fans they are more likely to fill theaters.

If one were to look back historically on the movie industry, in which period would filmmakers most likely achieve success showcasing economic struggle? The answer would be the Great Depression. Those interested in thirties' movies would immediately cite the films at MGM starring Judy Garland, Mickey Rooney, and Lewis Stone in the Andy Hardy series along with those at Twentieth Century–Fox showcasing the precocious talent of a very young Shirley Temple.

The Hardy and Temple series epitomized feel-good entertainment. They provided a momentary escape to an America that desired the contrast of an easier reality, one devoid of crushing poverty and want of basic necessities. Based on these films, the Depression can be seen as a creative catalyst for light fare, which provided theatergoers with a reason to laugh, smile, and feel good about themselves.

The other type of film that captured audiences during the Depression reflected the hard times that were so familiar. The element of struggle was often associated with crime films emphasizing the battle between good and evil. The Depression, characterized in its earliest phase by prohibition, was marked by speakeasies and illegal liquor trade. This gave rise to a host of syndicate crime activities with Al Capone surfacing as a notable example.

Out of the crime movie genre came a figure who loomed as an object of rebellion, a loner battling the system. His loner status enabled him to appear in films as a gangster or honest victim fighting corruption. He was the hero of an emerging genre of cinema, based on American detective stories, that post–World War II was labeled "film noir."

If any actor was born to play the jaded hero of film noir, it was Humphrey Bogart. Bearing a swarthy visage and the kind of expressive face that could alternate between toughness and sensitivity, Bogart was perfectly cast as a rebel mired in struggle. It was only fitting that Bogart would team up with a John Huston, another rebellious free spirit, who was making his directorial debut. The result would be what film historians deem the first film noir, the 1941 Warner Bros. hit *The Maltese Falcon*.

The Maltese Falcon was adapted from a novel by Dashiell Hammett, a former Pinkerton Agency detective whose sleuthing experiences led to the creation of a fictional alter ego known as Sam Spade, the character portrayed with fidelity by Bogart. Hammett suffered from tuberculosis and writing about his experiences afforded a chance to make money at home dealing with familiar subject matter that was marketable in the pulp detective magazine field that thrived during the Depression.

It is also significant to note that the studio boss who gave the green light to the project was Warner Bros. Studio chief Jack Warner. The Warners were first generation Americans who grew up in Youngstown, Ohio, and used enterprising resourcefulness to achieve the American dream. During the Depression period Jack Warner was a staunch liberal Democrat and ardent supporter of President Franklin Delano Roosevelt's New Deal. Warner Bros. was a studio that presented tough Depression-oriented fare that dovetailed with Jack Warner's strong identification with the struggle Americans endured during that period.

Captain Joseph Shaw was the creative genius behind *Black Mask*, the most prestigious detective magazine of a highly competitive field. Shaw carefully nurtured the talents of the two leading detective writers of the period, the aforementioned Dashiell Hammett and Raymond Chandler. Under Shaw's creative lead a different American detective style evolved. The traditional English model focused on a detective pursuing a series of clues, culminating with a surprise twist ending in which the crime is solved. Shaw, in concert with writers like Chandler and Hammett, developed a new detective story concept, with an emphasis on character over plot that adapted brilliantly to the screen.

Along with the character driven element of these stories, another feature that made them particularly well-suited to film is that they were often set in major cities. Hammett and Chandler each lived in the one of the two largest cities in California, representing the northern and southern parts of the state, respectively. Hammett lived in and wrote about San Francisco while Chandler became the laureate of Los Angeles. Chandler's love-hate relationship with Los Angeles imbued the setting of his novels with an ambivalent atmosphere that translated well on the screen.

Another author whose writing was deeply influenced by the Depression and who got his start in pulp detective magazines was Horace McCoy. A Dallas journalist as well as an operator of a local theater in which he performed, McCoy eventually made his way to Hollywood and would succeed only minimally as a screenwriter. It was when he took a job as a bouncer at a ballroom on the Santa Monica Pier, which would eventually become the site of *The Lawrence Welk Show*, that the seeds were sown for his most memorable work.

McCoy found temporary employment as a bouncer for an event that became a staple of Depression-era entertainment, the dance marathon. His short novel *They Shoot Horses, Don't They?* (1935) showcased the peculiar nature of the Depression's impact in Hollywood and the 1969 movie, filmed long after McCoy's death, made director Sydney Pollack famous.

During World War II an influx of directors fleeing The Third Reich infused Hollywood film noir with a European sensibility. Before emigrating Fritz Lang was a heralded director who had to his credit the futuristic *Metropolis* as well as the bleak yet fascinating drama *M*. The latter work presaged the film noir movement by presenting Berlin in the midst of the serial killings of female children. The impact of Lang's films was not lost on major Hollywood industry players and with him in the director's seat RKO became a noir factory in which sleek films were made on trim budgets.

Viennese director Billy Wilder was another great talent who came to Hollywood during the war. He collaborated with Raymond Chandler on the screenplay adaptation of James M. Cain's runaway bestseller, *Double Indemnity*. Wilder was awarded an Oscar for "Best Director" for his work on *The Lost Weekend*. Based on a Charles Jackson novel the film traces the path from degradation to redemption for a New York City writer in the throes of alcoholism.

Introduction 3

When Otto Preminger came to the United States he received, in an ironic twist, opportunities on the New York stage to portray imperious Nazis when he was Jewish. His acting led him to Hollywood where he pursued directing and found himself in frequent conflict with President of Fox Films Darryl F. Zanuck. They worked together on the noir classic *Laura* and *Fallen Angel*.

It was the chemistry of collaboration between the directors and actors and writers that made film noir such a phenomenon, but its success was also due to the mystery that often remained beyond even the creators' grasp. When Chandler's first novel, *The Big Sleep*, was adapted to the screen with Bogart cast as Phillip Marlowe, the actor wanted to know to the identity of the killer of the story's chauffeur.

This prompted Howard Hawks, the film's director, and William Faulkner, one of the movie's screenwriters, to telephone Raymond Chandler and pose the question. Chandler answered that he had no idea concerning the identity of the chauffeur's killer.

Hawks, one of the premier directors in film history, revealed that directing *The Big Sleep* taught him an important lesson. Chandler's frank response brought Hawks to a realization regarding the lure of film noir: the true source of menace could remain mysterious to the viewer — one didn't have to understand the storyline to find the movie entertaining.

Chapter One

Film Noir and the Great Depression

> At MGM in the thirties the thing that they talked about over and over was stories.
> — Mervyn LeRoy

Devotees of film noir, from movie historians and cinema magazine authors to a loyal and vitally interested fan base, have fastened their attention spans on the roots of the genre along with the arrival of this new topic of interest. "What could be more conspicuous timing than the end of World War II?" so many film noir devotees ask.

The war heightened true reality, and what could happen in a world where the acquisition of power unattached to moral responsibility coupled with military might brought on a tragic international consequence resulting in the loss of 50 million lives. To fully explore the foundation of film noir, however, it is essential to explore in historical rewind the America of the thirties and the response to the Great Depression.

The response to any question relating to film noir's foundational roots provides a plausible explanation. Any semblance of innocence in the American psyche ended during a traumatic war with the resultant paradigm shifting. One moment America was saluting Mickey Rooney and his movie father Lewis Stone, the thoroughly wholesome and likable young Andy and Judge Hardy, respectively. Metro-Goldwyn-Mayer studio head Louis B. Mayer would be the first one to trumpet the success of the Andy Hardy series in terms of capacity theater throngs and a solid impact on studio dividends with ultimate smiles on the faces of dividend holders.

What kind of actress was an ideal onscreen match for clean-cut and energetic Mickey Rooney? It was none other than the young girl with the sweet, sensitive face and the golden voice, Judy Garland. It was no accident that the girl audiences loved in the Andy Hardy films was selected by producer Mervyn LeRoy ahead of even Twentieth-Century–Fox's child phenomenon Shirley Temple for what proved to be the role of her lifetime in the runaway international hit *The Wizard of Oz* (1939).

While acknowledging Temple's rare talents, LeRoy believed that Garland represented the ideal casting choice for the role of wholesome Kansas girl Dorothy, who is spun into a world of make-believe amid allegorical messages to appeal to all ages. To demonstrate that the film industry survived on the instincts of successful producer-director types such as LeRoy, MGM top brass initially decided on cutting one song sung by Garland in *Wizard*.

LeRoy pled with MGM's moguls to at least let the song appear in the studio preview of *Wizard of Oz* slated for the familiar venue for many such previews, San Bernardino, deemed a typically American, middle-class city located some 60 miles east of Los Angeles. On the audience cards filled out to determine individual and group responses to the overall film product, fans singled out "Over the Rainbow" as *Wizard*'s most memorable musical selection. It became the signature selection from the career of the magnetic Garland. This was the song that studio moguls had deemed expendable.

Years later when performing in San Francisco, venerable singing legend Tony Bennett referred to Garland as "the most talented performer in the history of our industry." Given such an impressive recognition bouquet from one of the recording industry's immortals, it was understandable why Garland tugged at the hearts of Americans beginning with a turbulent Great Depression period.

Depression Light and Dark

The world of solid American values, along with dynamic color fantasy as represented by *The Wizard of Oz*, revealed bases of reaction on the part of Americans to the tumultuous upheaval of the Great Depression.

What do psychologists pose as the great antidote to pain? The answer is laughter. Pain can be dulled if people can be induced to laugh. This was another prescription served up with great panache by Hollywood with grand results.

The woman who kept Paramount from bankruptcy during that studio's most traumatic financial period was a strutting, confident blonde from New York, whose clipped wisecracks were often inserted at her own creation into scripts that, when the lines were crisply delivered, prompted audiences to roar with laughter. Mae West not only possessed a solid instinct to make people laugh; like Mervyn LeRoy and other industry creative giants, her knowledge extended to the casting realm.

There was that day when, while being driven down a street on the Paramount lot, she observed a tall, dark-haired young man. When she asked his name she was told that he was a British actor of no consequence, someone whose Paramount contract would shortly be dropped, whereupon he would be return to his native England.

The fates of the industry being what they are, Cary Grant may well have gone home to his native Bristol had Mae West not stunned those in her party by stating that "if he can talk" he will be starring with her in her next film. The result was a co-starring role for the handsome Britisher with the distinct Cockney accent in the 1933 release *She Done Him Wrong*. Following that major comedy success another film starring the duo was released later that year, *I'm No Angel*.

The Grant magic enabled him to combine a dynamic charm along with a farcical comedy manner. If Mae West could leave audiences laughing with sexy camp that demonstrated a brilliant touch at weaving her way around the prudishness of industry censors, Grant, as illustrated in his 1940 vehicle with Rosalind Russell, *His Girl Friday*, could keep viewers in stitches with his unique comedy talent.

Grant was a master at dashing off lines with rapidity. The staccato blasts proved useful in the comedy sphere. It was no surprise in Hollywood, where industry insiders delighted in playing after-dinner games, that when Grant would host guests at his Beverly Hills home he would reign as an accomplished master at a tongue-twisting game. Guests would challenge the master on his own turf at their prospective peril.

Two films that have received the ultimate in international exposure and popularity through the decades were forays into the new adventure of color. It was no surprise that MGM, the industry's biggest studio, would produce both.

The films were released the same year and had the same director, home grown product Victor Fleming, with the aforementioned *The Wizard of Oz* and *Gone with the Wind*. The latter film endured a staggering amount of production problems. They included leading lady Vivien Leigh and director Fleming loathing each other so much that he walked out on the project at one point.

At a time when hungry citizens sold apples on street corners and offered to provide work in exchange for meals, movie fans could temporarily escape their problems to worlds of spectacle, comedy, or viewing folks from mom and apple-pie America, but there emerged another world existing in the shadows and it was captured with haunting effect.

It was unsurprising therefore to receive the swift response I did from Mervyn LeRoy when I asked what it was like to be at MGM during its busy thirties period: "At MGM in the thirties the thing they talked about over and over was stories. When you went in to talk to Irving Thalberg you talked about stories. Thalberg had a story mind like Walt Disney."[1]

Eddie Muller on the Great Depression

San Francisco's Eddie Muller has played such an important role as an historian of the film noir movement that James Ellroy has called him "the czar of noir." Muller classifies the Great Depression as a thematic linchpin around which film noir grew.

"Frankly, I think the Depression was a bigger influence [on film noir] than World War II," Muller revealed. "The writers that influenced the more adult content and attitude found in film noir created their essential work in the thirties: Hammett, Cain, Chandler, Woolrich, Ben Hecht's big city style, all those *Black Mask* authors. These writers popularized the noir world that the mostly émigré directors so vividly visualized in mid- to late-forties noir."[2]

Black Mask, to which Muller alluded, emerged as the launching pad for Hollywood's forays into the visual field in which the characters developed by the aforementioned authors were seen depicted by charismatic performers in works that helped them become international stars. Much will be written about Captain Joseph T. Shaw, the editorial and publishing genius behind the success of *Black Mask* as a leader of the pulp magazine field. Shaw was a dynamic innovator who provided key ideas that helped writers such as Raymond Chandler and Dashiell Hammett achieve popularity.

Certain film noir analysts have focused strongly on the importance of World War II in shaping the genre. This view is popular in certain academic circles, where French existential intellectuals Albert Camus and Jean Paul Sartre enjoy great popularity. The influence of Camus and Sartre along with the impact of the Paris intellectual scene following World War II will also be evaluated.

It should be noted that a number of films that came to be regarded as a cornerstone of the noir movement had already been made prior to the pivotal event that intellectuals cited in propounding that post–World War II theory. The incident serving as a catalyst for those adhering to that view came in 1947 with the publication of an article that appeared in the prestigious French film magazine *Cahiers du Cinéma*.

Eddie Muller weighed in further on the issue of formative film noir influence. In so doing, Muller picks up on the aforementioned comment about the academic world's enthusiasm in linking film noir to the French intellectual movement, specifically the existential intellectuals Sartre and Camus. "I think the notion that film noir grew directly out of the Second World War is a little specious, a bit too convenient for grad student theses," Muller said.

"The movement was a long time developing, and was actually slowed down by the constraints of the Production Code, and the studios bosses' concerns that downbeat stories were inappropriate during wartime. I think the end of the war released noir, more than it created it."

Film noir, as the name implies, deals with shadowy figures engaging in dangerous actions in the darkness of late evening in American cities. To make the conversion from the printed page where authors such as Chandler, Hammett, and Woolrich exercised their considerable creative imaginations, it was necessary to cast characters that comported with the stories being adapted to the screen.

It so happens that Hollywood had just the right actor at film noir's christening period to intrigue as well as thoroughly entertain audiences that could not seem to get enough of him. In style and manner he fit the ideal conception of a film noir leading man.

Bogart's Brooding Presence

Humphrey Bogart was the son of two upscale New Yorkers. His father was a doctor and his mother the famous illustrator Maude Humphrey. Bogart turned out to be a rebel when he decided that the upper-class private schools where his parents had sent him were not to his liking.

Bogart, with his swarthy visage — a penetrating look that could take on a freeze-frame scowl when the occasion warranted — could make his brooding presence even more enduring in a black suit replete with matching hat. His clipped verbal manner could turn frostily sarcastic at a moment's notice.

After a stint on the New York stage, that all-intriguing element known as the camera's eye made it apparent to the Hollywood power brokers that here was a performer who had that indefinable, untaught magic to generate interest, the essence of star power.

In order to make the scowling visage and rebelliousness more richly perceivable, in a breakthrough Bogart drama, *The Petrified Forest* (1936), an adaptation of the Robert Sherwood play, he was blessed with a contrasting dramatic counterweight that gave the film more depth, and with it, Bogart's continuing screen persona.

The haunting story, aided by the presence of one of the cinema's most sensitive performers, Leslie Howard as Alan Squier, took a turn away from tough-as-nails, macho criminality.

Due to the unselfish and serene humanity of Squier, the relentlessly tough-as-nails criminal played by Bogart, Duke Mantee, sees a new side of life. He perceives a level of existence where one human being is willing to sacrifice his life for the benefit of another while considering the act no more than what one person should do for another.

This powerful 1936 drama, directed by Archie Mayo, has Great Depression written all over it. While Mantee sees society as "dog eat dog" and follows the rule of taking advantage before others can make you their victim, Squier, who sees his life as a failure, decides to exit a sad world of frustration and self-perceived failure by bestowing a kindness on Gabrielle Maple (Bette Davis).

In a unique story twist, Squier convinces Mantee to kill him as part of his overall armed robbery plan so that Maple will have the opportunity, by means of inheriting his insurance money, to move to Paris and begin a new life. The film invests both Howard and Bogart with opportunities to display their rich talents in varying roles. In Squier's case, he considers himself weak and a failure, and seeks to provide the young woman with an opportunity to advance her life.

While Duke Mantee initially displays a self-centered survivor's demeanor, through observing Squier at a time while he is being begged to be killed by the victim to be, he admires Squier's decency to the point where he tries to talk him out of his death wish. It is only after Squier convinces him that death is his best avenue that Mantee agrees to kill him, and does so while expressing admiration for his unique victim.

An Early Social Consciousness Film

A film released one year after *The Petrified Forest* permitted Bogart to reverse the pattern he dramatically pursued as Duke Mantee, of someone who concludes that there is fundamental decency in a society he had previously viewed as coldly anarchistic. *Black Legion* (1936), also directed by Archie Mayo, displays Bogart as factory worker Frank Taylor. The film begins with Taylor as a decent family man, but ultimately he becomes consumed by anti-immigrant hatred.

Taylor's life is changed when he listens to a racist demagogue on radio and becomes convinced that he is correct. His response is to join the Black Legion, which, though putatively a fictional group, was the identical name used by a derivative of the Ku Klux Klan's Ohio branch. The color variant was that their members dressed in black in contrast to the Klan's white, including hoods, with their uniforms bearing the symbol of the skull and crossbones. (The Black Legion was responsible for killing, among others, Earl Little, the father of Malcolm X. The group was centered in and around Detroit, with an estimated membership of between 20,000 and 30,000.)

Black Legion represented the kind of social-consciousness effort that was a hallmark of Warner Bros. during the Depression thirties. In his later years, Warner Bros. studio head Jack Warner became a staunch Republican, as did one of his contract stars, Ronald Reagan. During the Depression period, however, Warner was a stalwart supporter of President Franklin Delano Roosevelt and his New Deal.

Perceptive viewers can see Bogart's emergence as a complex rebel figure that can run from one emotional gamut to the other when evaluating the 1936 and 1937 Warner Bros. films. In contrast to the earlier film, when Duke Mantee felt a compassionate empathy toward the bravely tragic figure of Alan Squier, Bogart plummets from a man of decency toward one of ethnic paranoia as immigrants are blamed for America's ills.

The impressive element of two powerful Bogart performances in Warner Bros. vehicles was his dramatic skill in running the gamut from thorough ruthlessness to a man who can empathize in one instance and the opposite in the other, where he becomes gripped in Depression-era quick-fix paranoia and blames immigrants for America's economic problems.

Through examining Bogart's early performances via the prism of cinematic evolution, one can observe the man who would become a defining film noir symbol. Bogart was dark, he was brooding, he could become highly emotional, he could explode in bursts of righteousness or lawless rebellion. His dark, swarthy visage was perfect for the darkened world of cold realism that embodied film noir.

Steve Eifert and the Bogart Influence

Steve Eifert is the current guiding force behind the *Back Alley Noir* website. When asked about film noir influences he unsurprisingly mentioned Humphrey Bogart.

"My interest in film noir began when I was a kid watching old Bogart movies on WGBH in Boston with my old man," Eifert recalled. "It's interesting to see who are today's film noir fans. Some are like my dad. They grew up with Bogie being one of the biggest and coolest movie stars of all time. Other fans are like me. We grew up watching *Kay Largo* and *The Maltese Falcon* on *The Movie Loft* and tuned the TV set with a rabbit ears antenna. Now we have the Turner Movie Classic home video generation. The films are now classics and pieces of art and are easily found on cable, on DVD, or even by streaming online."[3]

With Bogart becoming an increasingly prominent presence in top vehicles at a studio eager to churn out social message films relating to Americans struggling against gigantic odds amid the Great Depression, he was an inevitable choice to become the leading man who was there at what was later deemed to be the christening of film noir.

Bogart worked in lockstep with another cinema legend also en route to the ranks of the immortals, whose crucial first step came in response to advice from his father. Bogart benefited as well.

A Rebel Teaming and the Birth of Noir

John Huston had the kind of knock-around life that was reflective of the idea that a writer assumed many identities before lifting his or her pen or striking a typewriter keyboard for the first time. In short, a writer learned to write about people after being a spectator and participant in numerous activities within scores of settings, therefore acquiring an education from the proverbial "school of hard knocks."

Huston conceded that he had failed at numerous jobs, including one as a newspaper reporter where his boss had re-hired and re-fired him on numerous occasions. While Huston would never attain the ranks of stellar journalist, writing would prove to be his ticket to enduring fame in the city where his actor father, Walter, a brilliant character actor, made his mark.

The field in which John Huston initially excelled was as a screenwriter. Not only would he blaze his own trail by chalking up numerous credits; he would, in the manner of William Goldman years later, also serve with distinction as a script doctor on properties for which he did not receive screen credit.

Since William Wyler and Bette Davis were both receiving stellar plaudits as director and superstar, respectively, during the thirties, Huston's standing was enhanced by crafting the screenplay for the 1938 Warners drama *Jezebel*. One year later, another film starring Davis that Huston scripted, *Juarez*, scored big, bolstered by a starring appearance by one of the century's great stars of the American stage, Paul Muni, in the vehicle directed by William Dieterle.

Huston came into the good graces of Jack Warner by crafting the screenplay of a Gary Cooper hit, *Sergeant York*, directed by Howard Hawks in 1941, which would prove to be the most pivotal professional year of Huston's career.

While Huston scripted an earlier Bogart film, the 1938 Warners release also starring Edward G. Robinson, *The Amazing Dr. Clitterhouse*, it was the 1941 Depression gangster epic *High Sierra* that would provide a stepping stone into a new world for Huston, that of directing, and with it foundational entry into the film noir realm.

High Sierra marked the union of three rebels who could empathize on such a project and working with each other. In addition to Bogart and Huston, the film was directed by

Raoul Walsh, a two-fisted, boilermaker-swilling type who began as an authentic cowboy and then, after a career in films, made his mark directing Westerns as well as other action vehicles for Jack Warner, including gangster movies.

Walsh, who wore a patch over one eye as a result of a stunt accident early in his film career, directed both Bogart and George Raft in *They Drive by Night* (1940). This film also blended sturdy action alongside Depression hard times, as evidenced by Bogart's character's plight in the film. Operating a small trucking business with his brother, played by Raft, he battles sleeplessness in order to deliver needed items to customers and loses an arm in an accident.

W.R. Burnett and Three Decades of Hits

On the *High Sierra* project Huston was able to hitch his creative wagon to a venerable star of the hard-hitting gangster fiction school. Huston assisted William Riley Burnett, better known as W.R., to adapt his novel of the same name to the screen.

Burnett's ride to film fame began one decade earlier after he crafted a book resulting from tragedy. Burnett, who grew up in Dayton, Ohio, and moved to Chicago, was listening to a live broadcast of a musical nightclub program when his entire life was suddenly and without warning, dramatically altered.

The Chicago of that period was dominated by criminal syndicates. As Burnett sat and relaxed, concentrating on the music, his attention was shattered by sound of gunfire erupting from a gangland battle for turf rights.

Burnett would later learn that his best friend, who had gone to the nightclub for an enjoyable night on the town, had been caught in the current of gunfire and was killed. In the manner of a purposeful writer, Burnett, armed with determination, turned the shocking experience into a novel carrying a sturdy ring of reality.

About the time that Burnett's novel was gripping the nation's attention, young Warners director Mervyn LeRoy, who had been invited to attend a Hollywood party that evening, decided to fill in time prior to leaving by reading a galley proof that had been recently submitted by an agent.

The key to a writer's success lies in gaining the attention of the subject. If you scale the level of riveting attention, so much the better, and such was the case with the galley proof of Burnett's novel.

LeRoy became, no doubt, convinced that this was a film he "had to do" by the time that he forgot about the party, read all night, and was beckoning a new morning. He took time enough to shave and then drove immediately to the studio to successfully plead his case.

The 1931 release *Little Caesar* became a gangster film classic. It promptly ushered LeRoy to the ranks of Hollywood's premier directors. It skyrocketed the film's star, a diminutive New York stage actor with the presence of an army of giants, Edward G. Robinson, into similar ranks while investing Burnett with the credentials on an important writer in that city of legend that was just beginning to turn its attention to that booming commodity, the talking motion picture.

The moving experience of LeRoy discovering the story roots of an enduring film classic was part of a process he explained to me years later in his Sunset Boulevard office.

In *Little Caesar*, Robinson is cast as an Al Capone style figure, no surprise since the muscular Sicilian gangster was Chicago's most notorious crime boss during the period Burnett depicted in his novel. The film culminated with the memorable line in which a dying Robinson asks rhetorically: "Mother of mercy, is this the end of Rico?"

The triumph of *Little Caesar* marked the beginning of a remarkable string for W.R. Burnett. Major Hollywood hits would be adapted from his books at or near the beginning of each of three decades, beginning with the end of the Roaring Twenties and subsequent early Depression period of the thirties, extending to the post–Depression, pre- and early–World War II segment, culminating in the middle mark of the twentieth century and the tensions of the Cold War with America and the Soviet Union amid a war caught in the specter of a potential nuclear conflict.

High Sierra would be released ten years after *Little Caesar*'s 1931 debut, with America joining a world conflict in progress following the December 7, 1941 bombing of Pearl Harbor by the Japanese navy. As will be seen later, Burnett's final triumph would come with a John Huston-directed film set in the crime world as well, *The Asphalt Jungle*.

A Bogart Figure Reminiscent of *Casablanca*

Casablanca (1942) is one of the most audience-acclaimed films in history. Its popularity can be attributable to a blend of romance and suspense intertwining through a sharp, witty, trenchant screenplay coming to life through superb interpretation by a stellar cast and attentive direction. At one point such a predicted resulted may well have caused Jack Warner and his studio minions to question the predictor's sanity given the fact that *Casablanca*, in the manner of the film noir gem *Laura* at Twentieth-Century–Fox, was considered to be the jinx project on the lot. It appeared that *Casablanca* might never even be cast, much less made and celebrated with distinction by global cinema audiences.

Much of the fascination among film historians and audiences lies in the unveiling of a character played by Bogart that is fascinatingly self-contradictory. He begins by presenting himself as Rick Blaine, the eternal nihilist. Bogart as Rick growls that he is in Casablanca running a nightclub as someone who cares not a whit about a world run amok in war, save for the conflict to end. As for love and women, we see him crush one admirer by telling her in the bluntest, most succinct terms that he never, in even the slightest way, gave her any reason to believe that she was anything but a mere passing interest, no more than a metaphorical case of two ships passing in the night.

A key period of *Casablanca* occurs when Ilsa Lund (Ingrid Bergman) arrives with the new man in her life, Victor Laszlo (played by the suave and mellow internationalist Paul Henreid). With Lund's arrival and the revelation that they had been lovers in Paris, the mask of Rick the nihilist is shattered and the real person emerges.

The fascinating suspense element in the audience discovery of the real Rick is how his false persona is peeled away layer by layer by Lund's re-emergence into his life. We see that beneath the tough outer veneer lies an incurable romantic and a political idealist willing to make the ultimate sacrifice of seeing the woman he loves leave him.

The same Rick who had snarled his nihilistic belief that it made no difference to him who won the war, giving the idea that humankind was born to fight and that he considered the whole process no more than the continuing process of human nonsensical behavior, demonstrates a different side during a key moment of the film after his regular customers from Nazi Germany's officer's ranks burst patriotically into song.

A system conceived by Hitler on extreme nationalism stressed frequent manifestations of support for Germany. After the Nazi officers burst into song an indignant Laszlo leads the opposing ranks to join him in a chorus of France's national anthem, "The Marseillaise." Laszlo asks Rick's pianist, Sam (Dooley Wilson), for accompaniment and all doubt is resolved by a silent but decisive nod from the presumed Rick the nihilist.

The sentimental side of Rick becomes paramount when Lund enters the scene for a post-business hours meeting. An emotional Rick forbids pianist Sam to play "that song" because it is reminiscent of those glorious days before the war in Paris and a brutal Nazi occupation.

Resolution and Bogart the Ultimate Idealist-Realist

The final plot point that swings the story convinces the audience that Rick was stringing everyone along with his early pronouncements. He turns out to be the ultimate idealist-realist in the interest of the world.

Rick was impressed by Laszlo and his international reputation from the moment he met him. In the end he tells Lund, apparently the only woman he has ever truly loved, that in the final analysis there were more important things than their love. No matter how much they meant to each other, the ultimate issue was that Laszlo led a cause bigger than the love they shared, no matter how sincere and meaningful it was to them.

The free world's ultimate destiny hinged on Laszlo's cause, and it was essential that it be served. If that meant giving up any claim to Lund, then that was the way that things had to be.

Casablanca represented tough story telling with a message. Even romance had to be sacrificed for the cause bigger than any romance. When the cover came off and the inner man was revealed, Rick was an idealist and a realist. The larger ideal held sway, that of humanity, which exceeded the personal future wishes of Lund and himself.

The manner with which Rick juggled the issue of his own happiness and ultimate satisfaction relating to the general good was reflective of the way that Bogart handled sociological complexity as he developed in his starring Warner Bros. roles.

"Mad Dog" Earle and Breaking Down the Inner Self

While film analysts and audiences alike considered *Casablanca* to be more of a romantic film than *High Sierra*, an expectation appearing all the more relevant in view of one containing a character called Rick who ran a night club while the other was a fearsome criminal bearing the nickname of "Mad Dog," the latter character role possessed traits in common with the great 1942 film.

Director Raoul Walsh was accustomed to directing gritty films involving cinematic tough guys, and while Bogart in *High Sierra* generated toughness, Roy "Mad Dog" Earle had a sensitive side that he sought to hide, but that came out nonetheless because it comprised an inherent part of the all-encompassing whole.

High Sierra fit definitely into the mold of so many other Warners films of the period, with the unmistakable mark of the Great Depression pervasive as an outsider attempts to tough it out against a system that looms as an enemy force daring to be overridden. Even though Earle is part of the underworld scene, and will be continuing in it after being released from prison, he still believes that there is an unwritten rule of integrity existing even in a world where lawbreaking is sought to be elevated to at least a livable professional enterprise.

Barton MacLane, someone who will cross swords with Bogart, as we will see, in *The Maltese Falcon*, plays Jake Kranmer, a cop gone bad in *High Sierra*. Earl lets him immediately know in their one and only meeting in the film that he is a man who retains certain standards of decency, even within an underworld framework, and that he believes Kranmer does not, and for that he does not wish to do business with him.

We see the idealistic side of the tough criminal known as "Mad Dog" soften as he meets a much younger woman, Velma (Joan Leslie), and falls in love with her. When he notices that she has a club foot and asks if something can be done for her, Earle is told that correcting the problem involves an operation that is too expensive for the family to afford.

Earle then swings into action. He is able to provide the funds for Velma to obtain a successful operation, correcting the problem and enabling her to then function normally without the handicap.

While he has received no indication that his love for her is reciprocal, Earle's romantic, idealistic side sees himself as the lover and protector of Velma. When he visits her after her successful operation, he is in for a rude awakening.

Casting Joan Leslie in a part in which the audience is expected to sympathize fully with her and, adopting Earle's viewpoint, sees her as a sweet, genuinely nice young woman worthy of his respect, proved to be a shrewd decision. Successful filmmaking, as revealed in particular with the works of Alfred Hitchcock, hinges on fooling the audience as a suspense ingredient and making it like it, and this is the element that is handled with consummate success in *High Sierra*.

Leapfrogging Against Type

The surprise that Earle receives along with the audience is when, following the successful operation, a different Velma is revealed. This is the first revelation of the practice of "leapfrogging against type" as Earle is jolted out of the kind of dreamy, idealistic love that Mad Dog of the gruff exterior would angrily snarl does not exist in the same manner that the actor as Rick in *Casablanca* sought to deny was a part of him before the arrival of Lund and Laszlo.

While she expresses gratitude toward Earle for being the guardian angel type that paid for her successful surgery, he is jolted when he is introduced to her husband-to-be. The entire atmosphere is non-conducive to what he anticipated. It is a party atmosphere, replete with loud music and drink. Also, Velma's fiancé comes off as smarmy and superficial. Earle leaves, partially in rage and partially in extreme disappointment mixed with sorrow, stopping just short of striking the man occupying the position in Velma's life where he had hoped he would be.

The use of Joan Leslie in *High Sierra* represented an excellent example of leapfrogging. Joan Leslie represented Warners' version of the kind of young woman that young men proudly take home to meet their parents, in the mold of Alice Faye at Twentieth Century–Fox and Teresa Wright at Samuel Goldwyn Studios.

The audience occupies the same position as Earle in the film in that Velma, in this instance, is eventually revealed as less wholesome than the tough holdup artist envisioned. The stern realization that Earle ultimately discerns is that he truly does live on a different side of the tracks from Velma and her crowd, as well as people who lead more conventional lives.

Enter Ida Lupino

Ida Lupino had acting in her genes. The daughter of prominent British actor Stanley Lupino, Ida possessed that unique charisma to command interest before the cameras. She soon became in great demand at Warner Bros. and even a brief analysis of Lupino at work provided solid indication of why she fit into their Depression style, black-and-white moody format.

Lupino was perfect in close-ups, which figured to make her popular with studio bosses, directors, and moviegoers. It was a face that was a natural for expressing pathos. She earned plaudits in a melancholy role in the Raoul Walsh vehicle, *They Drive by Night*, when she had a crush on a tough truck driver who had eyes for somebody else.

Initially, Marie (Lupino) is in the same position with Roy Earle in *High Sierra*. Earle instead decides to pursue a girl he is convinced comes from a different side of the tracks from him in Velma. After the aforementioned painful rejection from Velma, he begins paying more attention to Marie, someone he finds possesses genuine feeling for him along with more overall emotional substance than the disappointing Velma.

Earle finds himself playing a combination of boxing referee and minder to his two immature younger holdup team members, played by Arthur Kennedy and Alan Curtis. (As will be seen later, Curtis had the male lead along with Franchot Tone in the superb noir vehicle *Phantom Lady*.)

While Bogart, in the manner of his characterization of Rick the bartender in *Casablanca*, revealed a balance between his outwardly tough demeanor and inner sentimentalism. Fine tuning this balance is the stuff of great acting and successful cinema vehicles.

The final sympathetic touch displayed by this complex man of many parts, Earle finds a dog eager for a home. Earle has heard that the dog is considered a jinx due to the fact that previous owners have attained unhappy ends to criminal enterprises. Despite his misgivings, he agrees to let the dog stay.

Last-Ditch Effort

Due to the strict motion picture code enforced by Joseph Breen in what was called the Breen Office, Bogart as a hardened criminal was not about to escape an unsuccessful end. In line with Depression storytelling and with the Warner emphasis on tough guy survivors, the sharply honed John Huston script finds Earle taking on the police in the eponymous Sierra Mountains.

While Marie recognizes that the odds are impossibly stacked against Earle and prefers him to peaceably surrender, he is not about to do so. The sequence is stretched for peak dramatic impact, with the appearance of a familiar face to national radio listeners of the period and some film viewers as well: Sam Hayes. Hayes reigned for years as a network broadcasting pioneer, beginning in 1929. He scaled his peak as network radio's Richfield

Reporter. Hayes's dramatic rendering of news events made him a natural in *High Sierra*, giving the closing sequence, the do or die stand of "Mad Dog" Earle, a documentary flavor. Another point to be made is that Hayes became initially famous during the Depression period.

With the success of *High Sierra*, John Huston emerged as a red-hot writer on the Hollywood scene. He was ready to make his case to studio chief Jack Warner to enter the director's ranks.

The memorable film that would begin Huston's long and successful reign in the directing field would be classified as the opening chapter in the great and continuing film noir saga. Before analyzing *The Maltese Falcon*, it should be observed that a musical could perhaps be marked as a harbinger for film noir.

Busby Berkeley Noir?

Busby Berkeley would be one of the last persons ever mentioned in a list concerning film noir activity, yet one film he choreographed could be cited within the developmental history of the genre.

The Warner brothers, like many families of the American immigrant movement of the 19th century, had their roots in Eastern Europe, specifically Poland. The father of the clan worked long, hard hours as a butcher. Eventually the family established roots in Youngstown, Ohio, a great melting pot for immigrants located not far from Cleveland.

In addition to being the city where John D. Rockefeller established his Standard Oil Company dynasty, Cleveland, along with nearby cities such as Akron, which would become renowned as the home base of Goodyear Tire and Rubber Company, along with Youngstown became popular centers for Eastern European immigrants as well as for the budding labor movement.

It was, therefore, anything but surprising that Jack Warner, the member of the clan who began entertaining as a youngster on street corners, would in his early days be affected by the populist, social activist bent of President Franklin Delano Roosevelt's New Deal and its popularity among the immigrant classes, notably within the budding union movement.

When the Warner brothers moved to California and launched their own studio the Depression influence of the early thirties appeared in their work, along with the concurrent struggles of masses on the streets of large cities. As earlier mentioned, this factor was notable in director Mervyn LeRoy's blockbuster 1931 hit from Warners *Little Caesar*, which catapulted Edward G. Robinson, cast in the mold of an Al Capone style mobster, into the ranks of cinema immortals.

Just two years later, a LeRoy film would emerge that was one of the few in his long directing repertoire falling into the musical ranks. As a producer, however, LeRoy directed the musical classic *The Wizard of Oz*, with Victor Fleming scoring an incredible double in 1939 with *Oz* along with *Gone with the Wind*.

LeRoy's popular successes during the Depression period would, in addition to *Little Caesar*, include the 1932 film starring a famous Jewish actor from the New York stage, like Robinson, with Paul Muni starring in *I Am a Fugitive from a Chain Gang*.

Muni plays James Allen, a far more sympathetic figure than the terrifying mobster portrayed by Robinson. In Allen's case, he is a Depression victim without economic prospects who becomes an innocent victim in a robbery and ends up doing time.

It helps to have some luck in your corner when it comes to making hit films, and such was the case with Mervyn LeRoy and *Fugitive*. At the close of the film Allen, who has escaped from the chain gang and is a fugitive from justice, delivers the memorable line "I steal," meaning to stay alive. On the scene's first take, a mistake was made and there was no lighting. As a master showman the light went on in LeRoy's brain as he realized the symbolism in retaining darkness while Muni delivers the final and highly memorable line of the film. The darkness reflected the bleak existence of an American who, like so many others, was being done in by the grim reality of grim economic circumstances.

Imaginative Depression Musical

Just one year following the debut of *Fugitive* and two years after *Little Caesar* arrived in theaters, none other than musical choreographic genius Busby Berkeley teamed up with LeRoy in a most ironic blend of cinema talents. The young director with the ability to capture the true grit of conflict and Depression in America's cities combined talents with the young man notable for his ability to whip up a snappy chorus line and choreograph with mesmerizing musical results.

Depression musical choreography might seem like an oxymoron to some, with music serving as the destiny of lighter spirit to make people forget about their problems and live on the lighter side, and the skilled execution of *Gold Diggers of 1933* deftly accomplished this purpose.

Gold Diggers arrived at theaters the same year that Roosevelt was inaugurated and the New Deal began. The most memorable lines of Roosevelt's presidency (along with his war declaration against Japan in 1941 and words "a day that will live in infamy") were uttered just as he was being inaugurated for the first of what would be a record four times, that "the only thing we have to fear is fear itself."

Fitting Depression troubles into a musical delving into Depression activity was a tall challenge, but director LeRoy and choreographer Berkeley were more than up to it. A key message was surmounting class consciousness and economic calamity through citizen teamwork, an indigenous part of the Roosevelt administration message in the early thirties when the New Deal was taking shape.

Dick Powell portrays Brad, a happy-go-lucky songwriter seeking his first break to reach Broadway. The secret he holds is not revealed until he is thought to be a bank robber, at which time his real identity is unearthed. Brad is from old New England wealth and is willing to gain access to Broadway by investing his own money.

Broadway musical producer Barney (Ned Sparks), like so many Americans of his period, is out of cash and cannot move his career forward. Brad is greeted as an angel who has come calling. Meanwhile, a dramatic conflict ensues when Brad's older brother, who reflects the stodginess of old money country-club wealth compared to the songwriter's natural earthiness, seeks to torpedo his brother's self-financed Broadway adventure. The snobbishness directed toward any form of the acting profession was noted among upper-class wealth among well connected snobs of Britain and the U.S.

Busby Berkeley's genius lay in imaginative choreography. As in the pattern of Broadway and London West End musical hits, a pivotal scene is the elemental glue through which success is achieved. This was notably the case in *Gold Diggers* as Berkeley applied musical choreography to the panoramic sweep of America at the advent of the New Deal, extending back to World War I. It was a rare merger of a film musical with a political panoramic sweep, in some ways as if the talents of Vincente Minnelli and Stanley Kramer had bonded, entertaining musical and choreographical mastery merging with political message cinema.

The number loomed as a pep talk in Depression America. Scores of marching men were observed in a symbolic gesture of a nation seeking to unite to battle adversity.

From World War I to the Bonus March

The march continued from World War I to the then-current troubled times. In one scene, a man thought to be a vagrant is confronted by a policeman. At that point, the scene is dramatically heightened. The individual who is singled out pulls out of his pocket a service medal from World War I, which prompts the startled officer to walk away.

This magnificently choreographed scene was structured around an event that, in the minds of many historians, doomed the re-election effort of President Herbert Hoover in 1932 and threw the upcoming election irreversibly in the direction of his Democratic Party opponent, Governor Franklin Delano Roosevelt of New York.

The Bonus March, had it occurred in the kind of cable television market that exists today, would have been discussed exhaustively. Its strategic significance during that period in an era prior to talk radio, had to be analyzed instead on radio as well as by those who viewed that popular medium for keeping in touch visually, the movie newsreel.

The Bonus March involved World War I veterans, impoverished during the Great Depression, erecting tents near the nation's Capitol in what was called Hooverville. They sought bonuses promised to them under enabling legislation from their service in World War I.

What doomed Hoover as much or more than his decision to oppose their effort was the manner in which the opposition movement was handled. Army troops were called out. Among the Army officers responding to Hoover's call to break up the protest and demolish the tent facilities was a triumvirate of eventual World War II hero generals, one of whom, Dwight Eisenhower, would become a popular two-term Republican president of the fifties; the others being Douglas MacArthur and George Patton.

Numerous Americans viewing the images in newspapers and newsreels felt moral outrage over the manner in which Americans who had answered the nation's call in a world war were being treated. The harshness of the presidential action, the rejection of those who had served the nation during a global conflict, put Hoover in a highly vulnerable position. The saying of "a picture is worth a thousand words" had never been truer.

The then strongly liberal, highly pro–New Deal studio run by Jack Warner, a son of immigrants who grew up in the heartland of Middle America, made its impact devastatingly clear in capturing the mood of America during a critical period.[4]

Far from showing only the bleak side of the Depression experience and the tragic treatment of heroic veterans, the niftily choreographed scene ended on a note of Americans figuratively rolling up their sleeves in an effort to conquer the tragedies of poverty and forge a new beginning, something on the order of what young Jack Warner and his brothers had done as they forged a blazing trail in that exciting new world of talking motion pictures.

Warner Bros. was a highly innovative studio during that period, with a sensitive hand on the pulse of a nation amid a period of great challenge. It was Warner Bros., after all, that produced the groundbreaking part-talkie with Al Jolson leading the cast in *The Jazz Singer*.[5]

The realistic fashion in which the reality of American transition from World War I to the Great Depression in the gritty but highly entertaining fashion of the leading number of *Gold Diggers of 1933* by Warner Bros. could be seen in a broader historical context in the newly reshaped filmmaking evinced in film noir.

Jack Warner had to be talked into it, but an ambitious young writer on the studio lot was determined to make the jump into directing, and with it a broader control over shaping the ultimate product that would be released to American theaters.

John Huston was the director, and the actor he selected to bring his directorial debut to fruition was so letter perfect that, had he been molded from inception to fill this need, could never have been improved upon.

Chapter Two

The Hammett Touch and a Huston Launching

> When your partner has been killed you are supposed to do something about it.
> — Humphrey Bogart, *The Maltese Falcon*.

The famous character actor Walter Huston had told his son, John, that the launching pad to the power pedestal in Hollywood lay in directing. The time was ripe with a big hit notched into his writing belt with Bogart's 1941 winner *High Sierra*. It was a good as well as natural move for Huston to obtain Bogart's services to star in his directorial debut film, *The Maltese Falcon*, not only because the actor was riding the crest of a popularity wave, but also was a friend.

The future directing star knew the importance of casting, and Humphrey Bogart made good sense in the role of detective Sam Spade. Not only was this a role that fit into Bogart's niche, that of an actor who exuded a "no nonsense" touch with just the right measure of what to a future generation would be termed machismo. This role embodied that same blend of male toughness along with a sense of knowing right from wrong, of sensitivity to a cause.

The Sam Spade role was reminiscent of an element of Duke Mantee in *The Petrified Forest*. Despite Mantee's superficial air of anti-social behavior and blatant machismo, there is something lying deeper beyond. When it becomes apparent to the hardened criminal that Alan Squier is doing more than asking Mantee to bring an end to what the sensitive Britisher proclaims to be a hopeless life of suffering, it becomes obvious to him that his is a selfless act designed to provide someone else with an opportunity to survive and endure a painful Depression.

The 1936 film was an adaptation of a hit Broadway play by Pulitzer Prize dramatist Robert Sherwood, while Dashiell Hammett, the author of the novel Huston was bringing to the screen, brought the same type of tough guy sensitivity to Sam Spade. Experiences that notably made their way into Hammett's novel had been adapted for the screen twice before: in 1931 (with Ricardo Cortez) and in 1936 (under the title *Satan Met a Lady*, starring Warren William). Huston, the fledgling director, was provided a solid chance to validate the old saying that "the third time is the charm."

Hammett's Tough-Edged Morality

There was a tough-edged morality in the fiber of Hammett's character that was brought into play with his famous detective in a unique way. What better opportunity exists to determine character than the kind of situation that a lesser individual would shun, taking the easier route? Wouldn't it be far easier to look the other way and develop a lasting association, or at least the opportunity, with an incredibly beautiful woman that held overpowering appeal for you from the instant you met her?

Such was the case with the slender brunette with finely chiseled features, Mary Astor, portraying the intelligent, charismatic, but ruthlessly opportunistic Brigid O'Shaughnessy. When Spade's shrewd detective brain calculates that Brigid was the killer of his partner, Miles Archer (Jerome Cowan), a decision would become even more elementary in the mind of an individual less grounded in a toughened moral code.

Not only is Spade head over heels in love with his client O'Shaughnessy; his opinion of his deceased partner falls little short of contempt. On what basis, therefore, has Spade decided to turn Astor over to the San Francisco Police?

It all has to do with a deeply ingrained moral code. Amid painful rumination about giving up the potential of a future with the beautiful and desirable O'Shaughnessy, it all comes down to a basic decision in the world of detective Sam Spade, and beyond to that of author Hammett: "When your partner has been killed you are supposed to do something about it."

To any student of film or interested observer, the fundamental moral of the film — the clue to the essential ingredient of Sam Spade's code and basic plot point — boils down to that essential conclusion. Despite the personal feelings the detective holds for the individuals involved, strong love for the crime's perpetrator and gradations between disgust and contempt for the victim, in the final analysis we are left not only with a crime, but one committed against your partner, the one whose name was etched on the office door along with your own.

How the Hammett Code Developed

A sketchy study of author Dashiell Hammett's life is all that is required to understand why Sam Spade reaches the conclusion to turn Brigid O'Shaughnessy over to the police. Hammett, unlike most authors of detective fiction, had more than passing contact with the world of the private detective. Between 1915 and 1921, he had worked as a detective for the Pinkerton National Detective Agency, which was launched in 1850 by Allan Pinkerton. Pinkerton became famous by foiling a plot to assassinate president-elect Abraham Lincoln in 1861.

The Pinkerton Agency, whose operatives were known as Pinkertons, prospered and grew substantially by providing strikebreakers to the nation's corporate sector in the wake of a burgeoning organized labor movement. Pinkertons were used as strikebreakers in tenacious coal, iron, lumber, and railroad disputes. As a young man, Hammett was involved in such strikebreaking activities for Pinkerton, later generating a sense of guilt which he sought to expiate for the remainder of his life.

In his post–Pinkerton days, Hammett became one of the most active members of the American left. He was one of the founders of the Writers Guild of America West and championed the union movement and the rights of workers.

One distinct act in Hammett's life comparable to that depicted in *The Maltese Falcon* resulted in him accepting a federal prison term rather than divulge his political beliefs and those of individuals with whom he professionally interacted. As such he became one of the most frequently discussed figures of the McCarthy era.

When Hammett appeared before the House Un-American Activities Committee he expressed willingness to discuss himself but refused to reveal names. The position he then expressed would be later vindicated in a U.S. Supreme Court landmark case. In *U.S. vs. Watkins*, decided in 1958, Chief Justice Earl Warren broke fresh ground on the subject of HUAC and interrogation latitude. Committee supporters pointed out that earlier the Supreme Court had ruled that it was permissible to summon witnesses for interrogation pursuant to the pursuit of prospective future legislation.

In *U.S. vs. Watkins*, a clear distinction was drawn between inquiries pursued in the course of congressional legislative activity and what Warren referred to as exposure for its own sake. HUAC opponents saw the Warren Court majority as declaring that congressional committees were empowered to hold inquiries pursuant to legislative design but not to pressure citizens into "squealing" to snoop into the realm of personal beliefs.

An Adult Life of Personal Pain

Dashiell Hammett remarked that his early life was marked by good health, but that after serving in World War I, it was dominated by pain. His service was not unlike that of Ernest Hemingway. Like Hemingway he drove an ambulance. Unlike Hemingway he contracted tuberculosis as a result of his exposure to patients he transported at a time when the disease was rife.

Fox premier screenwriter Nunnally Johnson had been a friend of Hammett's since the twenties. The cynicism woven so adroitly into his fiction by Hammett (and captured with such performing dexterity by Humphrey Bogart in *The Maltese Falcon*) was a natural byproduct of the author's fragile health. In a letter written to Hammett biographer Julian Symons not long after Hammett's death, Johnson brought out two telling points.

"Apparently there was nothing in writing that interested him [Hammett] but the money," Johnson wrote. "He had none of the usual incentives that keep writers at their typewriters for as long as they have the strength to hit the keys. He had no impulse to tell any more stories, no ambition to accomplish more as a writer, no interest in keeping his name alive, as it is often described, or any other vanity about himself or his work."

The foregoing is comprehensible in view of the health element that Johnson saw as the paramount factor governing Dashiell Hammett's life as a creative artist and a man:

> From the day I met Hammett, in the late twenties, his behavior could be accounted for only by an assumption that he had no expectation of being alive much beyond Thursday.... Once this assumption was accepted, Hammett's way of life made a form of sense. Even allowing for the exuberance of youthfulness and the headiness of the certain approach of success, not to mention the daffiness of the twenties, no one could have spent himself and his money with such recklessness who expected to be alive much longer. For once in my life I knew a man who was clearly convinced that there would never be a tomorrow.... When the end approached, it was thirty years later than he had expected it, and Death owed him a genuine apology when eventually it made its tardy appearance.[1]

During the period that his writing career was commencing, Hammett survived economically by preparing press releases for a San Francisco jewelry store. Writing was something that the war veteran could do at his apartment, remaining his own boss. Detective writing proved a logical natural in the wake of his Pinkerton experiences. An interesting Hollywood connection prior to his successes with such future cinema matter involving Sam

Spade in *The Maltese Falcon* and Nick and Nora Charles in *The Thin Man* concerned Hammett's research for Pinkerton into the notorious case of silent film comedian Roscoe "Fatty" Arbuckle's alleged rape of film extra Virginia Rappé. Hammett was also involved in researching for Pinkerton the activities of notorious New York gangster Nicky Arnstein, the husband of famed Broadway and radio comedy star Fanny Brice, the duo portrayed in William Wyler's *Funny Girl* (1968) starring Omar Shariff and Barbra Streisand.

Prior to Hammett's authoring of the aforementioned books, he wrote a novel about big city political corruption, *The Glass Key*, which was adapted to the screen twice by Paramount. Initially it became a 1938 film starring noted noir screen tough guy George Raft with Edward Arnold. Directing that film was Frank Tuttle, who attained memorable heights by providing newcomer Alan Ladd with his breakthrough role in the noir smash hit *This Gun for Hire* in 1941 opposite the woman who became his most prominent leading lady, the diminutive and explosive blonde bombshell Veronica Lake.

The Glass Key was reprised in a 1942 remake starring Alan Ladd, Veronica Lake, and Brian Donlevy. This was an obvious effort to cash in on the popularity of the starring duo after their recent success in *This Gun for Hire*. Stuart Heisler, who later became a prominent television director in Western series (including *Gunsmoke*, *The Virginian*, *Lawman*, and *Rawhide*) directed *The Glass Key*.

Showcasing a Former Boss

Hammett broke into the book publishing world with two novels featuring a character modeled on someone he knew very well. The character appeared in Captain Joseph Shaw's popular magazine *Black Mask*, where Hammett catapulted quickly to the rank of top author, with his memorable character being adapted in the former Pinkerton's detective's two earliest published novels.

In 1929, Hammett's first two novels were published. Each was a detective work built around someone less physically imposing than the fearsome Sam Spade of *The Maltese Falcon*. The detective known as the Continental Op was featured in *Red Harvest* and *The Dain Curse*. The latter work became a successful television series that won an Edgar Award and received three prime-time Emmy nominations. James Coburn was cast as Hamilton Nash, Hammett's Continental Op character who had been given a specific name.

There was a physical departure as well between the muscularly lean Coburn and the Continental Op of *The Dain Curse* and its predecessor, *Red Harvest*. Hammett's Op was a heavy set man who uses guile to crack cases. The character was modeled after Jimmy Wright, Hammett's mentor during the Baltimore phase of his Pinkerton career. The tough, highly tenacious Continental Op was, in the final analysis, Hammett himself with the Op's cases thinly disguised versions of real ones that the author had worked as a busy Pinkerton detective.

As Hammett biographer William Nolan wrote, the Continental Op, who participated in the stories without a name, was based on someone for whom the author worked while in the detective field. The tuberculosis-ridden Hammett sat down at his Underwood typewriter in his San Francisco apartment and set out on a new profession better designed to work around his physical problems, providing him with independence, and fulfilling a creative need for which he was naturally gifted. Pursuing the path of a beginning writer, it was natural for Hammett to write about something he knew about, his experiences as a detective.

Biographer Nolan, who knew fiction in his own right as co-author of the acclaimed and successfully film adapted science fiction novel *Logan's Run*, explained Hammett's motivation and success:

> When he began developing his type of diamond-hard detective tale for *Black Mask*, Hammett was not setting out to innovate but was simply putting on paper, honestly and directly, the grim world he knew best. Reflectively, he brought the argot of the streets into print, portraying the people of his world with total authenticity, allowing them to talk and behave on paper as they had talked and behaved in his Pinkerton years. The inadvertent result was what Ellery Queen called "the first 100 percent American ... truly native detective story."[2]

A recurring staple in Hammett's *Black Mask* and the books adapted from them was the tough, organized, and professional manner in which the Continental Op stays on top of cases and ultimately triumphs. After two novels starring Hammett's Op were released, the San Francisco-based author introduced a detective based in Northern California's "city by the bay" who rivaled the earlier detective for what the French would term "savoir faire," as well as genuine toughness.

Enter Sam Spade

Little did Dashiell Hammett, John Huston, or Humphrey Bogart know, but the breakthrough of tough guy detective Sam Spade amid a fascinating constellation of character performers would break crucial new ground in what would later be termed film noir. A detective vehicle with a sure-footed professional seeking to solve crimes in atmospheric San Francisco, often amid darkness and fog, elements that enhanced the genre, were ingredients that brought fans to theaters.

The history of the falcon, as given to Spade by Casper Gutman (the character depicted by Sydney Greenstreet in the film), was partially based on fact. Hammett later recalled: "Somewhere I had read of the peculiar rental arrangement between Charles V and the Order of the Hospital of St. John of Jerusalem." He was referring to an agreement of 1530 between the order and Emperor Charles V, under which as "rent" for the island of Malta, which was then under Spanish rule, the order would pay the monarch an annual tribute of one falcon. One of these birds, according to Hammett's fictional account, was "a glorious golden falcon encrusted from head to foot with the finest jewels in their coffers."

Hammett reworked facts in that there was no jeweled bird. According to Diane Moore, curator of the order, the presentation each year of a Maltese bird of prey was "one of the conditions attached to the grant of Malta and Tripoli made to the Order by Charles V in 1530." The birds, however, were living and there was no jeweled falcon, which was a Hammett invention.

As a detective Hammett needed two traits, a patient investigator's analytical instinct as well as a capacity for research. In addition to digging out information concerning an ancient order with a fascination for falconry, according to Hammett ex-partner, fellow detective Phil Haultain, the bejeweling of the falcon and linkage to the ancient order stemmed from a possession of Haultain's that colleague Sam Hammett had seen.

Phil Haultain explained: "I had this jeweled skull when I knew Sam. Had it in my apartment. An uncle of mine, who lived in Calcutta, India, sent it to me. Had a gory history ... it was taken as loot by a member of the British Expedition to Lhasa, Tibet — the jeweled skull of a holy man.... When *The Maltese Falcon* came out, the book rang a lot of bells."[3]

Sam Spade as an Ideal and "Dream Man"

Dashiell Hammett put his own stamp of true grit on Sam Spade in *The Maltese Falcon* as an extension of the tough, no-nonsense Continental Op. Spade functions as a direct extension of former Pinkerton detective Hammett. As Hammett biographer William Nolan summarized, Spade "survives by following a rigid self-imposed code of honor, who seeks to sift truth from lies, who trusts no one but himself."[4]

Spade was given Hammett's own first name of Sam. The last name was said to have been connected to a boxer of Hammett's period, John Spade. In a swift summation of the detective he invested with fame in book form and Humphrey Bogart christened with his own unique stamp of no-nonsense machismo, Hammett stated, "Sam had no original.... He's a dream man in the sense that he is what most of the detectives I worked with would like to have been and what quite a few of them, in their cockier moments, thought they approached ... a hard and shifty fellow, able to take care of himself in any situation, able to get the best of anybody he comes in contact with, whether criminal, innocent bystander or client."

In his introduction to the 1934 Modern Library edition of *The Maltese Falcon*, which was honored as the first crime story chosen for the series, Hammett pinpointed the origins of the characters inhabiting his genre establishing milestone work:

> Wilmer, the boy gun-man, was picked up in Stockton, California.... He was a neat small smooth-faced quiet boy of perhaps twenty-one.... He was serenely proud of the name the local newspapers gave him — The Midget Bandit.... Brigid O'Shaughnessy had two originals, one an artist, the other a woman who came to Pinkerton's San Francisco office to hire an operative to discharge her housekeeper, but neither of these women was a criminal....
>
> Dundy's prototype I worked with in a North Carolina railroad yard; Cairo's I picked up on a forgery charge in Pasco, Washington, in 1920; Polhaus's was a former captain of detectives.... Gutman's was suspected — foolishly, as most people were — of being a German secret agent in Washington, D.C., in the early days of the war, and I never remember shadowing a man who bored me as much.[5]

Bogart's Sam Spade was the same type of symbolic, settling influence on crime-ridden city streets that John Wayne demonstrated in the cinematic atmosphere of the American West. Audience members find comforting release over seeing a strong force overcome evil. The world of film noir adapted from works of Raymond Chandler showed a more complicated, considerably grayer view of life riddled with anarchy and insolubility.

Bogart's Spade, as nurtured from the shrewd pen of Hammett, recognized, as did John Wayne in countless heroic Western roles, that to triumph against diversity one had to meet enemies on their own level. In one of the memorable lines of the 1941 film, Spade explains to O'Shaughnessy, "Don't be too sure I'm as crooked as I'm supposed to be. That kind of reputation makes it easier to deal with the enemy."

That statement had its dramatic showcase in an unforgettable scene in the hotel suite presided over by the placidly speaking but eternally double dealing Casper Gutman (Sydney Greenstreet). Bogart as Spade demonstrates the only outrage of the film as he shrieks in seemingly uncontrollable fashion while conveying the impression that he is about to destroy any object in the room that is handy.

With a flabbergasted Gutman seeking to calm him down and obviously shocked over the suddenness and depth of his outrage, Spade storms out of the hotel room. The camera then reveals how the detective actually feels as he stalks down the hall with a broad grin on his face, delighted that he has made an impression. Spade was using, rather than losing, his temper. In the manner of his statement to O'Shaughnessy, to defeat criminal elements one has to be prepared to behave in a like manner, his temper-erupting ploy was revealed to the viewer but not the gang seeking to acquire the falcon.

Noir Homophobia

The masculine images of fictional detectives could be enhanced by drawing sharp contrasts. Such masculinity enhancement was embroidered during the period with homophobia, a practice engaged in by both Hammett and Chandler, and that was adapted from their works to the screen.

In *The Maltese Falcon*, the tough-guy image of Bogart's Sam Spade is pitted against three stereotypical homosexual types. The obese, smooth-talking Casper Gutman fit the persona of the older, drawing-room type homosexual that was ridiculed with the title of "queen." The dapper Peter Lorre as Joel Cairo was depicted as being well perfumed, personifying the type ridiculed by homophobic elements of heterosexual society as the "perfumed dandy." As will be noted in the later analysis of Raymond Chandler, the perfumed type was exhibited in the portrayal of a pivotal character in the RKO classic *Murder, My Sweet*, an adaptation of Chandler's novel *Farewell, My Lovely*.[6]

The third character in the gay trilogy of characters depicted to cohere with early forties' homophobia was Wilmer, a ruthless gunman depicted by one of the most frequent and popular faces to appear in noir dramas, Elisha Cook, Jr. To broaden the illustration that Wilmer was a "kept boy" he was referred to derisively by Spade as a "gunsel," which was period slang depicting a kept male of the homosexual world.[7]

In a creative industry in which some of its most talented and in many instances most popular people, within the acting field, were homosexual and bisexual, it was particularly loathsome to see the kind of homophobic "piling on" depicted in movies. In the detective field in particular, however, this kind of bigoted depiction is understandable.

In some of the more physical depictions of slapstick, a straight man is often represented by someone to be made fun of and bullied verbally and sometimes physically by the comedian. Homosexuals revealed negatively in films could serve to make macho male figures look even tougher through expanding contrast. While the leading men were shown as tough and strong symbols, homosexuals were weak adversaries they could easily run over; the sturdy overpowering the vulnerable.

The subject will be further discussed in analyzing Raymond Chandler and his work with the homophobic segment of the blockbuster film *Murder, My Sweet* compared alongside the treatment of homosexuality in *The Maltese Falcon*.

Despite the aforementioned negative element employed against the criminal enterprise with which Sam Spade is confronted, the highly colorful and equally unique personas of Gutman, Cairo and Wilmer significantly figured in the film's popular and critical success. *The Maltese Falcon* served as a major launching pad for the triumvirate of actors portraying these characters.

Greenstreet would become an enduring figure in numerous character roles in Hollywood, his new home. His days of playing butlers in Broadway productions ended as a new career phase began. Lorre's trademark voice and manner made him a perfect character for foreign intrigue adventures, with one of his signature roles coming alongside Bogart the following year with the release of *Casablanca*. As for Cook, his roles in numerous film noir adventures made him a favorite at nostalgia festivals at which he was a presence to the time of his death. He will be further discussed in concert with one of his best roles in the Robert Siodmak film *Phantom Lady*.

Action and Characterization as Central Ingredients

John Huston, as a screenwriter nurtured in the Warner Bros. tradition, followed in *The Maltese Falcon* the concept of keeping the action moving. This was the studio that featured such men of action as Bogart along with James Cagney, George Raft, and Edward G. Robinson. Huston had to be also intrigued by Dashiell Hammett digging into his case histories and transposing some of the most fascinating characters he encountered into figures woven into his fictional framework of *The Maltese Falcon*. The villainous triumvirate of Greenstreet as Casper Gutman, Lorre as Joel Cairo, and Cook as Wilmer adapted colorfully to the screen. Characters of imagination entertaining readers on a printed page jumped onto a giant screen, where the camera's all-perusing eye could breathe a new kind of life into them, that of cinema magic.

Another element of the story that furnished solid entertainment value involved the police detectives who kept a careful watch on the activities of both Spade and the criminal trio seeking to acquire the elusive Maltese Falcon. As a seasoned Pinkerton detective, Hammett would be highly familiar with what has been termed in criminal prosecutorial circles as the Mutt and Jeff technique. The technique involves two police detectives who seek cooperation from criminal suspects through having one individual behave in an aggressive, nasty manner. This is contrasted with a smoother, non-confrontational type.

Police authorities achieved such a high level of success in using the Mutt and Jeff technique with suspects that many confessions were extracted using it. This technique was described and given as a reason in propounding Miranda rights warnings to criminal suspects. Chief Justice Earl Warren, a former successful prosecutor as District of Attorney of Alameda County, California (Oakland and surrounding areas), described the Mutt and Jeff technique in his majority opinion in the landmark 1966 case, *U.S. vs. Miranda*.

Playing the San Francisco plainclothes detectives were two veteran character actors who handled their roles with just the proper measure of contrast, leading those interested in criminal law to ascertain the psychological roots of them as screen versions of the Mutt and Jeff tandem technique. Barton MacLane plays Detective Lieutenant Dundy, a man who detests the confident independence of Spade and, at one point, punches him.

Moving in promptly to break up a potential fight and finesse the questioning process is Ward Bond as Detective Tom Polhaus. A former football player at the University of Southern California, Bond developed a lifelong friendship with a fellow Trojan footballer that benefited him when he became an actor. The friend was John Wayne, and Bond became one of the leading figures of the "John Ford Repertory Company" in vehicles starring Wayne.

Whereas Dundy is hot-blooded, Polhaus is lower-keyed, with the pride and independent nature of Spade. As a result Polhaus achieves success in dealing with him, talking to him in soft but earnest terms while Dundy speaks hostile words.

In the fiction of Hammett and Chandler, the key to success lay not so much in plot as it does in characterization. Take two fascinating California settings, the big city of the north, San Francisco, and the intriguing metropolis of the south, Los Angeles; inhabit each with a unique set of characters set amid detective stories with solid leading figures such as Sam Spade and Philip Marlowe seeking justice, and the judicious mixture marked success.

A Lost Assignment and "The Stuff Dreams Are Made Of"

Huston, a beginning director attempting to pump fresh film life into an adapted detective novel that had been unsuccessful in the first two efforts, made a believer out of initial skeptic Jack Warner. The studio head used his wiles to get a look at the rudimentary beginnings of the script and provided prompt approval. In the process, a top Hollywood writing professional lost an assignment.

Allen Rivkin was one of the founders of the Screenwriters Guild, later named the Writers Guild of America. An enthused John Huston told him that *The Maltese Falcon* had "never been done right" and thought they could get an assignment out of the project.

Rivkin ended up losing his assignment under the most flukish circumstances: enthusiastic intervention on the part of studio boss Jack Warner. Huston had his secretary break down the screenplay into basic shots, after which he and Rivkin would commence action. The secretary used the novel as a word-for-word guide. Somehow the working copy reached Warner, who declared it a "great script" and immediately supplied his approval for the project.

By Warner approving a scene breakdown precisely following the book's dialogue, Dashiell Hammett was fortunate enough to avoid the fate that many a dissenting book author delivered, notably Ernest Hemingway, that works had been substantially changed. In this case fidelity was scrupulously maintained while Rivkin became the writing project's casualty.

While Huston slightly trimmed the secretary's copy and added a few lines, in the final analysis he was substantially shooting Hammett's book. Critic Allen Eyles wrote, "Dashiell Hammett remains the real author of the film without ever having worked on it. Huston ... imposed no viewpoint of his own, but sought to realize on film the atmosphere of the book, merging precisely into the aloof position Hammett adopts in his writing. Hammett's style is tersely descriptive, involving no explanation of any set of his characters, and is entirely concerned in conveying a situation by its externals, letting events speak for themselves."[8]

One element of the book that was toned down by Huston was the homosexual aspects of the Cairo-Cook relationship. One of the most famous lines of dialogue in cinema annals was penned by Huston. It provided a perfect and evocative finale for the film as well as providing a universal comment about the human dream for fulfillment.

When Detective Polhaus asks Spade what the falcon is, the brilliantly succinct response is, "It's the stuff that dreams are made of."

Steve Eifert recalled how a Bogart renaissance coincided with linkage to his memorable Sam Spade role in *The Maltese Falcon*: "I loved *The Maltese Falcon*. I remember that Bogart had a bit of a resurgence in popularity in the seventies and early eighties. I had a Gordon's Gin ad for Bogart hanging on my bedroom door. It was great. Bogie sitting in his office with Spade and Archer etched on the door and San Francisco in the background. The black bird perched on his desk next to a bottle of Gordon's Gin, of course. You could stare at the poster and daydream about the adventures of Sam Spade."

Hammett's Changing Artistic and Political Temperament

Film historians have frequently noted the figurative passing of the baton between Dashiell Hammett and Raymond Chandler. Hammett was appropriately invested with the originative master of the "hard-boiled" school of detective writing, an essential launching pad for the film noir genre, but compared to Chandler, the former Pinkerton detective had retained some elements of the romanticist.

Bogart's Sam Spade character in *The Maltese Falcon* was both a moralist and romanticist. As someone who believed in fundamental honesty and moral order being preserved, the moralist in Spade superseded the romanticist. While Spade was adamant that O'Shaughnessy must pay for killing a partner he could not personally abide, the romanticist within him openly conceded to her his love while she begged him to drop his pursuit of justice so that romance would have an opportunity to bloom. Spade, the romanticist, talked about waiting for her until she finished her term of imprisonment.

In addition to the moralistic side of Hammett's detective characters, the Continental Op and Sam Spade, a world was presented in which their skilled efficiency, a composite of Hammett and his boss James Wright, were capable of thwarting and ultimately overwhelming the insidious forces of evil. It provided readers with a reassuring feeling to know that good would ultimately overwhelm evil.

The world was prepared following the brutal conflict of World War II, with at least 50 million lives lost, a Holocaust led by Adolf Hitler to eviscerate Jews, Czechs, homosexuals, Gypsies, as well as the physically and mentally challenged as unworthy of existence. Along with these atrocities came the unleashing of the deadly force of the atomic bomb and, shortly thereafter, the advent of the Cold War, to accept entertainment with less assuring messages. The world was a deadly realm of uncertainty where a Continental Op or Sam Spade would not necessarily surface to right wrongs and successfully combat adversity.

While it is true that Raymond Chandler would take over Dashiell Hammett's mantle as the king of the hard-boiled detective masters, this did not happen as a result of a different philosophy supplanting its predecessor. In fact, the passing of the baton, through the auspices of *Black Mask*, the nation's premier detective magazine, occurred because of a change in Hammett's thinking.

Captain Joseph Shaw, the flamboyant, public relations-oriented publisher of *Black Mask*, cajoled Hammett to the ultimate of his considerable powers of persuasion to abandon his thinking, but ultimately failed. As a result, Chandler took over Hammett's mantle through abdication.

Despite considerable health problems, Hammett nonetheless had earlier retained the measure of human optimism that spawned assertive crime solvers who conquered adversaries in the persons of the Continental Op and Sam Spade. Sober reflection on the march of human events left Hammett in a completely different mood. He moved into a somber phase, embraced by the kind of revolutionary politics the author believed were necessary to change the world.

His abandonment of the hard-boiled detective world in which he was a consummate master and trail blazer could also have been influenced over the then-public perception of the genre, as explained in one revealing paragraph by Hammett biographer Julian Symons:

> Hammett's success as a writer (distinct from the money he was soon to earn from films) must be seen in perspective. Despite the high critical praise of *The Maltese Falcon*, the hard-boiled crime story remained something that many readers of mysteries found too

violent and too crude for their taste. [S.S.] Van Dine faded from the scene during the thirties, but Ellery Queen flourished, and the small army of genteel women writers found it a steady market. Hammett's books had no great success at this time in Britain or the rest of Europe. The hard-boiled story was an indigenous American species and for some years did not flourish elsewhere. Pulp in general remained badly paid, and writers moved out of it if they could, as Erle Stanley Gardner did after the publication of his first Perry Mason novel in 1933.[9]

The Glass Key and a Turning Tide

While the Continental Op and Sam Spade were outsiders operating on the right side of the law, intervening forces on behalf of the good part of society, the chief figure of *The Glass Key* is Ned Beaumont, who is a definitive insider suffused in corruption. Beaumont plays people and situations to his advantage. Beaumont battles for control of a major city which, while not identified, bears a similarity to Baltimore, the city where Hammett was born and raised. Beaumont plays opportunistic right hand man to mob boss Paul Madvig.

Peter Wolfe in his work *Beams Falling: The Art of Dashiell Hammett*, summarized Ned Beaumont as someone who has "sold out to the machine. A believer in the spoils system, he hands out bribes, sinecures, and patronage jobs in return for political favors.... Beaumont's neglect of the poor, the sick, the jobless makes him ... an unlikely Depression hero."

Paramount filmed *The Glass Key* twice within a decade. The 1935 version, directed by Frank Tuttle, starred noir tough guy George Raft as Beaumont and Edward Arnold as Madvig. In the 1942 version, directed by Stuart Heisler, it was Ladd, capitalizing on his recently acquired popularity in *This Gun for Hire*, playing the role of Beaumont, with Brian Donlevy cast as Madvig.

The next work written by Hammett conjures up a more positive image by film viewers unaware of the differences between the book and what turned out to be a notably successful film series: *The Thin Man*. While the strong layer of charm applied for Depression movie audiences (along with the appealing performers paid major box-office dividends), the novel that spawned the films was a bleaker proposition. As Hammett biographer William Nolan noted, "*The Thin Man* is the bleakest of Hammett's novels." George Thompson weighed in on the same subject in the November 1974 edition of the magazine *The Armchair Detective*.

Thompson saw *The Thin Man* as an excursion on the dark side: "The moral vision of *The Thin Man* is dark indeed. The plot does more than unmask a villain; it shows that the villain survives only because of the corresponding greed and savagery in those around him.... Cannibals like Macauley the killer can feast off others because the world is so devoid of values that he can appear as a natural part of the landscape."[10]

William Nolan sees strong similarities between unprincipled opportunist Ned Beaumont and Nick Charles as embodying "Hammett's canon of antiheroes. Both are hollow men, empty of moral commitment. They are passive; they do not act, they react. A direct line can be traced from the reluctantly heroic Continental Op, through the more cynical Sam Spade, to the final emptiness of Beaumont and Nick Charles."

While Hammett focused on a bleaker vision of Nick Charles, Hollywood created a different persona in launching the successful Thin Man series. The focus was on style with the debonair, mellow-voiced, dapper William Powell portraying the detective. The casting addition of the comparably stylish Myrna Loy as his wife, Nora, doubled the panache ingredient.

Charles Tranberg wrote a book about the Thin Man film series, *The Thin Man Films: Murder Over Cocktails*. In analyzing Dashiell Hammett as a writer, he drew a line of demarcation between the cynical and brooding novel *The Thin Man* and what transpired in the films based on the Nick and Nora Charles characters as representations of New York chic and sophistication:

> Hammett is, of course, one of the pre-eminent examples of the American hard-boiled crime writer. I think he and Raymond Chandler are the best examples of this style from that era. My favorite book of his is *The Maltese Falcon*. Strangely I don't enjoy the book *The Thin Man* nearly as much as the film. The book follows the same basic plot, but it's also much darker and the characters are more cynical rather than playful. Of course cynicism has always been a hallmark of the Hammett style. Warner Bros. with *The Maltese Falcon* brought this hard-edged cynicism out well. Bogart was a perfect fit for Hammett because his screen persona was cynical and sardonic. The other hallmark of a Hammett book is the simplicity of the writing. He didn't try to go out and overpower his readers with his intellect. He told his stories very simply but yet the plots could be quite complex.

Tranberg draws a sharp distinction between Nick and Nora Charles as represented by Hammett and the characters who emerged on screen:

> Nick and Nora, in the book, are not nearly as much fun or as funny as they are in the film version of *The Thin Man*. I think the screenwriters, who were married themselves, Albert Hackett and Frances Goodrich, put a lot of themselves in constructing the film and the dialogue. It should be remembered that the director of the film, Woody Van Dyke, pretty much told them to downplay the mystery and conceive five or six good scenes for Nick and Nora. The Thin Man series was as much a comedy series as a mystery series. Yes, there is always a murder that needs to be investigated, but the real key to the popularity of the films is the interplay between Nick and Nora when you cast two such appealing and witty actors as William Powell and Myrna Loy it takes on a life of its own.[11]

The transformation from hard-edged cynicism to sophisticated humor and New York chic could well have stemmed from the prevailing outlook of MGM boss Louis B. Mayer. While Warner's fledgling director John Huston demonstrated an artistic side by beginning with a murder in the noir atmosphere of San Francisco fog and focused on the cynicism of Bogart's Sam Spade character, Mayer in the MGM tradition took a more upbeat, audience-friendly turn, fashioning a series based on the married detective team. W.S. Van Dyke, known as "One Shot Van Dyke" prompted by his swift pacing, as measured in musicals starring Jeanette MacDonald and Nelson Eddy, was the perfect MGM choice to influence the creative thrust of humorous spontaneity with a crafty duo of married screenwriters incorporating domestic chic into their adaptation, playing to the notable strengths of the popular stars Powell and Loy.

Hackett and Goodrich won a Pulitzer Prize and Tony Award for *The Diary of Anne Frank* and adapted their own drama to the screen in 1959. They also were among the collaborators on Frank Capra's *It's a Wonderful Life* (1946). In addition to penning *The Thin Man*, they also co-wrote the next two installments of the series, *After the Thin Man* (1936) and *Another Thin Man* (1939).

Hammett's Final Novel

The Thin Man was the final novel written by Hammett. His increasing cynicism can, with almost total certainty, be traced to his vision of America and the world. As times grew tougher in Depression era America, Hammett, like many Americans with a particularly pronounced propensity for the creative arts, turned sharply leftward in the belief that the political system had failed and that a new effort was needed to provide substantive change.

While Hammett, according to biographer Nolan, when asked if he was a Communist by his brother would say only "I am a Marxist," he was not bashful about supporting causes and joining organizations labeled as Communist front groups by the U.S. Attorney General's office. His position remained the same, that his ideas remained his own business and nobody else's and that acts rather than ideas represented prosecutable misconduct.

Despite suffering from tuberculosis and being significantly underweight, Hammett lobbied hard for World War II service duty and was eventually accepted into the Army. He spent most of the war in the Aleutian Islands, where he edited the base newspaper and would mentor two future network television commentators, the brothers Bernard and Martin Kalb. His perseverance assuredly related to his strong opposition to Nazism and Fascism.

With stern political pressure being applied by the Republican right, efforts that would culminate in McCarthy-style anti–Communism, Harry Truman, a Democratic president with solid liberal credentials on domestic issues and strong support from unions, felt the pressure as the war ended and the Cold War commenced.

Many historians believe that pressure from the right was a factor in Truman's eagerness to engage Communism in the Korean War. The stalemate, intensified by Truman's recall of the popular conservative symbol, General Douglas MacArthur, from Korea, resulted in sharp political division in America and increased concern about the Soviet Union.

Hughes and Anti-Communist Noir

Dashiell Hammett and other figures of the left, notably in the film industry, came under increasing scrutiny. Such scrutiny was facilitated by the passage of the McCarran-Walter Internal Security Act of 1950. The Cold War legislation mandated members of the Communist Party to register with the office of the U.S. attorney general.

The Smith Act, passed in 1940, made it a crime to preach for the violent overthrow of the U.S. government, and the Internal Security Act mandated Communist Party members to register with the attorney general's office. Senator Hubert Humphrey, a founder of the liberal Americans for Democratic Action and one of the most revered figures of the farm labor movement in Minnesota, the state he represented, like other Democrats saw the change in the wind when a 20-year executive reign of his party was snapped in 1952 with the election of popular World War II General Dwight D. Eisenhower. The campaign which successfully put the party in power during the conflict that concluded in 1945 was hammered by an invigorated Republican right with accusations that Democrats were being "soft on Communism."

Humphrey faced a re-election campaign in 1954 at a time when McCarthy and his ally, Vice-President Richard Nixon, were flexing their muscles. To shore up his anti–Communist bona fides McCarthy sponsored the Communist Control Act, which is generically known as the bill that outlawed the organization. Under the legislation members of Communist front organizations were barred from employment within the federal government, working in a private defense facility, obtaining passports, or receiving classified information.

It is understandable that, within this politically charged climate, films would be made denouncing internal Communism. One such effort that became a landmark of the film noir genre was the 1953 release *Pickup on South Street* starring Richard Widmark, a bright new Hollywood leading man fresh from a career as a radio film actor in New York, and Jean Peters, one of Howard Hughes's wives. The film, directed by Samuel Fuller, was essentially a crime story in which Skip McCoy (Widmark), a skilled pickpocket who falls in love with call girl Candy (Peters), helps police to nail a criminal syndicate. What made the film a product of the period with strong political overtones was that the ruthless gang leader ultimately hunted down by a persistent McCoy was a vigilant U.S. Communist. Playing the heavy was Richard Kiley, who would go on to starring fame on Broadway in the sixties in the highly successful musical *Man of La Mancha*.

While *Pickup on South Street*, along with some other films of the period, would use Communists as gangsters rather than typical routine criminal opportunists as heavies, it would be the controversial bashful billionaire Howard Hughes who tackled internal Communism with gusto.

The Woman on Pier 13 bore the pre-release title of *I Married a Communist*. It was directed by Britisher Robert Stevenson, who would become legendary better than a decade later for his work on several successful Walt Disney Studios hits, highlighted by the 1964 Julie Andrews classic *Mary Poppins*. *The Woman on Pier 13* was about as unlike Mary Poppins as any film could be.

While Hughes, according to his longtime former chief executive officer Noah Dietrich, did not even vote, when it came to recognizing the interrelationship of politics on his vast corporate empire, he was not averse to becoming involved in the process, such as his controversial loan to then Vice-President Richard Nixon. When it came to the strident anti–Communism that culminated in the Hollywood blacklist, Hughes was early on the scene, as evidenced by the fact that *The Woman on Pier 13* was released in 1949.

A note of supreme irony related to the fact that the film's male star was Robert Ryan, an unlikely performer due to his political views. In addition of being a strong backer and spokesperson in the presidential campaigns of Democrats Adlai E. Stevenson in 1952 and 1956 and John F. Kennedy in 1960, Ryan was also a prominent member of the Committee for a Sane Nuclear Policy, which advocated international disarmament at a time when "balance of terror" period bomb manufacturing activity was popular in many American circles, as well as the American Civil Liberties Union.

In *The Woman on Pier 13*, Brad Collins (Ryan), is a shipping magnate with a radical past. As a result he is blackmailed into cooperation of sorts with Communist leader Vanning (Thomas Gomez).

The script of Robert Hardy Andrews and Charles Grayson followed a formula encompassed in films of the fifties that would, in other periods, have been regular gangster films by casting Communists and the American Communist Party apparatus as evildoers of high magnitude. In *The Woman on Pier 13* Vanning runs an organization more closely akin to Murder Incorporated rather than the American Communist Party led for years by Gus Hall. One of the film's major figures is veteran character performer and film noir regular William Talman, a later stalwart on the *Perry Mason* television series, who plays Bailey, a ruthless assassin for hire employed regularly by Vanning.

The film's other major story element relates to a depiction of the familiar noir concept of "nice young man meets experienced ruthless woman" with John Agar (whose real-life divorce from former child screen idol Shirley Temple ended the year *The Woman on Pier 13* was released), as Don Lowry and statuesque RKO beauty Janis Carter as Christine Norman.

Lowry, the younger brother of Collins, is thoroughly indoctrinated by Vanning Communist cell member Norman. Her job is so effective that Lowry talks like a parrot that has memorized *Quotations from Chairman Mao*.

Film analysts frequently cite his role in *The Woman on Pier 13* as embodying Agar's finest acting opportunity. He handles his role with gusto, as does Carter as a sinister manipulator; the same can be said for the remainder of a cast top heavy with talented professionals. Director Stevenson was another professional of top standing in Hollywood who, earlier in the forties, had directed Orson Welles and Joan Fontaine in *Jane Eyre* (1944).

The film's problem stemmed from the stridence of the message. *The Woman on Pier 13*, from the standpoint of right wing propaganda, occupies a comparable position on the Hollywood firmament to the Sidney Bachman script in the apocryphal biography of Frederic Chopin, the 1945 release *A Song to Remember* starring Cornell Wilde, Merle Oberon, and Paul Muni.

Hammett's Imprisonment and Blacklisting

With the Cold War in full swing, membership in any organization designated by the attorney general's List of Subversive Organizations was a dangerous precipice to occupy. This is what occurred with Hammett as an organization he served as trustee, the Civil Rights Congress, was designated a Communist front group as directed by President Truman's Executive Order 9835.

To Hammett, someone who had served his country during two wars, revealing information about friends and confidantes was verboten. To him there was a code of honor involved in the manner that his detective Sam Spade in *The Maltese Falcon* would turn in the woman he loved upon recognizing that she had killed a partner he despised.

The government sought information from Hammett as a Civil Rights Congress trustee. The government believed that Hammett could assist them in tracing the organization's financial roots, but he steadfastly declined. Interrogating Hammett on July 9, 1951, in the chambers of U.S. District Court Judge Sylvester Ryan was U.S. Attorney Irving Saypol, who prosecuted Julius and Ethel Rosenberg and was described by *Time* as "the nation's number one legal hunter of top Communists."

When Hammett took the Fifth Amendment and refused to provide information regarding contributors to a bail fund on behalf of defendants convicted of violating the Smith Act, refusing even to identify his signature or initials on CRC documents the government had subpoenaed, he was immediately found guilty of contempt of court.

Hammett served a six-month sentence at the Federal Correction Institute at Ashland, Kentucky, after having been at the Federal House of Detention, a holding area on West Street in New York City. The process began on July 10, 1951. His time in Kentucky was shortened by 30 days for good behavior. Hammett was discharged on December 9, 1951.

The author found himself blacklisted in Hollywood, a common occurrence for many on the left in the movie colony at the time. Concurrent with that result was the Internal Revenue Service launching what was announced as "a careful investigation of Mr. Hammett's tax forms." The IRS ultimately billed Hammett for $111,000 in back taxes and attached all of his royalties.

A Confrontation with McCarthy

With Hammett, along with his companion of the last three decades of his life, playwright Lillian Hellman, becoming leading symbols of the Hollywood left, it could be classified as a form of historical inevitability for him to be ultimately confronted by the leading figure, along with Richard Nixon, of the political right's anti–Communist investigative pursuit. On March 26, 1953, Joseph McCarthy and Hammett locked horns before the Wisconsin solon's Senate Internal Security Subcommittee.

McCarthy asked Hammett if he had ever engaged in sabotage. The author answered, "No, sir."

Hammett's testimony concluded with a memorable exchange. It began with McCarthy asking, "Mr. Hammett, if you were spending, as we are, over a hundred million dollars a year on an information program allegedly for the purpose of fighting Communism, and if you were in charge of that program to fight Communism, would you purchase the works of some seventy-five Communist authors and distribute their works throughout the world, placing our official stamp of approval upon those works?"

The response by Hammett cut to the core of McCarthy's investigative technique by succinctly stating the end result he feared as well as loathed of such efforts: "Well, I think — of course I don't know — if I were fighting Communism, I don't think I would do it by giving people any books at all."[12]

In his self-designated role of America's censor, Senator McCarthy had combed the files of the overseas U.S. Information Service libraries to "root out" works by perceived Communist sympathizers. The creator of the Continental Op and Sam Spade saw 300 copies of his novels removed from those library shelves.

The copies were ultimately restored by an executive order by President Eisenhower. It was Eisenhower who had helped bring McCarthy down by instructing his aides not to cooperate with the committee headed by the Wisconsin senator.

It was Robert Vaughn, the actor who starred in the popular *The Man from U.N.C.L.E.* television series, who would provide the tragic Hollywood blacklist period with a two-word summation. In his doctoral dissertation from the University of Southern California, and what became a book superbly delineating the time and events, Vaughn's title said it all: *Only Victims*.

In the case of Hammett, however, like many on the left he turned a blind eye to the dangers of Soviet totalitarianism. In the manner of intractable party apparatchiks, Hammett took an isolationist stance regarding World War II until Russia was attacked by Nazi Germany. At that point he turned an about-face and became bullishly anti–Hitler.

"There is nothing unusual in such Communist about-turns, but it is shameful that a man of Hammett's independent mind should have behaved like any party hack," Julian Symons concluded. "Such behavior even extended to the characteristic denial of free speech to other opposition groups. When an objector at one meeting held in 1940 protested against the party's denial of election and civil rights to the Socialist party, he was hissed, and Hammett, in his role as chairman, said that only anti-democratic elements benefited from disturbing unity in such a way. Then and thereafter, the abnegation of his will in relation to the current party line was total."

A torrent of criticism would later greet Hammett's longtime partner Lillian Hellman's criticism of Nikita Khrushchev following the Soviet premier's 1956 harsh denunciation of the regime of Joseph Stalin.

When Hammett became disenchanted with detective authorship, his goal was to engage in what he termed "serious writing." This provided a cultured man who dressed regularly in tweed suits, had been educated in England, and spoke with an upper-class British accent, to ascend to the position Hammett vacated as initially king of the pulp story writers and, ultimately, that of supreme detective author.

Chapter Three

Raymond Chandler and His Symphony of the Streets

> There are two kinds of truth: the truth that lights the way and the truth that warms the heart. The first of these is science, and the second is art.... The truth of art keeps science from becoming inhuman, the truth of science keeps art from becoming ridiculous. — Raymond Chandler

With Hammett having his personal fill of the detective genre and hoping (without fulfillment) to move to a new career writing different types of novels, Captain Joseph Shaw of *Black Mask*, after failing despite numerous efforts to keep his famous author in the fold, would soon have reason to rejoice.

A silent symbolic passing of the torch would occur when Raymond Chandler, a former oil executive who bore the same motivation of Dashiell Hammett (that of trying to scrap out a living after being fired from his former occupation) took off where his successor ended. In fact, Chandler brought such meaning to the detective genre on an international scale that he would be appropriately christened as one of the founders of film noir after France's intellectual community, notably Albert Camus, had an opportunity to read and analyze his works.

While Chandler applied his talents directly to the screen, studios and their screenwriters adapted his printed work for years. Arguably the single best one scene application of the celebrated mystery author into cinema was a 1949 work that was not based on one of his novels and in which he was not involved in the script writing.

Criss Cross, a 1949 Universal production starring Burt Lancaster, Yvonne De Carlo, and Dan Duryea, contained a scene that brilliantly evoked the letter and spirit of what Chandler represented wrapped in a neat film noir package. A memorable figure emerged in that one scene, his only one of the film, that bore a closer resemblance to the detective author than any character he created.

Alan Napier as Chandler Stand In

Born in Chicago, Illinois, in 1888, Raymond Chandler spent his formative years in England, developing a refined British accent. Meanwhile, Alan Napier, born Alan Napier-Clavering in 1903, was reared in Britain's Midlands in Birmingham. He had distinguished lineage as a cousin to two of Britain's best-known political figures and one of Birmingham's most notable family names.

Napier was a cousin of Neville and Austen Chamberlain. Neville, after serving as Lord Mayor of Birmingham, became the prime minister. He was largely known for the Munich Agreement in what was a futile attempt to prevent, through negotiated settlement, Adolf Hitler's ascent as well as World War II. Napier's other famous Chamberlain cousin was Austen, who became one of Britain's notable foreign secretaries.

Though nobody in Napier's family had pursued a theatrical career, considering his commanding presence with an imposing height of six feet six inches and possessor of a voice that boomed as well as resonated with graceful command, the acting world would appear a natural choice. And pursue it Napier did. After graduating from Clifton College, he studied at the Royal Academy of Dramatic Art, which has helped mold many of its students to greatness. From there Napier became involved with the Oxford Players. He worked alongside such future acting greats as John Gielgud and Robert Morley.

While he appeared in some British films, Napier, as representative of so many serious dramatic talents hailing from the land of Shakespeare, Marlowe, and Wilde, was active on London's West End from 1929 to 1939. After he came to New York to co-star with Gladys George on Broadway in *Lady in Waiting*, Napier's career moved to a new level. With Hollywood then engaged in prolific film activity meant to appeal to an international audience, the cinema capital welcomed many well-trained British performers with elegant accents, and the rangy Napier cut a distinctive presence in character roles.

An early opportunity for Napier arrived when he performed in Val Lewton's 1942 cult classic *Cat People*, which was followed by roles in similar genre films *The Uninvited* (1944) and the 1946 release *House of Horrors*. Two years later Napier appeared as the high priest in Orson Welles's production of *Macbeth*.

One year after *Macbeth* was released, German director Robert Siodmak's *Criss Cross* appeared, with Napier cast in the role of Finchley. He appeared in just one scene. This could be arguably cited as the most thematically meaningful scene of one of the more representative noir works ever filmed.

The scene's setting was one not only used by Chandler, but a location where he lived not long after he moved to the city he both reviled and loved. Bunker Hill, a hilly slope removed from downtown Los Angeles, was generally reached not by walking up the sharp incline, but via funicular. The funicular route was known as Angel's Flight. Considering the style of living and type of individual typifying Bunker Hill, the Angel's Flight designation contains a note so ironic that it could have been invented by master ironist Chandler himself.

Bunker Hill was a location where a lot of youthful newcomers to the city — individuals who might be long on aspirations but short of cash — spent time before getting economic stability through gainful employment. Chandler was one of those young men looking forward to making his mark in the city. He not only made a mark in the city, he transplanted its geography and multi-faceted populace into the hearts and minds of millions of readers throughout the world. He was also able to capitalize on the experience in a way that nobody other than a writer of his piercing creative sensitivity could ever hope to achieve.

If Bunker Hill was affordable to Chandler and others like him who arrived in the city with limited funds, it appealed to another type as well. With the prospect of cheap rent, Bunker Hill became a boulevard of broken dreams, a location for those whose aspirations had dissipated long ago, or at least had been sharply curtailed. Such was the case with the older residents of Bunker Hill. The older residents — many of whom had brushes with the law and were not above doing whatever it took to claw out an advantage in a setting of shabby rooms endowed by drinkers of cheap wine, smokers of numerous cigarettes, and possessors of unlimited schemes — provided ample opportunity for study by the agile and fertile mind of the young Raymond Chandler. An education was being achieved that, from a practical standpoint, exceeded that which he received as a schoolboy at Dulwich College in London.

Noir and the Samson Effect

Director Robert Siodmak's brilliant instinct for noir had been earlier proven with *Phantom Lady* in 1944 and *The Killers* two years later. *Criss Cross* provided the same formula with a devastating and ultimately irresistible femme fatale, with the same actor playing the victimized character in each film. Burt Lancaster succumbed to the overpowering beauty and wily trickery of Ava Gardner in *The Killers* and Yvonne De Carlo in *Criss Cross*.

One of the noir tricks of the trade that enabled Siodmak to guide to fruition two such stellar classic noir thematic and dramatic efforts in *The Killers* and *Criss Cross* (with Jacques Tourneur doing likewise with the 1947 release *Out of the Past*) was to cast two broad-shouldered macho types in the leads, creating a greater feeling of all-consuming power wielded by the dazzling femmes fatale, Gardner, De Carlo, and Jane Greer, respectively.

Burt Lancaster was a former acrobat with a devastating manner to accommodate his build, the kind of man generally in charge of situations along life's highway. Robert Mitchum was a former semi-pro boxer who led a roustabout life before coming to Hollywood and ultimately pursuing an acting career. Mitchum even endured a period in the South on a chain gang, from which he escaped.

The sustaining element of Lancaster as Steve Thompson in *Criss Cross* is that he has no shortcomings in the brain department, a contrast from playing the hapless, hopelessly in love role of The Swede in *The Killers*. The fact that Robert Mitchum played a savvy, street smart private detective in *Out of the Past* who is lauded for his brain power by none other than crime boss nemesis Whit (Kirk Douglas), accents the clash at work when two rugged young males generally in control are thoroughly bowled over by two devastating and ruthlessly plotting women. They not only possess the requisite intellectual skills to know that they are dealing with deadly dynamite in the form of women who will stop at nothing to achieve their selfish goals; they have received warnings from others. In the case of Steve Thompson he is asked by his mother, "Of all the women in Los Angeles, why did you pick her?"

The idea of otherwise strong men turning against their intelligent and ethical selves to pursue dangerous and unprincipled women of beauty contains the clash of raw power revealed in the biblical account of Samson and Delilah, which was brought to the screen in 1949, ironically the same year that *Criss Cross* debuted. Cecil B. De Mille, biblical spectacle master, directed with ideal casting, pitting Hedy Lamarr, long acknowledged as one of the world's most dazzling beauties, haunting Victor Mature, touted in Hollywood press circles as one of the industry's handsomest hunks of man.

Mature, as Samson, was reduced to a highly vulnerable state he would not have occupied had it not been for the haunting beauty and controlling evil influence wielded by Vienna-born beauty Lamarr as Delilah. Samson derives power through his hair and, once Delilah convinces him to cut it, she assumes control.

The control of a wily woman of cunning coupled with beauty produces a Samson effect on leading men such as Gardner and De Carlo over Lancaster, and Greer over Mitchum, is accented due to their otherwise apparent strength. This makes the witch's brew concocted and wielded by the femme fatale appear all the more devastating.

A conflict of a differing nature occurred in the brilliantly constructed script that Raymond Chandler crafted along with the film's director Billy Wilder in the 1944 classic *Double Indemnity*. In this case, the brilliant sociopath Phyllis Dietrichson (Barbara Stanwyck) is dealing with a different type of man than that depicted by Lancaster and Mitchum. The psychological element pitting Dietrichson against Walter Neff (Fred MacMurray) is that he is a basically shallow and insecure man who attempts to appear self-assured through his salesman's façade. She seeks to put his knowledge as an insurance insider and successful bravado-ridden salesman to use in having her husband sign up for a policy with a huge ultimate payoff after she secures Neff's assistance as a partner in homicide.

Finchley as Revered Criminal Figure

While it is not apparent from reading major sources from Chandler's life that he even saw *Criss Cross* or, if he did, made any comment about it, the story thrust along with the appearance of revered criminal figure Finchley during a crucial point of the film represented a vintage application of Chandler tools of the mystery trade. These tools became an inherent element of film noir.

As for the British dignity that Alan Napier revealed in his brief but significant appearance on screen, his manner and dialogue, so quintessential of Chandler's grasp of criminal ways, harkens back to the one and only time that film noir idea master Chandler met definitive noir leading man Robert Mitchum. The future leading man was tending bar, one of the numerous jobs he had before reaching stardom. During a tribute to Chandler on the Arts and Entertainment cable television series *Biography*, Mitchum recalled Chandler's dignified British accent and the tweed suit in which he was attired. It was one of those meetings embodying two of the most significant molders of noir mystery, but according to Mitchum, it was brief and insignificant. Mitchum's conclusion was that Chandler seemed out of place in this seedy environment.

This did not mean that Chandler could not shine in a setting more befitting of his persona. When the highly regarded writer began working at Paramount Studios, a mutual admiration society ensued. Chandler often held court as a high-achieving elder statesman of writing during lunches in the commissary with younger and highly entertained writers. He also proved helpful and courteous when they dropped by his office for advice.

Teet Carle began his career in the publicity department of MGM. He was in charge of that same department at Paramount while Chandler was there and entertained literary ambitions, commenting to Chandler biographer Frank MacShane concerning Chandler's helpful manner: "He was incredibly friendly. I often sneaked up from my office to get close enough to talk to him."

Meta Rosenberg, then an assistant to William Dozier, head of the writers unit at Paramount and future studio boss at RKO, used to visit Chandler often in his office and recognized that, along with William Faulkner, Dashiell Hammett, John O'Hara, and F. Scott Fitzgerald, he "was obviously above the ordinary level of film writer. He was shy and diffident, quite unlike the many Hollywood writers who try to give the impression they are in control of everything."

Robert Presnell, Jr., was writing his first screenplay at Paramount and was understandably nervous over his debut effort. Presnell recalled, "Chandler was ironically sympathetic and encouraging and took time from his own work to talk to me practically any time I popped into his office looking forlorn. He said he loved interruptions more than anything — because things you do when you're supposed to be doing something else are always more fun. Digression is the spice of life. He told me to write whatever I wanted because no one in the front office could read anyway, and even if they could, they wouldn't know a good script from a bad one."

One important element that emerged from Chandler's letters is his keenly analytical dissection of criminal activity in a big city setting. His author's microscope calls to mind the kind of superior mental organization of a district attorney with a brilliant batting average. His was the rare ability to coolly see and analyze the entire picture. By putting those neatly nurtured instincts of a piercingly acute life experience on paper, it was understandable why he was so successful in the mystery genre.

Alan Napier as Finchley had the same microscopic brain in criminal dissection and was therefore looked at by a band of mobsters as a youngster at his first spring training in the Boston Red Sox camp would have reacted to Ted Williams. In the anarchistic, perpetually snarling world of actor Dan Duryea, immersed in one of his better roles as mob boss Slim Dundee, the hero worship for Finchley is especially noticeable. Given his dog-eat-dog style of cynicism, it is hard to imagine Duryea's Dundee respecting anyone, but Finchley is a revered figure to the ruthless criminal boss. Viewers have every reason to conclude that Finchley might be the only figure in the world that Dundee respected.

Bursting into a big smile at the sight of Finchley, greeting him like a youngster outside the home team's dressing room at Yankee Stadium, is Vincent (Tom Pedi). A familiar figure in noir gangster roles, the stockily built Pedi with his pronounced New York accent looms as the answer to a prayer at central casting. As a gangster he comes across on screen as the authentic article, just the type of individual who would be following orders from a Slim Dundee.

Contrasting circumstances make for great drama, a point accented in noir cinema. In the case of Finchley, viewers are asked to fill in the circumstances as the revered Napier speaks in the manner of an Oxford don, which is so ill befitting of his residential station. Dundee and his entourage climbed the well-worn steps of an ancient, badly preserved Angel's Flight residential building. It becomes clear why Finchley suffered such a sharp decline when he is informed that his valued advice would result in a week's credit at the liquor store down the hill from Angel's Flight.

Despite Finchley's dependence on alcohol, his common sense prevails when he is asked if he would like a drink before launching into the business at hand. Finchley shrewdly explains that he will have his drink after the discussion concludes. One derives the feeling that better judgment is at work since, otherwise, drinking would be the order of the day and there would be no meeting at all.

Finchley holds court in the manner of a highly paid lawyer discussing the dispensation of funds in a huge estate in front of family members. That analogy holds in that a big potential payoff is being discussed before the group that hopes to pull it off and move to a loftier economic status.

Familiar Duped Victim Noir Status

Criss Cross with its well-executed script by Daniel Fuchs, like *The Killers*, has Burt Lancaster portraying the victim of a niftily orchestrated sting. A shrewd criminal boss masterminds each undertaking. Albert Dekker in *The Killers* demonstrates more polish as a mob boss than the snarly Dan Duryea. What gives each film the kind of shrewd twist beyond noir male victimized by a cunning femme fatale is the manner in which the victim is conned.[1]

In *The Killers*, the husband and wife team of Big Jim Colfax and Kitty Collins (Dekker and Ava Gardner) dupe an unsuspecting Ole "Swede" Anderson (Lancaster). He is unaware of the fact that they are married and is suckered into an apparent double-cross to be ostensibly united with Collins, who talks him into robbing the robbery team of the factory payroll booty. That way, Colfax does not have to split the take with anyone, save his co-conspirator wife.

Anna (Yvonne De Carlo) exercises an equivalent level of cunning on Lancaster in *Criss Cross*. This time Lancaster, as hapless Steve Thompson, is aware of the fact that Slim Dundee (Duryea) has married his former wife, a woman he cannot remove from his passions and thoughts any more than Robert Mitchum was able to shake Jane Greer in *Out of the Past*.

A subtlety that Raymond Chandler would admire was at work in the plotting to get Thompson to cooperate with Dundee, someone he personally detests, without realizing that the mob chieftain is pulling the strings. It is all about convincing Thompson that he is helping free Anna in a faux "lady in distress" situation.

"It can't be done."

As soon as Steve Thompson explains to master criminal theorist Finchley that the criminal enterprise being planned is the robbery of an armored truck, the swift response is that "it can't be done." Thompson sparks curious interest by explaining just how this seemingly impossible criminal act can be accomplished. It involves having an insider, in this case armored vehicle driver Steve Thompson. He has clearly grasped the attention of the master.

The film's labyrinthine twist involves the brutally clever way that Anna's second husband Dundee, a mobster with a fearsome reputation, manipulates the situation along with his femme fatale spouse to maneuver a decent young man from Los Angeles to enter the criminal realm. The key is to make Thompson believe he has hatched a clever plan on his own to frustrate the nemesis Slim Dundee by accounting for time he knows the crime boss is aware that he spent with Anna.

The pivotal moment when audiences know that Thompson has been lassoed and is now under control of the mob is when Dundee, along with his stalwarts, show up unannounced while Anna is alone with the armored car driver. She has already shown him ugly scratch marks on her back where Dundee has injured her. She laments that she is in the hands of a savage batterer. Despite his fury, it must be controlled when Dundee and entourage surface since he is suspected of romantic activity with his wife while the mobster was "away on business" in Detroit.

Thompson thinks he has engaged in fast thinking when Dundee arrives, naturally expecting an answer on why he is in the presence of the mobster's wife. What makes the process such cunning psychological noir is that Thompson thinks he is the group's original thinker and has conceived a way to get himself and Anna out of harm's way for romancing his former wife, someone a highly proprietary Dundee believes belongs strictly to him.

So one fateful afternoon in Los Angeles, armored car driver Steve Thompson — believing that he has put himself in the driver's seat — is instead victimized by a shrewd sting process leading back to his nemesis Dundee, the man he loathes above all others. He genuinely believes he is protecting his former wife, along with his own life, by explaining that he can help the gang realize a big payoff by robbing an armored car.

Dan Duryea did not win acclaim as the perfect cad of noir by being anything other than totally convincing. He has never been more convincing than as Dundee in playing along, enhancing Lancaster's Steve Thompson that the prospective armored car robbery is his idea and that he has been earlier talking business with the brunette femme fatale.

"It can't be done!" Dundee initially exclaims, sitting and listening as Thompson beseeches him that it can, when a driver such as himself is leading the effort, heading the planning and execution. Dundee even feeds Thompson's ego at the appropriate points by appearing to begrudgingly acknowledge that in this enterprise his hated rival, the man who covets his wife, is "the boss."

Meanwhile Thompson can dream on — and does so. While Dundee and his gang plan to use Thompson's knowledge and expertise to make them rich, then abandon him as thoroughly used goods, this is an opportunity seen by Thompson as his big chance to win back permanently the woman he cannot let go and spirit her away to a new life, far away from the clutches of Dundee and crew.

Ideal Noir Atmosphere

The brilliant Chandleresque noir element captured in the scene is that Bunker Hill is used with total effectiveness to denote a host of points. First of all, there are the cramped quarters of a seedy hotel. In it resides perhaps the only man Dundee respects, while his gang members denote the same level of reverence toward the polished Finchley. Despite living in ramshackle quarters, they could not respect him more if he resided in the most celebrated mansion in Beverly Hills.

The noise from the busy street outside is heard throughout, but the group sharing the cramped quarters of Finchley's rundown residence is oblivious to it. A spark of triumph surfaces in Finchley's eyes the moment that Steve Thompson convinces him that an armored truck robbery is indeed possible, with himself as the enterprise's insider. He begins writing and planning, reminding one of Frank Lloyd Wright at his peak of creativity, designing a new and highly innovative building.

While Finchley is immersed in his planning, the camera of veteran cinematographer Franz Planer who, like director Siodmak, received his early cinema experience in Germany, reveals the tense interaction of the film's other characters. While the gang members, led by an enthusiastic Vincent, feel the same wave of creative exhilaration borne by Finchley as he works away, drawing up a plan of action, the film's tense trio reaches an accelerated moment of tension.

The emotions of Burt Lancaster, Yvonne De Carlo and Dan Duryea are pushed to a pyrotechnical zenith. Their expressions and inner nervousness tell the story, revealing how powerful a tool skilled noir filmmaking can be. On the printed page, much description would be needed and more words would be incorporated from the main characters to enhance story and mood. Given the mastery of mood in cinema by the teaming of former German cinema masters Siodmak and Planer we witness an emotional tug of war within the brutally confining circumference of Finchley's small and depressing quarters.

The moods of the characters are symbolically revealed by a flurry of activity of a major U.S. city observed through the spacious window. All the while, Finchley is immersed in creating his own symphony without music, chiefly how to pull off a seemingly impossible crime, the successful robbery of an armored truck. The ebb and flow of life, including the emotional intensity of Lancaster, De Carlo, and Duryea, are symbolized by the Angel's Flight funiculars moving up and down beneath the wires. One heads uphill to the west and a Bunker Hill destination while the other descends eastward toward the heart of downtown Los Angeles, filled with scores of people seeking to find meaning in their lives.

Anna has a reason to feel more tension than her two admirers, current husband, and previous spouse Dundee and Thompson respectively. She has two angry and frustrated individuals with whom to deal. As they steal glances she does her best to concentrate on a newspaper, but it is evident throughout that this is a losing battle, an attempt to appear preoccupied while it is obvious that she is the tense object of two determined men.

Dundee as a mob professional feels frustrated with the presence of Anna and the distraction she holds for himself and Thompson that he suggests she go to a movie, and that she is not needed for this session involving criminal planning. She spurns the suggestion, continuing to occupy her place as queen bee while criminal mastermind Finchley's creative wheels turn.

The confluence of activity and emotion summarize the essence of film noir, the final note of irony being that Finchley talks in the manner of Raymond Chandler, like a British intellectual with a smoothly elegant vocal manner. Chandler did much to show the way, and the scene is reflective of this meticulous planning. The scene reflects so much of the sharp bite of scenes from *Double Indemnity*, a script crafted by Chandler and the film's director, Billy Wilder. Lancaster plays the same kind of fall guy that MacMurray did in *Double Indemnity*.

MacMurray was an occupational necessity in his role of Walter Neff, a glib talking insurance salesman. He was needed as a helpful planner by Phyllis Dietrichson to kill her husband and profit handsomely from a double-indemnity insurance policy. In the same vein, Thompson was an insider whose expertise was vital. If your goal is to hold up an armored truck, then entice the driver onto your team, which the beautiful and seductive Anna was able to do, getting her former husband to work on the criminal enterprise with her current husband, the person he loathes more than any other.

As for the inimitable Finchley, once that the planning of the armed truck robbery had been completed, a construction project erected brick by brick, he was more than happy to accept a reward. He gulps thirstily from a whiskey bottle in the manner of a perilously thirsty man who has found an oasis in the desert. There was an even richer reward that was then provided. Down at the bottom of Angel's Flight in the heart of downtown Los Angeles, where Hill Street beckoned, Finchley could now look forward to that promised week of credit at the local liquor store. The warmth of whiskey tumbling into the palate was a staple of Chandler's Philip Marlowe, as well as the master who put the words into the detective's colorful first-person accounts.

Comparing Chandler and Hammett

Dashiell Hammett supplied an instance of someone working in a particular field and drawing directly from it as his books were drawn from detective experiences. Raymond

Chandler carved out a career as an oil executive in Los Angeles until his drinking and womanizing caused his dismissal. He ultimately turned to writing as a means of making a living during the Great Depression. Having carefully studied magazine detective writing through Joe Shaw's *Black Mask*, where Hammett had served as reigning star until his resignation from action, Chandler's forays into the Los Angeles streets through the voice and experiences of alter ego Philip Marlowe were drawn not from direct detective experience as in the case of former Pinkerton operative Hammett, but from his imaginative brain coupled with the setting of the city with which he would have a love-hate relationship for the rest of his life—Los Angeles.

The fact that Los Angeles was, at the time that Chandler wrote, expansionist and transitory gave him the creative grist for his tales of lone wolf Marlowe roaming streets that appeared dark with ominous danger. Even the most intense sunlight could not alter the mood of enveloping darkness that, in a darkened theatre, served up the unmistakable feel of film noir. A housewife or salesman playing hooky for an afternoon at the cinema was transported to a vastly different world from that in which they lived, yet Chandler's stories also gave the impression that the individuals encountered routinely by lone wolf Marlowe could be their neighbors.

There was a "you are there" camera's eye element and the disturbing thought that, with variant circumstances, they could be sitting in the same position as the characters depicted. Noir had that element of characters moving into an unfamiliar atmosphere they would never be able to understand any better than the lives of individuals caught up as perpetrators or victims of crime. When the suave actor Joseph Cotten was preparing to portray the psychotic murderer in *Shadow of a Doubt*, he asked his director, Alfred Hitchcock, exactly what a serial killer looked like. Hitch simply pointed toward the busy downtown Beverly Hills street where they sat parked in the actor's car. In short, the killer could be anyone.

Enduring Women, with Reversed Results

Both Chandler and Hammett had enduring 30-year relationships with women that provided important career impact, but in varying directions. In the case of Chandler the bedrock foundation of his beloved wife, Cissy, was cited by him repeatedly in letters and comments as providing a stabilizing influence on his career.

The three-decade relationship in Hammett's life that was captured in a famous film resulted in longtime partner, Lillian Hellman, jumping into upper-echelon status among America's leading playwrights. The influence Hammett held on Hellman and her development was a major feature of the 1977 Fred Zinnemann film *Julia* with Jason Robards, Jr., cast as Hammett, and Jane Fonda portraying Hellman.

When Hammett declared he would no longer be writing detective stories, his declaration (which was never realized) was to relocate to Italy and begin a new career phase as what he termed a "serious novelist." Instead, he became the celebrated tutor of Hellman as she achieved noteworthiness with a helping hand by Hammett in the shaping process of her playwriting.

Hammett exercised his researcher's craft to provide Hellman with a theme that, in completed play form, would catapult her to the top of new American playwrights. *The Children's Hour* was, in the Production Code world of 1936, considered too hot to handle when it was made into a film by Samuel Goldwyn. The film that resulted, *These Three*, was altered from the original storyline which involved an accusation of lesbianism flung by an angry student at two small-town teachers. In the film version, directed by stylistic master William Wyler, the plotting student (played by Bonita Granville) hurls the charge of heterosexual sex without marital foundation. That film starred Joel McCrea, Merle Oberon, and Miriam Hopkins. The 1961 remake was more daring, taking on the lesbianism theme, using the original title of *The Children's Hour* and starring Audrey Hepburn and Shirley MacLaine as the teachers, with James Garner assuming the male lead.

Hammett had pointed his astute protégée in the correct direction by saying, "If you're going to do another play, then start with something solid." The "something solid" proved to be a book by William Roughead, *Bad Companions*. He suggested that Hellman base her play on a chapter entitled "Closed Doors; or The Great Drumsheugh Case." This was the true narrative of an episode in 1810 wherein a pathologically disturbed girl attending a Scottish boarding school accused two teachers of a lesbian relationship. The accusation caused the school to be closed. The teachers sought a trial to prove that the student was lying, and the House of Lords ultimately exonerated them. Despite their legal exoneration, the excessive negative publicity had an adverse impact and the teachers were destroyed by the scandal.

In one instance, Hellman's playwriting industry paid directly substantial cinema dividends to mentor Hammett. With Hellman and Hammett being notable political figures on the American left, it was no surprise that subject matter would be developed concerning the evils of Nazism. The result was the hugely successful play *Watch on the Rhine* in which a Romanian pro–Nazi was pitted against a victim of Third Reich oppression. According to Hammett biographer William Nolan, "The villain was modeled on a nobleman Hellman had met in Europe who had been an international gambler. Such acquaintanceship and interest proved understandable in that both Hellman and Hammett possessed strong penchants for gambling."

Once *Watch on the Rhine* began packing in Broadway audiences it was only a question of time before Hollywood came calling. It was understandable that then New Deal FDR liberal Jack Warner would purchase the film rights, with Hammett being given what he recognized to be a "dream assignment" of crafting a screenplay.

In the spirit of a true professional, Hammett recognized the tender balancing needed to achieve a successful film result. Since the play was a hit, with the dialogue resonating on New York audiences, the key to a screen success was to retain as much of it as possible while "opening up" the action and extending several key scenes beyond the stage and into the streets of Washington.

Jack Warner's film and business instincts were sound enough to realize that this was a blockbuster project in the making. It was within that spirit that none other than his gifted contract actress Bette Davis was summoned to handle the female lead. Hungarian émigré Paul Lukas was invested with the male lead and won a "Best Actor" Oscar for his effort. Hammett secured an Oscar nomination for his script while Lucile Watson was nominated in the "Best Supporting Actress" category.

Watch on the Rhine also won the New York Drama Critics Circle Award for 1941, competing against such plays and writing talent as Maxwell Anderson's *Key Largo*, Ernest Hemingway's *The Fifth Column*, and Robert Sherwood's *There Shall Be No Night*.

While Raymond Chandler had, despite dalliances with secretaries during his oil executive days, an enduring marriage to his beloved Cissy that did not end until her death, and from which he never recovered, Hammett's enduring relationship over a comparable three-decade period to Hellman was without marriage. His first marriage, which produced a daughter, was put at a distance for medical reasons and was never reestablished. A doctor suggested a separation of Hammett to his wife and daughter after the author had contracted tuberculosis.

Despite compromised health that would never significantly improve, Hammett flung himself into extended sexual debauchery accompanied by heavy drink. The womanizing continued on a reduced scale even after Hammett met and established residence with Hellman. Understandably this element of Hammett's life would diminish based on extending age and diminished energy.

The Hammett who never fulfilled his desire to migrate to Italy and write what he termed "serious novels" instead "went Hollywood" in a way that Chandler never did. The trappings of wealth, albeit transitory, and tinsel town glitter resulted in Hammett having civil judgments rendered against him for his excesses. He never needed a mammoth suite at the Beverly Wilshire Hotel, nor was it necessary to have a chauffeur and limousine on call.

As for Chandler, he ultimately left Los Angeles area after renting numerous houses in Hollywood and near downtown locations with his beloved Cissy. He used his movie money to relocate south to the idyllic San Diego suburb of La Jolla, the same town where Gregory Peck and Raquel Welch grew up. His was a more modest lifestyle. His numerous letters that have so closely chronicled the great writer's life reflect on someone trying to keep pace economically. Far from bemoaning an absence of chauffeur and limousine, Chandler writes with humility about the importance of keeping up with his bills along with the prevailing economic uncertainty of a profession in which that element bore a deep imprint.

There was another element that troubled Chandler in his correspondence, and with the advantage of perspective and hindsight his concern is particularly understandable. Chandler had a permanent love-hate relationship. While the hate aspect of this dual-sided viewpoint made him delight to have a home overlooking the Pacific Ocean surrounded by affluent neighbors in a quiet community, this life removed him from access to the disharmonious, dysfunctional world that provided part of the magic ingredient resulting in highly functional works of art.

A quiet, more conservative and stable breed surrounded Chandler in La Jolla. In Los Angeles, his sharply honed writer's instinct drew from the activities and vibrations in his midst, the transient types that occupied small, desolate rooms in Bunker Hill rooming houses and tired, rotting apartment buildings on Hollywood cul-de-sacs.

There was one important creative link shared by Chandler and Hammett: Captain Joseph Shaw. To understand him and his philosophy of crafting a successful mystery story blended with the evolution and composition of film noir it is advantageous to explore that link.

Chapter Four

Captain Joseph Shaw and the Flowering of Film Noir

> The formula or problem emphasized character and the problems inherent in human behavior over crime solution. In other words, in this new pattern, character conflict is the main theme; the ensuing crime, or its threat, is incidental.—Joseph Shaw

When Captain Joseph Shaw took over publishing duties at the offices of the mystery publication *Black Mask*, his innovative editorial ideas and shrewd story eye launched both Dashiell Hammett and Raymond Chandler on paths to international fame. Shaw's ideas, transmitted to an interested world by these authors and others from the magazine's office on 43rd Street in midtown Manhattan, provided a formulaic framework for a new pattern of filmmaking.

Synergy is a strong fiber in the fabric of writing. Editorial leadership helps generate and channel this ingredient. French authors and formidable intellectuals Albert Camus and Jean Paul Sartre recognized the special magic of the writing of Raymond Chandler. Their astute thinking, as embodied in that formative article in *Cahiers du Cinéma*, served to generate interest in film noir in the intellectual community. This had its antecedent in an editor who won the respect of Chandler by the way that he was willing to fight a writer point by point on what should emerge on the printed page.

Shaw jump-started a giant in *Black Mask* and, in an introduction to a collection of short stories originally published in the magazine and edited by him (and which in 1946 became a hardcover edition), he provided details on how the publication created a new type of detective. The new pattern Shaw described represents in so many ways what emerged on screen in film noir drama. He sought something different from the universal concept of a detective story as accredited to the Chaldeans and "employed more recently" by Nicolas Gaborieau, Edgar Allan Poe, and Arthur Conan Doyle. Shaw described this working model as "the deductive type, the cross-word puzzle sort, lacking—deliberately—all other human emotions."

Dashiell Hammett immediately received a letter from Shaw about what lay on the *Black Mask* drawing board. Hammett responded that he shared the hope of Shaw and the magazine's staff, indicating that he had been working toward the same result, stating, "The field is unscratched and wide open."

Shaw's expressed boundaries constituted "simplicity for the sake of clarity, plausibility, and belief. We wanted action, but we held that action is meaningless unless it involves recognizable human character in three-dimensional form." Hammett's way of phrasing Shaw's point was, "If you kill a symbol, no crime is committed and no effect is produced. To constitute a murder, the victim must be a real human being of flesh and blood."

Shaw and *Black Mask* sought to take detective crime out of the deductive crossword puzzle realm and extend it to an intimate personal level. In short, what was being sought was a form of universal and spontaneous recognition. Through moving emphasis from problem solving and personalizing mysteries individuals would be drawn into the picture with an alertness and cohesiveness of identification never previously achieved.

Joseph Shaw explained his point in one illuminating paragraph:

> In physics, an explosion sends out sound waves. But if there are no ears within their range, there is no sound. If you read of a thousand aborigines wiped out by fire or flood, you are abstractly interested, but you are not disturbed. But let a member of your own family be remotely threatened and you are at once intensely concerned, emotionally aroused. This is true in real life. Why shouldn't it hold true in fiction, which must create the illusion of reality?

Shaw then traversed into a realm of familiarity to those who have viewed the works of one of filmdom's master directors. As Shaw explained, "The formula or pattern emphasized character and the problems inherent in human behavior over crime solution. In other words, in this new pattern, character conflict is the main theme; the ensuing crime, or its threat, is incidental."[1]

Hitchcock and the MacGuffin

In steering the focus away from the puzzle, the principal element toward which the story evolves and ultimately concludes, a characteristic seen repeatedly among fans of British mystery author Agatha Christie, Shaw was pursuing territory familiar to one of the cinema's most accomplished directors, Alfred Hitchcock, whose forte was mystery. His four devastating entries into film noir that are held by many to be the most accomplished works of his oeuvre, in chronological order, are *Shadow of a Doubt* (1943), *Strangers on a Train* (1951), *Rear Window* (1954), and *Vertigo* (1958). Each evolved in accordance with a central tenet congruent with that of Shaw and accompaniment of Hammett.

Hitchcock explained his working pattern of mystery development through an analysis that brought his frequently employed wry sense of humor to the fore, a trait that served him well in his later role as host of his own television program. In this case, Hitchcock used an anecdote to make his point.

The anecdote relates to two men traveling by train from London to Scotland. One man notices a long, oddly wrapped parcel in the overhead storage compartment. His curiosity leads to a brief dialogue exchange that has etched its way deeply into cinema annals.

> "What have you there?" one man asks.
> "Oh, that's a MacGuffin," the other man replies.
> "What's a MacGuffin?"
> "It's a device for trapping lions in the Scottish Highlands."
> "But there aren't any lions in the Scottish Highlands."
> "Well, then, I guess that's no MacGuffin."

The verbal byplay makes a significant point for Hitchcock. As explained by Hitchcock biographer Donald Spoto, "The point is that a MacGuffin is neither relevant, important, nor, finally, any of one's business. It simply gets the story going."[2]

In addition to moving the story along, the element of how to handle suspense was dealt with by Hitchcock in a manner consistent with the formula encompassed at *Black Mask* by Joseph Shaw and his editorial staff.

Homicidal Tradeoff in a Chandler Script

The plot in the 1951 noir classic *Strangers on a Train* contained not only a script co-written by Raymond Chandler, but used the concept of tradeoff with results which were at odds with Chandler's viewpoint. Chandler thought that the script and entire story concept involved such a muddled mess that he considered taking his name off the credits. Chandler, who worked on the script at his La Jolla home with Hitchcock (who was driven by chauffeur from his Bel Air home) did not get along any better with The Master than he had with Billy Wilder on *Double Indemnity*.

Chandler's relationship with Hitchcock plunged into a steady abyss from bad to worse, with the acerbic author on one occasion referring to the director as "the fat bastard." "He'll hear you!" his secretary warned. But Chandler did not care. Eventually, he quit the project.

Hitchcock standby Ben Hecht, one of filmdom's most famous writing names, was the logical choice to step in when Chandler abdicated, having assisted the great director mightily by scripting *Spellbound* (1945) and *Notorious* (1946). Czenzi Ormonde, who worked as an assistant to a then unavailable Hecht, took Hecht's place and shares the writing credit with Chandler for the adaptation of the book written by Patricia Highsmith that Hitchcock pridefully took credit in obtaining rights to for a small sum.

In the case of Chandler's well-publicized differences with Billy Wilder in collaborating on *Double Indemnity*, the detective author, who got along well with fellow writers at Paramount, was highly sensitive on the subject of the Hollywood hierarchy. It was, he felt, a hierarchy which fed on ego along with perceived talent he believed to be non-existent. Chandler believed he was being treated as hired help when Wilder asked him to open a window, leading to a statement of typed declarations regarding future conduct. Had the conditions not been met, Chandler asserted that he would no longer be collaborating on *Double Indemnity*. Thankfully the differences were patched up between Chandler and Wilder so that one of the wittiest, most acerbic scripts in cinema annals could be completed and the project filmed with devastating results.

In the case of Chandler and Hitchcock, an analysis of their methods and creative viewpoints points to a danger zone encompassed by two freight trains colliding at midnight on a dark track. Chandler was the man of words, whose bitingly descriptive prose encompassed, with devastating illumination, the transitory, "dog eat dog" side of Los Angeles. No wonder Chandler idolized British author W. Somerset Maugham, with the feeling being decidedly mutual. As director Ken Annakin noted, when Maugham attended a party the guests would become petrified. The sagacious Maugham would sit quietly and observe, then write up what he found interesting, a photographic camera's eye with its own ultimate word dispensary.

Chandler did not collect his argots from soirees involving the upper crust of society. Bunker Hill, Hollywood's Sunset Strip, or activities in nearby Santa Monica, referred to as "Bay City" by Chandler, would allow him to train his own camera's eye on the people and places. It was doubtlessly more than coincidence that Chandler and Cissy moved so frequently. A new location would afford Chandler's intuitive camera's eye an opportunity to take more pictures, which were then churned out with gusto by his verbal dispensary, capturing the city's dark spots even as a bright sun shone through his eyes and ears.

While Chandler operated as a camera's eye in encapsulating the world he knew and disseminated information through his alter ego Philip Marlowe, the mystery master was a man of words. His was a rich tableau of skillfully and colorfully transmitted information. Chandler launched his word procession of an unfolding Los Angeles by concentrating on its dark rooms and shadier people. Hitchcock, on the other hand, was a camera's eye first, last, and always, concentrating on original photographic technique. Capture the proper mood through the camera's eye and fill in the words to provide a talking tableau of rich imagery: this was Hitchcock's idea of approaching a script. In addition, Hitchcock, like Walt Disney, used the storyboard approach in crafting his films. Whereas most directors who used this technique worked in concert with a studio sketch artist, Hitchcock loved sketching. Hence, Hitchcock had a project worked out scene by scene, detail by detail. Chandler found the process severely suffocating, like being confined to a straitjacket.

While Chandler's own frustrated perspective restricted him from recognizing that greatness was afoot, Hitchcock turned *Strangers on a Train* into one of his most imaginative as well as enduring films, highlighted by parallel race sequences by the innocent tennis star Guy Haines (Farley Granger) seeking to save himself from incriminating evidence being planted by psychopath Bruno Antony (Robert Walker), capped by a risky, creatively daring merry-go-round crash sequence.

What provided the ingenious spark, along with the photographic pyrotechnics that put the film in such a unique category, was the idea of a murder tradeoff. A scion of Virginia aristocratic wealth, Antony believes he has made a compact to exchange murders with Haines aboard the train where they meet. In the novel, Highsmith has the tennis star complicit. In the film, Hitchcock shrewdly pushed the tradeoff concept one step further. Haines is a naïvely innocent nice guy who believes he has brushed off a madman when he responds to the deadly proposal with a "Sure, Bruno" response that he does not mean, presuming the relationship has thereupon ended.

Antony is maniacal but, in a certain worldly sense, miles ahead of the sure-footed tennis player Haines. The tennis star is stumble-footed socially. Antony telephones Haines and informs him that he has executed his part of the bargain. Now it is up to him to perform his part of the ruthlessly daring homicidal contract. The daring tradeoff proposal with an innocent victim confronted by a madman possessed of a special cunning provides the spark that makes this combustible noir gem explode with the fireworks of a Fourth of July gala.[3]

Once more, as in *Vertigo*, Hitchcock has chosen chilling suspense and psychological interaction in a brutal confrontational cinema clash over the classical detective format of withholding resolution of guilt and innocence.

Character Duality of Stewart and Novak

Hitchcock's masterpiece *Vertigo* has been termed an exemplar of voyeurism. Scottie Ferguson is hired by Madeleine Elster's alleged "husband" in the person of sinister Svengali mastermind Gavin Elster (Tom Helmore). One astounding element of the production deserving of multiple superlatives was how Hitchcock, always wily on the subject of wiggle room with Hollywood censors, was able to run Gavin Elster by them in that he was never punished and gives every evidence from the film's conclusion of relocating to Europe to live a life of opulence after inheriting his rich wife's money.

Retired detective Ferguson is mesmerized by stylishly dressed and coiffed Helmore clone Madeleine from the beginning. (Novak, unsurprisingly, was a model when Harry Cohn tapped her for stardom). The more Ferguson sees in his assignment for Elster to watch his wife, the more thoroughly head over heels he becomes, until, following a brilliantly conceived game plan by a fiendishly ingenious criminal, the time arrives for the statuesque blonde to meet her enamored pursuer. It happens through a shrewdly plotted potential "suicide leap" into the chilly waters of San Francisco Bay.

Hitchcock made his decision to forego that temporary moment of dramatic peak at the close of a film by resolving a mystery, and moviegoers can be delighted that he did. The psychological twists and turns of Ferguson coping with someone who resembled the fictitious and thoroughly trained Madeleine Elster but was, in reality, Judy Barton from Salina, Kansas, who worked as a sales clerk at I. Magnin's, are fascinating to behold. The battle for control is the pivotal element as, after retired detective Ferguson has taken Barton step by step into the world she dreads and knows is bogus, not to mention deadly, that of Madeleine, is ultimately resolved when the brunette is transferred back to Madeleine's shade of blonde.

Barton has held out on one point. She explains that it did not quite "work out" to have her hair worn in the bun that the erotically nostalgic Ferguson had requested. With momentum going his way and against Barton's, that last bridge is symbolically crossed when he sees the bun effect he desires to complete his own Svengali job.

The dramatic explosives then move into closing mode. How many times has Hitchcock and other directors exposed that ultimate flaw, the mistake that trips up someone seeking to hide the truth? This occurs when Barton wears a necklace that the well-trained Madeleine had worn previously at a time when Gavin Elster's cleverly developing escapade and trap door for Ferguson had his bogus wife seeking to emulate a painting of Carlotta Valdes, the tragic suicide victim of a century earlier, who allegedly had taken possession of Madeleine's soul.

This plot twist is followed by more spinning, this time within Ferguson. Spotting the necklace and realizing that he has fallen for a brilliantly conceived trap with himself the victim, he spins out of control. The devastating camera close-ups (by longtime Hitchcock favorite cinematographer Robert Burks) reveal a man of all-consumed rage dominated by helplessness, a turmoil over realizing he has been victimized and that the major performer orchestrating a criminal scenario was his former college chum, someone he thought was his friend. He heaps ultimate praise on Elster by conceding that he did a better job of creating the fictitious Madeleine than he had.

The ideally paced script of Samuel Taylor and Alec Coppel covers one more point before Elster-Barton plunges to an accidental death: Ferguson's vertigo, the dizziness he experiences when exposed to heights. It took one shock to induce it, and medical advisers reveal that it will take another inner jolt to remove it. This time, in contrast to the earlier death sequence at the climax of what has been termed Part One of the film, Stewart is able to make it all the way up to the bell tower. Because he is able to do so, Elster/Barton, who is compelled by the angry victim to accompany her, falls to her death after being startled by the sudden appearance of a nun. It has been frequently acknowledged that Kim Novak played a dual role in *Vertigo* in appearing in the first half as Madeleine Elster and Judy Barton in the second portion. The challenging element of Novak's performance as well as one of the film's most interesting elements from the standpoint of the audience is the sharp contrast of the two characters. Madeleine exudes the ultimate in sophistication, a beautiful, well-spoken, well-dressed, well-coifed San Franciscan who appears to belong in a large apartment on Nob Hill with an expansive view of the city. Judy Barton, on the other hand, looms as an ordinary figure who has migrated from Kansas to Northern California and is destined for an existence of little beyond going to work, putting in her hours, and receiving her paycheck at the end of the week.

This sharp contrast of the film's leading female character serves as a catalyst for a dual-character performance as well by James Stewart, one that needs to be fully explored. When he observes Novak and finally interacts with her as she is carrying out her well trained role for the sinister Elster as Madeleine, a character transformation occurs within Stewart. The expression on the face of the formerly "Reliable Ferguson," once the redone Judy Barton walks into her Empire Hotel room, reflects a man falling in love with a ghost (in the same manner that Mark McPherson [Dana Andrews] stares with transfixed lust at the portrait of Laura [Gene Tierney], then thought to be a murder victim). That expression will turn into a state of discombobulated rage when Ferguson spots the telltale necklace on Barton. This is in no way the man we see in the apartment of longtime college friend Midge Wood (Barbara Bel Geddes), to whom he was briefly engaged, and someone who makes him feel comfortable. There is nothing but high-level combustion whenever Ferguson is around Novak whether it is in the form of transformation one or two.

As a result James Stewart's part contains a duality of its own. There is the comfortable "old shoe" detective relaxing around longtime friend Midge, someone who will never light his romantic flame or prompt his imagination to soar in the manner of Elster/Barton, sharply contrasted with the man who, like the woman who transfixes him, is also a victim of the diabolical Gavin Elster, so smoothly played by Tom Helmore.[4]

Voyeurism Via Broken Leg and Binoculars

Another classic study of voyeurism (with the skilled camera work of Robert Burks working with microscopic fascination) occurs in one of Hitchcock's most celebrated artistic film efforts that was correspondingly appreciated at the box office. *Rear Window* is a suspense chiller based on a short story by Cornell Woolrich, who had numerous of his works adapted into noir cinema.

One important distinction exists between the book and film, and it was inspired by screenwriter Joseph Michael Hayes. Hitchcock and the veteran radio scenarist felt an additional element that would enhance the story was a love interest for the apartment-bound photographer Jeff Jeffries, played by Stewart, who is laid up with a broken leg, suffered as a result of his daring profession.

The inspiration on Hayes's part was home supplied. His beautiful blonde wife was a popular magazine cover girl. She bore a close resemblance to the cover girl and world-class blonde beauty who would later give up an outstanding career as a film actress to help preside over the principality of Monaco as Princess Grace. Bedazzling Philadelphia society girl Grace Kelly, through Hayes's astute story twist, provided an additional story conflict to synchronize with Stewart's character.

Once more the formula adopted skillfully by Captain Joseph Shaw's most celebrated *Black Mask* author Raymond Chandler was employed. As Shaw and Chandler asserted, what gave a murder mystery universal audience spontaneity was a bond of closeness. The story revolved around individuals about whom audience members knew and learned to care. The twists and turns, along with the intimacy of characterization, made the story a success.

In the case of Jeffries his yearning for adventure and travel inherent in his work provides a recipe for restless frustration beyond that of most other people. With little to do but bide his time until the cast comes off of his broken leg, the healing process is accompanied by constant viewing out of his New York City apartment window. He becomes obsessed with his neighbors' activities at another apartment building situated beyond a courtyard separating them.

At one point Jeffries is awakened by the shrill cry of a woman. The next thing he knows a burly, bespectacled man (Raymond Burr, who shortly after this role would go on to television fame as defense attorney Perry Mason) makes a series of trips to and from his apartment in the early morning, undeterred by a driving rain. At one point he is carrying a case.

Jeffries's suspicions have been aroused. He shares them with his girlfriend Lisa Fremont (Kelly) and physical therapist Stella (Thelma Ritter). He eventually convinces both women that his theory of Burr having murdered his wife is not the product of his fertile imagination. The last person that needs to be convinced is former World War II Air Force friend and current New York police detective, Tom Doyle (Wendell Corey).

The aforementioned elements would be enough to constitute a solid story, but Hitchcock and his peripatetic camera along with other accompanying plot elements, particularly an unconventional romance between Fremont and Jeffries, are juxtaposed with the skill of a master juggler. In this case the juggling is made all the more fascinating by the series of windows in which Jeffries views various activities. The apartment building across the courtyard provides a virtual city, and the voyeuristic Jeffries takes advantage of every opportunity to view events.

The unique story twist that was created for the screen version is the awkwardness of Jeffries (amid his concern over proving, at one point over the ridicule of his friend Doyle, that a murderer resides in close proximity) and his relationship with Lisa. The dashing and debonair Fremont makes him jittery because she, alas, is "too perfect." While it might be natural enough for many to question the photographer's sanity, there is plausibility in what develops onscreen.

Photographer Jeffries fears commitment to Fremont because he does not feel that he could live up to what would be expected in a marriage with someone he is convinced epitomizes female perfection. She even summons a waiter to serve a lobster dinner and wine from New York's famous 21 Club. He concedes, with a weary resignation of a trapped man, that nothing could conceivably be improved upon in his estimation. The perfection standard is used to convey his hopeless situation, an endless tangent. The meal was, like Lisa Fremont herself, perfect.

Enter Miss Torso

Even in comparison to *Vertigo*, which is highly voyeuristic with Ferguson's acceptance of a detective job which has him watching Madeleine and becoming increasingly obsessed with an image that never comported with reality, *Rear Window* contains voyeurism even beyond that. It could be convincingly argued that *Rear Window* was the most voyeuristic classic work ever filmed.

Hitchcock and screenwriter Hayes reveal their thinking on voyeurism when wisecracking Stella (an Eve Arden with a New York accent) enters Jeff's apartment and begins by delivering her tart and sassy one-liners as the wheelchair-bound photographer continues staring out his window. Stella warns that "there is a law against Peeping Toms." The voyeurism element is extended in her dialogue when she exclaims that "we" (presuming mid-20th-century Americans) have become "a race of Peeping Toms."

On another occasion the wily nurse, who has been sent to look after Jeffries on behalf of the insurance company for which she works, refers to his constant preoccupation with looking out the window. When he begins a gentle protest she defends the veracity of her comment by referring to the restless photographer's bloodshot eyes.

Someone who is as used to perpetual activity as Jeffries, who is confined to a wheelchair, would construct a Virtual City by looking out his rear window. The voyeurism also enters into the sexual realm. This by itself would be anything but original, but the fascinating spin placed on this element (through the fertile imaginations of writer Hayes and director Hitchcock along with the meticulous camera work of Robert Burks) puts *Rear Window* in a class by itself in the field of voyeuristic imagination.

Stewart becomes frightened at any mention of marital commitment. The fright accelerates after Kelly tells him that she can spend the night with him and poses holding a seductive negligee. But while he runs away from marital commitment to the "too perfect" Grace Kelly, he libidinously hungers for a ballet dancer who works out in tight-fitting shorts in her apartment, giving him as well as his lusty appetite a viewing workout. He christens the object of his viewing affection "Miss Torso." When his fascination continues even in Lisa's presence, she ends the activity by pulling down a window shade and announcing that "the show is over" for the night.

The script spells out where Jeff's psyche lies. While he fears intimacy and a marital future with Lisa, he has no compunctions letting his libidinous imagination soar well beyond New York's speed limit while viewing Miss Torso (played by Brooklyn born ballerina Georgine Darcy).

While he lusts for Miss Torso, Stewart compassionately frets for another Virtual City resident he terms Miss Lonelyhearts (Judith Evelyn). Not only does Miss Lonelyhearts sit in her apartment, she plays romantic music. She sits at her table and pours wine for her ideal (albeit non-existent) fantasy date. When she meets a younger man at a bar across the street and brings him back to her apartment, he is quickly evicted when he begins kissing her.

Her life is saved by another lonely person, The Songwriter (Ross Bagdisarian) who, in his melancholia, takes to drink. As he plays a portion of a lovely composition in process, Miss Lonelyhearts becomes so illuminated that she does not take what the audience would presume to be a potentially lethal dose of pills. By film's end they meet and are in the midst of a blooming romance. He then introduces his completed song bearing the title "Lisa," appropriate in view of the Kelly character in the film, the ever-perfect Lisa Fremont.

Another couple viewed by Stewart that bears a name as obvious as the others is The Newlyweds. By film's end their marriage has soured while the romance of The Songwriter and former Miss Lonelyhearts is proceeding promisingly. As for Miss Torso, her husband (or at least a serious boyfriend) has arrived home in uniform, his Army duty presumably completed.

All of these events and people occupy Jeff's interest, as they do Lisa and the blunt-talking Stella (who tells him he is a fool if he passes up the opportunity to wed the beautiful model). Meanwhile, old Air Force compatriot Doyle tells them they are dead wrong in their suspicion of burly neighbor Thorwald (Burr). But Thorwald's attempt on the photographer's life to save his own almost succeeds before he is apprehended by the police, with former skeptic Doyle leading the police team.

Joseph Shaw could not have been more correct. With as many dramatic wheels spinning as those employed by Hitchcock in concert with Hayes, it is not necessary to develop a suspense story that culminates in a crime being solved at its conclusion. The labyrinthian twists make a tremendous difference in the minds of shrewd artistic tail spinners on top of their game.[5]

Creative Continuity and the Shaw Clan

As befitting a successful magazine publisher, Joseph Shaw resided in the elegant New York City bedroom community of Scarsdale. The Shaws are an old line American family with Scottish roots extending back to Roger Shaw. Captain Shaw's grandson Chris related, "The first generation of Shaws arrived from Scotland in 1636. My dad had an artist that he knew at work draw a family tree about forty years ago based on the 1904 book *A Memorial of Roger Shaw, 1594–1661*, by Harriett F. Farwell. I am a tenth generation American Shaw."

Captain Shaw's son attended Williams College and Yale University. He went to work at ABC after Navy World War II duty in the fifties, eventually becoming a cameraman doing live television. Shaw finally became involved producing and directing live television shows and commercials. "Eventually he was offered a job with the Madison Avenue advertising agency Dancer, Fitzgerald, Sample," Chris related. "He moved up to the position of senior vice president. The firm merged with Saatchi and Saatchi in the eighties and my father retired from there in 1989. He and my mother then moved to their dream home on Cape Cod. When we visited there last weekend my dad began telling all these stories about the days of live TV and had us all laughing."

As for Christopher Shaw, he became involved in engineering with National Video Center. "I began as a junior video engineer," he explained. "We were a post-production house. At our peak we had three studios, eight or ten suites, and five audio suites. We did work for all the major television networks as well as the movies, including *Tootsie*. MTV was launched there."

Eventually Shaw would go to work for a company in Connecticut. "After 14 years and the son preparing to take over at National Video Center it was time for me to move on and I found a job with CBS Cable Group, Group W, in Stamford, Connecticut," Shaw revealed. "Now instead of being in the position of making commercials and shows I was in the position of broadcasting them and doing what I like, engineering. In 2003 or so CBS Cable was sold off to Ascent Media. For the past five years I have been working as a project engineer and I have been at Ascent Media now for 10 years."[6]

Christopher Shaw as the grandson of the great editor of *Black Mask* who was a primary catalyst of film noir, in an interesting twist of fate, works at Ascent Media with a current prime mover in the film noir field. Steve Eifert, about whom more will be written, is the editor of the Internet *Back Alley Noir* site. Eifert's site utilizes film technology by presenting, along with penetrating essays analyzing noir entries, key scenes along with trailers of movies being evaluated.

Chapter Five

Horace McCoy's Dance Marathon

> There can be only one winner, folks, but isn't that the American way?—Gig Young, *They Shoot Horses, Don't They?*

On only one occasion did the two masters of hard-boiled fiction known as film noir—Dashiell Hammett and Raymond Chandler—meet. It was no surprise that the magazine publisher who provided a great national showcase for each author, Joseph Shaw, arranged that sole meeting.

If hindsight came even reasonably close to foresight, then the two masters would surely have been interconnected through the efforts of commentators and reporters in a manner that would have pleased the readers of the crime genre. There is no reported instance of the two detective-writing masters even speaking, though they may have, given that each was aware of the other's credentials and that they were the two stars of Shaw's *Black Mask*.

A photograph taken at the First West Coast *Black Mask* Dinner on January 11, 1936 shows tall, gaunt Hammett standing on the far right of the second row. Chandler stands second from the left in that same row.

A pervasive element of that one and only meeting of the two hard-boiled fiction giants is that each wears a look of sober concern and appears to be preoccupied with his own thoughts. There is a third member of the group that also appears similarly preoccupied, while the remaining *Black Mask* authors face the camera and many are smiling: Horace McCoy forged his own solid imprint on Great Depression writing. Actually, McCoy's chief work, for which most mystery and noir genre followers know him, came closer to directly encapsulating the Depression period in an intimate way than any work written by the two masters, who tapped into that segment of history primarily through mood.

The Depression period was highlighted by individuals seeking to survive brutal socioeconomic elements through flexibility of occupation and place. Such was the case with Horace McCoy, who worked at a variety of jobs and moved from the South, where he had grown up, to the lotus land of Southern California and, ultimately, the film industry.[1]

Chandler and Hammett both plied their writing talents in the screenwriting field, but McCoy has been identified more closely to another Hollywood scenarist of the period: Nathanael West. The reason for the linkage is obvious. Both McCoy and West never felt comfortable with the Hollywood scene or screenwriting, but pursued it as a way of remaining afloat. Their names are associated with many B-level films written at a time when the Hollywood dream factory needed a seemingly endless supply of scripts for the numerous films being churned out to provide moviegoers with a temporary respite from economic problems, a fantasy contrast during a time of acute national need.

McCoy and West could see the intellectual vapidity of a lotus land where individuals arrived by the score to seek cinema fame and fortune. They knew that they had survived long odds to reach the station they occupied as frequently employed script writers for a vast machine. All the same, they saw their respective plights as dead ends, and longed to express themselves on what they deemed to be a higher and more meaningful artistic level.

Readers of fiction on the Hollywood scene repeatedly place two works at the top of the mountain on the subject of books most closely capturing the town. While F. Scott Fitzgerald's unfinished novel made a decided impact on readers, it was for a different reason. *The Last Tycoon* was said to be roughly based on the life and times of MGM's "boy wonder" Irving Thalberg. That work made its mark as a profile of an enigmatic figure who lived and worked in Hollywood. The works of West and McCoy made gigantic social statements of period and locale.

West's *The Day of the Locust* cuttingly encapsulated the vacuousness of transitory types who populated a slice of the American dream turned sunshine-laden tragedy. While those who could not make a living in Tinseltown might have envied those who did, often leaving to return to the lands of their roots, the ones who found employment plunged into a world of escape highlighted by frequent and unfulfilling sex, along with escapist bouts with drugs and alcohol.

Britisher John Schlesinger was a seemingly good choice to direct *Locust*, given his success in capturing sixties' restlessness and debauchery in his own London in the 1965 Julie Christie vehicle *Darling* and the 1971 release *Sunday Bloody Sunday* starring Glenda Jackson and Peter Finch. On the other side of the Atlantic, Schlesinger traced the experiences of penniless country boy Joe Buck (John Voight) in New York City and his interaction with tragedy-plagued Ratso (Dustin Hoffman) in the 1969 release *Midnight Cowboy*.

West's work was brought to the screen in 1975. The script adaptation was by Waldo Salt, who had earlier written *Midnight Cowboy*. While deemed brilliantly evocative of time and locale, *Locust* was defined even by its admirers as sad and depressing, but with a strong ring of reality, the kind of reality that would not be recognized in small-town America, but typical of Depression-era Hollywood.

William Atherton plays Tod Hackett, a young man fresh from Yale graduation who migrates west to find employment in Hollywood as an art director. His concentration toward achieving career success is disrupted, however, by his infatuation with Faye Greener (Karen Black), a talentless acting aspirant he seeks to promote. Along the way he meets social misfit Homer Simpson (Donald Sutherland) who, when pressed, can think of only one song he knows—"The Star Spangled Banner," and cynical, sly fox veteran Harry Greener (Burgess Meredith).

Those who appreciate the slice-of-life element of actual history intermingled with fictional depiction appreciated the role of Big Sister (Geraldine Page), recognizable as Aimee Semple MacPherson, the most flamboyant and best-known charismatic preacher in Los Angeles. In her heyday, Pentecostal sermonizer MacPherson packed Angelus Temple in the Echo Park district near downtown. She has been associated with the invocation of quiet collections notable for their "rustling of paper" rather than the "noisy jangling of coins."

A clever twist was inserted in the casting of a thirties' musical shown in the film. The person being shown was Depression-period song-and-dance man Dick Powell, later to become known as one of the industry's most versatile figures, moving on to dramatic star and then to director, actor, and producer while becoming one of the legendary figures of television through the company he founded, Four Star Productions. When Schlesinger needed someone who resembled him from his early period he tapped Dick Powell Jr., who indeed bore a close physical resemblance to his father.

A Story from a Bouncer on the Pier

As for Horace McCoy, his rendezvous with writing destiny commenced with a brief job designed to do little more than stave off hunger and keep a roof over his head. McCoy, whose varied background included stints as a boxer and wrestler, was given an employment opportunity as a bouncer. The venue for McCoy's activity was along Santa Monica's famous pier next to the Pacific Ocean. The indoor setting was a ballroom in which a brutal, agonizing, but ultimately popular Depression fad activity known as marathon dance contests were held.

Being a creative writer and, hence, a natural observer, McCoy's creative brain began ticking as he worked on the shore of the Pacific. The result was a shrewdly crafted novel of a little less than 150 pages called *They Shoot Horses, Don't They?*

There is one basic difference separating the works of Nathaniel West and Horace McCoy and the films adapted from them. While each focused on the film industry during the Depression, *Locust* bore a more direct link. More characters in the West book and subsequent Schlesinger film have survived the first hurdle of obtaining work in Hollywood. West and the film that evolved from his book focus like a laser on the emptiness in lotus land of those who comprise the industry, wanderers who encompass a virtual Tower of Babel, failing to understand themselves and those with whom they interact. In the case of McCoy and *They Shoot Horses*, acute frustration results from not being able to get a foot in the door. The two lead characters are an odd couple consisting of Robert (Michael Sarrazin), a young man with childlike simplicity and willingness to please, and Gloria (Jane Fonda), a young

OUT ON THEIR FEET— Robert (Michael Sarrazin) and Gloria (Jane Fonda) continue dancing in a supremely exhausted state in Sydney Pollack's devastating 1969 mood piece *They Shoot Horses, Don't They?*

woman who never hides her abiding depression in a society ravaged by the Great Depression.

The more that Gloria snipes at others and refuses to speak kindly to those who seek to be kind or at least civil to her, the more resolute the analytical conviction becomes that the only man in the marathon competition who could contend with and become a dance partner of hers is Robert, the person least likely to clash with anyone.

In this cleverly constructed pairing of two of many who came West and sought work in the film industry, each character feels a strong desperation, but Robert's is less demonstrable. Robert's desperation is passive, as befits his personality, while Gloria's conversely is weighted down heavily with chips on both shoulders and will verbally bite without any provocation.

Gloria's desperation reaches the point where she offers unsolicited advice to kindly fellow marathon competitor Ruby (Bonnie Bedelia). It bothers Gloria that Ruby is pregnant. Her message, delivered more than once, is that it is wrong to bring one more person into such a tortured and ultimately pointless world.

The repeated efforts by Gloria to influence Ruby results in intervention by her husband, James (Bruce Dern). (Fonda would later be paired with Dern in the highly successful 1978 anti–Vietnam War film *Coming Home*.) Initially, James tells Robert to make his partner stop bothering his wife. When an unrelenting Gloria continues her comments about Ruby's pregnancy, the result is that she refuses to back off and shows no fear of James. When the angry husband makes a move toward her, Robert steps in to defend his partner.

After order is restored and Gloria exclaims that the much bulkier James "would have killed you," the response is consistent with Robert's passivity, a quiet "I guess so." The words are spoken in a manner to beg the question that in the final analysis Robert does not care any more about life than Gloria — he is just quieter in his despair. Unlike Gloria, however, Robert does reveal a desire to become a movie director in a wistful phase contrasted with the suicidal despair of his dance partner. It is obvious from Gloria's consistent pattern of words and actions that any hope she had of achieving anything, or even hoping for anything, had passed.

McCoy and Symbolic Link of Marathon and Hollywood

Horace McCoy was Tennessee born and came West to Hollywood in 1931 following a period in which he had served as sports editor for the *Dallas Journal* and co-founded the Dallas Little Theatre. After moving to Los Angeles he tried his hand at acting, without success. Having written short stories from the late twenties for *Black Mask* and other publications, his experience as a ballroom bouncer prompted him to write his first novel, *They Shoot Horses*.

McCoy's tour de force lay in linking two of the biggest pursuits at garnering gold at the end of a proverbial rainbow. Scores of aspirants arrived daily in Hollywood determined to become the next Clark Gable or Carole Lombard. The marathon was created to attract survivors who were willing to battle staggeringly long odds, along with the normal cycles of their bodily systems, to stay on their feet for abnormal periods of time to achieve prize money.

These two efforts to strike gold in the midst of poverty and heartache were interlinked by McCoy as Hollywood film aspirants joined the ranks of marathon participants. Yet another link involved the dual aspirations of those marathon competitors. Not only were they vying for prize money, they also hoped to gain notice of film bigwigs through their involvement in the competition.

Gig Young as Carnival Barker

When it came to listing jobs, the one that stood out in any word association study or game was that of "blarney" in connection with carnival barkers. The popularity of carnival barkers in 19th century America was attached to the view of showman P.T. Barnum, who thought the entire world was a carnival. It was Barnum who coined the term "There's a sucker born every minute." Barnum was so tuned into mob psychology that he would hire two people to start a fight in the middle of downtown areas where his shows were slated to play. This was Barnum's way to assure a crowd when he began advertising his upcoming shows.

Playing the pitchman for a marathon competition that viewers ultimately learn is a rigged game is veteran actor Gig Young. The emcee of the program was what a later Madison Avenue America would term a "hard sell" sales type. Considering the fact that this marathon was being conducted on the Santa Monica pier so close to Hollywood was foremost on the pitchman's mind as he calls out names of anyone associated with the industry who appeared to cheer on the contestants.

Gig Young got off to a start that involved an instant career identity shift. Young's real name was Byron Barr. After starting his career under his actual name in 1941 in the film *You're in the Army Now*, he appeared in *The Gay Sisters* (1942) in a larger supporting role. The character he played in his second film was named Gig Young. The short, catchy, marquee-friendly name would be revived as his professional moniker after going by Byron Barr for a while longer.

Byron Barr was a good marquee name as well, containing alliteration as well as being short. The problem posed by using it was that Paramount had under contract a young player seeking to move up the ranks at that same time named Byron Barr. While the Paramount Byron Barr would never attain the star standing of Gig Young, he would appear in one of the great noir triumphs, and overall cinema successes, of all time: Billy Wilder's 1944 gem *Double Indemnity*. Barr scaled his career highlight in playing the hot-tempered Nino Zachetti. He clashes with Walter Neff in his initial scene, set at the corner of Vermont and Normandie, a short distance northwest of downtown Los Angeles.

Zachetti is the boyfriend of femme fatale Phyllis Dietrichson's stepdaughter, Lola (Jean Heather). Jumping to immediate jealous rage, Zachetti raises his voice immediately at Neff after he has done no more than give Heather a ride to Vermont and Normandie, where she was slated to meet her boyfriend. Neff calms him down with a "Don't get excited, sonny" rejoinder, explaining why Heather is riding with him.

Toward the end of the film, Neff realizes that wily and conscience-free user and ultimate killer of men Phyllis is setting up Zachetti in the way that she has previously used him. Now, after sexually enticing Zachetti and turning him against former flame Lola, who detests her stepmother and sees her for what she is, Phyllis is setting up the much younger man to eliminate Neff.

Barr's second and culminating scene of the film is also a dramatic attention getter. In this scene he becomes a calm listener as the badly wounded Neff, fresh from his climactic gunshot exchange which has left Phyllis lying dead inside her home, reaches into his pocket, yanks out a coin, and hands it to Zachetti. Explaining that the young man is being used by an evil woman in the same manner that he had been earlier, Neff implores Zachetti to go to the nearest pay phone and call Lola. The same Zachetti who had exploded at Neff in his first scene, listens to the insurance agent and apparently takes his message to heart, as he turns and walks away.

When Barr received another opportunity to appear in a visible feature role it was again a noir drama in which he played a hothead, but unlike his role in *Double Indemnity* where Walter Neff's intervention saves him from tragedy, in the 1948 release *Pitfall*, his misunderstanding of John Forbes's (Dick Powell) intentions results in his death. The film, directed by André de Toth, features Forbes as a successful Los Angeles insurance executive who has become bored with his life. He has a brief affair with Mona Stevens (Lizabeth Scott), with whom Barr's character Bill Smiley is passionately and jealously in love. While Forbes has no desire to push the affair further and wants to keep his marriage to Sue (Jane Wyatt) together, an enraged Smiley, convinced that much more is involved, is killed in a shootout with the insurance executive.

Such are the fates of unpredictable Hollywood. Smiley's swift death at the hands of Forbes marked the manner in which his career abruptly ended. His final film appearance was an uncredited role as a policeman in the 1951 Alan Ladd film *Appointment with Danger*.

The Byron Barr who had been born in St. Cloud, Minnesota, and changed his name to Gig Young, would go on to a long and sustaining career in film, albeit frustrating. The actor with matinee idol looks was used in repeated assignments as a type of relief for people thanking goodness over a type of physical perfection being brought to earth with a thud.

The handsome man with the excellent physique and well modulated voice became the movie equivalent of the bright, well prepared student who seemingly always delivers the right answer. A reverse culture sets in under those circumstances among fellow students who resent the bright man of preparation and desire him to experience ultimate frustration.

A classic case of Young used as the other man involved an opportunity to work alongside two of the most popular and celebrated stars of film. In *Teacher's Pet* Young was cast with the naturally masculine, never artificial, always popular Clark Gable. The star of *Gone With the Wind*, *It Happened One Night*, and numerous other successes was so popular with the film community that his nickname was "The King."

The film was released in 1958. It was perfectly natural that a reigning box office queen was selected to play opposite King Gable. Doris Day was repeatedly selected as female box office champion during the fifties. It would figure that given such a brilliantly conceived box office jingle pairing that Gig Young, cast as Dr. Hugo Pine, was being set up for foil and such was the case. In fact, Young's classic features and youthful appearance were used against him for comedy purposes in one of the film's memorable scenes.

After a rocky start, veteran journalist James Gannon (Gable) seeks to woo teacher Erica Stone (Day). He becomes jealous when he learns about Pine being a professional colleague. When Gannon sees the impressive list of books that Pine has written, he scoffs that the professor must be a very old man. The comedy element occurs when he turns a book written by Pine around and observes his face, promoting instant shock.

Veteran husband and wife team Fay and Michael Kanin secured a "Best Screenplay" Academy Award nomination in the popular film directed by George Seaton, who in the early fifties had won a "Best Director" Oscar for *The Country Girl* (1954). Such a blending of talents could be expected to generate fast-paced comedy with multiple laugh lines. They did not disappoint, and Young became a beneficiary of opportunity by being nominated for "Best Supporting Actor." His acting talent had been previously recognized by the Academy when he received a nomination in the same category for the 1951 James Cagney vehicle *Come Fill the Cup*.

The good news is that Young was impressing Academy members and other insiders for his solid professionalism. The disappointing news for Young is that he fell into that Hollywood trap door known as type casting. His professionalism kept him employed, but repeated use of Young in roles where producers and directors felt comfortable, using him for his reliability and shunning use of him in the kind of glossy leading roles being played regularly by the likes of Gable, James Stewart, Cary Grant, Burt Lancaster and other stellar male leads of the period.

Young was solid in his comedy in *Teacher's Pet* but was, unfortunately for him, still foil rather than lead. When Gannon, the hard-crusted managing editor asked by his boss to assist Stone with her journalism class, finally meets Pine and the three sit down for drinks, the younger man demonstrates his professor-cum-author encyclopedic knowledge in an area where old school, common folk sort Gannon would be expected to prevail, that of major league baseball. After discussion turns to the 1920 World Series and the legendary unassisted triple play, the only one in the horsehide classic's history, achieved by Bill Wambsganss, second baseman of the Cleveland Indians, against the Brooklyn Dodgers, Gannon is corrected by Pine. The correction relates not to the Wambsganss history maker, but the fact that the film's lead wrongly states that the Indians won the series by a margin of four games to two. Pine becomes one of the few people around, even among baseball fans, who knows that this World Series was the second to last played under an abandoned rule that, in some instances, compelled a team to win five games to prevail.

The three leads played beautifully together, with Gannon frowning and becoming frustrated over the sweeping intellectual grasp of the younger Pine, who made matters worse by being so youthful in appearance as well as good looking. Audience members could feel an empathy toward Gannon when he ultimately wins the girl, the screen equivalent of the smart youngster in school finally missing an answer as classmates smile with relief, concluding, "He's human after all."

Young would appear with Doris Day in another successful comedy, the 1962 release *That Touch of Mink*. Again, Young was compelled to ply his talents in a showcase role for another larger than life leading man, the enduring Cary Grant.

Good Again, but Hayworth Is Celebrated

When Young had an opportunity to appear with a star-laden cast of proven talents and a screenplay by one of Broadway's finest playwrights, Clifford Odets of *Waiting for Lefty* and *Golden Boy* fame, he had every reason to believe that perhaps now true stardom beckoned. In the second and final film directed by Odetts, Young was paired with a celebrated leading lady and never lost her to another performer. In *The Story on Page One* (1959) Young is paired opposite Rita Hayworth. The dazzling redhead became renowned for the glamorous image she conveyed in two glossy Columbia musical hits, *Cover Girl* (1944) and *Tonight and Every Night* (1945).

Hayworth appeared in two black-and-white noir films: *Gilda* (1946) with fellow Harry Cohn contractee Glenn Ford, and *The Lady from Shanghai* (1947), opposite husband Orson Welles, who was also the film's director. *Gilda* once more showcased Rita's glamour and was remembered for the Helen Hunt hairstyle which enabled her to toss her head in a manner that her hair twisted and turned in a sensual way. The second film proved more of a showcase for Welles's creativity, highlighted by the famous mirror scene at the end along with turning the world's most famous redhead into a blonde.

Rita had recently appeared in *Separate Tables* (1957) under the banner of then-husband James Hill's production company, Hecht-Hill-Lancaster. She won plaudits as the former wife of Burt Lancaster who reignites old flames with him in a Bournemouth, England, boarding house. Co-stars David Niven and Wendy Hiller copped Oscars in the "Best Actor" and "Best Supporting Actress" categories.

There was good screen chemistry between Hayworth and Gig Young in *The Story on Page One*. This film that had mixed reviews delivered tremendous praise for the dynamic redhead, whose role possessed a better opportunity for enhancing dramatics, especially when she broke down under cross-examination from prosecuting attorney Phil Stanley (Sanford Meisner, a legendary drama coach making a rare screen appearance). Anthony Franciosa had a showier role among the male performers, playing a win-at-all-cost defense attorney, while the luminous cast also included Hugh Griffith and Mildred Dunnock.

Bosley Crowther put the issue accordingly in the final paragraph of his *New York Times* review: "Perhaps Mr. Odets intended his drama to be barren of spice, the morbid and mysterious flavorings that put murder stories on page one. Perhaps he figured he could fashion a furor over an incident that is drab. If so, he miscalculated the public's discrimination in such affairs and depended too heavily on the acting of a good but essentially hamstrung cast."[2]

In addition to Young's earlier mentioned Oscar nomination in a 1951 James Cagney vehicle, he had one starring role in the 1953 *City That Never Sleeps* which prompted insiders to take note of his talent and tap him for future assignments. The problem is that this is a film that has taken hold in time for its obvious raw human power and story energetic. *City That Never Sleeps* was not a major production with resultant public relations firepower and advertising that would have provided the young veteran, who had been in Hollywood films for almost a decade and a half when the movie was released in 1953, with the kind of career thrust that his excellent performance in a quality film deserved.

The screenplay was written by the prolific Steve Fisher, no stranger to film noir enthusiasts. Fisher penned two noir films that appeared in 1947, the Humphrey Bogart-Lizabeth Scott drama *Dead Reckoning*, directed by actor-turned-helmsman John Cromwell, and the much discussed, innovative *Lady in the Lake*, adapted from a Raymond Chandler novel featuring his shrewd, streetwise alter ego Philip Marlowe. Fisher felt comfortable in the noir genre, a factor doubtlessly enhanced from his experience as a Los Angeles crime beat reporter whose sphere of activity during the same year that the aforementioned two films were released included the city's most notable unsolved murder, the brutal slaying of Elizabeth Short, the woman known as "The Black Dahlia."

Robert Montgomery was a screen innovator who used film noir along with imaginative technique in *Lady in the Lake* and *Ride the Pink Horse*, released the same year. He used the "I am the camera" technique as leading man Marlowe in the Chandler work adapted by Fisher. The audience stepped metaphorically into the detective's shoes. Perhaps the two most evocative scenes of the film involved the detective being struck. In the first instance he is struck and knocked unconscious by the unprincipled playboy Chris Lavery (Dick Simmons). The audience can then see Marlowe peering into a mirror at his apartment, where his black eye serves as a vivid reminder of the meeting. In the second forceful confrontation it is the longtime nemesis of Marlowe, Lieutenant DeGarmot (played with the proper level of sadistic force by character acting great Lloyd Nolan) who pummels Chandler's famous detective at the police station.

Montgomery's leading lady in the film, Audrey Totter as Adrienne Fromsett, who is deeply in mutual love with him at the fadeout, stated in recent interviews that the reason the film failed to capture public imagination when it was initially shown was that it was technically ahead of its time.

The same can be said with Fisher's imaginative and swiftly paced *City That Never Sleeps*. Young shares star billing with Mala Powers, who would triumph opposite Jose Ferrer in his tour de force starring role in the 1950 release *Cyrano de Bergerac*, for which he won a "Best Actor" Oscar.

Young proved that he could rise well above the "second banana" status and the man-who-does-not-take-life-seriously roles he had so often been given. In this film Young, playing Johnny Kelly, a dedicated uniformed police officer, takes life in a most serious manner. While plagued by guilt, he is still determined throughout a large part of the movie to leave his loving wife, Kathy (Paula Raymond). He seeks to depart the rat race of a night beat in a vast metropolis for life with Sally "Angel Face" Connors (Mala Powers), a nightclub performer, and a fresh lease on life that encompasses moving to a less hectic lifestyle in California.

The city that never sleeps in this case is Chicago, and the photography by John L. Russell gives an insightful look of the place poet Carl Sandburg called "the city of the big shoulders." One pivotal evening on Chicago patrol duty, in which the pace swiftens even beyond the normal pace for Officer Kelly, causes him to return to his life with his loyal wife. He now sees his role in life in an expanded, highly appreciated vein, in the same way as George Bailey's epiphany in Frank Capra's heartwarming 1946 classic *It's a Wonderful Life*.

Giving *City* a unique spiritual element with a surprise twist is the role of Sgt. Joe (Chill Wills), who mysteriously fills in for Kelly's regular partner at the last moment. He greets every negative, depressed comment of a then-cynical Kelly with positive rejoinders. The rejoinders are delivered in such a kindly, fatherly, old-school, soft-sell manner that the police officer never thinks of them as argumentative. We realize at the film's conclusion that Sgt. Joe's soft spoken, gently presented wisdom has, along with unfolding events, generated appreciation on Kelly's part for his life as it exists, ultimately causing him to opt for continuity and his current marriage rather than abrupt change and moving to a distant locale with another woman.

Kelly (and the viewers) gradually learn that Sgt. Joe is a spirit, guardian angel, godly presence who, through the process of a miracle, has come to provide counsel to a troubled young man during an hour of need. The conclusion arises after Kelly is informed that his fellow station officers have no idea what he is talking about and that Sgt. Joe is someone they know nothing about.

Budapest-born director John Auer did a superb job of developing pacing after receiving a well-honed script by Fisher. No matter how rich a performance Young gave, this low-budget film could not enable him to step up to the top ranks of leading man stardom.

When the great dramatic opportunity of Young's film career arose he was in his mid-fifties and had passed the point of competing for leading man roles and being saddled with the image of the handsome young man who loses the girl. Interestingly, the role of Rocky, the ruthless master of ceremonies and commercial operator of the marathon conducted in a ballroom along Santa Monica Pier, was not originally slated to go to Young. The first choice was Lionel Stander, a standout "Best Supporting Actor" nominee who played the studio public relations trouble shooter to alcoholic performer Fredric March in the 1937 William Wellman directed hit *A Star is Born*. Stander would later win enduring television fame with his continuing role on the series *Hart to Hart* starring Robert Wagner and Stefanie Powers. He had earlier appeared regularly with Wagner in the series *It Takes a Thief*. With his fog-horned voice, made even gruffer with his notable Bronx accent, which was Stander's passport to fame, he would have made an interesting Rocky in *They Shoot Horses, Don't They?* The veteran character performer who had been in the middle of the investigations into Communist influence in the film industry would have assuredly rendered a solid performance as Rocky. One could easily see and hear him delivering the classic blarney lines of the rosy and positive showman on the outside and ruthless, conniving operator on the inside.

The Stander participation never reached fruition, however, and Gig Young stepped into a different role type than that he had played on so many occasions. Rocky is a tough man operating during a rugged period of American history; he could connive his way to

BLARNEY MASTER—Rocky (Gig Young, right) is the master of ceremonies of the marathon dance competition serving as the basis for the film *They Shoot Horses, Don't They?* (1969). He won the highly praised film's lone Oscar for "Best Supporting Actor." Young's assistant, Turkey (Al Lewis, left, who achieved fame as Grandpa in *The Munsters* television series), has apparently heard Rocky's spiel many times before.

possess the things he wanted, whether it was money or women. Hence, this was a role of contrasting challenge for an older and more experienced Young and he surmounted it well enough to win an Academy Award in that same "Best Supporting Actor" category for which he had been twice nominated.

Sydney Pollack's Artistic Conception

The setting for the film was Lick Pier. The marathon set was an exact replica of the old Aragon Ballroom at Ocean Park. (The Aragon was the location for orchestra leader Lawrence Welk's "champagne music" in a program that became a Saturday night staple in homes throughout America for a staggering three decade period encompassing 1951 to 1982.) The realistic venue was matched by the film's director. Sydney Pollack was born in Lafayette, Indiana, but by his late teens he was in New York City forging a mark in the career where he would become celebrated. As with many directing giants, he would reach his pinnacle through other, earlier means. He studied with acting instructor Sanford Meisner and began teaching and performing. One movie assignment that took the New Yorker to California resulted in him launching into directing. During a break in filming Pollack discussed how he would play an upcoming scene with fellow cast members. A fascinated listener sitting nearby was Burt Lancaster, who asked, "Hey kid, how would you play my scene?"

Pollack explained to the superstar performer how he would approach the scene. Nothing more was said, the film ended, and as Pollack was preparing to fly back to his wife and family in New York, he received a call to be interviewed, a meeting suggested by none other than Lancaster. Pollack initially balked. He was not making a lot of money at the time and did not want to forego the cost of his return airfare to New York. The voice on the other end of the line emphasized the importance of the putative meeting, suggesting that Pollack would be wise to forego the ticket cost.

Lancaster suggested that Pollack be given an opportunity to direct television dramas at a time when major studios were in need of knowledgeable and motivated young talent. Lancaster had reportedly quipped in recommending Pollack, "He can't do any worse than the guys you've already got."

This enabled Pollack to enter a new field. Before moving into feature films he would do two stints on *The Alfred Hitchcock Hour* while also directing on such prestigious small screen dramas as *Kraft Suspense Theater* and *Bob Hope's Chrysler Theater*.

Pollack took over the *They Shoot Horses, Don't They?* project from James Poe. It took 35 years to bring the movie to the screen. In the early stages, not long after McCoy's work was published, Charlie Chaplin had shown interest in making the film.

While recognizing that the book by Horace McCoy constituted raw power of its own and the danger of tampering with it, the director felt that one sequence adjustment needed to be made for the benefit of film audiences. McCoy's literary work delivered immediate impact by describing the plight of the hapless Robert Syverton as he admitted in court that he had killed Gloria. Pollack conceded the importance of retaining fidelity to McCoy's work, and Robert E. Thompson (who completed the final version of the script in six weeks) did so, but one important element was changed. While much of the flash-forward technique employed in the book was deployed in the Thompson screenplay, the film's first scene differed from McCoy's beginning.

"[I]t seemed very important in the film to create a sense of immediacy in the marathon itself," Pollack observed, "and thanks to the acceptance into the syntax of film of the flash-forward, we chose to reverse McCoy's structure. The marathon is established as time present and glimpses of Robert's trial are interspersed through the film as flash-forwards. The reversal may be considered only a technical change: the 'facts' of the story are delivered to the film's viewers in substantially the same order as they were to the readers of the novel; but it is by just such nearly undetectable devices — when they're properly chosen and well executed — that all narrative art is made to realize its fullest potential."[3]

Pollack saw the strong Depression symbolism and sad inevitability of McCoy's creative purpose in the book and brought that quality to the film. He sees the marathon competitors as searching for a "pot at the end of a rainbow" and continuing "because the prospects of reality in the outside world are just too tough." The film culminates with no winner in the marathon. Pollack believes that for McCoy to culminate the marathon with a winner "would have been antithetical to his concept, which was what we have since learned to call existential and absurdist."

McCoy had the marathon aborted due to a shooting with the police closing the dance hall and competition down. As a shrewd story analyst, it was Pollack's desire to retain the strong element of suicide lurking within Gloria as well as the "no winners" concept that was so inherent in McCoy's hard-hitting Depression novel. Pollack, via screenwriter Robert Thompson, substituted another route to defining his point, which will be thematically examined shortly.

The Film's End and Thematic Synthesis

Pollack declared that he had "a personal aversion to ending a film at its precise high point." He cited as an illustration that Blanche Dubois' classic line at the close of *A Streetcar Named Desire* of "I've always relied on the kindness of strangers" was followed by a character at the poker table exclaiming, "The name of this game is Seven Card Stud."[4]

On the subject of playing cards, Horace McCoy as an author masterfully played his deck from the standpoints of character, story development, and searing conclusion integrated into the fine-tuned fabric of thematic synthesis embodied by an important period of American history.

The "no winners" concept was carried to creative culmination by McCoy as a number of story elements merged. Jane Fonda (not long after playing an intergalactic fantasy sex symbol in *Barbarella*) was invested with the most formidable challenge of her career to that point. Then in her early thirties, Fonda deposited into the persona of the tragic Gloria Beatty the embittered cumulative life experiences of a woman who had lived many years.

Whereas Michael Sarrazin's Robert, despite receiving his share of jolts, can still talk about a dream to become a film director, the wily Gloria has been to one studio cattle call too many, jostled through too many lines, and sees the marathon competition as a one-way stop to oblivion. If ever the term "misery loves company" held meaning, it does within the context of Gloria interacting with so many like her, drifting in the midst of an all-engulfing economic tide pool.

The book and film's totally evocative title embraces the singular line in each vehicle that explains the thinking of Robert as he grants Gloria's wish of destruction. This creature who no longer has any tangible reason for existence needs assistance to bring life to an end.

Since this thought-provoking film containing multiple layers of ideas was released four decades ago, the issue of suicide has become far more widespread as political reality as well as a continuing discussion point. Diane Sawyer on ABC's popular weekly magazine program

20-20 showed an assisted suicide in the home of a terminally ill cancer patient in which his doctor participated in that final ultimate step. It occurred in Holland, where the practice is legal. The state of Oregon enacted the Death With Dignity Act on October 27, 1997. Its neighbor to the north, Washington, enacted Initiative 1,000. It was modeled closely on the Oregon law and took effect March 5, 2009.

Rest assured that the three aforementioned instances were not referenced as analogies. What is depicted at the close of the film would constitute a step in a drastic direction to extend suicide to such a level. The point that is relevant is that the issue raised involved a woman who finds herself totally devoid of hope seeking assistance from an empathic soul since she is afraid to carry out the ultimate act of suicide herself. Robert can empathize with Gloria on a basic level because he does not consider his own life a cause for optimism, but there is more, an event from his youth that makes him identify more strongly with the totally crestfallen young woman than he might otherwise do so.

Young as Blarney Master Meets Depressed Fonda as Gloria

In numerous of his foil roles to major leading men during his younger days Young played a character who does not take life all that seriously. In the major dramatic role of his career for which he won an Academy Award, rather than being a fun loving but harmless

OFF THEIR FEET—Gloria (Jane Fonda) and Robert (Michael Sarrazin) are exhausted, pain-ridden competitors seeking to push on to the next level of competition in *They Shoot Horses, Don't They?* (1969).

person who does not take life seriously, as Rocky the marathon master of ceremonies he does not take people seriously. They are mere instruments toward his stab at prosperity. Rocky, like Gloria, but without her sensitivity, sees a world without hope.

In the manner of a demagogic politician, Young's Rocky will say anything to build an audience. Early in the action he explains that the marathon is like the spirit of America in 1932, intoning, "Those who give up ... those who give out ... those who give in — OUT. Tough rules but these are tough times."[5]

At one point Rocky reveals his inner hardness to an assistant. He explains that while he lacks formal education, he learned all he needed to know observing his father — a faith healer. With unbridled cynicism he learned all he could from his father and went on to con audiences. He freely admits to being a con artist in every respect, carrying his activity in Depression times to making money on the tragic plight of masses willing to do virtually anything to prevent starvation. Rocky uses the marathon as a symbol of American competitive zeal rather than the rigged game designed to benefit himself that it realistically symbolizes, philosophizing, "There can be only one winner, folks, but isn't that the American way?"

Gloria sees things in a different way. On the issue of the film industry and her efforts to get ahead in it, the following exchange occurs:

> ROBERT: Have you met anybody who can help you?
>
> GLORIA: In this business how can you tell who'll help you? One day you're an electrician and the next day you're a producer. The only way I could ever get close to a big shot would be to jump on the running board of his car. Anyway, I don't know whether the men stars can help me as much as the women stars. From what I've seen lately I've been letting the wrong sex try and make me.[6]

Rocky's Derby

As the action is set in Southern California's film capital, inveterate promoter Rocky exploits that element to its zenith. One of the thirties' most popular comedians was Ben Bernie. Rocky repeats the word that Bernie popularized in the American lexicon of that period, "Yowza, yowza." Film industry personalities have been invited to watch the contest. The shrewd Rocky loves calling out their names, knowing that so many of the marathon's participants hope to achieve success in Hollywood. Rocky nurtures the dream that perhaps one of these famous marathon watchers will observe a contestant and see that he or she gets a break. As long as they are in the presence of successful Hollywood personalities, who knows? So the dream continues.

When it comes to conceiving ways to grab public interest, Rocky would make even P.T. Barnum sit up and take notice. As a means of generating added audience interest the grand spieler has introduced a brutalizing periodic method of eliminating participants. The slowest couples are terminated through a grueling event existing within the main contest called "The Derby." It is a hectic race to the finish line tape. The hour-by-hour human meltdown is not enough. The thoroughly opportunistic Rocky must carry the competition to an extended level.

In one particularly rugged derby competition late in the film, Red Buttons, playing a veteran sailor that Young as Rocky refers to as "our Ancient Mariner" collapses and is carted away on a stretcher. It is unknown whether he is alive or dead. Young instructs his assistants to "get him out of here. The back way." Meanwhile, he later assures one concerned participant who asks if Harry the Sailor is dead that he "will be fine." Never at a loss for words, the marathon's master of ceremonies takes the mike and glibly exclaims: "I've just had a message from our House Physician — a little touch of heat prostration. Nothing in the least serious. I understand that Harry, crusty old salt that he is, wants to stay in the marathon. But the Doc says No. And when it comes to something like this, the Doctor's word is law."[7]

Susannah York: From Turning Down Role to Oscar Nomination

One of the film's nine nominations went to Susannah York, who initially turned down her role, only to be contacted anew, and ultimately garnering a "Best Supporting Actress" nomination. Her appearance in *They Shoot Horses* served as a stepping stone on an international level that shortly gave her the chance to win "Best Actress" Cannes Film Festival honors in the 1972 Robert Altman film *Images* that was shot in Ireland. One year before *They Shoot Horses* was released she appeared in the controversial *The Killing of Sister George*, an adaptation of a successful play focused on the then-highly daring subject of lesbianism.

Susannah York has been renowned as an international film star from the sixties onward. I caught up with her at a time when she was busily engaged in stage activity in her London home base.

It was a bright afternoon and sunshine filtered onto the lawn as shadows lengthened behind the large Victorian home set near the sprawling green fields of Wandsworth Common, a colorful section of Southwest London near the Battersea section of Lavender Hill, the setting for one of Britain's greatest cinema comedies, *The Lavender Hill Mob* (1950) starring Alec Guinness. The name Guinness rings a bell in York's mind since her film debut came in the 1960 war drama *Tunes of Glory* directed by Ronald Neame and also starring John Mills, with the blonde actress cast as Guinness's daughter.

It was tea time and York moved with an elegant, supple grace, the movements of a performer equally at home before cameras or on stage. Before the subject of *They Shoot Horses, Don't They?* she mentions her early life. After being born in London she moved with her family northward and Scotland, living on a small farm. Her expressive blue eyes reflected back in time:

> We lived out in the country in Ayrshire County. The nearest town of Troon was five miles away. It was a relatively lonely type of existence since we were in such a remote setting. Perhaps the setting stimulated my creativity. I was always creating. By the time I was seven or eight I was writing plays that were being performed at school. They were about 20 minutes in length so I guess you'd call them playlets. I was always imagining myself to be other people. I would imagine what it would be like to be a coal miner, a school boy, or a secretary. I was always encouraging my playmates to take part in these games with me.[8]

These early indications of imagination and interpretive creativity led Susannah back to the great city where she had been born, the land of Shakespeare, Marlowe, Shaw, and Wilde. She moved to London at 16 and was accepted at the Royal Academy of Dramatic Art. Tackling the classics regularly honed her skills and brought her recognition in winning the Ronson Award, which is bestowed on the person selected as the Royal Academy's "Most Promising Student."

One evening while performing in a RADA production of Henrik Ibsen's *A Doll's House*

Susannah was spotted by veteran Hollywood agent Al Parker. He recommended that she be tested for the part of Guinness's daughter, and a star was ultimately born.

York received strong reviews for her initial screen effort. Two years later she received one of her showcase opportunities working with one of the film industry's most brilliant actors in Montgomery Clift and legendary directors in John Huston in the 1962 release *Freud*. Huston called the blonde British performer "an acting prodigy ... one of the greatest actresses of our time," comparing her to Katharine Hepburn and Ingrid Bergman.

Clift became good friends with York during the shooting of *Freud*. "Monty was a wonderful actor, one of my tops," she related. "He was a very truthful actor. Instinctive. He combined great truth and instinct in his work and was a perfectionist. He was incapable of cheating or letting you cheat. He was very encouraging to me."

Another film of eminent international import in which Susannah York starred was the 1963 adaptation of the Henry Fielding picaresque novel *Tom Jones*. Tony Richardson, who had made his mark by directing John Osborne's "angry young man" tour de force *Look Back in Anger* at the Royal Court Theatre, directed *Tom Jones*. Susannah needed to be enticed by Richardson to accept the role. His advice was stellar, providing her with one of her memorable screen roles as the prim and proper young woman pursued by a bawdy and rebellious Tom Jones (Albert Finney). A play on contrasting opposites evolved as Jones enjoyed romantic adventures with a ribald Molly Seagrim (Diane Cilento) in a film that received a "Best Film" Academy Award.

Decline and Acceptance

The vagaries of the film industry were once more in vogue as Susannah York wrote a polite letter declining an opportunity that eventually arguably provided the single-best scene opportunity of her eventful career, and perhaps her finest role opportunity alongside her Cannes winning performance in *Images*. James Poe, the then-intended director of *They Shoot Horses*, sent her a script that he had penned and for which he would receive co-authorship along with Robert E. Thompson, who honed the screenplay into its final form in six weeks.

"I wrote back, detailing my reasons for declining to appear in the film," Susannah explained. "I did not feel that the character was right as written. It was a character I could not feel and did not believe in. I began detailing the reasons why I did not feel the character was believable. Much to my surprise, they called me in to talk about the changes that I felt were needed in the script to make the character believable."[9]

The hairstyle and blonde tint displayed by Susannah as Alice LeBlanc in *They Shoot Horses* was reminiscent of Marilyn Monroe, a point made repeatedly by film reviewers throughout the world at the time. The character she endowed with such raw power was a woman of dramatic skill who had not received a break in Hollywood. Gig Young's Rocky might have possessed the morals of a rattlesnake, but displayed an impressive and unceasing level of native intelligence. When he hears the elegant voice of the struggling Alice, his showmanship flair prompts him to tap into her talent. She performs a scene reading at his behest to please the audience sitting in the bleachers. The scene is rendered along with her marathon partner, who is also struggling to break into films.

Viewers observe a rattled, angry Alice shriek at female marathoners during a break, claiming that someone has stolen her dress. She later seduces Robert and induces him to leave partner Gloria, who is obliged to dance solo and search for a new partner. Gloria is reminded in the process by Rocky that unless she finds a partner within the allotted time, she cannot continue in the competition.

York's culminating scene is that which assuredly clinched her Academy nomination. Her final scene is riveting. She stands in a shower with water pouring on her and goes insane. It is a swift descent into insanity registered largely through expression, one of the most difficult dramatic challenges, but one which she powerfully surmounts.

Rocky's Marriage Stunt Effort and Gloria's Tragic Demise

Two steady patterns emerge during the film. One is the exhausting relentlessness of the determined marathoners and the other is the steadily clicking brain

MARILYN MONROE LOOK-ALIKE—Susannah York was said by reviewers and filmgoers to resemble Marilyn Monroe in the British performer's role in *They Shoot Horses, Don't They?* (1969).

of the opportunistic Rocky—one of the most disliked characters ever on screen. While his nonchalant, ruthless opportunism does not reach the level of screen killers in film noir, he can be said to be a serial killer of sorts—along with his sociopath's business persona. Rocky will kill off human spirit and expose helpless Depression victims pursuing a dream with nary a thought. It all falls within his cynical view of life.

After Gloria and Robert are reunited with partners following the tragedy of Alice (along with Fonda's partner leaving her for a brief stint at Monogram), those steadily clicking wheels within Rocky's calculating brain discern yet another angle for him to peddle in the manner of the 24-hour bunco man, someone so concentrated in his efforts that he perhaps sees exploitation angles even in his sleep. During a break he summons Gloria and Robert to his office. It would be a great stunt, and one that the crowd would embrace, if the relentless marathon survivors married.

The respective responses on the part of Gloria and Robert delineate their personality differences. The nonchalant, acquiescent Robert is neutral about this as he seemingly is to everything else. Gloria, on the other hand, is a swift decision maker. She refuses to participate in a sham ceremony, even after Rocky explains that perhaps he could send one hundred or two hundred dollars to the "newlyweds" to entice her. When she delivers her initial response,

Rocky seeks to use Robert's diffidence as a plus, trying to convert it into a "yes," meaning all that she has to do is assent and his scheme can be brought to fruition.

When the no nonsense Gloria, who clearly despises Rocky's "all for a buck" cynicism, remains adamant, the enterprising promoter reveals that the ceremony is their only opportunity to gain anything from the marathon. Gloria mentions her desire to seek the grand prize of $750, more money than she has ever seen. Rocky has a ready answer: "Don't be naïve. Nobody's getting a full 750 bucks. What the hell you think I'm running here—a charity? (points to desk) I got bills stacked up. Every day. This Marathon don't run itself, you know. Not with what you kids are costing me. It's all right there."[10]

Gloria had been so dismally concerned about what she saw as the hopeless plight of civilization that she had pursued a pregnant Ruby with the sincere belief that she would be better off aborting the child she carried, infuriating her burly farmer husband, James. Despite her supreme cynicism that resulted in razor-sharp one-liners delivered with helpless despair and occasional anger at other marathon contestants, it is obvious from her crushed expression that she had believed a $750 first prize, as advertised, would be bestowed on the final competition survivors.

Even that dream was squelched as cool and methodical businessman Rocky provides her with itemized figures. He lets her know that she and her partner also figured in that tabulation.

With that Gloria departs. A final fleeting flicker of purpose, for remaining around a world she believes to be ultimately hopeless, is dashed. Before her departure she delivers a final shout to the few tired remaining marathon participants, telling them they have been suckered.

Gloria had earlier likened herself and other participants to animals in cages, wondering if people would "throw peanuts" at them. Just when the audience becomes convinced that a thoroughly despondent Gloria had seen it all, she receives a literal "run" of bad luck. The pair of stockings she wore were purchased by giving up streetcar rides.

When Robert exhibits his apologetic sorrow, Gloria sees the stocking tear as the final of a series of events. "Oh shut up!" she snaps. "It's not the goddamned stocking anyway.... What the hell difference does it make? Forget it."[11]

Two more penetrating Gloria comments complete her summation: "Maybe it's just the whole damn world's like one big Central Casting—and they got it all rigged before you ever show up." After Robert asks what she intends to do, the reply is straight and to the point ala Gloria: "I'm going to get off this merry-go-round. I'm through with the whole stinking thing."[12]

Gloria removes a snub-nosed .38 caliber revolver from her purse but is unable to carry out the suicide act, imploring of her former marathon partner, "Help me." After he complies, a policeman later asks, "Why'd you do it, kid?" Robert reflects back to his childhood when his favorite horse was shot by his grandfather after its leg was broken in a fall.

"They shoot horses, don't they?" the ever soulful, wide-eyed Robert declares with a sad moroseness containing an appropriate ring of inevitability, the kind Gloria would have fully appreciated.[13]

Nine Oscar Nominations

The nine Oscar nominations received by *They Shoot Horses, Don't They?* was the most in the history of the Academy bestowed on any picture that failed to win "Best Film" honors. The single Academy statuette garnered by the Depression classic went to Young.

Young's victory was one of the strongest in his category in Hollywood history. It is exceedingly difficult to master the role of a total cynic without either undershooting the mark or overdoing it. Young's balance was remarkable as the devil-may-care charlatan who had rigged the game but admired the plucky courage of the marathon participants and even waved the American flag, symbolizing their efforts with the fighting spirit of its citizens and exclaiming with full-throated optimism, "What Depression?"

The tone and spirit of the film, carried forward by the direction and writing, and rendered visually with consummate impact by close-ups that showed the agony of souls seeking to lift themselves up from want, is symbolized down to playing the soothing ballad "Easy Come Easy Go" in a note of stinging irony.

Fonda received a "Best Actress" nomination for her stellar work. Director Pollack was also nominated, as was the team of Poe and Thompson in the "Best Adapted Screenplay" category. The other Academy nominations were garnered by Harry Horner and Frank McKelvy for "Best Art Direction-Set Decoration," Johnny Green and Albert Woodbury for "Best Musical Score," and Donfeld for "Best Costume Design."

Young also received a Golden Globe Award for "Best Supporting Actor," while Pollack was honored as "Best Director" and the film triumphed in the "Best Drama" category. While Young failed to secure a British Academy Award, Londoner Susannah York took home honors as "Best Supporting Actress" with Fredric Steinkamp triumphing as "Best Editing."

The soulful-eyed Sarrazin secured a British Academy Award as "Most Promising Leading Newcomer to Films" after winning that same Golden Globe distinction one year earlier for *The Sweet Ride*. The sensitive expressions displayed by Sarrazin were reminiscent of Montgomery Clift in *I Confess*, the 1953 Alfred Hitchcock release shot in the city of Sarrazin's birth, Quebec City.

Regrettably, Sarrazin did not receive enough film opportunities to live up to the promise of his talent. The seventies found him appearing in such films as *Sometimes a Great Notion* (1971), *The Life and Times of Judge Roy Bean* (1972), and *The Reincarnation of Peter Proud* (1975); he eventually found a busy career on television.

On to Further Glory

Made at a time when Sydney Pollack was entering his mid-thirties, *They Shoot Horses* proved a springboard to a brilliant career. The same year that it was released the war film *Castle Keep*, starring Pollack's mentor Burt Lancaster, also debuted. In 1973 one of the screen's finest romances was released: *The Way We Were* starring Barbra Streisand and Robert Redford, which Pollack directed.

Two years later the diverse director's CIA political intrigue drama *Three Days of the Condor* debuted in theaters. In 1982 it was on to rollicking comedy with *Tootsie*, starring Dustin Hoffman as an ambitious actor who masquerades as a woman to land a role on a television soap opera. Jessica Lange won a "Best Supporting Actress" Oscar as his co-star, who believes for most of the film that her close friend and fellow soap opera performer is a she. Pollack portrayed Hoffman's agent.

While Jane Fonda would win an Oscar for her portrayal of aspiring New York City stage actress and high-priced call girl in *Klute* (1971), a case can be made that her performance in *They Shoot Horses* was even more powerful, making so infinitely believable a tough role of a complex young woman who had reached the end of the road.

There would be some other great roles as well for Fonda in her halcyon period, beginning with the Depression drama and extending beyond *Klute* to another "Best Actress" Oscar in the anti–Vietnam War film *Coming Home* in 1978, to her portrayal as playwright Lillian Hellman opposite Jason Robards, Jr., as Dashiell Hammett in *Julia* one year earlier and alongside her father Henry and Katharine Hepburn in their Oscar-winning performances in 1981's *On Golden Pond*.

James Poe, the initially intended director of *They Shoot Horses*, would never direct a film, but had a brilliant career as a screenwriter, with an Oscar for Mike Todd's multi-starred classic from 1956, *Around the World in Eighty Days*, an honor which he shared with John Farrow and S.J. Perelman. He was nominated three other times: for *Cat on a Hot Tin Roof*, shared with the film's director Richard Brooks, the 1963 Sidney Poitier Oscar vehicle *Lilies of the Field*, and for *They Shoot Horses*.

Poe's fellow Academy Award nominee for *They Shoot Horses*, Robert E. Thompson, would, oddly enough, not author another movie screenplay during his entire career, nor had he received any such credit previously, but as the seventies beckoned he crafted an early draft for director William Friedkin for his 1971 "Best Picture" Academy Award winner *The French Connection*. Ernest Tidyman, author of the finalized screenplay, won an Oscar in the adaptation category in shaping Robin Moore's novel into film form, while director Friedkin and leading man Gene Hackman also took home statuettes.

It was Thompson who took Poe's earlier work and, in six weeks, honed a finalized screenplay. Thompson, who had a long career writing teleplays for some of the smaller screen's biggest vehicles (such as *Bonanza* and *Mission: Impossible*) was the perfect one to call upon to reshape an earlier draft, given the deadline constraints of television writing.

The Final Tragedy of Gig Young

With an Oscar under his belt, Young received plaudits as the father of a bride-to-be in the 1970 hit *Lovers and Other Strangers*, which garnered a Golden Globe for "Best Comedy." It was a sharp departure from his performance as Rocky in an area he considered to be more challenging than drama since comedy involves "offbeat roles."

His agent and longtime friend, Martin Baum, to whom he bestowed his Oscar after crediting him with his help in winning it, landed the aforementioned role for the actor after Young's *They Shoot Horses* triumph as well as the 1974 Sam Peckinpah film *Bring Me the Head of Alfredo Garcia*.

Young was cast as the Waco Kid by Mel Brooks for *Blazing Saddles*, which was ultimately one of the madcap director's biggest hits. He was replaced shortly after filming began by Brooks with Gene Wilder after he suffered from delirium tremens on the set.

Drinking plagued Young throughout his life. He dreamed of a comeback on Broadway and had appeared in a Canadian tour of the play *Nobody Loves an Albatross*. He married 21-year-old German actress Kim Schmidt. They shared a Manhattan apartment without windows, perhaps thereby enhancing a troubled, depressive state all the more as his heavy drinking persisted.

On October 19, 1978 tragedy struck, shocking the show business community. Young fatally shot his much-younger wife and then turned the weapon on himself, resulting in murder and suicide.

Young had been married five times. His third wife was popular television actress Elizabeth Montgomery, daughter of actor-director Robert Montgomery. She starred in the popular television series *Bewitched*.

According to Elaine Young, the actor's fourth wife: "What he was aching for, as he walked up to collect his Oscar, was a role in his own movie, one that they could finally call a Gig Young movie." She believed the actor was shattered when that opportunity did not materialize. "For Gig, the Oscar was literally the kiss of death, the end of the affair," Elaine concluded.

As for Young, he cynically summed up his professional career as "30 years and 55 pictures — not more than five that were any good, or any good to me." On the subject of his acting specialty, he was at his most acidic: "My specialties are corpses, unconscious people and people snoring in spectacular epics."

Personal problems plagued Young throughout his career. When his former agent Martin Baum became president of ABC Pictures he insisted that Young play Rocky in *They Shoot Horses*. There was opposition to Young from certain backers of the movie as well as female lead Jane Fonda. The opposition centered on two points: Young's widely known, myriad personal problems along with a belief that his forte was comedy and that he was therefore not as suitable as certain other performers who specialized in drama.

Not only had his critics not recognized Gig Young's versatility, they overlooked the fact that their other reason for concern — personal problems — constituted a plus for him playing such a unique and specialized role as that of Rocky.

Great performers are noted for tapping into inner roots in specialized roles. This role was specialized for Young given the fact that, while he in real life could display charm and affability, there remained the deeply troubled inner persona. He was plagued by a drinking problem and so was his brilliantly captured character. Also, like Young, Rocky exuded charm and affability to the audience viewing the marathon contest.

Rocky sought to leave behind the seamier side of himself by providing assurances that the American spirit would defeat the Depression as he extolled the determination of the couples competing in the grueling marathon. All the while his other side had worked painstakingly to dupe participants into thinking they had a chance to win a grand prize of $750, unaware that he had cleverly and ruthlessly rigged the game.

This was a role that involved a turbulent bravado as well as profound sensitivity, the story of a troubled man, an opportunist seeking to convey patriotism and bonhomie to the audience. While Gig Young remained immersed in personal problems, he apparently failed to recognize the breadth, the all-encompassing scope of his dramatic triumph as Rocky in *They Shoot Horses*.

The brilliantly rendered noir classic was Young's great opportunity, his picture, his grand chance to show his dramatic greatness. Flanked by great co-stars: Fonda, Sarrazin, York, Buttons, Bedelia, and Dern — Gig Young proved he was a truly special actor.

Perhaps the grandest irony of all was that Young's tragic end was evocative of how the outer bravado-etched but deeply inner conflicted Rocky's life might also have ended.

At his memorial service Martin Baum, who knew him so well, stated, "Gig knew real pain."

Pain was such a huge component on all sides in the breathtaking team achievement of *They Shoot Horses, Don't They?* In retrospect, can we conceive of anyone better equipped or more understanding of the role he played than Gig Young?

Chapter Six

Chandler's Blueprint for Mystery and His Career in Hollywood

> Hammett wrote at first (and almost to the end) for people with a sharp, aggressive attitude to life. They were not afraid of the seamy side of things; they lived there.
> — Raymond Chandler, *The Simple Art of Murder*

That January 11, 1936, *Black Mask* convocation that brought together three eventual giants and creative founding influences of book noir (ultimately developed into film noir) revealed interesting portraits of themselves. McCoy looks both distinguished and camera-ready, just the pose for a man who started a theater in Dallas and, after acting there, sought to make the grade by performing in films. He looks the part of a dapper actor.

As for Hammett and Chandler, they too blend with the images constructed in their hard-hitting fictional works. Hammett conveys an expression of boredom and wanting to get away from it all. His is the palest complexion of all the authors in the picture, not surprising in view of his fragile health. The former Pinkerton detective has the pasty look of the inmates that he had helped send to places where people are compelled to spend all but exercise periods indoors.

Chandler appears just as he was written about. Augmented by the pipe that so frequently hung between his lips, the bespectacled author looks like an Oxford University don, master of all he surveys, and surveying with a sense of detachment. That natural expression of the wise old owl seasoned by experience prompted thoughts of the wily Philip Marlowe. Marlowe was a sociological quick study whose knowledge was updated daily by experience as he encountered people in and around Los Angeles on detective assignments that would never make him rich in the coin of the realm, but rendered him significantly wealthy in the dominion of human understanding.

Raymond Chandler wrote about the *Black Mask* dinner and meeting Hammett in a letter to Alex Barris, stating, "Often wonder why he quit writing after *The Thin Man*. Met him only once, very nice looking tall quiet gray-haired fearful capacity for Scotch, seemed quite unspoiled to me." Chandler put on record what he thought of Dashiell Hammett's contribution to the detective suspense genre. As someone who began writing during the Depression after losing his job as an oil company executive, he appreciated the exigencies of the moment and the need to make a living. He recognized that Hammett had the unique advantage of having worked in the field into which he plunged. Chandler recorded his impressions of Hammett as an artist in his essay *The Simple Art of Murder*: "I doubt that Hammett had any deliberate artistic aims whatever; he was trying to make a living by writing something he had firsthand information about. He made some of it up; all writers do; but it had a basis in fact; it was made up out of real things."[1]

In the pages that preceded his comments about Hammett, Chandler pointed out what he considered to be factual flaws in what had been praised as detective novel masterpieces, mentioning *Trent's Last Case* as well as the problem-solving activities of Agatha Christie's memorable Belgian detective Hercule Poirot. He contrasted writers of the traditional British detective school, stating tartly, "The only reality the English detection writers knew was the conversational accent of Surbiton and Bognor Regis. If they wrote about dukes and Venetian vases, they knew more about them out of their own experience than any well-heeled Hollywood character knows about."[2]

Chandler then went on to say more positive things about Hammett as he contrasted the style he brought to detective novels compared to traditional British detective writing as adopted by predecessors of the San Francisco author. In Chandler's view, Hammett "wrote for people with a sharp, aggressive attitude to life." He believed that Hammett "gave murder back to the kind of people that commit it for reasons, not just to provide a corpse; and with the means at hand, not hand-wrought dueling pistols, curare and tropical fish. He put these people down on paper as they were, and he made them talk and think in the language they customarily used for these purposes."[3]

According to Chandler, Hammett "had style, but his audience didn't know it, because it was in a language not supposed to be capable of such refinements." The style of Hammett, in Chandler's view, did "not belong to Hammett or to anybody, but is the American language." Chandler pointed out that, while detractors asserted that Hammett lacked heart, the story he thought the most of is the record of a man's devotion to a friend. In Chandler's view, "He was spare, frugal, hard-boiled, but he did over and over again what only the best writers can ever do at all. He wrote scenes that seemed never to have been written before."[4]

In praising Hammett for blazing the trail for a new kind of detective-suspense style, Chandler fired what those of the traditional British detective school style regarded as a shot across the bow. The writer, who was proud of his Dulwich British school experience and who grew up in London, contrasted the man-of-the-street style of the former Pinkerton detective to what he considered to be a stodgier world of drawing rooms removed from what he considered the thrust of action on the streets of a major American city, traversing the flesh-and-blood lives of Americans of contrasting experiences.

Chandler summarizes his view in the final paragraph of *The Simple Art of Murder*:

> The story is this man's adventure in search of a hidden truth, and it would be no adventure if it did not happen to a man fit for adventure. He has a range of awareness that startles you, but it belongs to him by right, because it belongs to the world he lives in. If there were enough like him, the world would be a very safe place to live in, without becoming too dull to be worth living in.[5]

Carr Strikes Back

Chandler's essay titled "The Simple Art of Murder" was revised, rewritten, and published by Houghton Mifflin in a new book containing twelve of his old novelettes. It was reviewed by John Dickson Carr in the *New York Times Book Review* on September 19, 1950.

Carr was a writer of the type of detective mysteries derided by Chandler, who would later complain about his selection in a letter to Dale Warren of Houghton Mifflin. Chandler complained that, by selecting someone critically opposed to his style of detective writing, the *Times* was using a back-door approach to attack him.

Critic Carr began by attacking Chandler's "thesis that murder become realistic." He followed by stating Chandler's view "that murder must become realistic. It must be taken out of the Venetian vase and dropped into the alley. It must be handled by men who understand it, who use the Luger and the Colt for real reasons, undismayed by violence, all rawhead and bloody-bones. Besides, he says, this makes the writing of a detective story good fun."[6]

Warming up to his task, Carr asserted, "He is pitiless, this austere fellow. He will not even allow English writers the negative virtues of background or culture. They speak in what Mr. Chandler calls the 'conversational accent'—as opposed, perhaps, to the non-conversational accent?—of Surbiton or Bognor Regis. They write about dukes and Venetian vases, but they don't know a thing about dukes or Venetian vases either."[7]

Concerned about covering every aspect of Chandler's essay, the detective author of a distinctly different school took umbrage over his criticism of the Detection Club of London, of which Carr himself was a member. Carr cites that "the club contains only one peer of the realm, one baronet, one O.B.E., and two lowly knights. There isn't a duke in it. Mr. Chandler, who modestly claims affinity with Aeschylus and Shakespeare, will have to debate only with Miss [Dorothy] Sayers ... and perhaps a dozen others.... And, of course, these people know nothing of violence, especially those who lived in London and were on duty from 1940 to 1945."[8]

Another major area where Carr took exception was with Chandler's comment in *The Simple Art of Murder*: "The cool-headed constructionist does not also come across with lively characters, sharp dialogue, a sense of pace and an acute sense of observed detail." In rebuttal, Carr supplied a list of authors on "both sides of the Atlantic" who "joyously wrote bloods as well as detective stories" and "were cool-headed constructionists." Carr's list included Edgar Allan Poe, Nathaniel Hawthorne, Mark Twain, Charles Dickens, Wilkie Collins, Robert Louis Stevenson, Thomas Hardy, Joseph Conrad, John Galsworthy, Hugh Walpole, and G.K. Chesterton.

John Dickson Carr allowed that "Mr. Chandler is a serious-minded man, and it would be unjust not to take him seriously." He then levels sharp criticism in the realm of damning with a certain amount of faint praise, writing, "His similes either succeed brilliantly or fall flat. He can write a scene with an almost suffocating vividness and sense of danger—if he does not add three words too many and make it funny. His virtues are all there. If ... he could add the fatigue of construction and clues ... then one day he may write a good novel."[9]

After stating that Chandler has no "new ideas or plot twists," Carr examines the novelettes in *The Simple Art of Murder* and concludes "that it is an admirable collection." Having said that, the reviewer ends on a biting note by exclaiming, "Mr. Chandler will do even better when he discovers that you cannot create an American language merely by butchering the English language."[10]

Dale Warren was publicity director at the company that published *The Simple Art of Murder*, Houghton Mifflin of Boston. Since Chandler corresponded regularly with him on the subject of shop talk, namely the marketing of his works, it was far from surprising that Warren would be the party to whom Chandler would vent his creative soul in responding to the John Dickson Carr *New York Times* review.

Chandler was displeased not only with the Carr review, but with one written by Anthony Boucher in *Time*. He conceded to not seeing the Boucher review but told Warren that the *Time* reviewer was taking "deadly aim" at him. Chandler wrote that it was obvious that "people like Boucher and Carr are committed in advance to disliking me, because they are well aware that I regard their kind of detective story as apt to be a crashing bore.... If they don't like my opinions, why don't they sit down and refute them on the same level instead of waiting until I write something else and then take their spleen out on that? I could write a better defense of the deductive mystery than they could."[11]

Two Distinct Schools; Two Strong Believers

Chandler's essay in *The Simple Art of Murder*, sharply contrasted with Carr's review in the *New York Times*, demonstrates a clash of two distinct schools of detective-mystery thought delivered by two practitioners of writing with strong beliefs. In delivering their viewpoints it is natural to expect some exaggeration on each side. Chandler's disdain for the traditional style could prompt the uninitiated to believe that traditional detective stories contained esthetes with overly starched collars. Analyzing Carr from the sternest perspective, one could believe that the Hammett-Chandler school contained uniformly pesky panhandlers with cheap wine on their breath.

Given the rapier, blistering attacks on each side, it is necessary to take a step back and weigh the central thrust of each argument. The traditional viewpoint contains many adherents of the Arthur Conan Doyle school who enjoyed the foggy atmosphere of old London and a dazzling intellect (as embodied in Sherlock Holmes) who could unravel the most complicated mysteries by peeling off layer by layer. Hammett's Sam Spade and Chandler's Philip Marlowe peeled off layers as well, leading up to an ultimate solution, but in the manner of common folk mingling within the elements rather than cogitating and delivering finely reasoned results to his alter ego in the manner of the ever-astute Holmes touching base with Dr. Watson.

As for the issue of where the film industry was proceeding in following one direction or another, a powerful voice was emerging. It was a merger of places and time with the steadily developing popularity of film noir.

Raymond Chandler wrote in the March 1948 issue of *The Atlantic*, "Not only is the motion picture an art, but it is the one entirely new art that has been evolved on this planet for hundreds of years. It is the only art at which we of this generation have any possible chance to greatly excel."

As for adherents of traditional detective form such as John Dickson Carr there would be the smartly packaged Sherlock Holmes films of the forties. Basil Rathbone, a British transplant to Hollywood with exceptional sword-fighting skills, demonstrated the right panache and analytical facility to convince audiences as Sir Arthur Conan Doyle's popular detective of the late 19th- and early 20th-century fiction world.

Playing Holmes's loyal friend and ardent case-solving cohort was another British product, Nigel Bruce, also a veteran of the character acting ranks. Bruce was ideally tapped to play a certain variety of friendly foil to the genius crime solver since he had sometimes been selected to play a bumpkin role. A memorable instance of Bruce as a well-intentioned bumpkin used to enhance homicidal ends was when Geoffrey Carroll (Humphrey Bogart) insisted on retaining the heavy drinking, far from diagnostically astute country physician Dr. Tuttle (Bruce) to remain on his wife's case in the Broadway stage hit brought to the screen, *The Two Mrs. Carrolls* (1947).

Ironically, neither Rathbone nor Bruce, two of the definitive Britishers of film, was born in England, although both were raised there. In Rathbone's case he was brought to England at the age of three after being born in South Africa. His father was believed to be a British spy in the leadup to the Boer War involving Britain and South Africa. Bruce was born to an English family while on vacation, which explains why he was born in Ensenada on Mexico's Baja Peninsula.

Chance for Rathbone to Be on Winning Side

For years Basil Rathbone was cast as a suave villain with an egotistical, smirking self-righteousness to serve as a devastating contrast to the leading men with whom he would clash, making them by contrast all the more appealing to the audience. An irony of Rathbone in real life contrasted with the villainous characters he played was that he was long considered one of the most talented swordsmen in Hollywood. All the same, the scripts called for him to lose climactic fencing battles at the close of action films. He fell prey to Warner Bros'. swashbuckler Errol Flynn in Michael Curtiz's 1938 action epic *The Adventures of Robin Hood* and to Tyrone Power in Rouben Mamoulian's *The Mark of Zorro* (1940).

Mamoulian, a director who thrived on experimentation, had some misgiving in accepting *The Mark of Zorro* in view of the earlier Curtiz action epic. With such a drawn-out sword fighting scene involving Flynn and Rathbone encompassing so much ground, the one thing Mamoulian did not want to do was engage in anything resembling repetition in a film that involved the same smarmy adversary to a dynamic and handsome leading man, in this case Power.

"It finally came to me," Mamoulian recollected. "The other scene had covered so much ground. I had asked myself how to make this sword fight unique and I decided what I should do was confine it to a very small area."[12]

The scene was praised by the critics and received approval from Columbia boss Harry Cohn, but it did not come off without a hitch. Rathbone, during one take, and in front of friends visiting from England who were taking in the filmmaking activity, had his toupee accidentally removed from one swish of Power's sword.

"Tyrone Power was such a gentleman and he felt so sorry," Mamoulian revealed. "He apologized profoundly to Rathbone and his guests for what he had done. We all explained that it was understandable, the kind of thing that can happen when you are shooting a rapid action scene."[13]

He might have been one of Hollywood's top swordsmen, but the twice Oscar nominated Basil Rathbone won very few on-screen sword fights, actually only one. Longing for some triumphs, it was no surprise that Rathbone jumped at the chance to play the literary world's most eminent detective, the renowned Sherlock Holmes, in a finely crafted series of films produced by Universal, all based on stories from Arthur Conan Doyle's series. "I got to beat the bad guy instead of play him," Rathbone delightedly explained.

As for Bruce, his career was earmarked playing a distinctly patterned character as surely as was fellow Brit Rathbone. Some purist lovers of the Doyle mystery series demurred over Bruce playing a bungler as a comedic foil to Rathbone in the Universal films. The stories written by physician Arthur Conan Doyle while awaiting patients revealed a more suave and intellectual Doctor Watson than that played by Bruce. As first-person narrator, the literary persona of Doctor Watson, revealed as a distinguished doctor, stands as closer to an equal in the relationship, but one that stands in awe of the brilliant powers of detection of Holmes, building up his image within the pages of each well-constructed work.

Bruce on film appears as comedic foil rather than as an erudite partner. Two apparent reasons surface as to why the Watson persona differs on screen as contrasted with print. The first is that the erudition by description of a sage first person narrator could not be captured on screen. Granted this would not prevent a smoother, more erudite Watson from later appearing on film as someone embodying more of an equal in the relationship. The second reason is that audiences were familiar with Bruce in this role and he portrayed it in a unique fashion that bears his individual trademark. This element achieves two other results. By injecting a comedic element into the films, a contrast is achieved away from the grisly element of murder. A second reason is that by Watson bungling as he attempted to assist Holmes in solving crimes, the detective appears to be all the greater genius.

The ultimate lesson to carry away from the teaming of Rathbone and Bruce is that two veteran performers appeared with two well-developed personas plumbed repeatedly by directors and producers due to their perfection of those roles. In the Sherlock Holmes series one performer donned a fresh mantle removed from his traditional screen image while the other remained the same. Since Holmes was formal and articulate in manner, going with the brilliant deductive detective's persona as developed by Doyle in the literary series, Rathbone only needed to fine-tune his traditional character, making his screen presence formal but positive rather than brilliantly arrogant as befitting a formidable villain. Oddly enough, the old Rathbone-style villainous character was compatible with Holmes's long time adversary, Professor Moriarty.

As for Bruce, his hilarious bungler persona remained a perfect counterweight to the dignified formality and refined detection skills. The series maintained an edge of humor through Watson's good-hearted fumbles offset by machine-like efficiency and sturdy brain power by a master detective.

Enter Chandler and the New Wave

While there would continue to be some films made in the old tradition of Sherlock Holmes, including a glossy, well-done British version of *The Hound of the Baskervilles* (1959, directed by Terence Fisher and starring Peter Cushing, Andre Morell, and Christopher Lee), this type of product would increasingly fall into the domain of the public broadcasting format.

Agatha Christie's colorful detectives Miss Marple and Belgian Hercule Poirot would entertain television audiences in series of enormous popularity on both sides of the Atlantic with Joan Hickson and David Suchet rendering the main characters with a fidelity that Christie would have lauded. Between 1987 and 2000, the idyllic beauty of Oxford would serve as the backdrop in the series *Inspector Morse* with John Thaw cast in the lead as an educationally overqualified police officer with a penchant for pub stops and quoting the poems of Keats and the sonnets of Shakespeare with Kevin Whately cast as his faithful partner ever seeking to understand Morse's ways.

The tradition of the London school of detection and progeny of a comparable school of step-by-step clue finding would not die, as exemplified in an American context by Peter Falk as the seemingly plodding but ultimately shrewd Lieutenant Columbo. The *Columbo* television series began in 1971 and had an incredible run with periodic made-for-TV movies co-featuring leading guest performers up to 2003.

While there is sufficient interest in traditional detective methods to ensure that this form of entertainment will not die, by the time that the spirited essay debate pitting Raymond Chandler and John Dickson Carr was published, the issue was already settled on the busy sound stages of Hollywood studios. A new voice took over suspense films as forties' entertainment became dominated by that French-sounding name that was in practice so thoroughly American.

The Outsider and Film Noir

Raymond Chandler was a man who kept very much to himself. The one defining person in his life following the death of his mother was the woman he married at that same juncture, his beloved Cissy. He shared his creative ideas and intimate feelings with her, but for the most part, kept within himself. After losing his job as an oil executive he positioned himself in front of his trusty Underwood typewriter, wearing gloves. With a bottle of whiskey perched next to him, Chandler turned out brilliantly crafted detective suspense initially for Captain Joseph Shaw's *Black Mask* and from there, full-length novels and shorter works for the book market. Ultimately he would move into a screenwriting field where his voice and subject matter selection would play a sharply defining role.

Los Angeles author Judith Freeman was intrigued by Chandler's solitariness and his reposing of confidence almost exclusively in the woman 18 years his senior, trusted confidante Cissy. Freeman noted how many different residences the Chandlers lived in during his productive Los Angeles writing phase, before he moved to the quietly idyllic San Diego suburb of La Jolla. Freeman reported that it was at his La Jolla residence that Chandler mutually fulfilled high expectations in meeting British novelist Somerset Maugham. In his phase as an author writing about his craft in works such as *The Summing Up,* Chandler was one fellow writer whom the British craftsman held in high regard. Chandler reciprocated in his own articles about the writing craft, and in his vigorous personal correspondence. The meeting was arranged by Maugham's close personal friend with whom he stayed on Southern California visits, film director George Cukor.[14]

Freeman describes a meeting filled with mutual praise and bonhomie, but asserts in another context a point made frequently by those who followed Chandler's creative activities. The tranquility of La Jolla, with Chandler and Cissy having a splendid view of the rolling waves of the Pacific Ocean, resulted in the kind of creative restlessness that produced finely crafted works such as *The Big Sleep, Farewell, My Lovely, Lady in the Lake,* and *The High Window.*

While it is true that Chandler wrote much of *The Little Sister* at the La Jolla residence, the two works he produced that were most associated with this period of his writing life were *The Long Goodbye* and an unfilmed screenplay, *Playback.* Neither of these works contained the crispness of movement and varied characterization associated with the melting-pot element of Los Angeles. In this connection it must also be granted, as numerous Chandler watchers have deduced, that his energy was flagging after so much recent work on screenplays. That energy diminution could possibly have related to the fact that he never felt at home in the Hollywood scene (but for his camaraderie among fellow screenwriters) and considered the writer to be the slave of an insensitive, highly commercial system.

There are some plausible reasons that Chandler's voice would surface in the noir world of the forties, and that the stories would be centered in and around Los Angeles, often Hollywood, where the author's alter ego detective Philip Marlowe resided. Two practical reasons arise. One relates to the ever-ascending popularity of film production. The movie industry was America's second leading industry, surpassed only by the nation's automobile makers in Detroit. A second reason also pervaded, and was linked to its predecessor. Just as the nation's thriving automobile industry had its home in Detroit, America's film capital was Hollywood.

As has been recently noted by knowledgeable American film industry insiders, such as producer and director Rob Reiner in an insightful interview with Jeff Greenfield on CNN, the current film industry is based more strongly on international distribution. Much of this is interrelated to a strong current video game market. Successful films feed into the video market, increasing productivity through further popularizing a film, series of films, movie personality or personalities. A Terminator video game featuring Arnold Schwarzenegger's film character or one based on the fantastically successful Harry Potter series have already been internationally and prolifically presold before arriving in a video game context. Also, as the demand to please the international market increases, the use of language becomes a diminished factor while special effects and chase sequences assume increased importance compared to dialogue construction and development.

With Hollywood the unrivaled movie capital and so much product needed to continue a successful process, it is logical and thoroughly anticipated that audiences would be seeing fewer films starring detective characters such as Sherlock Holmes, Hercule Poirot, and Miss Marple as opposed to hard-hitting works about servicemen returning from World War II and adjusting to circumstances in a tough world existing in America's cities.

By the same token, most Americans regarded World War II as a fight both necessary and worthy. In that context the detective persona (crafted initially by Hammett in film noir with *The Maltese Falcon* and followed up by Chandler in *The Big Sleep*) stressed the importance of honor. In the world of a tough, often cold and anarchistic large city teeming with people, honor still counted for something.

With most Americans going to the cinema at least once a week, and with stadiums increasing attendance for sports events, people were spending more money with returning veterans re-emerging on work forces. A boom was in progress, with more dollars being made and spent.

It is easy to see why Americans would be looking for films denoting the national experience. A nation needed to both sacrifice to endure and struggle during the Depression, then brace itself and participate in a global military conflict that ultimately resulted in the loss of 50 million lives.

By the time Raymond Chandler emerged in print with his first novel, *The Big Sleep*, he was 51 and filled with the kind of cumulative experiences that presented intrigue on paper. Readers analyzed Philip Marlowe, the detective the author had honed to a razor's edge in the pages of Captain Joseph Shaw's *Black Mask*. Also of interest were the people and adventures Marlowe encountered in the streets in and around Los Angeles, where people came and went, identities were acquired and lost with staggering rapidity, and people moved around restlessly from place to place as the author and Cissy did.

In terms of laying out story and perspective swiftly with descriptive as well as sledgehammer prose, Raymond Chandler shone like a beacon. Consider the three brilliantly crafted paragraphs that launch *The Big Sleep*:

> It was about eleven o'clock in the morning, mid October, with the sun not shining and a look of hard wet rain in the clearness of the foothills. I was wearing my powder-blue suit, with dark blue shirt, tie and display handkerchief, black brogues, black wool socks with

dark blue clocks on them. I was neat, lean, shaved and sober, and I didn't care who knew it. I was everything the well-dressed private detective ought to be. I was calling on four million dollars.

The main hallway of the Sternwood place was two stories high. Over the entrance doors, which would have let in a troop of Indian elephants, there was a broad stained-glass panel showing a knight in dark armor rescuing a lady who was tied to a tree and didn't have any clothes on but some very long and convenient hair. The knight had pushed the vizor of his helmet back to be sociable, and he was fiddling with the knots on the ropes that tied the lady to the tree and not getting anywhere. I stood there and thought that if I lived in the house, I would sooner or later have to climb up there and help him. He didn't seem to be really trying.

There were French doors at the back of the hall, beyond them a wide sweep of emerald grass to a white garage, in front of which a slim dark young chauffeur in shiny black leggings was dusting a maroon Packard convertible. Beyond the garage were some decorative trees trimmed as carefully as poodle dogs. Beyond them a large greenhouse with a domed roof. Then more trees and beyond everything, the solid, uneven, comfortable line of the foothills.[15]

Any writing instructor needing to provide an example of a "narrative hook" to readers need not look beyond these three purposefully constructed paragraphs. Chandler has told us that his first-person detective narrator is a careful man of detail who observes all around him. His manner of dress is professional and prideful.

Detective Philip Marlowe as a scrupulous man of detail and circumstance is very well aware of where he is proceeding. Part of the narrative hook's appeal in these first three paragraphs of *The Big Sleep* is the descriptive manner in which Detective Marlowe introduces the world to another style of life far removed from what he (as well as almost all of his readers) is accustomed. This is the world of the super rich choosing to shut off at least some of their inner lives to others by hiding behind huge gates and hiring others to retain privacy.

When Marlowe and his readers enter the world of the Sternwoods, the family living in the huge, cloistered mansion, they learn that the hiring of go-betweens along with structured distance does not protect against tragedy and conflict. Beginning with the Sternwoods, Marlowe encounters a panoply of characters, consisting of drugs, nymphomania, mob activity, pornography, and sadistic hired killers. In the film version, after a conference call involving director Howard Hawks, his project screenwriter William Faulkner (a future Nobel Prize laureate in Literature), and Chandler, the detective author's inability to answer the question troubling the film's leading man Humphrey Bogart of "Who killed the chauffeur?" was ultimately shrugged off.

Howard Hawks would later say that *The Big Sleep* taught him a vital lesson. The director who had soared to success with sharp repartee male-female love duality comedies learned that he need not have the answer to every question. The important thing was to keep the action going and have a dynamic interplay involving characters. It was not important to comprehend every aspect of the plot of *The Big Sleep*, but it was essential to keep the audience entertained. In short, keep the flow of activity involving an interesting variety of characters occupying the screen moving and you have the ingredients of success.[16]

The Big Sleep presented a series of fascinating film personalities who delivered gusto entertainment value. This began with tough but fair and sensitive Philip Marlowe (Humphrey Bogart). The sister tandem of Vivian Rutledge (Lauren Bacall) and thumb-sucking, pervasively trouble seeking Carmen Sternwood (Martha Vickers) provided continuing fascination, as when Marlowe abruptly seeks to take the "spoiled rich girl manner" out of Rutledge.

Marlowe shows his compassionate side over the brutal murder of Harry Jones (Elisha Cook, Jr.) by sadistic killer Camino (former screen cowboy Bob Steele) and responds to the overture of the glamorous and amorous Acme Book Shop proprietress (Dorothy Malone in her screen debut). Marlowe's relentless gumshoe pursuit of answers makes it seemingly inevitable that he will clash with mob boss Eddie Mars (John Ridgely).

The writing team of Faulkner, Jules Furthman and Leigh Brackett was shrewd enough to remain within the context of Chandler's story development and characterization. The original novel contained the ingredients for solid, non-speed action involving a superb mix of characters, evocative of Los Angeles as the post-war melting pot that it was when the film was ultimately released following delay in 1946.

The film ended with mobster Mars meeting his ultimate death fate and Marlowe winning former spoiled rich girl and ultimately broader-visioned Rutledge. (In real life Bacall, by the time of the film's release, was Mrs. Humphrey Bogart.) Chandler's conclusion in *The Big Sleep* is grayer, more murky than the end of the film, which, not unpredictably, provides a positive closing note with Marlowe and Rutledge seemingly cementing a gradually flowering romance. The tough world of Philip Marlowe on the streets of Los Angeles (as delineated in Chandler's hard-hitting style) results in a different ending, true poetry of the somber in the final two paragraphs:

> What did it matter where you lay once you were dead? In a dirty sump or in a marble tower on top of a high hill? You were dead, you were sleeping the big sleep, you were not bothered by things like that. Oil and water were the same as wind and air to you. You just slept the big sleep, not caring about the nastiness of how you died or where you fell. Me. I was part of the nastiness now. For more a part of it than Rusty Regan was. But the old man didn't have to be. He could lie quiet in his canopied bed, with his bloodless hands folded on the sheet, waiting. His heart was a brief, uncertain murmur. His thoughts were as gray as ashes. And in a little while he too, like Rusty Regan, would be sleeping the big sleep.
>
> On the way downtown I stopped at a bar and I had a couple of double Scotches. They didn't do me any good. All they did was make me think of Silver-Wig, and I never saw her again.[17]

The book's conclusion provides evidence as to why French intellectuals would applaud Chandler's work and make him a popular favorite before he won acclaim in America. While he is now routinely studied in literature classes, there was a long period when he was dismissingly scoffed at as a detective writer.

To bring Sartre and Camus back into the discussion, it is easy to see them soberly reflecting on the conclusion of *The Big Sleep* over drinks at a Left Bank café near Sartre's apartment in the Paris university district. This was an ending with which existentialists could easily identify. After all the fast-paced fireworks and the stench of death, Philip Marlowe as putative existential hero has the gravity of all the destruction on the seemingly anarchistic streets of Los Angeles land in the manner of a swift solar plexus shot. In the manner of the determined warrior that he is, Marlowe stops to have two double Scotches. The drinks have no impact in shaking his melancholia, but everything in his character, all that the reader had absorbed in the preceding pages, led to the inexorable conclusion that the tough, uncompromising detective, warrior of righteousness in the same manner of Dashiell Hammett's Sam Spade, would be back, fighting the same cause, patrolling the same troubled streets.

Merging Chandler's Voice into Film Noir

The voice that Chandler incorporated into *The Big Sleep* and other works was one that adapted superbly to film. What an adaptable feat when the restless land of transients that Chandler found as a home base and conveniently wrote about also happened to be the thriving film capital. If, as in *Double Indemnity*, Walter and Phyllis needed a clandestine meeting spot at a local market, all that Paramount and director Billy Wilder needed to do was shoot those scenes just a short walk away. As for a Spanish-style home such as the one appearing in the film and the Cain novel, that location was found in the stylish Los Feliz area nearby.

Chandler's setting of stage and tone alongside his perfectly blended fiction voice proved ideal for translation to film. With the Depression and a world war we had become a more brooding world. Chandler's novels could serve as ideal treatments for films examining the brooding, rapacious, and anarchistic sides of a restless society. In *Double Indemnity*, Billy Wilder shrewdly brought Chandler along on the ride of a lifetime as he co-wrote the film with the wily director. Chandler would not be involved in the screenplay adaptation of *Farewell, My Lovely*. That event occurred some three short blocks to the southwest at RKO while the master of brooding fiction remained under contract to Paramount. RKO's master film noir scenarist-in-residence, John Paxton, caught the tone involving individuals seeking to survive in a society that makes little if any sense, along with capturing the fascinating array of characters that Chandler wrote about.

Murder, My Sweet would debut in 1944, a gigantic breakthrough year for Chandler since *Double Indemnity* made its bow that same year. In addition to Chandler not being able to adapt or co-adapt the RKO work due to his contractual commitment, the title was changed from *Farewell, My Lovely*, but not due to any inherent dissatisfaction. This was Dick Powell's breakthrough opportunity as a dramatic actor after a promising career as a song-and-dance man. RKO did not want audiences to gain any misconceptions about the subject matter of the tough Los Angeles city streets from a title that could be misconstrued as a musical with dancing and comedy. The new title *Murder, My Sweet* was provided to invest a film set primarily in the darkened settings of the city at night with the heightened gravity that the word "murder" portended.

The launching of Chandler's novel was similar to the start of the film. One major difference, however, from a scenic standpoint is what John Paxton's script and Edward Dmytryk's direction contributed. The change was reflective of the substantive difference separating writing for the printed page and readership as apart from the eyes used for entertainment purposes following sharply constructed objects on a wide screen.

In Philip Marlowe's first-person account in the book he is looking for a relief barber named Dimitrio Aleidis who might perhaps be working on Central Avenue. Marlow had visited what he termed "one of the mixed blocks," the ones that had not become "all Negro." In that presentation Chandler, through the omnipresent eyes of detective Marlowe, was providing emerging Los Angeles history. Central Avenue would shortly become almost totally African American in South Los Angeles.

While Marlowe stands outside the barber shop he looked up "at the jutting neon sign of a second floor dine and dice emporium called Florian's." It is at that point that Marlowe first encounters the hulking presence of Moose Malloy (the role of a lifetime for legendary character actor Mike Mazurki). In the script the action is shrewdly centered in Hollywood, narrowing the perimeter of action, making everything simple to follow in a film that relies heavily on smooth but rapid-fire transition of events.

In the film the narrative technique is used to commence action, but this time Marlowe is sitting in the darkness of night all by himself. We see that his office is in the center of a swirling Hollywood hub of activity. Outside his window a constellation of neon lights burn brightly. The contrast is stark, that of a dark office inhabited by a lone detective and Hollywood by night with brightly burning lights revealing various forms of activity as Marlowe sits by himself, mentioning that a woman has stood him up.

Hollywood screenwriters earn a lot of their money for their expertise at changing elements of a finely crafted novel which provides a bountiful nest of characters from which to draw. This was a particular hallmark of Chandler works featuring Marlowe. A skilled scenarist such as John Paxton could move action along in the manner for which the masterful Alfred Hitchcock was preeminent, in ways that feature camera technique-enhancing action.

Murder, My Sweet provides an excellent example of this process at work. The contrast between the steady stream of lights in the Hollywood world below and that of a detective, a lone wolf of society, sitting by himself in darkness illustrates where he works and what he represents. Philip Marlowe lives in a world of darkness interspersed with light.

Moose Malloy then makes his entrance, startling Marlowe, who stares at his hulking presence, which is made more potentially menacing in the darkness and stillness of the office. Mazurki's character is established in his first meeting with the detective he will hire to "find my Velma!" Malloy's hiring of Marlowe shortly after his release from prison to find his former nightclub entertainer girlfriend extends to murder, jewel theft, blackmailing, and the world of the high-powered, finely dressed, smooth-talking local underworld kingpin Jules Amthor (Otto Kruger).

In the manner that Chandler described him, Moose Malloy is a hulking figure whose awesome size and muscularity overwhelm any scene of which he is a part. His slow wit combined with a hair trigger temper, especially if he believes, wrongly or correctly, that someone is lying to him, carries the constant potential of murder. His huge hands are a strangulation weapon. They are used against Amthor in *Murder, My Sweet* just as Mazurki, playing a wrestler who has been used and humiliated, exacts vengeance at the conclusion of Jules Dassin's 1950 noir classic *Night and the City*, with his strangulation of con artist Harry Fabian (Richard Widmark). In that film, dark and brooding cinematography substitutes London for Hollywood, the focal point of *Murder, My Sweet*.

More Homophobia

It was earlier mentioned in analyzing Hammett's supreme screen triumph, *The Maltese Falcon*, how conspicuously homophobia was evoked. While not threaded as comprehensively throughout *Murder, My Sweet* as was exemplified in a film whose entire trio of criminals (in the estimation of historians and critics) consisted of homosexuals, the 1944 classic demonstrated homophobia in the case of one character who represents a stereotypical pattern.

Toronto-born Douglas Walton was cast during the thirties and forties in foppish roles that reflected homosexual stereotypical affectation. He was cast in such a role in *Murder, My Sweet*. Before Walton's character, Lindsay Marriott, appears on screen he is established in one evocative line delivered by the elevator operator in the building where Philip Marlowe has his office. The detective is told that the man who is waiting to see him smells good.

The cologne element is mentioned in later dialogue. The pattern has been set when Detective Marlowe meets Marriott. The prospective client exudes a foppish, affected manner.

On a day when it does not appear to be chilly, and in a city where neck scarves are not generally worn, the prospective client is wearing one. This is further evidence of stacking the deck through attire to make him look considerably less masculine than Chandler's detective.

While Powell's depiction of Marlowe is breezy and nonchalant throughout the film, an element of naturalness that endeared him to Chandler, in his scene with Marriott the manner is flippant as well as insulting. At one point, after the prospective client explains that he wishes for Marlowe to accompany him to a clandestine meeting in a canyon as part of an exchange and payoff relating to a valuable jade necklace, Marriott mentions Marlowe's nasty behavior, to which the detective breezily acknowledges that he has received many complaints about it.

When Marlowe's level of insolence reaches the point of stopping just short of calling Marriott an opportunistic blackmailer the detective is asked, "How would you like a punch in the nose?" The detective coolly responds that he "trembles" at the thought of "violence." (In the book, *Farewell, My Lovely*, the meeting occurs at Marriott's apartment. When the question is asked about a punch in the nose the detective begins walking toward the door, with further conversation from the prospective client prompting him to return.)

Eventually a deal is struck and Marlowe accompanies Marriott to the designated site, but is unable to prevent his death as he has been knocked out by the killer. At subsequent intervals of the film a theme prevalent in homophobia is discussed. The Lindsay Marriott character is one who could be counted on to keep women company, to take them dancing and get involved in various forms of double dealing on their behalf. This typifies the association between Marriott and his social relationship with blonde and very homicidal femme fatale Velma Valento (Claire Trevor), the individual who will ultimately waylay her homosexual friend and his detective partner in the darkened canyon.

Homosexuality and Building Up Detective Images

One motivator to use stereotypically foppish and effeminate homosexual types opposite Humphrey Bogart in *The Maltese Falcon* and Dick Powell in *Murder, My Sweet* is that in doing so a contrast is presented. The difference makes leading men like Bogart and Powell appear all the more masculine. The term "real men" was often employed to demonstrate differences between the effeminacy perceived to be a standard pattern of homosexuals and masculinity displayed by heterosexual males.

A conditioning pattern existed previously that is still accepted by many in society about the standard line of demarcation between heterosexual and homosexual men where the former is associated with masculine activity such as playing sports and the latter with needlepoint and interior decoration.

Not only have medical studies refuted such simplistic stereotyping, so have instances of courageous individuals in the professional sports world who have come forward to reveal their homosexuality. Testing has revealed that, while some male homosexuals are effeminate, the same applies to certain individuals in the heterosexual community. It has also been revealed (through conducting interviews among the heterosexual population) that some men with more-than-average male hormones than the general populace prefer other highly masculine males to the exclusion of females.

Some two generations ago one of the most famous baseball players of all time, someone with no known links to homosexuality, played a major symbolic role in deflating the canard that fragrance wearing bore a symbolic identification with homosexuality. Willie Mays, the great centerfielder of the New York and later San Francisco Giants, did a commercial for a men's cologne manufacturer that went far in destroying stereotype. Mays made the succinct point that it was important for men to make the best possible impression, which could be enhanced not only by wearing fine clothes but through exuding a positive fragrance.

A more direct shattering of stereotype occurred in 1975 with the publication of the autobiography of college and professional football star Dave Kopay. In the 1977 publication *The David Kopay Story*, co-written with Perry Dean Young, he reveals growing up gay in a conservative Roman Catholic family, in which he attended parochial school through graduation at Notre Dame High School in Sherman Oaks, California. He proceeds forward to his years at the University of Washington in Seattle, where he became an All-American his senior season and captained the team, and from there to a career from 1964 to 1972 with the San Francisco Forty-Niners, Washington Redskins, and Green Bay Packers.

A major part of Kopay's much-discussed work pertained to an affair he had with a teammate who was tormented over the discrimination and double standard of society. The sensitive teammate was troubled by alcohol and died prematurely, feeling the stigma of a society he believed did not understand him. Kopay asserted later that he should have "outed" his teammate then rather than assist in keeping his identity secret. Kopay's conclusion was that by doing so he then could have faced reality and not operated in a false world, believing that the teammate would have lived had he taken that step.

Chandler, Montgomery and Trouble with Police

Chandler's story craft, in print or adapted to the screen, was notably different than forays through small British towns collecting evidence, balancing and analyzing it, then drawing conclusions in an orderly psychological process. The world of Philip Marlowe was one of an anarchistic society which comes to life by night. The two keys are disparity and characters, making use of the gigantic cross section that constituted life in the city with which Raymond Chandler had his lifelong love-hate relationship.

One element with which Raymond Chandler clashed in print was the police department of a beach town, aptly named Bay City. Its reality counterpart was Santa Monica. At the time Chandler was busily at work on his trusty Underwood writing his works and basing Marlowe's activities on numerous realities occurring within the contemporary Southern California area, Santa Monica was linked in various controversies, some of which involved its police department.

Southern California was gaining large numbers of residents and anarchy clashed with elements of control. Roman Polanski's 1974 film noir masterpiece *Chinatown* starring Jack Nicholson and based on a taut script written by Robert Towne dealt with the growing pains of Southern California in 1937. *Lady in the Lake* covers a period one decade later during an epochal movement of returning servicemen from World War II. Many of the men, grown used to the war climate of the area during basic training and regular stays at military bases, frequently in and near San Diego to the south, returned to try their luck in various enterprises, some legitimate and some not. When certain enterprises fell outside the purview of legality, police were frequently paid off handsomely to allow criminal activity to continue.

Philip Marlowe had frequently clashed with Lieutenant DeGarmot of the Bay City Police

Department. These confrontations could be made more scenically physical in the shape being devised for a new type of film that, while not greatly appreciated by audiences upon its release, has generated widespread discussion and generous praise as increasing numbers of film viewers and critics have seen the film in the now better than six decades since its 1946 release.

Audrey Totter and Praise for Montgomery's Daring Approach

Robert Montgomery scored one of his major acting triumphs in an unconventional film in which he portrayed a dead professional boxer brought back into the story as a part of the spirit world in the 1941 film *Here Comes Mr. Jordan*. As he returns to earth in a bid to make things right and do some of the positive things he could not achieve in a life cut short in his boxer's prime, he is aided in his return trip by Mr. Jordan (Claude Rains), a distinguished, astute, and thoroughly proper angel.

Here Comes Mr. Jordan was successful enough to inspire a remake with the 1978 fantasy triumph *Heaven Can Wait* with Warren Beatty reprising the Montgomery role, but this time as a quarterback for the Los Angeles Rams of the National Football League. James Mason, a distinguished British performer like Claude Rains, served as the assisting angel.

Montgomery, president of the Screen Actors Guild and a performer who exuded the dapper style of an executive, possessed a creative daring of an actor looking for challenges. This desire took him into the realm of directing two interesting film noir projects, both released shortly after the war. *Ride the Pink Horse*, released in 1947, was filmed in New Mexico and involves an avenging serviceman coming home to make things right in the death of his fellow military mate amid the rugged intrusion of a gang led by mobster Frank Hugo (Fred Clark) while local girl Pila (Wanda Hendrix) seeks to supply assistance.

A period dealing with exploration in the film noir realm provided the perfect opportunity for Montgomery to extend his horizon into the directing field. His versatility would lead him in the fifties to serve as the first television advisor to an American president as he instructed Dwight D. Eisenhower in adjusting on camera to the ways of the new technological tool. This medium would ultimately and ironically serve as a boon to the candidacy and two term presidency of fellow Screen Actors Guild President, governor of California and U.S. president, Ronald Reagan.

Montgomery used a unique camera that no doubt confounded filmgoers of his era. His leading lady in the film, Audrey Totter, explained in a December 1999 interview that *Lady in the Lake* revealed Montgomery as a director of gifted creative imagination. Totter, a Joliet, Illinois product, possessed a combative sauciness and energetic sexuality that directors and producers found a plus on screen. She attracted notice in 1946, the same year that *Lady in the Lake* was released, playing Madge Gorland, the young woman with whom Frank Chambers (John Garfield) becomes acquainted while fixing her car outside Union Station after putting Cora Smith (Lana Turner) on the train in Tay Garnett's *The Postman Always Rings Twice*. Fireworks erupt between Chambers and Smith later after the latter learns that he has been spending time with Gorland.

The half decade following World War II became a productive professional period for Totter. She almost received the opportunity to star with Burt Lancaster in the 1946 Robert Siodmak noir classic *The Killers*, adapted from one of Ernest Hemingway's Nick Adams stories. Producer Mark Hellinger became so impressed with Ava Gardner's screen test, however, that she was offered the part instead of Totter.

"I couldn't do both *The Killers* and *Lady in the Lake*," Totter explained. "I was delighted with *Lady in the Lake*, but it would have been great to do *The Killers* as well. They also wanted me for *A Place in the Sun* (1951), but Metro didn't want to lend me out for it. Shelley Winters got the part, and she was great. She got an Academy Award nomination for it [for 'Best Supporting Actress']. I would have liked the opportunity to do that part. That was the film version of Theodore Dreiser's *An American Tragedy*, and my character was the one killed when the boat overturned."[18]

Three 1949 Totter starring vehicles were mentioned along with Montgomery's film as among those holding special interest for the blonde performer. "I am proud of *Lady in the Lake*, *The Setup*, *Alias Nick Beal*, and *Tension*," Totter told her interviewers. "They really are all excellent, and people seem to have responded well to them."

Asked if there was any one performers with whom she particularly enjoyed working, Totter responded, "I enjoyed working with all the actors and actresses in these films. If I had to name just one it would be Robert Montgomery, since *Lady in the Lake* was such an innovative film."

Montgomery did a scene with Totter and "went to the producers" and said, "I want Audrey for this part!" A versatile performer who got her big early break on radio in Chicago, the big city closest to where her roots lay in nearby Joliet, Montgomery knew that the subjective camera technique with the scrutinizing focus it provided necessitated a performer who could convey truth and convince the audience of it.

Totter's first scene as Adrienne Fromsett with Montgomery is a classic. When he is taken aback after believing that he has been contacted by her to sell an article and that she seeks to put him to work contacting the missing wife of her boss (Leon Ames), tempers flare. Montgomery delivers Philip Marlowe's lines at their most direct and salty, testing Fromsett, who strikes back in kind. All the while the audience sees a romantic tension developing, prompting much of the mutual sniping. Audrey Totter is at her craftiest and most seductive at the same time. Only a performer of skillful versatility could bring off such a delicate balance.

Another challenge lay in the fact that, using the subjective camera approach, the scenes were long.

"Yes, they were quite long," Totter concurred. "Bob tested five or six actresses for the part, and they had difficulty acting directly to the camera. They began to shift their attention to Bob instead because he was feeding their lines. In motion pictures, you are taught to ignore the existence of the camera, and here you had to treat the camera as another actor. I was able to do this because of my background in radio. When you did radio, you had the script in your hands, and you spoke your lines to the microphone, not the other actors. I played to the microphone for years, so it was easy to play to the camera."

Cameraman Paul Vogel mastered the technique that Montgomery, very much in command while directing his first film, sought to achieve. "The cameraman kept his camera on his shoulder," Totter explained. "It was very unusual, and I had never encountered this technique before. Bob stood right next to the camera at all times. He had his lines to deliver, of course. But everyone had to respond to the camera, not to Bob."

There was one point to which MGM studio boss Louis B. Mayer objected: the scene in which Adrienne got up in the middle of the night, and her hair was tousled. According to Totter, Montgomery exclaimed, "For heaven's sake, Mr. Mayer, she just got out of bed!"

"When my actresses get out of bed, they look like they just got out of the beauty shop," Mayer retorted.

"Not this one!" Montgomery replied.

Totter noted that the director ultimately won his point. Montgomery had a better semblance of realism over the perfectionist standard of a studio head wanting to see his actresses look as perfect as possible at all times.

As for the actress's experience with cinematographer Paul Vogel, she would also appear with him in one of her major roles one year later, in the 1947 release *The High Wall*, directed by Curtis Bernhardt. She plays a doctor seeking to prove the innocence of a patient (Robert Taylor) who has confessed to a murder. As for Vogel, his camera work was lauded in another challenging work better than a decade after *Lady in the Lake*, in the 1960 release of the H.G. Wells novel *The Time Machine*. That film, in which debut director George Pal exercised his special effects artistry, starred Rod Taylor, Alan Young, and Yvette Mimieux.

Lady in the Lake contained both a prologue and epilogue. Audrey Totter explained that audience preview comments registered concern over not getting a chance to see her kiss leading man and director Montgomery.

"It was not enough for me not to kiss the camera," Totter explained. "Bob and I thought it was so silly that when we shot our kiss, we couldn't stop giggling. Someone said, 'Come on, you amateurs! Do the kiss and get this thing over with!' Bob did yield on the kiss because the audience wanted it."

UNIQUE APPROACH—Robert Montgomery, shown with *Lady in the Lake* love interest Audrey Totter, both directed and starred in this 1947 film adaptation of Raymond Chandler's novel.

You Are the Detective

The film begins with an interesting musical touch. Due to the 1942 musician's strike many famous recording artists of the period — including Bing Crosby, Frank Sinatra, Dick Haymes, and Perry Como — substituted group vocals as backup support in lieu of orchestration. The choral effect proved uniquely interesting in certain recordings of that interval such as "You'll Never Know" with Sinatra and Haymes, and "Long Ago and Far Away" featuring Perry Como.

Perhaps this factor flowed through Robert Montgomery's fertile mind while filming *Lady in the Lake* since it is used throughout. It was particularly effective in the opening sequence of the film when Detective Philip Marlowe walks into the office of magazine editor Adrienne Fromsett to sell a magazine article about his experiences as a private detective. She immediately offers him the assignment of locating her boss's missing wife.

The choral effect seems well suited to a Christmas format. It is in this scene that Montgomery's "You Are the Camera" element is creatively employed. It provides filmgoers with a different approach in seeing inside the world of a professional detective. Rather than seeing a series of camera angles providing introductions of characters from a variety of viewpoints, the audience is hoisted into the mind's eye of Detective Marlowe as he surveys employees of a publishing empire and ultimately focuses on two of the major characters of the film, Derace Kingsby (Leon Ames), boss of a magazine publishing empire, and Marlowe's love interest, Adrienne Fromsett. Marlowe and the magazine editor initially engage in verbal combat, realizing gradually that the sparks portend mutual romantic desire.

As could be anticipated by the nature of film detective subject matter, the most graphically memorable elements of veteran Paul Vogel's cinematography related to physical exchanges involving Marlowe. The first was sparked by a surprise element and the second a gritty and realistic look at police brutality. In each instance, given Montgomery's selected viewpoint of the audience stepping figuratively into Philip Marlowe's shoes, a searing realism unlike other combative scenes emerges.

A Playboy's Sucker Punch

Marlowe has been informed that Kingsby's missing wife had been involved with local playboy Chris Lavery (Dick Simmons). Lavery is appropriately tanned and muscled to fulfill his function in life as someone whose living and lifestyle are provided by women. He speaks with the bourbon and branch water patrician manner of a Southern country gentleman, the kind of demeanor that a streetwise analyst such as Philip Marlowe can instantly perceive as contrived to serve a purpose with vulnerable ladies.

The charm runs thin when Marlowe's direct questioning peels off the playboy's veneer. Direct anger is the result. Marlowe is nailed by a sucker punch. Given the personal viewpoint camera approach of director and star Montgomery, viewers experience the rude awakening of being sucker punched as clenched fist makes impact with target. The playboy who threw the sucker punch suffers a fate far worse and shortly after the incident becomes a murder victim, with a detective just regaining consciousness taken to the police station as temporary suspect.

The other run-in with clenched fists, rather than the brief impact of a playboy's sucker punch of a detective, is sustained and, hence, more brutal. Handing out the beating on this occasion is the nemesis of Marlowe, Lieutenant DeGarmot, played by Lloyd Nolan, a film character acting legend at home playing an honest cop, a street smart hood, or, as in *Lady in the Lake*, a sadistic police detective who will stop at nothing, including murder.

The city where DeGarmot serves as a police lieutenant is one that is familiar in the Chandler world, delineated in first-person fashion by mouthpiece Marlowe. It is Bay City in Chandler lexicon. Its vivid description and clues as to its locale make it a giveaway to those paying attention that the author is referring to Santa Monica. While much of Chandler's invective through the mouth of narrator Marlowe is directed toward his dislike of what he perceives as the idle rich, he takes dead aim at the city (in the words of Chandler biographer Frank MacShane) "representing an independent part of Los Angeles life in which the extent of corruption in California life is more vividly demonstrated."

In Marlowe's words, "It's probably no crookeder than Los Angeles. But you can only buy a piece of a big city. You can buy a town this size all complete, with the original box and tissue paper."

Chandler began training his verbal guns on Santa Monica when he was writing the stories on which his first novel, *The Big Sleep*, were based. As MacShane wrote in *The Life of Raymond Chandler*:

> It [Santa Monica] is less elegant than Beverly Hills or San Marino, a middle-class town with Spanish-style houses in stucco with wrought-iron grilles and tiled roofs built along clean, wide streets that are lined with palm trees. The commercial district is limited to a few streets, and the place has an air of universal propriety. For Chandler, Bay City was a symbol of hypocrisy: he hated the pretense of uprightness in a place virtually owned by a few people with money. "This Grayle packs a lot of dough in his pants," says Marlowe of the millionaire in the novel. "And law is where you buy it in this town."

When Chandler's creative brain was stirred to critical cutting edge it operated at its most effective — as well as at its most entertaining. As MacShane wrote, Chandler "was continually fascinated by the ludicrous, comic-opera quality of the place."

If Chandler found a kindred spirit who empathized with his aims, his critical facility was enhanced all the more. A 1944 correspondence Chandler sent to Charles Morton of *Atlantic Monthly* revealed how he could make use of his sociological view of Santa Monica. It also demonstrated how creatively skilled writers, seeking to dig all the verbal nuggets possible out of a promising mine, often visit the same places for inspiration. (This was a spot found creatively enriching by Horace McCoy and put to good visual use in the film version of his epic work, *They Shoot Horses, Don't They?*, Ocean Park, along with adjoining Venice, were used by cinematographer Ernest Laszlo and director Joseph Losey to captivating effect in the 1951 remake of Fritz Lang's 1931 classic *M*.) Chandler brimmed with creative delight as he revealed his thoughts about Bay City as fertile ground in his letter to Morton:

> The other day I thought of your suggestion for an article of studied insult about the Bay City (Santa Monica) police. A couple of D.A.'s investigators got a tip about a gambling hall in Ocean Park, a sleazy adjunct to Santa Monica. They went down there and picked up a couple of Santa Monica cops on the way, telling them they were going to kick in a box, but not telling them where it was. The cops went along with the natural reluctance of good cops to enforce the law against a paying customer, and when they found out where the place was, they mumbled brokenly: "We'd ought to talk to Captain Brown about this before we do it, boys. Captain Brown ain't going to like this." The D.A.'s men urged them on heartlessly forward into the chip and bone parlor; seized for evidence (a truckload of it) was stored in lockers at local police headquarters. When the D.A.'s boys came back the next morning to go over it, everything had disappeared but a few handfuls of white poker

chips. The locks had not been tampered with, and no trace could be found of the truck or the driver. The flatfeet shook their grizzled polls in the bewilderment and the investigations went back to town to hand in the Grand Jury story. Nothing will come of it. Nothing ever does. Do you wonder why I love Bay City?"

Chandler proves his point through the sad words of a tragically dumb cop named Hemingway who appears in *Farewell, My Lovely* and mourns, "A guy can't stay honest if he wants to. That's what's the matter with this country. He gets chiselled out of his pants if he does. You gotta play the game dirty or you don't eat."

After Raymond Chandler bowed out of the script assignment (a point that will be more broadly discussed in the next chapter), producer George Haight turned over the responsibilities to experienced hard-boiled noir screenwriter, novelist, and crime journalist Steve Fisher. At the time he went to work for Haight, Fisher had secured an Oscar nomination for "Best Original Story" for the 1943 war drama *Destination Tokyo* starring Cary Grant and John Garfield.

Two years earlier Fisher's novel *I Wake Up Screaming* was adapted to the screen by Twentieth Century–Fox into a memorable noir drama starring Betty Grable, Victor Mature, and Carole Landis under the direction of H. Bruce Humberstone. As earlier noted, Fisher also chalked up a notable reputation in the Los Angeles area as a local crime beat reporter. One of his assignments was the Black Dahlia murder case.

Fisher wrote the screenplay for the 1945 film noir *Johnny Angel* starring genre regulars George Raft and Claire Trevor. In 1947, the same year that *Lady in the Lake* debuted, Fisher wrote *Dead Reckoning*, another noir drama featuring two other genre favorites, Humphrey Bogart and Liz Scott, with actor-turned-director John Cromwell.

Fisher delivered a power-edged script that heightened dramatic conflict between Philip Marlowe private detective opposite his nemesis, the tough, hard-edged Lieutenant DeGarmot of the Bay City Police Department. Director Montgomery scored a casting coup in securing the perfect actor to give DeGarmot just the right measure of brutal toughness amid an anxiety to get his nemesis out of the way permanently.

Lloyd Nolan, Perennial Authority Figure

Lloyd Nolan personified an authority figure with plenty of savvy. His New York accent and no-nonsense manner typified the air of a worldly Manhattan figure capable of figuring out difficult situations in a flash. So many who observed him in action in scores of films assumed, based on his accent, that Nolan was New York bred and born. In actuality, his roots lay some three thousand miles removed, in San Francisco.

Nolan grew up in an affluent household. His father owned a large shoe factory and Lloyd was sent to Stanford University. His mind was not on joining the business community but on amateur theatrics and he flunked out of the prestigious Palo Alto school.

Lloyd Nolan, committed to the art of acting, continued his pursuit after the Stanford episode ended by attending Pasadena Playhouse, where such great performers as Robert Taylor, Gregory Peck, Dustin Hoffman, and Gene Hackman pursued their thespian interests. In the cases of Hoffman and Hackman, a supreme irony intervened as they were dropped by the playhouse for displaying insufficient promise.

As for how Nolan spoke with such a distinct New York accent, that came after the Pasadena Playhouse phase of his career when he made his mark on Broadway. The period proved to be beneficial beyond the experience and noteworthiness he acquired since the distinct accent became a trademark during his long career.

Nolan not only was what film noir needed in persona, he was able to add the charismatic spice that produced low-budget winners. A classic case in point was his role in the 1941 Depression story set around an orchestra, *Blues in the Night*, directed by Anatole Litvak. This film is a trivia questioner's favorite since it has been noted for the feature role of brilliant director of the future Elia Kazan.

Nolan's character, worldwise gangster Del Davis, fits his authority persona like the proverbial glove. After he has been befriended by members of a traveling band of young men and seeking to survive during Depression times, he is able to obtain a nightclub for them to play, cutting himself in on the action. When Ginger Powell (Priscilla Lane), the unfaithful wife of the band's trumpeter, attempts to play the wily, older Davis in the same manner that she does husband Leo (Jack Carson) and other members of the group, she receives a distinctly different response.

In the film's most dramatic encounter, Davis demonstrates experience and authority as he informs the spoiled and glamorous Ginger that he sees through her. Since she has become so accustomed to having her own way with the younger, less experienced orchestra members by exercising her considerable charms, Ginger is taking thoroughly aback by Davis's knowledgeable and brusque response. Her dramatic effort of being thoroughly stunned is in perfect contrast to that of Davis. The result is superb and perhaps the major reason the film holds up so well and has received so much recent positive attention among film nostalgia enthusiasts.

The hard-hitting dialogue for *Blues in the Night* was adapted from an Edwin Gilbert play by Robert Rossen, who later combined his writing and directing skills on such prestigious screen works as *Body and Soul* (1947), *All the King's Men* (1949), and *The Hustler* (1961).

Hollywood was developing a solid appreciation for Nolan in the forties. After his performance in *Blues in the Night*, the following year found him cast in the role of popular detective Michael Shayne in no less than four films: *Blue, White and Perfect*, *The Man Who Wouldn't Die*, *Just Off Broadway*, and *Time to Kill*. The significance of *Time to Kill* relates to its having been adapted to the screen from Raymond Chandler's novel *High Window*. Rather than adapting it as a vehicle for Chandler detective Philip Marlowe, it was instead switched to one for Michael Shayne, with Nolan in the lead.

In the 1945 espionage noir thriller *The House on 92nd Street* Nolan switched from a private detective to an agent of the Federal Bureau of Investigation. During the war period and the years that followed, semi-documentary films involving the dangerous world of FBI agents became popular. FBI Director J. Edgar Hoover, eager to enhance the bureau's image with the public, cooperated with the film community in the effort to provide movie patrons with stories showing dedicated agents determined to assist the public and solve crimes.

The House on 92nd Street, directed by Henry Hathaway, was based on a true story of a Nazi spy operation run out of a building on Manhattan's exclusive Upper East Side. William Eythe (a young star from the "victory casting" system of developing male stars while most leading men were involved abroad in the war effort) as Bill Dietrich was eager to assist in exposing and ultimately stopping the activities of the well-coordinated network run out of an elegant clothing store by Elsa Gebhardt (Swedish acting star Signe Hasso). The film was developed by Charles G. Booth, who won a "Best Original Story" Oscar. He and co-writer Barre Lyndon honed a screenplay ringing with dramatic realism.

The objective was to prevent the Nazis from tapping into American development of the atomic bomb. Dietrich is recruited out of college by the FBI and trained to serve as a double agent, infiltrating his way into Gebhardt's Nazi group.

Assisting Dietrich in the young man's efforts to penetrate a cell run by a shrewd woman of espionage expertise in the person of the icy, cold-blooded Gebhardt, is a man of authority and from the FBI, Agent George A. Briggs (Nolan). The cool-under-fire Nolan in *The House on 92nd Street* went over so well that he reprised Briggs as he assists young agent Gene Cordell (Mark Stevens), who has infiltrated an operation run by ruthless gang leader Alec Stiles (Richard Widmark) in the 1948 William Keighley-directed film *The Street with No Name*.

The House on 92nd Street and *The Street with No Name* both fit into the realm of film noir semi-documentary realism. In each instance a coolly analytical, veteran agent played by Lloyd Nolan appraised the actions of young agents. In the 1946 film noir release *Somewhere in the Night* Nolan is cast as Lieutenant Donald Kendall of the Los Angeles Police Department, where he keeps close tabs on returning World War II veteran George W. Taylor (John Hodiak) in seeking to resolve a mystery. More will be revealed about this film in the next chapter.

Nolan's Sharp Clash with Montgomery, Followed by Comedy

Lloyd Nolan's challenging role of Lieutenant DeGarmot in *Lady in the Lake* represented this character actor of supreme versatility in his meanest role. He hates Marlowe with a seething passion. The Fisher script throws the audience an interesting curve when Marlowe is arrested on Christmas Eve. DeGarmot is in anything but a mood of good cheer toward one fellow man, the detective he despises. As DeGarmot moves into close range and strikes Marlowe, the camera eye technique, given the close-up range, captures the seething hatred of DeGarmot, the burning cauldron within him. Never has hate been more effectively captured at close range.

Although DeGarmot thoroughly enjoys beating up his victim on his home turf, the Bay City Police Station, Marlowe defends himself by delivering a swift kick that knocks his stunned attacker to the floor. When DeGarmot jumps to his feet and prepares to launch a fresh attack, his boss, Captain Kane, restrains his officer. Portraying Kane was Tom Tully, a popular character performer who, like Lloyd Nolan, conveyed authority and was accordingly often cast as a police officer.

Tom Tully did such an effective job playing Captain Kane that this could have been a factor in him receiving the part in which he would make his mark as a star. The opportunity came on television as Tully starred alongside Warner Anderson in the popular police series *The Lineup*. The series, which was so popular that it was later reprised in rerun form under the name *San Francisco Beat*, had a robust 185 episodes and appeared in its original form from 1954 to 1959. What enhanced the robust quality of *The Lineup* was the authentic San Francisco's interesting and always-photogenic street scenery. It was a forerunner to the popular seventies' police television drama *The Streets of San Francisco*, with veteran Karl Malden and youthful Michael Douglas paired as police detectives.

After Kane calms down a raging DeGarmot and sends him home for the night, Fisher employs the kind of contrast exercised by a smoothly functioning script professional. He sought to lighten the mood temporarily following the fierce scene by injecting a brief note of humor.

The in charge Kane, who runs the office of a major Southern California city's police department, receives a call that proves embarrassing due to Marlowe's presence. The telephone call involves Kane's young daughter and his wife. After talking in the manner of a doting father preparing to return home to help his daughter celebrate Christmas Eve, he conveys a manner in the conversation with his wife that embodies anything but that of the tough, in charge police captain he seeks to convey toward others. Eventually Kane, while attempting not to convey the awkwardness he inwardly feels over Marlowe's presence, gruffly tells him to go home.

Kane and fellow Bay City officers are around to assist when his corrupt and homicidal detective seeks to kill Marlowe. A neat touch applied by script master Fisher is the way that veteran officer DeGarmot believes that he is being decoyed by private detective Marlowe when informed that the officers, headed by his boss, Captain Kane, have arrived.

Just as Tom Tully made a mark as star of a network television series, the same held true for Lloyd Nolan as well as another member of the cast, Leon Ames. Nolan's penchant for conveying authority marked him well as he starred as a doctor alongside Diahann Carroll and Lurene Tuttle in the sixties' sitcom hit *Julia*.

During the fifties Leon Ames also starred opposite veteran character performer Tuttle in the popular comedy series set in turn-of-the-century New York City, *Life with Father*, based on the novel by Clarence Day. Tuttle was also one of Hollywood's premier drama coaches. She was saluted posthumously by former student Helen Hunt when she won her "Best Actress" Oscar appearing opposite Jack Nicholson in *As Good as it Gets* (1997). Ames and Tuttle achieved such widespread recognition for *Life with Father* and developed such a good dramatic rapport that they reprised their roles periodically on stage for many years.

Ames's appearance in *Lady in the Lake* came one year after his memorable role as the district attorney who successfully vows to put John Garfield behind bars in *The Postman Always Rings Twice*. In that film he convincingly plays a man of authority. His role in *Lady in the Lake* finds him cast as Derace Kingsby, the authoritative publishing empire mogul. When the film opens he is engaged to Adrienne Fromsett, but Marlowe's appearance changes everything. Ames also played a prominent role in the 1952 film noir that will later be addressed, *Angel Face*, starring Robert Mitchum and Jean Simmons.

While Kingsby, given his astounding business success, is comfortable in his own publishing world, there is a perpetual bafflement concerning the detective who begins by seeking to sell a story about his true life experiences to Fromsett and eventually works his way into her heart, but not before plenty of fireworks. Fisher has woven a clever romantic element into the film in which combative sparks represent the seeds of eventual intense romance.

As the definitive professional that he was, Ames played his role with the proper measure of helplessness along with the aforementioned bafflement. As for Totter, her lengthy first meeting with Montgomery might well represent the highlight of her film career. The all-seeing camera's eye remains fastened to her every movement. As in the case of convincing cinema acting, so much is represented in eye movements. Totter is particularly effective at conveying anger at Montgomery's Marlowe as he fires verbal salvos, to which she responds sharply in kind.

Performer Making Headlines for Another Reason

As noted in the case of Audrey Totter, the camera's eye technique used in the film made it easier to be noticed. This factor proportionately increased in the case of someone blonde and beautiful. This worked not only in Totter's favor but for another blonde performer hoping to use the film as a launching pad toward bigger parts.

Lila Leeds had come to Hollywood from her native Kansas and, with her flawless features and excellent figure, obtained a job as a hatcheck girl at the famous Sunset Strip nightclub Ciro's. Before long Leeds was married to Jack Little, a bandleader and racehorse owner. A problem arose when Little failed to tell her the truth about a divorce that never occurred, providing her with grounds for an annulment.

Leeds took an acting course at the Bliss-Hayden School of the Theatre in Beverly Hills. After appearing in a school production farce called *Campus Honeymoon* she received what she described as "three good offers" among the contingent of Hollywood talent scouts who viewed the production, signing with MGM.

Director Montgomery provided Leeds with a great opportunity to be seen as the camera followed her in and out of scenes. Before long she became known throughout America for a reason MGM did not appreciate. After meeting Robin Ford, who unsuccessfully pursued her for a date, he aroused her interest by introducing her to his movie star friend Robert Mitchum.

The evening of August 31, 1948, Mitchum and Ford visited the Laurel Canyon home she was renting and called upon Leeds and his girlfriend, dancer Vicki Evans. There were other visitors as well — detectives from the Los Angeles Police Department. They confiscated the marijuana being smoked and made arrests, taking the foursome to police headquarters.[19]

After finding both Mitchum and Leeds guilty at trial, Judge Clement D. Nye sentenced them to one year in county jail, but suspended both of them for a period of two days. He mandated that 60 days be served within the confines of county jail. Mitchum spent his jail time at the state honor farm in Castaic, 40 miles north of Los Angeles. He came out weighing less and proclaimed to be much more fit than when he arrived.

Many in Hollywood circles speculated that Mitchum's career would be doomed by the scandal. Paramount studio boss Hal Wallis, fearing such a result, refused to allow his top leading lady Liz Scott to work opposite a performer convicted of a felony on the grounds that she may suffer from a ripple effect from the negative public reaction to Mitchum. Mitchum's leading lady from *Out of the Past*, Jane Greer, was brought in at the last moment to appear with him in *The Big Steal*.

The public reacted favorably to Mitchum for two reasons. For one thing there was great suspicion that he had been set up in a sting. Second, he bore up under the circumstances without complaining, doing his time and returning to civilian life without bitterness or rancor.

Mitchum headed for Mexico to report for work on *The Big Steal* for director Don Siegel. The caper film proved to be a major RKO success upon its release in 1949. Not only was Mitchum vindicated with the public, which flocked to theaters to see him, he ultimately received good news from the justice system. On January 31, 1951, just after Mitchum completed his parole period, Judge Clement D. Nye, who had found Mitchum guilty and sent him to jail, issued a statement quashing the conviction: "After an exhaustive investigation of the evidence and testimony presented at the trial the court orders that the verdict of guilty be set aside and that a plea of not guilty be entered and that the information or complaint be dismissed."[20]

Lila Leeds was not destined to experience the same career surge as Mitchum after doing her 60-day stretch. She starred in an anti-marijuana film that was an attempt at an updated version of the 1936 cult classic *Reefer Madness*. Instead a flop resulted for *Wild Weed*, released in 1949, the same year that Mitchum enjoyed success with *The Big Steal*. *Wild Weed*'s only claim to fame (other than Leeds's appearance) was that it marked the film debut of prominent character actor Jack Elam. Leeds's career bowed out in 1949 with an unbilled role in another forgettable low-budget film, *The House Across the Street*.

Chapter Seven

The Outsider and Film Noir

> At first sight, the Outsider is a social problem. He is the hole-in-corner man.—Colin Wilson, *The Outsider*

George Haight, producer of *Lady in the Lake*, employed Raymond Chandler to adapt his novel to the screen. When he began reading portions of Chandler's screenplay in progress Haight expressed surprise. He liked the original product sufficiently to want to develop a film from it. The producer expressed surprise to Chandler that the screenplay pages written by the detective writer were veering considerably from an original work he admired.

It took little time for what interest Chandler might have originally possessed in adapting his novel to dissipate. Ultimately he withdrew from the project, upon which Fisher was summoned like a relief pitcher from the bullpen to provide George Haight and his director-star Robert Montgomery with a shooting script.

Once the film was released and Chandler saw it, his response was the same as that of some of his other filmed works. Chandler disliked *Lady in the Lake*, but, if anything, Haight and Montgomery could well have considered his reaction good news. After all, Chandler abhorred another screenplay on which he worked. In the case of *Lady in the Lake* Chandler sought to have his name removed altogether from the project, as a result of which Fisher received sole screen credit.

The other screenplay for which Chandler ultimately received credit occurred after his one and only collaborative effort with screen giant Alfred Hitchcock in the powerful 1951 release *Strangers on a Train*. Chandler seethed with disgust over what critics and viewers consider not only one of Hitchcock's finest efforts, but one of the best movies ever made by anyone.

There is ample evidence that Chandler fit into the category of a definitive outsider. He never appeared to enjoy any aspect of screenwriting except for conversations with fellow writers at Paramount, and that had less to do with working on a screenplay than enjoyable conversation with members of the craft in general. When it came to dealing with those in positions of creative authority, be they directors or producers, Chandler was ill at ease.

An exception was when he worked with fellow Dulwich College graduate John Houseman when the latter was producing *The Blue Dahlia*. Since Alan Ladd, the most popular male star on the Paramount lot, was faced with service recall, the studio was highly desirous of getting one more film under his belt before he left. As it turned out, Ladd was never obliged to face any World War II combat action and was released shortly afterward, but the tension was on during that period to get the film made promptly.

Many Hollywood observers were convinced that Chandler saw an opportunity and grabbed it. He told his friend Houseman that the only way he could deliver a script under such pressure was to work at home. In that respect Chandler resembled William Faulkner, who detested the obligation of working in the formal office-style atmosphere of a studio writer. Chandler and Faulkner both made their mark working at home as fiction authors writing books and gravitated later into the cinema field. Each professed a marked discomfort for that type of writing compared to the free-flowing atmosphere of working on your own typewriter in your private residence.

Chandler insisted on working at home while the studio supplied a driver to pick up pages of the work in progress. He explained that it was necessary for him to be fortified with alcohol to be able to deliver a completed script under such a tight deadline. The game plan was to ply himself with alcohol and work on the script, then take breaks as necessity dictated to sleep off the alcoholic effects, after which he would return to the script.

Although the conditions were met by Paramount and the script was done by Chandler without any conferring or any other type of interference, he was dissatisfied with the results of *The Blue Dahlia*. And, despite the fact that Alan Ladd clicked with leading lady Veronica Lake, Chandler had a profound dislike for her and referred to the Florida-born blonde star as "Moronica Lake."

While the film, directed by George Marshall, was a commercial success, the script was not up to the Chandler standards exemplified by the two classics on which he labored, his collaborative effort with Billy Wilder, *Double Indemnity*, and Hitchcock's masterpiece *Strangers on a Train*. Then again, with not one but two films ranking among the greatest of all time, it is also safe and reasonable to state that such lofty perches are visited only on rare occasions, even by the finest talents.

As for *The Blue Dahlia*, a major complaint was that Veronica Lake and Alan Ladd's initial meeting (when she picked him up while she observed him walking in the rain) was seen as pat. To those critics the initial meeting of Paramount's popular stars could have been invested with a more thematic foundation.

In terms of what the script and finished film product provided, it contained solid pacing with good characters. Along with Ladd and Lake, William Bendix, Howard da Silva, and Doris Dowling all contributed commendable efforts. (More will be written about *The Blue Dahlia* later in this chapter.)

The act of writing is a solitary pursuit. It is therefore understandable that so many writers were solitary listeners and stood outside anything embodying a social milieu mainstream. When they did mix in social gatherings, it was often with the purpose of listening and understanding, then writing about their observations. As Ken Annakin told me about the great Somerset Maugham, when he attended parties, "The other guests were terrified. He would sit, watch, and listen. They knew that he would be writing about them and he did."

It is axiomatic that, for a writer to have subject matter, it necessitates using powers of observation. A direct relationship exists between writing expertise and observation. Ask any diligent reader what sets an excellent writer apart from others in the field and the answer, in one form or other, will come back that the author of consummate skill possesses an eye and ear for detail, along with the requisite skill to set such acquired information on paper.

It was no surprise to anyone familiar with his fascinating and highly unconventional life that British author Colin Wilson in *The Outsider*, his penetrating work on individuals who combined genius with outsider status, that T.E. Lawrence, known to the world as "Lawrence of Arabia," fell into that category. Despite failing to meet the required minimum height standards for the British Army, Lawrence not only found a way to get in, but eventually gained an international reputation for the ingenious manner in which he took a group of Arab irregulars and turned them into a desert guerrilla style force that aided in overcoming Turkey's Ottoman Empire in World War I.

Not only was Lawrence a natural outsider who did things in his own particular manner, like so many in that distinct category he had a strong penchant for recording his experiences on paper. While some would question the veracity of certain content in his masterpiece *The Seven Pillars of Wisdom*, none disputed his gift for linking event and detail in a colorful fashion. Lawrence's life was seemingly made for film.

Fortunately when the time arrived it was a fellow Britisher, genius, cinema director, and noted outsider named David Lean, an international traveling vagabond, who formed a creative bond with the long-deceased desert warrior with the 1962 classic *Lawrence of Arabia* the brilliant result. Playing the lead was a performer known for blazing his own trails and marching to his own tune: Peter O'Toole.

Lawrence would ultimately retreat from the same society in which he had become an international figure. He became an enlisted man in the British Royal Air Force. Lawrence even took a new name, that of Shaw. The legendary playwright and social critic George Bernard Shaw and his wife became his adoptive parents.

Colin Wilson sums up his definition of the outsider in one far-reaching paragraph:

> The Outsider's case against society is very clear. All men and women have these dangerous, unnamable impulses, yet they keep up a pretence, to themselves, to others; their respectability, their philosophy, their religion, are all attempts to gloss over, to make look civilized and rational something that is savage, unorganized, irrational. He is an Outsider because he stands for truth.[1]

Wilson's encounter with the outsider and what produces the species led him to the last published work of H.G. Wells, one of Britain's most prodigious creative and intellectual talents. It was appropriately titled *Mind at the End of its Tether*.

Wells explains the obligation humanity feels to clarify the world and ideas to maximum capability: "His renascent intelligence finds itself confronted with strange, convincing realities so overwhelming that, were he indeed one of those logical, consistent people we incline to claim we are, he would think day and night in a passion of concentration, dismay and mental struggle upon the ultimate disaster that confronts our species. We are nothing of the sort. We live with reference to past experience, not to future events, however inevitable."[2]

Wilson defines Albert Camus, that early champion of Raymond Chandler, as one whose "tone of indifference" generates throughout his famous work *The Stranger*. To Wilson, Camus's outsider "has hardly any feelings at all."[3]

When Camus read Chandler he certainly observed a thematic synergy between characters of his own, such as Mersault, the Algerian first-person narrator of *The Stranger*. Chandler's riveting first-person narrative of his alter ego, detective Philip Marlowe, sharply evaluated human nature in a comparable manner to Camus in the aforementioned work. Chandler's love-hate relationship with Los Angeles stemmed largely from the fact that a rootless city with a transient population coming largely from elsewhere made it an ideal target.

Apart from his mother, the only person who had any kind of a sharply defining influence on Chandler following his schoolboy days at Dulwich College in London was his wife, Cissy. Theirs was an enduring relationship severed only by her death.

Chandler and Cissy

Despite the fact that Chandler was reputed to have had a number of extramarital affairs, it was obvious from observing his life that the only woman who truly won his heart (apart from his mother) was Cissy. A full 18 years the author's senior, Cissy did not marry Chandler until after the death of his mother.

In the manner of a T.E. Lawrence or David Lean, Chandler was a wanderer and definitive outsider. While Chandler lived most of his life in Southern California, his addresses were more numerous than his collective writing enterprise. While it is true that Chandler's Los Angeles experience was always a love-hate relationship at best, and he chronically complained about the area's absence of culture and identity, the vagueness that so many others have also complained about, it was every bit as true that his creativity was jump-started by those same elements. From the time that Chandler got his first experience of Angel's Flight and the transitory element of Los Angeles and its citizens, his prose took off.

It was a classic example of a creative symbiotic relationship, one based to a large extent on opposites. The sophisticated, tweed suit wearing, pipe-puffing Chandler would sharply denounce the Los Angeles area. Los Angeles was not really a city. It was a way station to wealth that never materialized involving dreamers who never got their wishes and became transients instead. In Chandler's view there was corruption galore, particularly evidenced in the Bay City Police Department with the infamous Lieutenant DeGarmot, brought to life with such conclusive reality by Lloyd Nolan.

Chandler, as the city's ombudsman traversing in the realm of fiction, let those who wished to know that his criticisms were based on cold, calculating reality that produced incendiary sociological sparks from his trusty Underwood. Santa Monica had its share of critics who made the same points that Chandler did in his fiction.

In 1938, Mayor Frank Shaw became the first mayor ever recalled from office in the U.S. He was replaced by Los Angeles voters that same year by reform candidate Judge Fletcher Bowron. Los Angeles District Attorney Buron Fitts was also the target of reformers and was voted out of office by John F. Dockweiler in 1940. Dockweiler was presented upon assuming his position with an impending prosecution of mobster Bugsy Siegel for a Hollywood murder in 1942. The judge dismissed the case when it went to trial after the prosecution's star witness fell to his death from a New York City hotel window.

That brutal Los Angeles reality reads like fiction pouring from Chandler's typewriter. An astute man who kept careful track of what was happening in and around Los Angeles, Chandler merely converted the facts to fictional characters and provided his own insights and microscopic penetration. A writer with the rare gift of creating detective fiction that Chandler possessed could use actual events and people for outlines as he breathed fresh life into situations with his sharp characterization.

Philip Marlowe served Chandler superbly as his own insights and beliefs regarding the city and some of its most unique people were served up by that clever alter ego. While Marlowe maintained his own standards of probity as a detective he was ever mindful of the greedy, grasping nature of society in the same manner that Chandler observed, from the outside.

The fiction of Chandler accordingly dovetailed not only in motion picture adaptations of his own works, with a brilliant effort added to the mix in the case of a James M. Cain novel with *Double Indemnity*, but in film noir cinema in general. Camus and the French wave of creativity was in its element watching works from Hollywood that showed outsiders doing battle with the forces of nature that sought to exterminate them. This battle of forces was repeated in scores of films following World War II.

Chandler, Corruption and the Suburbs

Los Angeles author Judith Freeman sought to unearth patterns of Raymond Chandler's life in the city and how it, along with his outsider status, had an impact on his fiction. Freeman meticulously traces the steps of the author and his wife, Cissy, as they moved to numerous locations within the city. It is significant to note that after the Chandlers moved to the quiet and affluent San Diego suburb of La Jolla that the restless dissatisfaction abiding within Chandler diminished, as did his output, even extending to witty letters to friends and professional colleagues.

Freeman provides insight on the subject of Los Angeles and the evolution of Chandler's craft:

> Chandler once said that when a civilization is in the process of getting rotten, you will always find the symbols of this rottenness in the suburbs, in the lives and homes of supposedly decent people.
>
> Los Angeles was (and still is, as the trope goes) nothing if not a vast collection of suburbs (all that rottenness in search of a center). To become the capital of noir, all L.A. needed was the perfect bard — the poet of the common who, rising out of the sleaze and junk material of the city, could capture it with a voice like no other. And it found him, in the owlish, bespectacled former accountant who, after his sacking from Dabney Oil and humiliating fall from grace, was ripe for reinvention.[4]

The twin elements of film noir and the fiction that helped serve as a launching pad were the Great Depression and World War II. Combine the Los Angeles popularized by Chandler, the series of suburbs searching for a city, a place where the rootless from elsewhere converge to bask in the city's sun-baked streets and overarching rootlessness, alongside the element of returning service veterans following World War II, and a natural element for drama surfaces.[5]

One film that debuted in 1946 not only featured a returning soldier attempting to find his identity in Los Angeles, the element of amnesia was also added. An exciting young leading man merged his talent with a new director.

John Hodiak as a Pawn of Fate

The term "pawns of fate" was used to describe the universal victimization of humanity in the novels of hard-bitten realistic novelist Theodore Dreiser, whose principal works, *An American Tragedy* and *Sister Carrie*, were adapted into major films, the former under the title of *A Place in the Sun*. That term could also be applied to the male stars in film noir efforts beginning in the period immediately following World War II.

At a time when so many service personnel were returning from duty, it was a natural to present works demonstrating a return to America. The big twist is that they encountered much more than the type of economic and social readjustments that America's returning veterans face. With the film noir trademark of alienation and pawns of fate and heroes being overwhelmed and frequently destroyed by external forces, these returning veterans sought to survive in a brutal world.

John Hodiak received one of the finest opportunities of his career in a 1946 release in which Joseph Mankiewicz was in the early throes of his transition from screenwriter to screenwriter-director. *Somewhere in the Night* is a film meant to keep audiences guessing in the manner of a detective story, but in this instance George W. Taylor (Hodiak) is a pawn of fate who suffers from amnesia. All he has when he leaves the Army hospital where he has been treated is a letter from his former wife and a letter of credit, under the name of George Taylor, with funds to be received at a Los Angeles bank.

When a woman comes into a noir leading man's life, it can mean eventual curtains (consider what occurred with Robert Mitchum when he encountered beautiful but ruthless and homicidal sociopath Jane Greer in *Out of the Past* or the different Humphrey Bogart result with Lauren Bacall in *The Big Sleep* and *Dark Passage*, and from Lizabeth Scott in *Dead Reckoning*). The woman who walks into Hodiak's life at a moment when he has every right to believe he is one man against the world is supportive.

Christy Smith (Nancy Guild) is a nightclub singer who is genuinely nice and immediately empathizes with the thoroughly befuddled Taylor as he seeks answers, hoping that they in turn will free him from the oppressive element stemming from his amnesia. Smith begins by threatening to get the nightclub bouncer to throw Taylor out. She then feels sorry for him in his tragic state, and shortly thereafter begins falling in love with him.

Guild blended well enough with Hodiak so that Twentieth Century–Fox teamed her with George Montgomery in the 1947 release *The Brasher Doubloon*, the film adaption of Chandler's novel *The High Window*. Hodiak had starred for Twentieth opposite Gene Tierney in the 1945 adaptation of the John Hersey novel *A Bell for Adano*.

At the time that Guild appeared in *Somewhere in the Night* she was married to Edward Lasker, then a prominent agent and later a famous movie attorney. Lasker was linked to three famous noir leading ladies. While Guild was cast in a supportive woman noir role, the other two female stars with whom he was romantically linked were femmes fatales. After his divorce from Guild, Lasker was engaged to blonde British star Peggy Cummins, who starred with John Dall in the 1949 low-budget *Gun Crazy* directed by Joseph H. Lewis. Lasker then married Jane Greer.

A FRIEND IN NEED—Nightclub singer Christy Smith (Nancy Guild) befriends and ultimately falls in love with George W. Taylor (John Hodiak) in ***Somewhere in the Night***.

Pursued by the Mob

The element of being pursued by the mob, such an inherent part of *Somewhere in the Night*, is reminiscent of a plot device in *Out of the Past*. As will be seen, this element is also present in *The Blue Dahlia* with the presence of Howard da Silva, and was a strong element in the form of Richard Widmark in his classic role of psycho mobster Tommy Udo in *Kiss of Death*, a Twentieth triumph from 1947. Along with laughing crazily throughout and throwing wheelchair bound Mrs. Rizzo (Mildred Dunnock) down a flight of stairs, Udo actively pursued victim Nick Bianco. Udo realizes that on the subject of whether or not he will remain free in New York City rather than rotting in Sing Sing, Bianco holds the prison keys in his pockets.

Much of *Somewhere in the Night*'s fascination stems from the audience being in the same position as Taylor. Here is a man devoid of memory. By having no past, an intrigue is present with viewers that exceeds another type of noir drama in which the male star is aware of who he is, investing George Taylor with a definitive outsider status. When he becomes a creature of the night in the true noir tradition, he is literally in the dark beyond a station that the likes of Bogart and Mitchum scaled in their roles. In this instance Taylor is literally "in the dark," unaware of who he is and where he is going.

As revealed by this author in *Hitchcock and the Methods of Suspense* and Otto Friedrich in *Hollywood Nets*, with the immigration of numerous disciples of Sigmund Freud from Europe (particularly Germany and Austria in World War II), psychiatry became a lucrative profession in the movie colony. Prominent figures of the film industry had both the money and active curiosity to explore the depths of psychoanalysis. With Alfred Hitchcock along with producer David Selznick and screenwriter Ben Hecht all fascinated devotees, it was unsurprising that they pooled their considerable talents to generate two memorable films dealing with psychological subject matter.

Both films starred Ingrid Bergman, the most famous leading lady to come to Hollywood from Sweden since Greta Garbo. Her roles covered both elements of psychology. In *Spellbound*, Bergman is cast as a psychiatrist probing for answers on behalf of John Ballantyne (Gregory Peck), the patient with whom she has fallen in love. The film was released in 1945 while the second film, *Notorious*, was released one year later in 1946, the same year as the debut of *Somewhere in the Night*.

In *Notorious*, Bergman is Alicia Huberman, a woman who has jumped from nymphomania amid the rich of Miami to falling in love with FBI agent Devlin (Cary Grant), who has a fear of romantic commitment. One more psychological twist involves the man with whom Devlin and the U.S. government asks Huberman to become involved, extending ultimately to marriage. Alexander Sebastian (Claude Rains) is one of a contingent of Nazis living in Rio de Janeiro, seeking to keep the quest for an international Third Reich alive. Sebastian's psychological complication is his tie to a mother who competes with Huberman for her son's attention and is perennially suspicious of her.

Somewhere in the Night, *Notorious*, contains the Nazi element amid local intrigue. In this case amnesia sufferer George Taylor is an innocent victim in a $2 million money laundering mystery involving a Nazi seeking to send money out of rapidly crumbling Third Reich Germany. Taylor finally realizes why a local mob element and other fortune seekers are after him, since he learns that his former profession before going abroad to fight was that of a Los Angeles private investigator.

Richard Conte plays Mel Phillips, the owner of the nightclub where Christy Smith sings. She introduces Phillips to Taylor in hope that her boss can provide assistance. It is learned that Phillips's self-interest is much involved and this is the element that seeks him to become interested in Taylor.

Taylor's Adventures and the Characters He Encounters

Any story theme such as this film possesses provides ready-made opportunities for character performers, talents meant to sparkle often with one or at most a small handful of scenes. One of the familiar faces of film noir and comedy during the period was Sheldon Leonard. (He would later gain fame on a related entertainment front as one of television's most prominent producers; he cast the first African American ever to star in a regular series, Bill Cosby, who performed opposite Robert Culp in Leonard's hugely popular sixties' *I Spy* series.) Leonard's character, Sam, appears in one scene and makes it memorable, aided by a clever script twist. He answers the door of his apartment clad in his undershirt, telling Taylor to leave in a manner evidencing more bluster and disgust than anger. The woman with whom he is living, Phyllis (Margo Woode), had been pursuing Taylor for what he correctly suspects was an effort to aid his enemies. While Sam blocks the doorway and insultingly and repeatedly tells Taylor to leave, that he has come to the wrong address, the vigilant amnesia victim persists. He continues asking questions. The fascinating twist is that, while Sam continues telling Taylor that Phyllis has no information, she provides clues while superficially presenting the image of someone sarcastically stonewalling Taylor's efforts. Phyllis is so successful that Sam is convinced, repeatedly telling Taylor that his efforts are futile and to immediately depart.

Another interesting figure who engages Taylor in one extraordinary scene is Josephine Hutchinson as Elizabeth Conroy, a lonely woman beset by tragedy. By patiently listening to her disclosures he is provided with important information about her father, then confined to a local mental institution. (Hutchinson, a brilliant character performer, received one great starring opportunity playing Marie Pasteur opposite Paul Muni as the famous scientist in *The Story of Louis Pasteur* [1936], the biography of the French chemist and biologist.)

When Phyllis directed Taylor to a fortune teller in San Pedro, doing so in a sarcastic manner and fooling Sam in the process, by following up Taylor finds and obliterates the false cover of Anzelmo, a.k.a. Dr. Oracle (Fritz Kortner), who had earlier sought to convince the ex-soldier that he is a prominent mob figure. The bluff is made more convincing since Oracle has a husky, broad-shouldered enforcer to administer beatings. The doctor tries vainly to obtain information from Taylor concerning the missing $2 million. Despite being subjected to beatings by Oracle's enforcer, the efforts prove futile since Taylor, like Oracle, is seeking to obtain information to unlock secrets from his past.

Lou Nova and the Cosmic Ray Punch

Perhaps it was inevitable for Lou Nova to enter the ranks of show business after a career that included a fight against Joe Louis for the world's heavyweight championship in 1941 and a victory over Max Baer, a former titlist in that same division. Nova, a California native born in Oakland, was one of the few pro fighters of his day to receive a college education. His career demonstrated a propensity for skillful self-promotion, a trait that is helpful in show business. Nova touted a "cosmic ray punch" in his boxing repertoire. He also entertained newsmen at workouts by demonstrating yoga technique, sometimes standing on his head.

While Nova received continuing opportunities to play roles in movies and on television involving fighters and mob tough guys, his most available opportunity to seek steady income in show business was in the nightclub field. Nova was particularly prominent in Las Vegas. Perhaps his most memorable line was, when inebriated hecklers sought to interrupt his act, a reminder that "I do my own bouncing."

Nova was one of the regulars of the group that Mike Mazurki along with successful boxing promoter George Parnassus formed as a meeting place for former professional boxers and wrestlers, many of whom were film and television regulars, the Cauliflower Alley Club. The club began when Mazurki and Parnassus co-owned a downtown Los Angeles restaurant. When they observed how many former boxers and wrestlers frequented their restaurant, the co-owners decided to launch a club and hold weekly meetings, concluding that it was a great opportunity to draw additional numbers from those ranks.

Lou Nova was a regular at the Cauliflower Alley Club. His role in *Somewhere in the Night* as Oracle's enforcer, Hubert, is reminiscent of longtime club president Mazurki's in the latter's most memorable film opportunity, *Murder, My Sweet*, in which he dogs seemingly every move made by Philip Marlowe. The ploy was highly effective in that viewers, aware of Malloy's menacing presence, began looking for him, just as Marlowe did on screen. While Nova is not showcased to the same extent as Mazurki in *Murder, My Sweet*, he maintains a brooding presence. Taylor remains apprehensive about him appearing on the scene to harass him or worse.

As for Taylor, one of the most puzzling aspects of his persona as someone who has returned to Los Angeles from the war asking questions about his past in his amnesiac state is that those who deal with him are unaware that he looked different three years earlier, when the stash of $2 million was taken and a murder was committed that has been wrongly attributed to him. The reason is that, at the time he was wounded in battle and lost his memory, Hodiak's face was badly injured and he required extensive plastic surgery.

In order to solve the mystery of his own identity, Taylor learns that he is the Larry Cravat character for whom he has been searching. His efforts lead him not only to a grim San Pedro apartment and the realization that Dr. Oracle is a down-at-the-heels fortune teller and all-purpose con artist, but that he might have killed a man when caught up in activities relating to the $2 million sent by a Nazi in the final throes of the Third Reich's defeat.

The person he needs to see is Michael Conroy. Here the plot procedure of throwing a score of roadblocks into the path of the outsider leading man seeking to unearth answers takes an imaginative turn that takes this device to its highest level of achievement. Taylor has previously conversed with Michael Conroy's daughter, Elizabeth, and his search to find him leads to the mental institution where he has been confined. Every effort is extended to prevent Taylor from meeting Conroy. He is able to speak to Conroy but not to prevent him from ultimate death at the hands of the same criminal element seeking to dispose of him.

Conroy is played by the prominent character actor Houseley Stevenson. More will be revealed about Stevenson in the analysis of *Dark Passage*. His craggy face in the brooding darkness makes his brief scene with Hodiak stand out in the way that the aforementioned scene with Josephine Hutchinson as his lonely daughter, played out in her small apartment in daylight, also commands attention.

Somewhere in the Night was made before the conclusion of World War II, depicting activities in and near Los Angeles. As an expanding city into which many residents of other states were pouring, the need became acute for housing. This, coupled with the war time exigencies of production to aid that cause, left many residents struggling to make do with less, meaning frequently cramped quarters. One of the most natural aspects of writing is reflecting what is occurring in the environment in which such efforts were being produced. The awareness of what was happening in Los Angeles with housing scarcity achieved a natural harmony with an essential ingredient of film noir.

One of the most impressive ingredients of *Somewhere in the Night* is the brooding darkness of night captured in the deeply shadowy cinematography of Norbert Brodine, who was nominated three times for an Academy Award. This compelling element of incorporating moodiness into a film drama is linked to the natural restlessness of the film's main character. In this case it is an amnesia victim seeking to re-establish his identity while unlocking the mysteries of his earlier life. This story element complicates but increases fascination with his pursuit, which puts him in the same category with audiences seeking the same answers without any clues provided by revelation of past events.

Taylor's outsider persona is enhanced by the trap doors by which he is frustrated in his attempt to unravel mysteries surrounding him. He meets characters trapped as well, existing in cramped quarters. He moves from a small hotel room to sleeping on a couch in the small apartment of Christy Smith. Elizabeth Conroy and Dr. Oracle are confined in small spaces, frustrated, alone and trapped in their worlds. The exterior of the apartment that Phyllis shares with Sam indicates small quarters containing confined, frustrated people trying to break out of their mold.

Lloyd Nolan as Cool Authority Figure

It is thematically important to note that Lloyd Nolan in his role as Lieutenant Donald Kendall of the Los Angeles Police moves throughout the film with an air of brisk authority that Taylor wishes he possessed. Nolan's presence bespeaks of analytical professionalism. He does not appear often, but when he does it is to inform all that he is on the case and observing everything interesting that occurs. On one occasion he appears late in the evening at Christy Smith's door, asking questions about Taylor. In an earlier scene he had discussed a missing man by the name of Larry Cravat with Taylor, Smith, and her boss, nightclub owner Mel Phillips.

The film's conclusion involves a gun battle between the two characters who have keenly observed from the periphery. Smith had introduced Taylor to Phillips as her "nice guy" boss. She hopes he can assist the returning soldier as he seeks to find the mysterious Larry Cravat. Phillips possesses the true air of power and authority as well as knowledge of the case that Oracle only bluffed about. Lt. Kendall arrives to rescue Taylor and Smith. The analytical police detective is shrewd enough to conclude that Taylor's natural propensity of tracking down clues arose from his earlier pre-war occupation of private detective.

In concluding analysis of this film, its release year of 1946 corresponds with story trends pertaining to returning veterans falling into dilemmas in their crucial early readjustment period. The film that is most associated with Samuel Goldwyn is the widely heralded 1946 classic *The Best Years of Our Lives*. To understand the approach taken in so many fascinating noir films released in the period immediately following the war it can be instructive to analyze what master director William Wyler generated sociologically concerning the period.

Since this was not a noir film based on mystery and resolving deaths, the Goldwyn-

GOOD COP, BAD COP—Lloyd Nolan, center, played the honest and shrewd Captain Kendall in the early Frank Mankiewicz drama *Somewhere in the Night* (1946).

Wyler effort resulted from a magazine story by MacKinlay Kantor. Kantor's story was adapted into an Oscar-winning screenplay by the prolific Robert Sherwood. Standing a gigantic six feet eight inches, Sherwood emerged as a tall talent indeed. His distinction was being the only Pulitzer winner from the fields of playwriting and historical non-fiction. Sherwood won Pulitzers for his plays *Idiot's Delight* (1936), *Abe Lincoln in Illinois* (1939), and *There Shall Be No Night* (1941). His other Pulitzer for historical writing was for his 1949 work *Roosevelt and Hopkins*. Sherwood had a distinct advantage in writing such a book since he had served as a speech writer to Roosevelt as well as Director of the Office of War Information. It was Sherwood who spawned the quote "arsenal of democracy" used by Roosevelt during the war period.

In a noir context, Hodiak along with Alan Ladd and Humphrey Bogart all played characters who were seeking to re-adjust following military conflict, but the democracy they sought was resolution, resolving conflicts associated with returning to civilian life after engaging in conflict abroad. While Al Stephenson (Fredric March) and Fred Derry (Dana Andrews) were battling the ravages of returning to the job front and life in general in *The Best Years of Our Lives*, in *Somewhere in the Night*, released that same year, George Taylor was fighting to regain his identity, to learn who he really is, and what he had done prior to losing his memory. He learned that he was Larry Cravat, the same person he was seeking to locate, but was he a killer, as was being alleged, or a victim of circumstances?

One factor that provides Taylor's seemingly instinctive talent for ferreting out information and acting upon it, along with digging for clues and people, is that in his pre-war period as Larry Cravat he worked as a private detective in Los Angeles. At the end of the film Lt. Kendall compliments him on his efforts and suggests that perhaps he might wish to return to his former occupation. Taylor demurs. After an arduous battle to survive, which he indelibly linked to uncovering the mystery of who he really is before it is too late, Taylor is ready for a quieter life with Smith, who is more than ready to share hers with him.

Somewhere in the Night was released during the important early to mid-forties phase of John Hodiak's career. Alfred Hitchcock provided him with a solid boost in casting him in his 1944 production *Lifeboat*, adapted by Jo Swerling from a story by future Nobel Prize–winning novelist John Steinbeck. The film was notable in that it was one of the few film roles for Broadway stage giant Talullah Bankhead.

Twentieth Century–Fox was impressed enough with Hodiak to put him in two more successful vehicles, one of which provided his first meeting with a woman he would eventually marry. The 1944 film *Sunday Dinner for a Soldier* found Hodiak starring opposite Anne Baxter. The granddaughter of famed architect Frank Lloyd Wright had something in common with her male lead in addition to marrying him. Hodiak and Baxter had two of their choicest roles in films directed by Joseph Mankiewicz. He directed Hodiak in *Somewhere in the Night* the same year that he would marry Baxter; the elegant female star won a "Best Actress" Oscar nomination in the legendary role of opportunistic Broadway performer Eve Harrington in the 1950 blockbuster *All About Eve*. She had earlier achieved a "Best Supporting Actress" Academy Award for the 1946 release *The Razor's Edge*.

In 1945, Hodiak starred in the adaptation of the John Hersey novel *A Bell for Adano*. It was directed by prolific Twentieth Century–Fox veteran Henry King. Hodiak starred opposite Gene Tierney and William Bendix, along with his nemesis and would-be killer from *Somewhere in the Night*, Richard Conte.

During this same period—the most productive of his career—Hodiak had a staunch ally in Twentieth's studio boss Darryl F. Zanuck. Hodiak was Zanuck's first choice for the plum role of Detective Mark McPherson in *Laura*. Even after shooting had commenced with Dana Andrews cast in the role, Zanuck at one point suggested to director Otto Preminger that Hodiak possessed more of the kind of assertive masculinity that he believed reflected a New York City police detective. In the final analysis, however, Zanuck deferred to his director and Andrews remained as star of the 1944 noir classic.

Hodiak had been the beneficiary of launching a film career during the period when so many major male leads were involved in wartime service duty. Once they returned he found it more difficult to obtain lead roles and appeared in subordinate parts opposite male stars who had returned from the war. This was the case with Mervyn LeRoy's 1948 release *The Homecoming* with Clark Gable, Lana Turner, and Hodiak's wife, Anne Baxter.

John Hodiak received plaudits for his role as a stoutly determined district attorney and courtroom adversary of Glenn Ford in the hard-hitting 1955 release *Trial*, directed by Mark Robson. On October 19 of that same year Hodiak died of a heart attack while shaving at his Tarzana home.

Alan Ladd and Post-War Conflict

Johnny Morrison did not suffer from amnesia in the manner of George Taylor in *Somewhere in the Night*, but the two shared one common plot point in Paramount's release that same year, *The Blue Dahlia*. That catchy film title was such a natural that, following the brutal murder of Elizabeth Short less than a year after the Ladd film was released, local journalists named her "The Black Dahlia." This case remains one of the best-known unresolved murders in Los Angeles history, the story of a young lady who came west from Medford, Massachusetts, and ultimately met a brutal end.

Johnny Morrison (Ladd) has returned from military service to learn that his wife, brunette beauty Helen (Doris Dowling), has fallen out of love with him. Helen appears to care for only one person in life, namely herself. Helen lets Johnny know that she is interested in a good time and that he holds no bearing in her future plans.

Morrison is jarred by their meeting and leaves in a state of angry frustration. While in this state, which becomes cinematically enhanced by an evening walk in the dark amid rain (a familiar noir style scene), he is picked up by Joyce Harwood (Veronica Lake), who happens to be driving by. As we will see, *Dark Passage* is marked by the initial meeting between the leading man and lady involving the same action, but under different circumstances.

The element of the impact of war on returning veterans is made clear in *The Blue Dahlia* with the presence of Buzz Wanchek (William Bendix), Morrison's old service friend. Morrison is compelled to watch Wanchek carefully since he sustained a head injury from combat that leaves him vulnerable to periodic attacks, in the course of which his actions are not only volatile, but often violent as well.

Veronica Lake falls into the noir category of strong supporting women that includes Nancy Guild as Christy Smith in *Somewhere in the Night*. Joyce Harwood comes to the aid of Morrison, a returning veteran who is linked to the murder of his wife. George Taylor faced a similar predicament with Smith assisting him in seeking to tie together mystery elements and reach a conclusion, with the added albatross of him not being able to remember. Morrison is not suffering from amnesia and does not have a tragic war-related injury in the manner of loyal sidekick Buzz Wanchek, but has another problem not confronted by Taylor, that of being under suspicion for killing his wife.

While *The Blue Dahlia* does not possess the explosiveness and sharp story impact of other filmed Chandler works (such as *Double Indemnity*, *Murder, My Sweet*, or *The Big Sleep*), it is a serviceable effort that utilizes familiar film noir formulas and maintains steadily paced action.

Much of the action centers around noted character actor Howard da Silva as Eddie Harwood, with whom Morrison's unapologetically disloyal wife has become romantically involved during his service absence. As will be seen later, da Silva and Dowling appear as prominent companion figures in Billy Wilder's noir gem released just one year before *The Blue Dahlia*, *The Lost Weekend*, starring Ray Milland and Jane Wyman.

In *The Blue Dahlia*, da Silva's character falls into the familiar character pattern of mob figure. In this regard *Somewhere in the Night* serves as a comparative example in that, just as pre-amnesia private eye Taylor unlocks the mysteries surrounding his life through uncovering the real background and activities of Mel Phillips, the man Christy Smith introduced to him as someone who will help him, Morrison unlocks secrets that propel him toward learning about his wife's real killer.[6]

Chapter Eight

Bogart's Dark Passage and Moorehead's Blockbuster Performance

> I've cried myself to sleep at night because of you.—Agnes Moorehead to Humphrey Bogart in *Dark Passage*

The third film of the triumvirate featuring an outsider returning to resolve a murder mystery is *Dark Passage*, released in 1947 one year after *Somewhere in the Night* and *The Blue Dahlia*. In the manner of the latter film, Vincent Parry (Humphrey Bogart) seeks to unravel the murder of his wife, but unlike Alan Ladd's character, who pieces together the mystery before he is tried, much less convicted, Vincent Parry has not only had his markedly unsuccessful "day in court," but has gone to San Quentin Prison and done time for a crime he did not commit.

Dark Passage was the third teaming of Bogart and Lauren Bacall. Warner Bros. presented a trailer that enticed fans back into the theaters to herald a team they solidly endorsed in two films directed by Howard Hawks. After tall, leggy Bacall was culled from the ranks of New York fashion models while still in her teens, in her first role in the screen adaptation of Ernest Hemingway's novel *To Have and Have Not*, fate knocked at her door a second time. Her older leading man, a fellow New Yorker, was destined to become her husband. Hawks, possessing the eye of a great director and the air of a realist who reacts to box-office briskness, brought the team back a second time in an adaptation of Chandler novel *The Big Sleep*. By the time the second film was released after some delays, Bogart and Bacall were man and wife.

The clever trailer introducing the dynamic duo in *Dark Passage* uses a simple and effective "just plain folks" approach. A pleasant looking young man attired as a movie usher reminds moviegoers of how much they loved the electric team of Bogart and Bacall, whose personal romance sizzled just as the same fireworks loomed on the big screen for all to see with the price of an admission ticket. After the movie usher-narrator tells his audience that in his job he "sees them all," he reminds theater patrons of how much the cash customers loved the Bogart-Bacall team in *To Have and Have Not* and *The Big Sleep*. He concludes with the revelation that the explosive love team is back again in *Dark Passage*.

Delmer Daves, the film's director, had, in the tradition of Billy Wilder and John Huston, learned his craft as a screenwriter and concluded that he could best guide his own material through the final celluloid process by directing as well. Daves also produced many of his films, but with *Dark Passage* familiar Warner Bros. figure Jerry Wald produced with studio boss Jack Warner serving as executive producer.

Daves received a law degree from Stanford University, but any thought of a legal career was permanently supplanted when he became immersed in the film industry. While still a college student, he served as prop boy on the 1923 release *The Covered Wagon*. Once he graduated from Stanford he was put to work by several studios as a technical advisor on films with collegiate backgrounds. His experience served as a stepping stone into the field of film writing. One of his credits enabled him to see the special magic of Bogart at work in the actor's breakthrough role of Duke Mantee in Daves's adaptation of Robert Sherwood's successful play, *The Petrified Forest*.

Now, one decade later, as a director as well as screenwriter, Daves adapted the David Goodis novel *Dark Passage* to the screen while assuming the director's reins as well. His experience as a screenwriter prompted him to use cinema technique in action settings to create a steady pace that never falters. The film is enhanced by the location of the film — cinematic San Francisco — a setting that enhances mood.

Dark Passage is launched with a unique and imaginative opening. A truck has just exited San Quentin Prison and moves along a road. We see a large barrel perched in the back of the truck swaying back and forth. Eventually it tumbles off of the truck and falls to the ground, with Vincent Parry along for the tumble. The intriguing opening continues with the swirling can rolling around until it comes to a halt. Finally Vincent emerges in prison grays. He immediately buries his shirt, then heads promptly for the road. A voice-over reveals Vincent's conclusion that he has perhaps 15 minutes to make an escape or he will be captured. Siren sounds accent the drama.

He knows that time is anything but his ally and that he must move fast or be caught and sent back to San Quentin. In this tense period the action continues with Vincent being picked up by Baker (former Our Gang member Clifton Young), a stocky young man in a convertible with unique striped seat covers. He becomes immediately curious about his passenger.

That troubled look on Bogart's swarthy visage that held him in good stead in noir drama is clearly seen when the questioning becomes brisk and aggravating. Vincent realizes he has done wrong in grabbing a quick ride as a hitchhiker. His questioner soon becomes more than curious. Vincent, doing time himself and therefore experienced in the ways of criminal types, can see that Baker's perceptiveness marks him as someone experienced in that realm. He will later learn that Baker, a person who will plague him beyond this meeting, is himself a graduate of San Quentin.

The criminal on the run has his predicament extended when a message is flashed onto the radio concerning the escape of a prisoner doing a life term for murdering his wife. The car comes to a grinding halt and Baker stares at Vincent in stunned silence, then pleads for him to stop when the desperate escapee begins pummeling him with his fists, knocking him out.

Vincent is shortly thereafter offered a ride from Irene Jansen (Lauren Bacall) as the statuesque beauty pulls her station wagon to a halt. Her offer of a ride when the male lead is wrongly suspected of killing his wife involved the same circumstances of the introductory meeting of Johnny Morrison and Joyce Harwood in *The Blue Dahlia*. The difference between the scenarios is that Vincent Parry has been convicted of the crime and has done time for it, hoping that his escape and resurfacing in San Francisco will enable him to solve the crime.

This type of first meeting between a male lead in deep trouble with authorities and a sympathetic female holds a powerfully dramatic ring for two reasons. First, there is an element of surprise with a beautiful young woman offering assistance to a man who is a victim of circumstances, in this case someone wrongly accused of killing his wife. Secondly, the story is quickly framed by an early meeting between the film's two leads. The woman emerges as a vigilant partner seeking to help a wrongly accused victim prove his innocence. In *Dark Passage* Vincent's innocence cannot be proven due to circumstances that will be later revealed, but Irene Jansen is able to provide her partner with time to plot an exit strategy from San Francisco.

After his experience with Baker, Vincent is reluctant to accept another ride, even from a beautiful woman. She makes a good point, though, that persuades him. If he does not get far away from the prison he will soon be caught in a floodtide of approaching police vehicles. As it is, she is barely able to move past a roadblock where an officer reaches into the back of the vehicle. While Vincent lies stretched out on the back floor, the officer misses him by inches as he inspects the back of the vehicle, which Irene, a landscape painter, assures him contains nothing but paints and canvases.

One justifiable criticism of *Dark Passage* is that Daves's script involves too many coincidences, and as such the scenes often appear contrived. While in a logical context many events would not occur, noir adventures that deal with a circumstantial chain of scenes frequently rest on acceptance of coincidence, a cinematic license that enables a director-screenwriter such as Delmer Daves to craft a film where a main character is constantly besieged by forces that threaten to overwhelm him. Still, this film, it will be seen, contains more coincidences than the norm for noir and general mystery format films.

The drama of *Dark Passage*, as well as other numerous noir dramas, stems from the tension of erecting sets of barriers. These are barriers that the leading man and the elements operating to assist him are constantly grappling with, a dramatic tension stemming from the steady clash of opposing forces. In *Dark Passage* the competing forces involve in convergence consisting of a group of fascinating character performers who appear briefly but create indelible impressions. On one team we have Vincent and Irene while others appear along the way who seek to help a man they like and believe received a raw deal. On the other side there are those who seek to thwart Vincent, led by the police, who are eager to put a convicted killer back in prison.

One Small Group

When Vincent is taken to Irene's apartment his curiosity about why she is interested in his welfare is disclosed. He learns that her own father was tried for murder and sent to prison, dying in San Quentin. She had attended Vincent's trial every day and even wrote a scathing letter to the editor of the local newspaper accusing it of witch hunt tactics against the defendant.

The wealthy Irene is able to advance money to Vincent. When she leaves him alone to shower and rest after he has arrived, he cannot relax for long. There is persistent knocking at the door; the female caller complains that she can hear the phonograph playing and knows someone is there. Vincent calls out gruffly for the woman to go away. The woman at the door is the perpetually meddlesome, always pestering Madge Rapf. (The role of Madge is played with a sturdy conviction by Agnes Moorehead, one of the screen's premier character performers. A product of Orson Welles's Mercury Theater, she appeared in both *Citizen Kane* [1941] and *The Magnificent Ambersons* [1942], winning one of the four "Best

Supporting Actress" nominations of her career in the latter film. She good-naturedly quipped that perhaps she was destined to be a "bridesmaid" where the Academy was concerned.)

After hearing about Vincent's escape from prison, an agitated Madge has arrived at Irene's apartment. She begs Irene to allow her to stay with her at least until it is presumed that the escaped convict is not in San Francisco. Madge insists that he will kill her just as he did his wife. Vincent, meanwhile, stands in a bedroom, able to hear the discussion and becomes alarmed with each passing moment. He becomes even more alarmed when Bob (Bruce Bennett) arrives. Bob has unrequited romantic feelings for Irene and had formerly been engaged to Madge. Irene, eager to get back to Vincent, persuades Madge to leave. Even though he wants nothing to do with a former fiancée he obviously loathes, Bob agrees to drive Madge to a point where he can locate a taxi to transport her home.

Before leaving Irene's apartment, Madge offers to call her the next day. Irene bluntly tells her that she expects to be busy thereafter, an obvious hint that she does not wish to see her. Madge, ignoring the implication, promises to call her in two days. Bob responds with biting sarcasm by suggesting that Irene "pick up the sofa and throw it at her" and that then, possibly, Madge will get the point that she wishes to have nothing more to do with her. Vincent is naturally most concerned about Madge since her testimony resulted in him receiving a life sentence for his wife's death.

Outstanding Character Performers, All on Vincent Parry's Team

Another coincidence of the film relates to Irene just happening to have money along with the willingness to impart a significant amount to Vincent to help him elude capture. Her reason for picking Vincent up alongside the road also involves coincidence. She had been nearby working on a landscape painting and heard the radio flash regarding Bogart's escape.

The coincidence factor is further extended with Madge being gruffly told to leave by Vincent seeking to hide in Irene's apartment. Madge just happened to be the leading witness against Vincent. Madge then arrives at the apartment fearing for her life with Vincent now free and, presumably, back in San Francisco. Bob, Madge's former fiancé, is now dating Irene regularly and is obviously in love with her at a time when she is seeking to tactfully break off the association.

Anyone reading a critical review of *Dark Passage* might decide to avoid watching a film so rife with implausible coincidences, but there are compelling reasons as to why it has endured. As an experienced screenwriter and director, Delmer Daves recognized the significance of swiftly paced, cinematic scenes and a cast inhabited by fascinating characters. *Dark Passage* provides the opportunities for leads as well as brilliant character talent to make a strong impact on audiences.

After thanking Irene for all she has done, Vincent concludes that it is in her best interest for him to leave her life as swiftly as he had entered it. Her association with Madge renders that conclusion all the more necessary in his eyes, along with the fact that he does not want her to get hurt.

The ideal San Francisco evening setting generates classic noir effect as Vincent steps into a taxicab, destined to meet someone who feels for the underdog and wants to be on his team. Initially, Vincent tells cab driver Sam (Tom D'Andrea) that he is not in a mood to be sociable and does not wish to speak with him. When Sam persists, Vincent realizes

FINAL CLASH—Vincent Parry (Humphrey Bogart) and Madge Rapf (Agnes Moorehead) in the pulsating 1947 hit *Dark Passage*.

just how essential it is to allow the plain-speaking cab driver to join his team. Sam explains that he believes Vincent received a raw deal and would like to see him get a break. His friend, as coincidence would have it, is a facial reconstructive specialist. An appointment is made for them to meet later that evening at the surgeon's office.

Vincent's Closest Friend

It is anything but surprising that an outsider like Vincent, someone who appears destined to fight forces of injustice, would have as his closest friend an individual of similar circumstance. When Vincent enters his small apartment a close-up reveals surprise and concern on the face of his friend George Fellsinger (Rory Mallinson). The individuals Vincent meets receive close-ups from cinematographer Sid Hickox that enable them to display interpretive acting talent, that which lies beyond dialogue. With Daves to that point using the same technique as Robert Montgomery in *Lady in the Lake*, a natural curiosity builds about the persona of George Fellsinger.

With a small apartment setting in San Francisco, the brooding darkness of evening is enhanced by the periodic sounds of fog horns. The reclusive George Fellsinger appears to have but one friend besides escaped con Vincent Parry, that being his trumpet. When he is asked about his trumpet playing, he responds that he plays it only when the neighbors are out.

Fellsinger is revealed as a gentle soul. He is not only considerate of his neighbors; he sounds guilty in admitting that it was hard for him not to hate Madge Rapf for her testimony against his friend Parry. The fact that hatred would bother him in such an instance demonstrates how hard Fellsinger concentrates to be one of society's decent as well as gentle souls.

Vincent explains to his friend George Fellsinger about his visit to the plastic surgeon to have his face restructured and asks if he can stay with him during the recovery process. George is agreeable, but he expresses concern that Vincent, in staying in the city that long, runs an increasing risk of being caught. He ultimately accepts that such a move might be his friend's only chance to avoid detection.

Doctor Outsider Meets Escapee Outsider

In the analysis of *Somewhere in the Night*, Houseley Stevenson was mentioned as the man in the sanatorium that George Taylor speaks with shortly before he is killed due to fear about what he might reveal concerning Mel Phillips's activities. His craggy face looked lived in, as if the man inside had endured a great deal of hard living and frustration.

Houseley Stevenson was born in London and worked in a San Francisco glass factory until making a career switch in his thirties. From that point forward he became immersed in the world of drama. He became a prominent drama instructor and director at Pasadena Playhouse, performing in plays there as well. With his craggy face and mellow voice which contained just a hint of a British accent, Stevenson appeared frequently on screen.

Stevenson was showcased one year later in *Dark Passage*. His craggy, lived in face is given even closer scrutiny this time due to the subjective camera that director Delmer Daves employed until a strategically important milestone point of the film. Stevenson portrays Dr. Walter Coley, the surgeon recommended by Sam the cab driver as a means of helping escapee Vincent Parry elude authorities. The camera closes in on Coley's appraising face as he stares closely at his patient. Sam agrees with the insight that Vincent has a good nose and he will not change it. He explains that he will make Vincent appear ten years older, but that the patient will always be aware that he is a decade younger than his appearance conveys.

Once Dr. Coley has completed his work a look of sad disappointment registers on his face. He expresses satisfaction with his work, but is saddened that he will never see the finished product. He explains that he has been stripped of his license to practice medicine and is taking enough of a chance in performing reconstructive facial surgery on Vincent and that he dare not press matters further.

Sam drives Vincent back to his friend's apartment, where he expects to stay during the recuperative period before the bandages are removed. By then a strong bond of empathy has emerged between two outsiders who met in the darkness of the city. They know that it is too risky for them ever to meet again. When Vincent seeks to give Sam a tip for his beneficial services, the cabbie initially balks, but relents when his determined friend places the money in his hand.

A Friend Is Killed and Irene Resurfaces

When Vincent unlocks the door to George Fellsinger's apartment he finds him sprawled on the floor dead, his trumpet lying next to him. Vincent's voice-over reveals that poor

George wanted nothing more in life than to play his trumpet and travel one day with him to Peru. The mention of Peru will hold great significant as the story progresses.

Vincent recognizes quickly that there is only one place for him to go. As much as he sought to leave Irene's life for her sake, he has no recourse but to recuperate at her apartment. As he staggers in his post-surgical state in the beckoning dawn up a flight of wooden steps, Vincent endures a loud crack from a wise guy who teases him for having had a bad night and wondering if an argument with his wife triggered his difficulty.

A weakened Vincent is barely able to make it to the elevator and ring the bell. His rocky state becomes all the more agitated when he sees the car of his old nemesis Baker in his parked car near Irene's apartment building. After ringing the doorbell, he collapses.

His problems are compounded with the local news report that he is the suspected killer of Fellsinger. Irene shows him the headline story and asks if he is guilty of the killing. Told by his doctor not to speak until the bandages are removed, he asks for writing materials. He writes in a tablet, with the camera panning in dramatically, "He was my closest friend."

A Story of Contrasting Women

The film noir exemplified by Bogart's powerful role in *The Maltese Falcon* and Robert Mitchum's tour de force in *Out of the Past*, released the same year as *Dark Passage*, reveal conclusions in which a positive resolution cannot be reached in the wake of homicidal characters of femmes fatales.

Lauren Bacall as a strong supportive woman in *Dark Passage* is reminiscent of her character in *The Big Sleep*. Despite numerous roadblocks that Bogart's Philip Marlowe character is able to surmount, experiences out of the dangerous streets of Los Angeles in the darkness of evening and confrontations with desperados willing to kill with impunity, Bacall remains a sturdy presence and the couple is united at the film's conclusion.

Edward Dmytryk's 1944 noir gem *Murder, My Sweet* bears thematic similarity to Jacques Tourneur's *Out of the Past* with contrasting women, a femme fatale and a strong supporting woman, but with differing conclusions. *Murder, My Sweet*, in the manner of *Dark Passage*, opted for a "love team unites" conclusion that would not have occurred in the hard-boiled fiction world of Hammett's detective Sam Spade and Chandler's alter ego Philip Marlowe.

RKO opted for a satisfying conclusion when moviegoers left theaters. The film contained a homicidal femme fatale willing to do anything including kill to get her way. Claire Trevor played her role as Helen Grayle (a.k.a. Velma Valento) to icy blonde perfection. The counterpoint was provided by her stepdaughter, Ann (Anne Shirley, who would in 1945 marry the film's producer Adrian Scott). Shirley provides a symmetrical fit as the strong supporting woman to Dick Powell's Philip Marlowe characterization. His decency prompts him to reject Helen Grayle's overtures and fall in love with Shirley.

Robert Mitchum as Jeff in *Out of the Past* possesses both the street smarts and essential decency of Powell, but the script by Daniel Mainwaring, writing under his pen name of Geoffrey Homes, takes a different turn from that of John Paxton in the 1944 release. The latter RKO release fell into the hard-boiled film noir pattern of Billy Wilder's *Double Indemnity*, with one differing twist. Whereas Walter Neff was thoroughly bowled over by the calculating ruthlessness of Phyllis Dietrichson, and is revealed as anything but the shrewd person that his own pretenses seek to assert, Jeff possesses a street savvy that is absent in Walter.

Much of the noir power of *Out of the Past* evidences from the brutal reality that, while Jeff, following an early period of romantic ecstasy, is well aware of what homicidal sociopath Kathie (Jane Greer) represents, he continues to deal with her. Jeff's tart as well as weary admission at the end of the film explains his dilemma. After Kathie advocates that they team up and go to Mexico, stating, "We deserve a break," he replies with appropriate film noir fatalism, "We deserve each other."

In *Out of the Past* beautiful blonde Virginia Huston is cast in the role of the supportive Ann, but what prevents Jeff from spurning Kathie and finding true love with her is timing. It turns out to be all wrong for former detective Jeff Markham who changes his name to Bailey, opens a gas station in Bishop, and falls in love with appealingly innocent small-town girl Ann. Her decency is revealed after Jeff has explained his past, highlighted by his romantic involvement with Kathie. Ann suggests that he search his heart to see if any love for her remains. "Nobody is all bad," she concludes. In one of the most memorable, succinctly tart lines in a script containing many, Jeff responds, "She comes the closest."

As someone who, beneath a tough, impassive interior, is a moralist and a realist, Jeff realizes that he made decisions regarding Kathie and serving as a client of Whit (Kirk Douglas), the mobster set into motion forces that overwhelmed him. He realizes that his chance for a different and preferable life with Ann has come too late. Whit is not willing to let him go until he performs one last job for him, and Jeff is enough of a realist to recognize that he may never complete the job. Even if he does, he knows that he still may never endure and might well be done in by Whit.

Even if he should somehow be able to surmount the difficult hurdle of Whit, there is the presence of Kathie. He recognizes that he will probably never be able to say no to her. In his frank conversation with Ann as she drives him from Bishop to Whit's Lake Tahoe mansion for the "final job," there is the sense of inevitability overwhelming him, the feeling that he has traveled a long road and that there is no turning back.[1]

"Too Marvelous for Words"

While the superb Daniel Mainwaring script of *Out of the Past* was a perfect representation of hard-boiled film noir to impress the Chandler-Hammett school as well as existentialist devotees of Sartre and Camus, the mission of Jack Warner being fulfilled by Delmer Daves as director-writer was different. While elements of film noir were definitely to be featured, especially as applied to Bogart's prison escapee character, Warner had a clear idea of where he wanted his productions to proceed. He based his decisions on star power.

Warner's concern was with fulfilling audience expectations. As such he frequently ignored requests from the stars in the Burbank studio's constellation, traveling a safer route than the likes of Bogart, Bette Davis, and Errol Flynn sought to pursue. These dynamic talents wanted to take chances. Warner preferred the tried and true, meaning what corresponded to studio grosses, the cash flow that kept a board of directors happy.

Bogart had that same world-weary look of Mitchum. They were clearly men who had seen it all, shrewd outsiders who frequently tired of uncovering the dirty deeds that people played on each other. That was part of the Bogart audience expectation, but, then again, as evoked in two Howard Hawks films that were smash hits, the Bogart-Bacall team spelled romance, and this was the second part of the equation.

The neatly tailored Delmer Daves script split the difference judiciously. The noir romance included incorporation of a tune sung by Jo Stafford, "Too Marvelous for Words." The lyrics were written by hit master Johnny Mercer and the romantic and catchy music was by Richard Whiting. It was initially written for film, but one produced a decade before *Dark Passage* premiered, the 1937 Warner Bros. release *Ready, Willing and Able*, starring Ruby Keeler.

Mercer, the longtime hit lyricist, and music master Whiting formed a great team, but Whiting, who wrote the spirited "Hooray for Hollywood," was struck down at the peak of his creative powers. He died in 1938 of a heart attack, one year after collaborating with Mercer on "Too Marvelous for Words." He had two daughters, Margaret, a popular songstress, and Barbara, a talented performer who launched her career in her early teens in the 1945 release *Junior Miss*.

As for the popular success of "Too Marvelous for Words" and how it fit into the Bogart-Bacall romance element in *Dark Passage*, Margaret Whiting incisively commented that it was a way to say, "I love you, honey." Jack Warner would have responded, "Exactly!"

Not a Femme Fatale, but a Murderous Meddler

Creating an entertaining film can be like conducting a political campaign. Propaganda is used to create effects, to generate stark differences between individuals. In *Dark Passage* there are sharp delineations between members of Vincent Parry's team, the people who sympathize with him, and those who oppose him. The sharpest delineation is presented, however, in the expansive contrast between the film's two pivotal women, Irene Jansen and Madge Rapf.

Madge looms as the film's heavy, but she is not a femme fatale. Men run away from her as fast as they can, making the meddlesome, thoroughly unwanted and brassy woman all the more determined to see that, if she cannot have a man she seeks then nobody else could have him either.

In terms of story propaganda, consider the differences in the names of the sharply contrasting characters. Repeat the name Irene Jansen several times. It contains a soft, resonant sound. A character associated with it could, in public estimation, be associated with a chic woman of glamour who carries herself with dignity, speaks in soft, resonant tones, and looks good in her clothes. In contrast, what does the name Madge Rapf conjure up? A woman who is loud, abrasive, and shrill. Irene Jansen sounds mellow and seductive when she speaks, always in a calm tone. The perpetually hyper, always intrusive Madge Rapf sounds unpleasant and scratchy, the kind of person that makes one run away. As foil to Irene the strident antics of Madge are perfect. The wider the line is drawn the more appealing Irene becomes to audiences.

Consider the following fact. In the next Academy Awards program held in 1948, the first following the release of *Dark Passage*, Agnes Moorehead became the first woman to host an Oscar presentation, co-hosting with Dick Powell. Her stirring performance as the meddlesome murderer Madge Rapf had made her famous.

Tranberg Analyzes Agnes Moorehead's Special Magic

Charles Tranberg is in a unique position to evaluate Moorehead's genius. As a superb biographer he captured the careers of both Moorehead and Fred MacMurray, two important figures of film noir, given the former's stellar effort in *Dark Passage* as Madge Rapf and the latter as the unforgettable Walter Neff in *Double Indemnity*. The two names even have a similar ring in Rapf and Neff.

When asked what impressed him about Moorehead, Tranberg replied: "First, I would say her incredible versatility as an actress. She played spinster aunts, temptresses, courtesans, career women, vicious gossips, royalty, murderesses, frontier women, schemers, and good-hearted women. She could play any type of role and do them each very well. Second, I would say that there was a sense of mystery about her. She rarely spoke of the private woman and I guess I was fascinated by that. To Agnes it was the public persona that counted — not the private person. She didn't understand why the public was so fascinated by what a public person does in his or her private life."

Tranberg targeted an interesting element about character performers in detailing some of the numerous characters Moorehead played in her career. Variety is a spice that generates continuing challenges for character performers. Certain lead characters, even those with gifted acting skills, conversely, are often compelled to remain within carefully defined roles. Studio executives did not want to take chances with proven box-office talents toward which audiences had preconceived expectations. Studio contract writers were ordered to generate scripts within those structured guidelines.

Jane Greer, for instance, lamented in an interview with me about how sad it was that the brilliantly executed 1947 RKO film noir drama in which she starred alongside Susan Hayward and Robert Young, *They Won't Believe Me*, was rejected by film audiences of that period. A superbly paced drama with excellently drawn characters was rejected for one reason. "The public did not want to accept Robert Young when he played a cad," Greer explained. The womanizing, opportunistic Young is ultimately tried for murder when, in fact, he is an innocent victim. The public saw him as a perennial nice guy in the manner of Jimmy Stewart and Gary Cooper, as evidenced in his other film roles along with his successful television lead roles in *Father Knows Best* and *Marcus Welby, M.D.* A character performer such as Moorehead, however, is invested with myriad opportunities, presenting a different challenge with each varying role.

"I grew up watching Agnes as Endora on *Bewitched*," Tranberg said. "To me the most fascinating element of that show, when viewing it today, is the dynamic between the Endora and Darrin characters, especially when Darrin was played by Dick York. But as I got older and became a fan of classic films it eventually occurred to me how many times Agnes appeared in some wonderful films. They weren't all classics, but she was always good. I think her five-minute role as the mother who sacrifices her son in hopes of a better life for him in *Citizen Kane* is the best performance in the film. Her Aunt Fanny in *The Magnificent Ambersons* is one of the most outstanding pieces of work by an actress of all time. You feel for her when the Joe Cotten character ignores her and doesn't realize how much she loves him. I think her performance in *Dark Passage* is one of her best. And each of these film characterizations is different from the others. In *Ambersons* she is vulnerable. In *Passage* she's a vixen and murderess."

After studying Moorehead's career exhaustively, Tranberg's key area of admiration for her is unsurprising, a trait that generates strong admiration. "What impresses me most about Agnes is the work she put into being an actress," he explained. "I researched her papers, which include tons of scripts and almost every scene that she is in has notations and underlined words for emphasis. She would note a pause here before completing a line or to downplay this line and emphasize another. Agnes had an incredible work ethic. She was always on time and always knew her lines. Directors loved her because she came prepared and always had an idea of how she would play her character."[2]

Switching Back to Outsider Battling Forces

The romantic element with Irene Jansen is played with a focus on the unselfish attitude of Vincent Parry. Even though Irene becomes teary-eyed the early morning of Vincent's departure, he explains that he has a penchant for bringing people bad luck. He cares too much for Irene to subject her to a life on the run with him. The parting is so lengthy that the cab driver complains about the long time he spent ringing the doorbell.

Irene is determined to help Vincent and suggests he take a new name to go with his reconstructed face. After rejecting her first suggestion as too much like the name of a man he did not like, Vincent assents to her second recommendation of Allan Linnell, the name by which he would thereafter be known.

In a scene reminiscent of Edward Hopper's famous "Nighthawks" painting, Vincent — now Allan — is next shown entering a small diner amid fog and darkness combined with a tinge of light from a beckoning morning. The proprietor hands him a newspaper to read while he prepares Allan bacon and eggs. Attempting to appear knowledgeable, Allan mentions he is interested in reading race results from the Bay Meadows race track. When the proprietor informs him that the Bay Meadows season has concluded, the tall, muscular man sipping coffee alone in the back of the diner moves forward to talk with him. His demeanor and air of authority stamp him immediately as a policeman. The powerfully built Detective Kennedy (Douglas Kennedy) becomes interested in Allan, having heard him make an error about the Bay Meadows racing season after indicating that he had an interest in horse racing.

Allan's trembling hands and evasive answers about who he is and where he comes from — he claims to be on business from Portland — along with inability to provide identification arouses Kennedy's suspicions. He tells him to accompany him to police headquarters. Allan pulls a bluff, telling him that he has identification at his hotel room.

As the detective and Allan leave the diner the proprietor mumbles to himself that he has opened his "big mouth" and is clearly disgusted about accidentally arousing suspicion toward his customer through his remark about Bay Meadows Racetrack. Once more we see the tugging of forces between two teams consisting of those who empathize with someone they see as a lonely man immersed in tragedy and those who for various reasons seek to thwart him.

When an oncoming truck proceeds into their area, Allan sees an opportunity to make a break. He eludes Kennedy and checks into a hotel room, hoping that after a brief respite he can make a successful escape.

Once more outsider Bogart becomes a victim of forces hunting him, this time with the reappearance of Baker, who has followed him since he left Irene's apartment. He brandishes a gun and demonstrates an immediate interest in Irene's money, informing Allan that he had been able to jot down her license plate number after awakening from the beating. He even knows that she has $600,000.

While Baker holds a gun on him, he ushers Allan out of the hotel and commands him to drive his car to Irene's apartment. Baker tells him that he has been a small-time criminal and hopes to escape with a nest egg, leaving by way of Benton, Arizona, where he will receive a fresh identification.

When it becomes obvious to Baker that Allan is not driving toward Irene's apartment in the city but to an area in the wilderness, the car is stopped. With a quick movement Allan seizes the gun from Baker. The now-desperate Baker, pleading for his life, swears that he never killed George Fellsinger.

Finally, the truth that outsider Vincent Parry, now Allan Linnell, has been seeking is revealed. There was a bright orange car following Baker's. As with the case of the information pertaining to Benson, Arizona, and a printing company that can provide needed fresh documentation, the revelation about the orange-colored car is also filed away.

The determined Baker, seeing his chances of leaving the country for a new life in Mexico slipping away, regains the upper hand with a deft move of his own, reacquiring his gun. A struggle ensues. Baker pins his opponent to the ground as the desperate outsider bites his tormentor's hand. Baker falls backward and plummets to his death.

Reemergence of Madge Rapf

At this point, the thoroughly meddlesome, thoroughly unlikable, thoroughly homicidal Madge Rapf reemerges. Allan presents himself at her apartment with his new face and new name. He tells her that he is a friend of her former fiancé and even bears a box of candy as an introductory present. Madge lets him into her neatly appointed penthouse-style apartment. He begins with flirtation, causing her to laugh. She tells him that there is something familiar about him. Allan then gets down to business. He lets her know who he is and mentions her infatuation with the color orange, right down to her car. Allan shoves a paper in her direction, demanding that she sign a confession, admitting that she killed his wife as well as his closest friend.

The cornered Madge admits to the murders but refuses to sign a statement. She delivers a declaration stating her motivation: "I've cried myself to sleep at night because of you. She's got you now. She wants you very badly, doesn't she? She's willing to run away with you and keep on running and ruin everything for herself. But she wouldn't care because she'd be with you and that's what she wants. Well, she doesn't have you now. She'll never have you. Nobody will ever have you! And that's the way I want it! You're nothing but an escaped convict. Nobody knows what you wrote down. They'll believe me! They'll believe me!"

After delivering her furious declaration, she lunges backward through an open window and meets instant death. Once again the outsider is confronted with a problem. He will be held accountable for this death as well.

As police arrive on the scene, Allan leaves the building and makes it to the bus station. Using the information he obtained from Baker, he buys a one-way ticket to Benton. The ticket seller tells him that he needs to sell two more before the bus leaves San Francisco. The last of the many coincidences occurs when Allan, after selecting his and Irene's favorite song, "Too Marvelous for Words" on a jukebox, steps into a phone booth and misses by a flash an inquiring police officer hoping to find him.

On the other end of the line, Irene listens once more with him to their song as it plays on the jukebox. He tells her about Madge Rapf's death and provides her with information about Peru and where they could meet again after a reasonable period, in a little town called Pieta. He warns her that for a time she will be watched by authorities due to her connection to him. That final conversation ends just after the police officer leaves with the ticket seller assuring him that he will be on the lookout. The final two tickets are meanwhile sold, meaning that the bus will depart immediately.

The spirit of people forming bonds and assisting each other is introduced by a man who looks as if he has had a hard time as he speaks to a woman with two small children. As they enter the bus and take seats next to each other they mutually smile, indicating that perhaps their loneliness and presumed struggles might end with them finding happiness together, just as Allan and Irene have formed a bond.

The film's final scene is just what one would anticipate. Allan sits in a beach-fronted Pieta, Peru nightclub while well-dressed couples dance. Suddenly "Too Marvelous for Words" begins playing, alerting Allan. Irene arrives and they move toward the dance floor together, dancing to their song, reunited and happy in a way they could not be before, when it seemed that their world would topple any second.

To make the film fit into the Jack Warner recipe for commercial success the struggles of Bogart's character would not reach the kind of ending endured by a Robert Mitchum in *Out of the Past* or a Fred MacMurray in *Double Indemnity*. Warner held a trump card with the Bogart and Bacall romantic team, one that had secured dividends on two previous occasions with shrewd veteran Howard Hawks in the director's chair. So, alas, *Dark Passage* was not a film that would follow a Sartre-Camus, hard-nosed existentialist premise to its logical conclusion. This was an outsider, man-against-the-elements format up to a point, in which case the romance element took over. The insertion of a song that fit the mood for romance was Jack Warner's recipe. He preferred to send audiences home happy.

The Special Magic of Bogart and Bacall; Rapf as Reverse Femme Fatale

Charles Tranberg has his view of what made Bogart and Bacall such a special team capable of motivating strong box office results: "I think Bogart and Bacall were so popular as a team because they were so much alike. In Bacall, Bogart found his perfect match. She was just as cynical as he was and they both had marvelous senses of humor. Watch the phone scene in *The Big Sleep*. I believe Bacall was referred to as the female Bogart. They did four pictures together — two before they were married and two after. Strangely, the only one which did not do well at the box office was *Dark Passage*. Maybe it was because Bogart's face was not seen on the screen until the middle of the picture. Bacall has said that the reason it didn't do well was because it came out around the time that she and Bogie went to Washington to denounce the House Un-American Activities Committee. Whatever the reason, *Key Largo* came out the following year and it proved to be very successful."[3]

There is one essential difference between the regular femme fatale construct and the persona of Madge Rapf in *Dark Passage*: "No, I don't really see Madge as the traditional femme fatale in film noir," Charles Tranberg revealed. "She is the murderer. Madge Rapf is the one who killed Vincent Parry's wife because she was in love with him. It wasn't the other way around. Vincent didn't reciprocate her feelings, so she got even by killing his wife and framing him. In traditional film noir, it's often the woman who drives a man crazy with lust — so crazy that he'll kill for her. The great example is Barbara Stanwyck manipulating Fred MacMurray to kill her husband in *Double Indemnity*."

Eddie Muller also weighed in on the topic of Moorehead's portrayal of Madge Rapf: "I love Agnes Moorehead, especially in *Dark Passage*. Her big scene with Bogart is extraordinary, the best in the film, even though I think that director Delmer Daves didn't get the full impact out of her suicide. In the book it's abundantly clear what she's doing, what her motivation is, but audiences don't quite 'get it' the way it's staged, behind the curtain. Madge Rapf is somewhat unique in noir, though certainly not in the stories of David Goodis, in that her behavior stems from wanting a man so badly, as opposed to the typical femme fatale, who only uses men, but doesn't really desire them. I suppose the character she's most like is Ellen Berent (Gene Tierney) in *Leave Her to Heaven*, another femme fatale who kills herself to get even with the man she loves."

In the traditional femme fatale situation, the man hungers for the woman. In the case of Madge Rapf, her former fiancé delivers a stinging mea culpa, a bitter self-denunciation for ever having been involved with her. With Madge Rapf intensely desiring Vincent Parry to the point that she would kill his wife separates her from the realm of the traditional femme fatale. She is, in fact, an example of a reverse femme fatale. Here is a woman willing to destroy because a man has rejected her following aggressive and thoroughly unsuccessful pursuit.

Final Cast and Author Notes

The film noir factor that gave *Dark Passage* its brooding mood and heightened dramatic empathy toward a haunted outsider trying to overcome obstacles involved the insertion of top character performers. Their talented efforts brought scenes alive and invested the film with a feel for life on the streets.[4]

A few cast notes should be made. In the cases of Bogart's ardent pursuers Clifton Young and Agnes Moorehead, tragedies befell them that loom as episodes from the annals of film noir. Clifton "Bobby" Young made his film bow as "Bonedust" during the Our Gang series transition to sound. During the same period as his appearance in *Dark Passage*, Young received other screen opportunities, appearing with Robert Mitchum in Raoul Walsh's *Pursued* (1947) and *Blood on the Moon* (1947) along with the Joan Crawford's 1947 noir film *Possessed*, directed by Curtis Bernhardt.

Young was seeking to break into leads during the same early-post World War II period as another cleft-chinned actor, Kirk Douglas, and with the exposure he was generating appeared to have a shot at top roles and breaking the "jinx" often associated with child performers.

Young fell on hard times as the fifties dawned. After a painful divorce he moved into a hotel and died there in a fire (he had reportedly been smoking in bed). The date was September 10, 1951, five days removed from what would have been his 34th birthday.

Agnes Moorehead's death from lung cancer (on April 30, 1974, at the age of 73) fell within a pattern of other cancer deaths befalling members of the cast and crew of the 1956 RKO film *The Conqueror*. Studio boss Howard Hughes wanted the film shot in the Utah desert and speculation continues that the deaths of numerous cast and crew members resulted from atomic testing during that period occurring in and around the area of filming.

John Wayne, who portrayed Genghis Khan in the film, died of lung cancer following a long illness. The film's producer and director Dick Powell also died from cancer, as did cast members Thomas Mitchell and Pedro Armendariz. A reported 90 people from the 220 cast and crew members working on *The Conqueror* later contracted cancer.

Recent television documentaries and articles centered around the city of St. George, the area where *The Conqueror* was filmed, have emphasized the disproportionate numbers of deaths of residents of the city at that time from cancer, continuing to fuel controversy that nuclear testing was either the catalyst or a contributory cause of so many lost lives. It must also be recognized that some of the deaths occurred with individuals known for excessive smoking habits.

David Goodis, Author from the Film Noir Tradition

The script director Delmer Daves wrote was adapted from David Goodis, as mentioned earlier by Eddie Muller. Goodis has become a recent cult figure in film noir circles. *Dark Passage* was initially serialized in the *Saturday Evening Post*, as well as being published by Julian Messner. Philadelphia author Goodis was in his late twenties and the newly acquired noteworthiness prompted an invitation to Hollywood along with an ensuing contract.

Goodis arrived in Hollywood as a young writer with dreams of achieving success and had a six-year Warner Bros. contract to fuel his optimism. *Dark Passage*, after all, reprised the dynamic team of Bogart and Bacall. Things started out promisingly for Goodis as a screenplay he wrote along with James Gunn, *The Unfaithful*, a remake of Somerset Maugham's *The Letter*, was released in 1947, the same year as *Dark Passage*. *The Unfaithful* involved Warner Bros. regular Ann Sheridan in the title role that Bette Davis assumed in the original version that was directed by William Wyler and premiered in 1940.

Film noir remained in Goodis's future as he penned an adaptation of Chandler's *The Lady in the Lake* that was never filmed. "Of Missing Persons" was another Goodis script that went unproduced.

Goodis's Warners period ended in the same kind of unfulfilling fashion as had the Hollywood phases of such prominent novelists as F. Scott Fitzgerald and William Faulkner. Goodis returned to Philadelphia and began frequenting the city's seedy nightclubs and bars. He lived with his parents, along with his schizophrenic brother Herbert.

Those evening excursions through Philadelphia's seedy side provided Goodis with the creative ingredients to craft more novels. *Cassidy's Girl*, which was published in 1951, sold over a million copies. At that point an interest was shown in Goodis's work. France led the way in popularizing Goodis's novels. Goodis had adapted his own novel *The Burglar* in a 1957 film directed by Paul Wendkos and starring veteran noir performer Dan Duryea, along with Jayne Mansfield and Martha Vickers. It received a French incarnation in a 1971 film directed by Henri Verneuil starring John Paul Belmondo, Omar Sharif, and Dyan Cannon. Shortly thereafter, Francois Truffaut, one of France's premier film directors, decided to adapt a Goodis work to the screen. The 1956 novel *Down There* was structured into a highly acclaimed cinematic work titled *Shoot the Piano Player*. The film, which was released in 1960, gained a solid cult following that has grown through the years and enhanced interest in Goodis's writing.

What Goodis observed combing the late hour streets of Philadelphia's bleakest neighborhoods as well as visiting its bars and nightclubs accomplished two things: spurring on the author's creativity while shaping a dark vision of society. This was a period when Goodis was published regularly in paperback form.

David Goodis died in 1967 of cirrhosis of the liver. His work went out of print in America following his death, although it continued to be popular in France. In 1987, however, Black Lizard began reissuing Goodis titles. In 2007, Hard Case Crime published a new edition of *The Wounded and the Slain* for the first time in more than 50 years. Also in 2007, *Street of No Return* and *Nightfall* were reissued by Millipede Press. A recent perusal of Internet bookseller giants Amazon.com and Abebooks.com revealed first editions of *Dark Passage* were being offered in the $400 to $500 range.

The Centenarian of Film Noir

While the annals of film noir include many tragic cases, one performer stands out as the centenarian of film noir, leading a sturdy life in which a strong body was nurtured into athletic prowess that was put to use to help forge a career as an actor.

Bruce Bennett was initially known to movie audiences as Herman Brix. He was born in Tacoma, Washington, on May 19, 1906, and ventured north to nearby Seattle to begin making his mark. He received a degree in economics and starred on the football team, playing tackle for the Huskies in the 1926 Rose Bowl, which was won in a 20–19 thriller by an Alabama team that also featured a future film performer in running back Johnny Mack Brown, who later starred in numerous westerns.

Herman Brix won a silver medal, placing third at the 1928 Amsterdam Olympics, in the shot put. It was only natural to put his ruggedly compacted six foot three inch frame to work in athletic film parts. In this area he received early acclaim, but his athletic heroics in one film cost him work in another. Brix sustained a separated shoulder making a tackle in the 1931 release *Touchdown*. His loss was Johnny Weissmuller's gain as the Olympic swim champ took the role intended for Brix in *Tarzan the Ape Man*, which was released the following year. Independent producer Ashton Dearholt would shortly provide Brix with an opportunity to play Edgar Rice Burroughs's jungle action hero in a 1935 series *The New Adventures of Tarzan*. The serial would be distinguishable from others bearing Tarzan's name in that it would follow the authentic Burroughs depiction of an English nobleman who chose to live in the jungle and enjoyed a rapport with the creatures living there by literally being able to speak their language.

After starring in the Republic Pictures 1938 serial *Hawk of the Wilderness*, playing a Tarzan-like jungle figure named Kioga, Brix dropped out of films for awhile. He took some dramatic lessons, reemerged as Bruce Bennett, and secured a Warner Bros. contract. One facet of the old Herman Brix remained in the actor's new image, that of demonstrating a man of strength. Bennett performed in feature roles of Warners classics with often only a few scenes and lines, but his strength and common sense shone through. In *Mildred Pierce*, the 1945 Michael Curtiz noir film that resulted in a "Best Actress" Academy Award for Joan Crawford, Bennett assumed a pivotal role as Bert Pierce, her husband, who falls on hard times as a real estate agent. Bert's decency in granting his successful wife a divorce so she can marry prominent socialite Monte Beragon (Zachary Scott) contrasts with the latter's brazen shallowness. When a triumphal Monte proposes a toast, he cynically exclaims, "One man's meat is another man's poison." Bert hurls the glass to the floor, where it shatters, after which he stalks away.

After Mildred Pierce is charged with Monte Beragon's murder (her spoiled daughter Veda [Ann Blyth] is the actual killer), Bert is at the police station to supply support. At the film's conclusion, Mildred leaves with Bert, furnishing the prospect of a reunion.

In 1948, Bennett was seen in the blockbuster Warners release *The Treasure of Sierra Madre*, a hard-edged story of greed with Humphrey Bogart playing a man so ruthless in his pursuit of gold that he sanctioned the killing of honest James Cody (Bennett). Later Bennett would say, "I wish I would have had more to do in the film. I hated to get killed so soon."

While Bennett's statement is understandable from the perspective of an actor preferring more screen time in one of the great films of the early post–World War II cinema, the fundamental, unchanging element about his performances was how he made an impact in so brief a time. Bennett's character was the one through whom decency shone to a point where the greedy gold miners believed it was necessary to kill him.

Bennett played a prominent role in another Warners film noir production, *The Man I Love* (1946). Leading noir actress Ida Lupino provides one of her typically fine performances as Petey Brown, a beautiful young singer who is employed by small-time mobster Nicky Toresca (Robert Alda) at his nightclub. Petey falls hard for San Thomas (Bennett), a formerly successful jazz pianist who has fallen on hard times. Rather than accept her affections, he straightforwardly tells Petey that he has never been able to free himself from the confining tentacles of his ex-wife, for whom an unrequited torch burns.

As for his performance as Bob in *Dark Passage*, Bennett serves as a one-person Greek chorus in extolling the truth about the homicidal and thoroughly selfish Madge Rapf. A plain spoken architect, Bob condemns himself for having been engaged to her.

Bruce Bennett's vigorous athleticism continued into his mid-nineties. He enjoyed parasailing and skydiving, leaping out 10,000 feet over Lake Tahoe at 96. "I feel sincerely that age isn't compatible by number of years," Bennett explained in a 1988 interview. "We know many young people of 90 and old people of 20. By my mind, I'm still young!"

While Bennett preferred spending most of his movie years out of the limelight, toward the end of his life, he found responsive audiences at fan conventions. With so much fan interest in Tarzan, he was a special guest at various seminars and conventions celebrating the series' book author Edgar Rice Burroughs.

Bruce Bennett died in Santa Monica, California, on February 24, 2007. He was 100, decidedly young to the end.

Chapter Nine

Berlin and Vienna, Film Noir Influences

A chance meeting in 1944 with Joan Harrison, Hitchcock's producer, led to one of Siodmak's best films, *Phantom Lady*. It is his first film noir—a name given to some American films of the mid–1940s and 1950s by French critics who noted in them a darkening, paranoiac tone, a preoccupation with the psychology of the criminal and social outcast, and an implicit critique of American society in the aftermath of World War II.—Christopher Lambert writing about Robert Siodmak

When a young and eager Alfred Hitchcock desired to obtain knowledge in the technique of camera work he traveled to Berlin, a hotbed of film activity. He learned from observing masters such as Fritz Lang, F.W. Murnau, and G.W. Pabst. A major reason for international film interest in German technique was the air of realism presented by directorial craftsmen living in a city of the kind of widespread activity that nurtured unlimited story potential.

Berlin was a lightning rod of busy creative activity during the pivotal period between the end of World War I and the outset of World War II. It was a veritable burning cauldron of dissolute activity with part of its citizenry caught up in waves of debauchery while others of its number sought to preserve order by working steadily and bringing up families.

The restlessness and debauchery caught the attention of filmmakers given the potential of stark human drama. Marlene Dietrich became internationally famous playing the role of Lola-Lola, a young Berlin woman with whom the respected Professor Immanuel Rath (Emil Jannings) falls hopelessly in love in *The Blue Angel*. This memorable 1930 film, based on Heinrich Mann's novel *Professor Unrath*, follows Rath's descent from a respected teacher to a clown in Lola-Lola's cabaret troupe. After an unsuccessful attempt to strangle her, the disgraced professor is released after having been beaten down and placed in a straitjacket by troupe members. He returns to his old classroom and dies.

The Blue Angel ushered in more biting realism in which a penetrating camera's eye revealed the cruel anarchy and resultant suffering of individuals caught up in the throes of a rapidly paced city. Berlin proved to be a springboard to fame for Joseph von Sternberg and his electrifying protégée Marlene Dietrich. The same could be said for Christopher Isherwood. As a young British writer who came to Berlin during the period when *The Blue Angel* was released, his experiences there resulted in *The Berlin Stories* and two major films defining a troubled city heading toward the abyss of calamitous war under the leadership of Adolf Hitler's Third Reich. A prevailing restless social anarchy resulted in a perpetual party atmosphere for numerous Berliners while Germany marched toward war.

The restlessness of Berlin's socially anarchistic side was exemplified in colorful personal form by the irrepressible party girl Sally Bowles and her interrelationship with Isherwood and others in her wide circle of friends and acquaintances. *The Berlin Stories* was filmed twice, initially with a 1955 release as *I Am a Camera*, a black and white British production directed by Henry Cornelius with Anthony Harvey cast as Christopher Isherwood and Julie Harris portraying the irrepressible Sally Bowles, with excellent supporting work from Shelley Winters.

The 1972 release was a colorful musical, *Cabaret*. Liza Minnelli received an Oscar for "Best Actress" as Sally Bowles, putting her singing and dancing talents to work. Michael York played the young British writer who comes to Berlin and learns about life. (In this version he is called Brian Roberts.) The robust spectacle won eight Oscars, with director Bob Fosse, by then already a Broadway directing and choreography legend, winning a statuette. Another was won by cinematographer Geoffrey Unsworth, with yet another garnered in the "Best Music" category. The tone of the times was set to musical numbers performed by Sally at the club where she stars with the Master of Ceremonies (Joel Grey, who secured a "Best Supporting Actor" Oscar).

That historically rich period in which Isherwood wrote was a fecund period for Fritz Lang. His 1927 silent masterpiece *Metropolis* was a frightening dystopian epic about a future city dominated by technology and devoid of humanity. Brigitte Helm, portraying Maria, serves as a symbol of conscience. "There can be no understanding between the hand and the brain unless the heart acts as mediator," is one of her aphorisms. The film also contains a meaningful allegorical commentary from the socially conscious Maria with biblical significance: "'We shall build a tower that will reach to the stars!' Having conceived Babel, yet unable to build it themselves, they had thousands build it for them. But those who toiled knew nothing of the dreams of those who planned. And the minds that planned the Tower of Babel cared nothing for the workers who built it. The hymns of praise of the few became the curses of the many—BABEL! BABEL! BABEL!—Between the mind that plans and the hands that build there must be a Mediator, and this must be the heart."

Innocent Victims Amid Restless Anxiety

It was only natural for Lang, after a number of successes in Germany's film industry, to approach the advent of talkies with a sonic boom. In 1931, one year following the release of Sternberg's *The Blue Angel*, the early international sound classic *M* debuted. The film revealed a Berlin amid a siege of panic and helpless fury. A serial killer of children has just taken his ninth victim. In a city of panic anyone perceived as suspicious is grabbed and recommended for arrest and trial.

The fascinating twist that gives *M* its own special stamp of uniqueness stems from the fact that, as baffled police authorities look for answers, the criminal element of the city becomes concerned over losing its status. It sees its shakedown operation as in jeopardy so the decision is made to hunt down the serial killer of children. The audience is aware (while the citizens of Berlin are not) that Hans Beckert (Peter Lorre) is the killer. The unique twist of the story emerges when the criminal posse not only apprehends Beckert, but seeks to decide his fate. With the criminal element loudly demanding Beckert's swift execution, he explains his inability to control what he realizes is a tragically sick impulse. The citizens of Berlin are hardly in a position to judge given their own less than sterling record. It is a fascinating discussion of what constitutes criminal behavior and who should ultimately pass judgment on such conduct.

TRAGIC ISOLATION—Hans Beckert (Peter Lorre) seems to know that his murderous deeds will bring him to a tragic end in Fritz Lang's 1931 German film *M*.

Two noir films that Lang made in his American phase bear thematic connection to *M*. Christopher Cross (Edward G. Robinson) is a meek, henpecked husband who ultimately takes a life after becoming involved with femme fatale Katharine "Kitty" March (Joan Bennett) in *Scarlet Street* (1945). After being swindled out of money to which he was entitled through his brilliant painting talent by Katharine and lover, Johnny Prince (Dan Duryea), the formerly timid cashier attains sufficient towering rage to kill her. Ultimately, Christopher becomes responsible for two deaths since Johnny is convicted of murdering Katharine and is ultimately executed at Sing Sing Prison.

The eventual plight of the victimized philanderer thematically represents Fritz Lang's belief in morality. In Lang's view, punishment relates to an individual having to come to grips with his or her conduct. In *Scarlet Street*, Christopher is so tormented after causing Johnny's death as well as Katharine's that he attempts suicide. He is unsuccessful and is forced to endure brutal psychological punishment for his conduct. Lang believed that this type of punishment was more conclusive than that any legal authority could engender.

Lang's other great social concern that is thematically transformed into his work is the restless anxiety of the citizenry and how the innocent become victimized in this process. In addition to *M*, Lang tackled this point in the 1953 American release, *The Blue Gardenia*. The period in which the film was made is key, that of the McCarthy congressional hearings, one in which guilt by association and jumping swiftly to unwarranted conclusions were the

HOLLYWOOD'S LEGENDARY HEELS— Johnny Prince (Dan Duryea) and Katherine "Kitty" March (Joan Bennett) are a ruthless con team in Fritz Lang's *Scarlet Street* (1945).

order of the day. The film was made so quickly that Lang was inclined to overlook *The Blue Gardenia*, as he considered it a film of minor consequence. Careful scrutiny reveals it to be a biting commentary about a period wracked with accusation.

In the story, Norah Larkin (Anne Baxter) becomes terrorized as an angry city seeks her capture and trial after she awakens following a confrontation where she repulsed the advances of amorous photographer Harry Prebble (Raymond Burr). Norah passes out from excessive concoctions of Polynesian alcohol-laced specialties, awakening to find Harry dead. Her plight is worsened by her faulty memory of events preceding her collapse from the devastating impact of drinks Harry had induced her to drink. Meanwhile, headline hunting columnist Casey Mayo (Richard Conte) appeals to the person he calls "The Blue Gardenia Woman" due to the fact that she was seen in the Polynesian restaurant (which, incidentally, bears a resemblance to the popular Hollywood eatery and drinking spot Trader Vic's). Casey promises that if the woman turns herself in that his newspaper will bear all costs for the best defense to be obtained. When she does so he is forced to admit that it was all a ploy to attract headlines and stay ahead of his competition.

A performer's connective link exists between *M* and *The Blue Gardenia*. Peter Lorre became internationally famous for his stirring performance as Hans Beckert in the Berlin-made film. In *The Blue Gardenia*, Lorre's former wife, Vienna-born Celia Lovsky, has a brief but pivotal role as a blind flower woman. Lovsky's elegant European accent makes her performance all the more fascinating.[1]

The Viennese Connection

Too frequently the talented filmmakers who came to America to escape the long arm of Adolf Hitler and achieved some of their most impressive efforts in the film noir genre have been referred to strictly as Germans. Just as Berlin deserves its recognition, so does Vienna.

Fritz Lang, thought of by many as the quintessential German film director, was born in Vienna. Billy Wilder, whose work will be analyzed in this chapter, was born in Vienna but generally recognized as stemming from the German tradition. Otto Preminger, who will be analyzed in the next chapter, has been referred to in various biographical accounts as having been born either in Vienna or on his grandfather's farm in what was then Austro-Hungary and is now Austria.

Both Berlin and Vienna were exceedingly cosmopolitan cities of bustling activity amid culture and sophistication. Vienna has long been renowned as a city where East blends with West. This was the case at the close of World War II, when Vienna was divided into American, British, and Russian sectors. Such a blending of creative minds came to pass with *The Third Man* (1949), a joint venture produced by America's David O. Selznick and Britain's Alexander Korda. The script and directorial assignments went to two eminent British talents, author and scenarist Graham Greene and veteran director Carol Reed. Selznick supplied contractees Joseph Cotten and Alida Valli with starring roles. Greene needed a story to match the fascinating setting. It surfaced after he went to Vienna and talked to a British army officer stationed there. Greene was told about an outrageously fatal black market scheme to dilute penicillin and sell it to Vienna's hospitals.

The story centers around a pulp Western novelist Holly Martens (Joseph Cotten) traveling to Vienna to assist an old friend by ostensibly writing publicity on behalf of his hospital charity efforts. The friend is Harry Lime (Orson Welles), who does not appear until the final third of the film. A memorable scene ingeniously photographed by cinematographer Robert Krasker, from the Ferris wheel located in the Prater amusement park in the Vienna Woods, finds Harry pointing far below to tiny specks of humanity walking to and fro. He shocks his lifelong friend by asking if it would bother him if "one of those dots" stopped moving.

The visiting American writer gets caught in a nest of ruthless racketeers as willing to kill to achieve riches as his friend. Anna Schmidt (Alida Valli) is the woman caught in between. While Holly has desperately fallen in love with her, the conniving Harry, who has earlier faked his death to achieve freedom of movement in a military-occupied city, barters with the Soviets. He has revealed information that could result in Valli's repatriation back to Communist-occupied Czechoslovakia while Holly seeks to spare her such a result by cooperating with British army officer Major Calloway (Trevor Howard) in seeking to rein in Harry's deadly racket and its operatives.

Carol Reed can be thanked (and was, profoundly, at the time by scenarist Graham Greene) for changing the movie's end and giving it a film noir feel that helped move it into the ranks of international classic. The response was so strong in Europe that a theater in Vienna has played *The Third Man* full time for years to enthusiastic audiences.

Throughout the film a bumbling, drink-plied, but sincerely intentioned Holly Martens attempts to resolve the mystery surrounding Harry Lime's fake death, all the while falling more deeply in love with Anna Schmidt. His romantic efforts correspond to dangerous efforts to play detective while Major Calloway begs him to go back to America before he is killed. While his efforts had been previously unrequited in seeking romantic interest from Anna, Holly makes one last attempt after the real Harry Lime is buried. When Major Calloway's Jeep passes Anna in the Vienna Woods after the funeral, Holly asks to be let out. Greene's script originally called for the two to walk off together. Reed, thankfully, saw that *The Third Man* needed to stand on a logical foundation rather than appealing to conventional tastes, a decision that enhances the film's overall impact. After all, it was Holly who had cooperated with Major Calloway in seeking to bring down his former friend. It was ultimately Holly at the unspoken request of a badly wounded Harry, who finishes him off with a single deadly shot. In addition, Anna remained hopelessly in love with Harry contrary to logic, considering Holly a turncoat even while his effort in assisting Major Calloway was to prevent her repatriation by the Russians back to Soviet-controlled Czechoslovakia.

The scene wherein Anna spurns Holly was done with such consummate skill that the unwary actor provided an unrehearsed touch that gave the final scene a spontaneous finality. Cotten described the event in his autobiography:

> Nobody uttered a word. The camera kept rolling. The special effects men from their high perches continued to drop toasted autumn leaves from above. I continued to puff on my cigarette, and began to get quite panic-stricken. Was there more to the scene? Had I gone blank? What was Carol waiting for me to do? I took one more puff, then in exasperation threw the cigarette to the ground, at which point Carol shouted through his laughter the word I had been waiting desperately to hear — "Cut."

In addition to the final rejection by Anna there is all the pondering about delivering the final deadly shot, ending the life of a friend from boyhood. This was the friend with whom he was planning to rekindle an association in what he initially believed to be a worthwhile hospital charities pursuit, what he obviously hoped would be a step up from writing his pulp novels. Not only did Holly find that Harry had turned into a sociopath who would stop at nothing to make money, he learned that he was even willing to turn a woman who loved him over to Communist authorities for repatriation. The fact that she continued to love Harry was perhaps the most savage cut of all.[2]

Reed Switches Suspense Scene to Berlin

Peter Ustinov, a neighbor of Carol Reed's on King's Road in the Southwest London borough of Chelsea, told an anecdote indicating the domination of film in the life of the famous director. Reed had innocently asked, "What's a Cold War?"

Despite this uninformed response, it would be but a short time before Reed would learn about the Cold War via the pursuit that dominated his thoughts — cinema. As Ken Annakin, a directing talent discovered by Reed, explained, "Carol's life was dominated by looking for stories to film."

This pursuit of story material led Reed to direct a film like his 1949 classic *The Third Man* with its fascinating international political dimensions of Vienna's control being divided up among three major powers in an early Cold War atmosphere. Just four years later another film under Reed's banner would be released with stronger Cold War overtones and undertones, *The Man Between*. While that 1953 film was not of the same classic level of *The Third Man* it was a shrewdly done, moody suspense piece that brought out the stark contrasts between East and West Berlin during a period of acute Cold War tensions. The Western powers exemplified by the North Atlantic Treaty Organization led by the U.S. were locked in stern competition which many thought could result in a nuclear confrontation against the Warsaw Pact dominated by the Soviet Union.

James Mason had starred for Carol Reed in the 1947 drama *Odd Man Out*. Mason is cast as idealistic Irish Republican Army member Johnny McQueen, who becomes involved in a bank holdup to secure needed funds in the campaign to nationalize Ulster. The effort goes awry and McQueen is fatally wounded. Before he dies he makes a series of stops in his desperate state, hoping to elude the police and make it to at least temporary safety.

The authentic Belfast locations add to the stirring tone of reality as the ever-weakening protagonist moves increasingly closer to death's door. Carol Reed's brilliant cinematographer Robert Krasker adroitly uses close-ups to heighten the action. Scenarists F.L. Green and R.C. Sherriff gauge that action, in accordance with Northern Ireland's division between Catholics and Protestants, to include McQueen's meetings with some believing him to be a patriot and seeking to help him and those who loathe his IRA link and desire him to be captured.

Lukey (Robert Newton) is an artist who seeks fame from McQueen's plight, hoping to capture the tragedy of a man in the throes of death. McQueen escapes from the pub where the two had met, moving onward toward the dock, where he will meet his ultimate end. Kathleen Sullivan (Kathleen Ryan), who had temporarily hidden McQueen in her home, receives word that he has been badly wounded in a bank robbery and sets out to locate him for one final meeting.

Reed's shrewd casting instincts could not have worked better in selecting James Mason for another role of great sensitivity. The Yorkshireman had a face that blended sensitivity with keen intelligence. Mason was born in the British mill town of Huddersfield. His father was a prosperous wool merchant. Mason received a degree in architecture from Cambridge University, but after being bitten by the acting bug his initial career objective was abandoned. Before reaching his ultimate pinnacle as a richly talented screen star, Mason, in typical British fashion, carved out a notable career in the theater as an Old Vic production regular.

Mason could become an instantly effective screen tragedian when his keenly intelligent expression was turned toward sadness. Mason played the tortured man of sensitivity to perfection in several films, including the 1949 release *The Reckless Moment* opposite Joan Bennett for German director Max Ophuls. Mason also played the alcoholic former Hollywood star turned has been Norman Maine opposite Judy Garland in George Cukor's 1954 musical drama *A Star is Born*. In 1962, he played Professor Humbert Humbert, a man so totally consumed with the nubile charms of pre-adult Lolita (Sue Lyon) in Stanley Kubrick's adaptation of Vladimir Nabokov's provocative novel that he kills his rival, Clare Quilty (Peter Sellers). Alfred Hitchcock turned Mason's intelligence in a ruthless direction in the 1959 vehicle *North by Northwest*, alongside Cary Grant and Eva Marie Saint. Just two year before his death in 1984, Mason received a "Best Supporting Actor" Oscar nomination for playing the smarmy corporate lawyer pitted against Frank Galvin (Paul Newman) in *The Verdict*. Director Sidney Lumet, like Hitchcock, saw that Mason was capable of playing a ruthless heavy.

Sacrificing His Life for Others

In *The Reckless Moment* Mason is Martin Donnelly, a man with a checkered past willing to sacrifice his life so that housewife Lucia Harper (Joan Bennett) is not arrested and prosecuted for the death of a ruthless criminal she kills while protecting her daughter, Bea (Geraldine Brooks). Martin deeply loves Lucia, knows he will never have her, but believes he can save her, even at the cost of his life.

The same conclusion is reached in *The Man Between* with Susanne Mallison (Claire Bloom) the woman he deeply loves, but with the ultimate futility of knowing that things could never work out in the manner that he desires. Ivo Kern (Mason), a lawyer by trade, is trapped in a cold, despairing existence capturing Westerners for the East German government in the midst of savage Cold War competition involving East and West Berlin. Susanne travels from her London home to visit her brother, Martin (Geoffrey Toone), a major in the British Army, where he serves as a doctor, and his wife, Bettina (Hildegard Neff). The plot thickens after Susanne meets Ivo, thereby enabling Martin and Bettina to discover that Ivo, presumed dead in the war, is very much alive. Since Martin and Bettina were married at the time of his presumed death, a cloud of legitimacy is accordingly thrown over their marriage.

The Cold War tensions are in evidence throughout, with the authentic Berlin locations enhancing the effect. The black and white photography of Desmond Dickinson imparts a message of troubled times and people, when those traveling into the eastern sector of Berlin are taking enormous chances. Carol Reed was one of filmdom's most effective directors at establishing mood, and it is achieved with a flair for the somber. The political danger of the period is enhanced by the proliferation of large pictures of General Secretary of the Soviet Union Central Committee Joseph Stalin. This conveys the impression of an Orwellian Big Brother watching at every turn.

Amid this backdrop, young and naïve Susanne Mallison receives a fast education, falling in love under such ponderous, ultimately impossible circumstances with the highly experienced, cynical Ivo Kern. A brief dialogue exchange from Harry Kurnitz's script between Ivo and Susanne reveals much about them:

> KERN (rubbing one of Mallison's feet): Are your feet cold?
> MALLISON: Yes, and my hands are cold. Your heart is the coldest of all.
> KERN : I can warm your feet for you. It's a pity you can't do anything about my heart.
> MALLISON : I could try.
> KERN : Why should you bother?

Ivo speaks as a dead man, someone who wishes he could have met a young woman like Susanne under different circumstances. He recognizes that he can do nothing but bring consternation into her life should any attachment be attempted. Susanne escapes with her freedom, returning to West Berlin.[3]

Burton Stars in British Cold War Noir

Richard Burton died in Celigny, Switzerland, on July 27, 1984. One week later, on August 5, James Mason succumbed to a fatal heart attack in nearby Lausanne, Switzerland. This marked one final linkage of many. The classically trained performers possessed handsome, refined features, conveying great intelligence. Along with the frequent concomitant of keen intelligence, there existed the melancholia of those recognizing the troubled side of humanity. How helpful this gift was for Burton and Mason in brooding black and white British noir dramas. How particularly notable it was in the realm of British Cold War noir.

Burton secured one of his seven Best Actor Oscar nominations for his tour de force as the cynical British intelligence agent in *The Spy Who Came In from the Cold* (1965). In this masterful film, the intelligence operatives fighting the Cold War are either not able to distinguish the competing sides or, if they can, they no longer care. The script, adapted by Paul Dehn and Guy Trosper, originally stemmed from a source highly knowledgeable about the coldly impersonal, deadly world about which he wrote.

David John Moore Cornwell was born in Dorset, England, in 1931. After studying foreign languages at Berne University in Switzerland he joined the British foreign service in 1950. Two years later he returned to his studies at Lincoln College, Oxford, while still undertaking assignments for Britain's domestic service MI5. After receiving his degree with honors and teaching French and German at Eton College, Oxford, Cornwell ultimately joined MI5 full time in 1958. His responsibilities involved running agents, conducting interrogations, tapping phones, and performing authorized break-ins. In 1960, Cornwell joined MI6, Britain's foreign intelligence agency. He worked under the diplomatic cover of the second secretary in the British Embassy in West Germany's capital city of Bonn. He was then transferred to Hamburg as a political counsel.

During this German phase Cornwell wrote two books, one of which would become his biggest seller. It was not acceptable for those working in the British Foreign Service to use their actual names as authors and Cornwell thereupon invented the nom de plume by which he would become famously known throughout the world, John le Carré, which in French means "the square."

In 1963, *The Spy Who Came In from the Cold* reached bookstores for the first time, hitting readers around the globe like a sharp punch to the solar plexus. Le Carré stepped well beyond the Ian Fleming world of glamorized fantasy in Cold War espionage, presenting a brutal reality from an insider's unique perspective.

John le Carré was one of three great British authors with intelligence backgrounds. The others were Graham Greene and W. Somerset Maugham. In the case of le Carré, however, his riveting analysis of intelligence operatives and those with whom they interact related to the dirtiest of double dealings on the part of governments claiming the moral high road as they competed for the minds of citizens of the global community during the peak of Cold War paranoia.

Director Martin Ritt had been one of many Hollywood victims of the Cold War, a casualty of the blacklist. His perspective gave him the knowledge and resolve to do a film on the topic as he turned in one of his supreme efforts directing *The Front* (1976). Woody Allen plays a docile New York restaurant cashier who becomes a front man for blacklisted television writers, posing as the author of scripts they provide. One novel aspect of *The Front* compared to other critical works on the blacklist period is the participation of individuals who directly suffered, such as Ritt, co-star Zero Mostel, and screenwriter Walter Bernstein.

The New York–born Ritt, up to the time he directed *The Spy Who Came In from the Cold*, had never tackled anything like the subject of Cold War intrigue, but had directed films dealing with the kind of hard-edged subject matter that unfolds in the 1965 British Cold War noir classic. Ritt made the move from television to film directing with two 1957 efforts that identified him as an uncompromising talent who tackled the tough side of life. *Edge of the City* found Axel Nordmann (John Cassavettes) befriending fellow New York longshoreman Tommy Tyler (Sidney Poitier) from the antagonism of racist co-worker Charles Malik (Jack Warden). *No Down Payment* focused on the suburban Southern California scene in the fifties and how young couples interact. The fact that Joanne Woodward was one of the film's stars correlated with where Ritt's career would take him from that point.

Ritt had trained as an apprentice actor during the final period of New York's famed Group Theater. It was the first theatrical group in America to put Stanislavski's practices into action. Ritt appeared as Sam and was an assistant stage manager for the 1939 premiere of Clifford Odets's *Golden Boy*. Appearing in that same production were future film greats John Garfield, Elia Kazan, and Michael Gordon.

As a technically trained New York City method actor Ritt could relate to Paul Newman, a product of the heralded New York Actors Studio. When he directed Newman in the screen adaptations of William Faulkner's *The Hamlet*, and *The Long Hot Summer* (1958), the sparks were rekindled from Newman's former association with Joanne Woodward as joint cast members for the William Inge stage drama *Picnic*. Shortly thereafter the two future Oscar winners married (after Newman was able to obtain a divorce).

It is understandable why, along with their shared New York method acting training, Ritt would form a creative association with Newman that would span five films, ending with *Hombre* (1967). The New York school, with the emphasis on Stanislavski's method technique, stresses adopting an objective and pursuing it within a scene. This type of acting involves seeking out creative challenges that prompt performers to shed a "beast from within." In method acting an emphasis is placed on the internal dynamics of a performance. By stressing tension through eye expressions and vocal inflections, a trained performer of the method technique and other schools in which such dynamics are emphasized can register discontent extending to acute hostility and rage without raising one's voice. In the hands of a film director possessing the creative ingenuity of a Martin Ritt, such a technique can be utilized to even greater advantage than on stage.

Burton's Electrifying Voice

The son of a Welsh coal miner, Richard Walter Jenkins, Jr., won a scholarship to study drama at Oxford University, thanks to the tutelage of his schoolmaster, Phillip Burton, from whom he later acquired his professional name. In the manner of Ritt and Paul Newman, Richard Burton then began a long period of stage activity, which started early in the forties. Like Newman, Burton had expressive eyes and a dynamic inner energy that could be internalized and drawn out by the intimacy of the camera. His major breakthrough came when he played the rebellious Jimmy Porter in the 1959 socially evocative *Look Back in Anger*, directed by Tony Richardson, who had earlier served in that same capacity for the John Osborne play. Osborne touched off a new movement in British intellectual circles: the "Angry Young Man" revolt. Richard Burton, then in his early thirties, depicted a character at least a half decade younger. While the play's plot revolves significantly around a love triangle consisting of Jimmy Porter's wife, Alison (played by dramatist Osborne's spouse at the time, Mary Ure), and Helena Charles (Claire Bloom, with whom Burton would be reunited in *The Spy Who Came In from the Cold*), the play and resulting film set off fireworks based on the loud eruptions of Jimmy Porter over his perceived purposelessness and inflexibility of fifties' British middle-class life.

A dominant aspect of Burton's persona in the film is the use of his effortlessly hypnotic voice. In *The Spy Who Came In from the Cold*, every tone, every nuance is fine-tuned to inform viewers of the quiet desperation of an agent who has spent his adult life in the dirty business of spying. This exposure has left him embittered and desperate to the point where he realizes it is impossible for him to extricate himself from his dilemma. He clearly expects to pass into the great beyond reserved for agents put out to pasture. The only question is when and how this result will occur. This is the point at which Burton's character, Alec Leamas, is introduced.

Readers of the John le Carré bestseller saw a craftsman in control of his subject matter use the narrative process to describe the combustible inner rage felt by the British MI6 foreign agent. In order to depict this kind of deep character insight, it is essential for an actor to invest, through expression and inflection, an internalized performance that creates audience awareness. The thorough professionals can accomplish this objective through a subtle facial expression or change in voice tone. Lesser performers feel compelled to shout, gesticulate, or generate more expansive expressions to make their points.

Burton presents the complex character of Alec Leamas through a commanding subtlety of tone and expression. Here is an intelligence professional who has kept his true feelings bottled up for years. Ultimately what do those true feelings really constitute? A political agnosticism results as Leamas, seeing so much double-dealing in Cold War political chess playing, concludes that ultimately nothing makes sense. This is an atmosphere where the players often change sides, or appear to do so, with the twinkling of an eye.

In from the Cold, Into the Freezer

The film and the le Carré novel from which it was adapted could be alternatively titled "In from the Cold, Into the Freezer." Leamas's boss, known in intelligence parlance as Control (Cyril Cusack), brings him in from active service, but the operative has participated on the active front so long he has no taste for a desk job in the banking division. Control tells him the agency wishes to keep him in the cold for one more assignment.

In the labyrinthine system of which he is a part, Leamas moves from the cold into the freezer. He is tricked to the point that the veteran intelligence operative expresses professional admiration for the way that he, as well as Nan Perry (Claire Bloom) have been effectively played by Britain's MI6.

The assignment that Control reveals is different from what was actually concocted, as Leamas will ruefully learn. The ostensible purpose for the assignment is to thwart East Germany's intelligence chief, Hans-Dieter Mundt (Peter Van Eyck), someone who has been killing Britain's secret agents posted there, including one recent operative of Burton's.

Martin Ritt, in his dual capacity of producer and director, made a deft move in selecting veteran scenarist Paul Dehn to hone le Carré's novel into a screenplay. Britisher Dehn secured an Oscar for the team of Roy and John Boulting for the 1950 spine-tingling thriller *Seven Days to Noon*. Dehn secured an Academy Award along with James Bernard for "Best Writing" and "Best Motion Picture Story." Dehn also displayed his deft touch for exploring with intelligent subtlety the world of espionage in the 1967 spy film *The Deadly Affair*. Not only did Dehn exhibit a flair for the realistic, black and white spy film, he also mastered the subject from the splashy, romantic world of color with the James Bond thriller *Goldfinger* (1964).

Guy Trosper shares writing credit with Dehn on *The Spy Who Came In from the Cold*. Trosper was also an experienced scenarist who had co-written the heartwarming script for the James Stewart baseball vehicle *The Stratton Story* (1949) and the Burt Lancaster true-life drama adaptation *Birdman of Alcatraz* (1962).

The Spy Who Came In from the Cold is that rare film that does not disappoint those who love the novel from which it was adapted. The cold murkiness and savage opportunism of opposing Cold War forces was adapted into the film. The twin components of personal anarchy and doom are etched into Burton's expressive features as he brings the le Carré creation of Alec Leamas dramatically to life on screen.

Creating a New Persona

The assignment for which Leamas was selected involved the creation of a new persona. In order to make him look like a good candidate to go over to the other side (East Germany, in this case), the impression must be made that he has truly gone to seed. Hence a piece of dirty work is undertaken that will put him at odds with authorities.

Leamas's acting assignment for MI6 finds him entering a London market run by a mild-mannered proprietor who has extended credit to him in the past. He enters the market in an inebriated state and makes obnoxious comments to other shoppers before setting down some selected items and demanding additional credit. The incident has been timed in a manner whereby Leamas is certain that the soft-spoken store owner will turn him down this time. Violence results when Leamas administers a beating to the store proprietor. From there the action shifts to Wormwood Scrubs Prison, north of Notting Hill Gate in Kensington, a familiar area of Southwest London in which a good deal of the film takes place.

The idea behind Leamas going to prison was for the East to make contact with him; that happens once he is released from Wormwood Scrubs. Pursuing him is Ashe (Michael Hordern, an even more familiar figure on the London stage than on the international screen. In the fifties, Hordern befriended a young Richard Burton. The future superstar was resolutely learning his craft following his earlier Oxford training. Later in his career Hordern would become renowned as one of England's most notable King Lears. Hordern worked with Burton in eight films). Ashe makes contact with Leamas in a London park. Even though subterfuge is employed as Ashe explains that he represents a group that seeks to rehabilitate former prisoners, he shifts quickly to the real purpose in explaining that Leamas could assist in providing valuable information to assist writers on articles about international politics. He is clearly being asked to move to the other side — for a price. As damaged goods, he will never again be used by MI6.

British Noir Homophobia

Leamas needles Ashe from the beginning and clearly holds him in utter disrespect, but the feeling is rooted in his distaste for the spy game. Toward the end of the film Leamas tells Nan Perry, the only person toward whom he holds any genuine feeling, about "queers and henpecked husbands" who gravitate into the spy game. He explains that it is a way in which the vulnerable seek to make themselves appear important. Leamas's point is shrewdly made in the scene where Ashe invites him to meet his superior, Peters (Sam Wanamaker, who, like Martin Ritt, was a victim of the McCarthy blacklist. In Wanamaker's case he moved permanently to London. Near the end of his life he became prominently involved with the effort to reconsecrate the Globe Theatre). When Leamas once more insults Ashe in Peters's presence at the strip club where they meet, the organization's courier reacts for the first time. He tells Leamas that he will accept insults in private but not in front of someone he respects. Ashe's low status is exposed when Peters, rather than being touched by the courier's respect for him, dismisses him. Ashe is told to leave as Peters explains that he has business to discuss with Leamas. Ashe departs without saying another word, indicating his meek subservience and low position within the spy world's organizational structure.

Love in Bloom and George Smiley

When Leamas is invited to Nan Perry's apartment for dinner, he learns that she is an active member of the London branch of Britain's Communist Party. Leamas laughs resoundingly

LONELY MAN FINDS LOVE—Alec Leamas (Richard Burton), a lonely and cynical British intelligence operative, finds love with equally isolated librarian Nan Perry (Claire Bloom) in *The Spy Who Came In from the Cold*, a 1965 Cold War noir epic adapted from a bestseller by John le Carré.

upon learning of Perry's affiliation. His reason stems, not from any opposition to Communist ideology per se, but to a broadly based nihilistic viewpoint that nothing matters in a thoroughly disjointed world. Leamas's view is that the Number 11 bus will take him to his flat in the Hammersmith section of Southwest London but that he does not expect it "to be driven by Father Christmas."

Leamas will learn in time that Perry was meant to serve a strategic purpose in the cunning plans of MI6, and that it would be every bit as surprising and unexpected as what his agency had in store for him. Ensuing events only strengthen his core belief that the Cold War is no more than a sad and tragic development in a world that is devoid of purpose.

Leamas accepts the offer extended by Peters to travel abroad and provide information to East Germany. George Smiley (Rupert Davies) visits Perry on the pretext of helping her. Instead, Perry will later become a pawn along with Leamas in the machinations of British intelligence. By contacting her, Smiley intentionally establishes a record of contact with British intelligence. Later, Perry is given the opportunity to visit East Germany. She believes that her sincere efforts as a London Communist Party member is the reason for the invitation. She will ultimately learn that she has been duped, as has Leamas.

Leamas visits Smiley at his flat, located in Chelsea near Kings Road and Sloane Square, where the Royal Court Theatre is situated. Smiley hosts the meeting between Leamas and Control. When Leamas leaves on his trip to meet his East Germany contact, Smiley tags along to see that he gets there and initiates contact.

Oskar Werner as Interrogator

Leamas initially flies to Holland to be interrogated by Fiedler. (Oskar Werner, whose Golden Globe-winning role bore resemblance to his own life. An avowed pacifist, Werner used resourcefulness after being conscripted into the German army to avoid conflict and involved himself in kitchen duties by feigning incompetence. His position was made more tenuous by the fact that he married a woman who was half Jewish. They had a child and were forced to hide out in the Vienna woods to escape from both the German and Russian military after Werner's home city was besieged.) He lashes out at him angrily when he learns that his missing-person status has been reported in a London newspaper, meaning he has been outed. Fiedler responds with equivalent anger, then coolly tells him that the information was not leaked by East German intelligence and must have been revealed by MI6. This provides a valuable clue as to where the story is headed, with British intelligence setting Leamas up while rendering Fiedler vulnerable. Fiedler's angry rebuttal to Leamas's outburst is highlighted by the revelation that, as a "traitor" passing secrets to a former enemy, this marks him as the "lowest currency" of the Cold War.

Werner does his best to see that his interrogation of Burton is accomplished. His professional intelligence instinct tells him something is awry and he announces that the interrogation will resume in East Germany since Holland no longer seems safe. Something has been compromised somewhere and this is just the beginning regarding what both Fiedler and Leamas will ultimately learn.

The passionately committed Fiedler is immersed in a power struggle with the sadistic Mundt. Their control struggle is augmented by the brutal reality that Mundt is a former Nazi, and Fiedler is Jewish, resulting in seething hatred and distrust on both sides.

Double Dealing Minus Femmes Fatales

Two events prompt Alec Leamas to recognize that he has been used as a pawn by his own agency. Suddenly the tide is turned on a flabbergasted Fiedler, who shifts from the prosecutor in the trial of hated rival Mundt to the prosecuted. A linchpin in the strategy is unwitting innocent Nan Perry. By presenting evidence more apparent than real, suspicion of a relationship between the MI6 agent and his Communist Party girlfriend, facts are twisted to shift the onus of traitor to the East German cause to Fiedler. Leamas does his best to shield Perry, explaining that she knows nothing, and indicating his willingness to accept whatever punishment will be ultimately meted out by East German Communist authorities.

When a ruling is made that Fiedler be put on trial it is obvious that his destiny will be a firing squad, a penalty imposed by the very government to which he was faithfully committed. Leamas is distraught when Perry is jailed and treated as bearing guilt equal to his own. Just as Leamas has decided that his fate will be as grim as that of Fiedler, and silently bemoans unwittingly involving Perry in such deadly circumstances, he is summoned in the darkness of early morning. He is told by Mundt that he, along with Perry, must leave immediately. He will drive to a certain point and abandon his car. An escort will then be provided to drive them to Checkpoint Charlie, where they will be afforded just enough time to jump from the wall and into West Berlin and ultimate safety. Mundt explains that the incident will be passed off as a prisoner escape.

Leamas sardonically explains everything to a dumbfounded Perry. Mundt visited London as an ostensible part of a steel delegation from East Germany, his cover for his spy status with East Germany's Secret Police. When he killed a man while in England the stage was set for British intelligence to move in, enabling him to return to his own country, on the condition that he thereafter serve the interests of MI6. He had, after all, moved from the Nazi youth movement to Communism, and was resourcefully pragmatic to switch again, given the hold that England held over him. He was compelled to cooperate with the British or face a murder charge. Mundt's persona is explained in one succinct sentence: "Before he was evil and my enemy," Leamas says. "Now he is evil and my friend."

The entire premise of the picture could be summarized in another of Leamas's statements as he attempts to obliterate what is left of Perry's idealism: "What the hell do you think spies are? Moral philosophers measuring everything they do by the word of God or Karl Marx? They're just a bunch of squalid, seedy bastards like me: little men, drunkards, queers, henpecked husbands, civil servants playing cowboys and Indians to brighten their rotten little lives. Do you think they sit like monks in a cell, balancing right against wrong?"

Leamas, in his sharp exchanges with Fiedler, reveals how little value he places on himself. "I reserve the right to be ignorant," he exclaims at one point. "That's the Western way of life." He offers more in the same vein: "I'm a man, you fool. A plain, stupid, muddled, fat-headed human being. We have them in the West, you know." At another point in the film he explains his romantic relationship with Perry: "She offered me free love. At the time it was all I could afford."

A Vapid, Endless World of Darkness

One way of injecting mood into a film is through dialogue, in this case terse, sardonic words expressed by a veteran intelligence agent in the midst of a Cold War. Another is through the camera, and in *The Spy Who Came In from the Cold* this is superbly done. Cinematographer Oswald Morris, who would later receive an Oscar for his work on *Fiddler on the Roof* (1971) and nominations for *Oliver!* (1968) and *The Wiz* (1978), creates a dark, vapid world. When Alec Leamas flies from London to be interrogated initially in Holland and flown to East Germany for more of the same, filmgoers are shown open spaces on a seeming road to nowhere. Even when Burton and Werner walk along a beach during the Holland interrogation phase it is amid daytime darkness, with nary a soul in sight.

The interrelated twin themes of loneliness and purposelessness are carried forward to the film's conclusion. It is obvious from all that has occurred that the only influence prompting Leamas to care about living is Perry. When they reach the wall at Check Point Charlie, he carefully guides her up the ladder. Just then, she is fired upon and killed immediately. Nan Perry, the young librarian who had joined the Communist Party for idealistic reasons, had been found expendable. The peripatetic George Smiley, the eyes and ears of British intelligence, is on the scene. "Jump, Alec!" he beckons from the other side of the wall. Leemas has no intention of jumping. The only person he cares for in the world has been gunned down before his eyes. What reason does he have to live?

The film comes to an abrupt and logical end. Leamas knows he will have only a few precious seconds to make his leap from East to West. He stands there, knowing what will happen and presumably welcoming the finality of the moment. Gunfire ensues and Alec Leemas is dead.

Richard Burton was an actor of commanding presence. His voice of many inflections was a developed gift, generating fascination. Burton conveyed an electricity and intelligence that was demanded for the role of Alec Leemas. He never faltered for an instant, delivering perhaps the most truly memorable performance of his career.

Chapter Ten

Siodmak's Phantom Femmes

> If she'd been trading one-liners with Dennis O'Keefe and Dan Duryea, she'd have a much more memorable screen persona.—Eddie Muller on Ella Raines

Robert Siodmak was a graduate of the Berlin cinema school who applied his lessons with consummate brilliance after emigrating to the United States during the massive creative talent exodus from Europe during the World War II period. His productive Berlin period caused him to recognize the magic that the camera can produce in the world of film and *Phantom Lady* is a glittering testimony of his enriching imagination at work.

Siodmak was born in Dresden. An injury sustained as a result of a school fight left the boy with reduced vision. With his trademark glasses he was stamped in acting, his early profession of choice, as a heavy. Recognizing his reduced opportunities to move up the acting ladder, his focus shifted to directing, for which the Berlin and Hollywood film communities along with a constellation of international movie viewers can be thankful.

Siodmak as well as his brother, screenwriter Curt, were among the talented ranks relocating to Hollywood during the Third Reich war period. Initially Robert lived in frustration, awaiting a project into which he could eagerly sink his teeth. That opportunity came with *Phantom Lady* and Siodmak's skilled hand wove a rich tapestry across a cinema canvas that breathed creative life and vigorous imagination.

The Berlin training of Siodmak served him well with his imaginative sketches along with his brilliant depiction of New York City within the confines of Hollywood sound stages. Economy was the watchword and Berlin-trained cinema geniuses such as Siodmak, Billy Wilder, and Fritz Lang could produce the intimate feel of a major city without the necessity of location filming. Such was the case with Siodmak and his enriching portrait of New York in *Phantom Lady*. Contained within America's largest city are scores of diverse people with stories of their own. Siodmak let the camera speak for him as its exploring intimacy detailed two characters around whom memorable scenes were etched by cinematographer Woody Bedell.[1]

Phantom Lady was adapted to the screen by Bernard Schoenfeld from a novel by Cornell Woolrich. The unique mastery of suspense fiction by Woolrich involves zeroing in on characters within a busy city and provides a voyeur's touch by exploring intimate details of their lives. Such an approach is readily adaptable to film, providing numerous enriching opportunities for imaginative directors and scenarists.[2]

This film revolves around the film noir dilemma of a man trapped by circumstances. Young and handsome engineer Scott Henderson (Alan Curtis) would seemingly have the world at his feet with an opportunity to flourish in Manhattan. At the film's outset, however, we see a troubled man of 32 who sits in a bar with a lonely, troubled expression. He has temporarily retreated from his apartment and a loveless marriage to a bar for a few drinks before attending a popular Broadway musical. Henderson has an extra ticket. His wife will not be at his side, and he dreads going alone.

Ann Terry (Fay Helm), a woman wearing a distinctively colorful hat, sits next to him in the bar. Henderson approaches her in a shy manner. He explains that he has an extra ticket for the show and nobody to use it. She mulls his unique request to accompany her, but refuses to tell him her name. Terry explains that this will be their sole meeting and that it is better for them not to know each other's names.

Ann Terry's insistence on anonymity forms an important building block in the story. By not having a name the important noir suspense element is enhanced through the important story mechanism of barrier creation. Suspense is enhanced by meeting barriers, surmounting them, then confronting new ones.

Enter Detective Chewing Gum

After watching the musical together they go their separate ways. Upon entering his apartment, Henderson receives a jolt. He finds it occupied by Inspector Burgess (Thomas Gomez) and his fellow New York Police Department associates. Henderson's astonishment reaches advanced shock level as he learns that his beautiful wife has been killed.

A ploy is used in the scene that demonstrates the position Henderson occupies, as someone who is the logical suspect in the strangulation of his wife. Regis Toomey, a fixture in many dramas of the forties and fifties, is cast simply as Detective Chewing Gum. He has no name nor does he need any. Nor does he need dialogue, of which he has precious little. What Pittsburgh-born Irish character actor Regis Toomey becomes is a gnawing presence whose perennial pacing almost wears a hole in the rug; his is a symbolic role in the progression of events.

The incessant staring at Henderson by Chewing Gum illustrates the vulnerable position the handsome young architect occupies. The relentlessness of the gum chewing beckons thoughts of the wear and tear confronting an innocent victim beset by the law of averages, the statistical awareness that the most likely perpetrator of the homicide death of Curtis's wife is her husband. This is a scene played without histrionics and marked by the symbolism of one officer chewing gum and another seeking answers from Henderson that he cannot supply, enhancing suspicion in his direction. If such a woman existed as the attractive woman in the hat, then why is he so glaringly absent of information about her?

While viewers are aware of Henderson's innocence, his comments appear to a trained eye to be far-fetched. Why did his wife not accompany him to the show? Would he really give a spare ticket to a strange woman he met casually in a bar and then not learn anything about her, not even her name?

Both cinematically, with Toomey looming large with his restless walking and gum chewing, as well as dramatically with Gomez seeking answers that Curtis is unable to supply, the scene is a rousing success. It sets the stage at a crucial early juncture for what is to follow in the film's story development.

An important thematic thread is established in this scene. Detective Chewing Gum's pattern of silence is broken at the end of the scene as he tells Henderson that his wife was strangled with a necktie that was tied so tight that it was necessary to use a knife to remove it from the victim's throat.

The ingenuity of the interrogation scene when Henderson returns home from the show and finds his wife strangled is notable for its effective three-tiered approach. The unfolding activities prompt the stunned Curtis to veer from sadness to helplessness to anger. The anger occurs with the questioning of Detective Tom (Joseph Crehan). Due to his disbelief over Henderson's explanation of where he was when the murder was occurring, the case-hardened detective lashes out with sarcastic comments at the suspected husband, letting him know that he finds his explanation implausible. This leads to disgust since Tom feels that the police detectives are being deceived in a manner that angers him since he believes that their collective intelligence is being insulted.

Siodmak along with scenarist Bernard Schoenfeld have presented a taut, snappy noir scene that projects the story forward into the realm of a defendant whose story is not believed and the race to save him from execution for a murder he did not commit. While a thoroughly frustrated, totally stunned Henderson faces a nightmare of questioning over the murder of his wife, a trio of sharply defined New York police detectives operates as a functioning Greek chorus demanding answers. Meanwhile, lead detective Burgess pursues a middle ground, patiently probing Henderson.

Two Hats and Scenic Symbolism

A creative tour de force of *Phantom Lady* is constructing a film noir drama around a mystery lady wearing a large hat. This element is underscored with unique effect when that lady shows up at the theater with Henderson and draws the immediate ire of the show's hot-blooded Brazilian singing and dancing star. (If the performer is reminiscent of Fox's Brazilian bombshell Carmen Miranda there is a good reason beyond their joint national heritage. Playing the role of Estella Monteiro is Aurora Miranda, Carmen's younger sister by six years. Unlike her career-ambitious older sister, Aurora Miranda preferred married life and raising a family to a show business career and returned to Rio de Janeiro to raise a family.)

Once again, the camera reveals dramatic sparks. In this case the clash involves the identical hat that each woman wears. The film audience learns later that the hot-blooded performer has reason to be furious when she observes Ann Terry in a front-row seat wearing an identical hat. With hats being a trademark of her musical act, she insists on originality. Much later, and after much investigation, it is learned that a woman working for the company making the hat engaged in secret action to enable it to be made again in violation of an agreement, of which Ann Terry was unaware.

The use of the hat is a clever ploy. It provides a visual mystery element that compounds the plot. Not only is a mysterious woman with no known name being sought. In addition there is the element of the hat. Perhaps the hat can be found and then the woman can as well. The hat element is suggestive of two later film noir efforts involving Raymond Chandler and German directorial giant Fritz Lang, *The Blue Dahlia* and *The Blue Gardenia* and the visual emphasis on flowers as part of evolving mystery dramas.

A Drummer's Wild Eroticism

The creative scenic innovation of Siodmak extends to an imaginatively suggestive sequence taking place in the same theater where the two hats and frazzled women wearing

BATTLE OF WITS—Carol Richman (Ella Raines) plays the role of a crude flirt to extract information from Cliff the drummer (Elisha Cook, Jr.) in *Phantom Lady* (1944).

them occurred. Carol "Kansas" Richman (Ella Raines), Henderson's faithful secretary who is deeply in love with him, is extending every effort to prove his innocence in the face of increasingly long odds. Richman is a highly dignified, naturally reserved young woman from Kansas. The one thing she is not is a flirt, but she assumes that role in an effort to assist her boss by playing up to a drummer named Cliff (Elisha Cook, Jr.).

Elisha Cook, Jr. fit the bill as a vulnerable figure in the early stage of his career. The short, wiry actor looked even more youthful than his actual years and possessed the vulnerable look of someone seeking to find his way. Cook's role in *Phantom Lady* marked a partial departure from his roles in *The Maltese Falcon*, *I Wake Up Screaming*, and *The Big Sleep*. There is a wild air of bravado in the theater sequence with Cliff engaging in his wild-eyed flirtation with Richman. It later becomes apparent, however, that much of his persona consists of wild bluff. By the time that he met his timely demise at the hands of a sociopathic killer, Cook appeared every bit as timid and vulnerable as the characters he played in his other memorable forties noir appearances. Cook can be viewed in sharply contrasting scenes. There is a tremendous contrast between the early cockiness of Cook beating his drum on stage and exuding libidinous urges and the vulnerable soul begging for life.

Steve Eifert, editor of the *Back Alley Noir* website, recognizes the cinema magic and raw power of the scenes involving Richman and Cliff. He notes that Raines seeks to play "the tramp groupie" while Cook is "wonderfully creepy" as the drummer. As he states, "You can almost smell the sweat and booze when they enter the place. Cliff puts on a show. [Richman] continues to play hot-to-trot for Cliff when she's clearly repulsed by him."[3]

Fast forward two years to another Siodmak noir classic, *The Killers*, and a scene representing commanding sexual energy emerges. In this case a man is surrendering his individuality and eventually his life to a captivating femme fatale. When the slow-witted boxer Ole Andreson (Burt Lancaster) initially sets his eyes on singer Kitty Collins (Ava Gardner) you also see the white heat of passion electrifying the screen.

In one respect the two scenes are eerily alike. Cliff is captivated by Richman to the point where he will be her willing victim, as is her calculation. Andreson's passion pushes him to the same crescendo of erotic desire. The scenes differ in that Richman seeks information for a positive purpose to help clear her boss, whereas Andreson's all-consuming passion for the charismatic singer enables him to be used by the ruthless mob run by the man to whom she is secretly married (played with opportunistic aplomb by Albert Dekker).

Done In by Henderson's Best Friend

Adapting a Cornell Woolrich story involves transferring a narrative hook followed by a sharp narrative pull from literature to screen. In two cases, *Phantom Lady* and *Rear Window*, sharply honed love interests enhanced story appeal. To do so expanded audience interest in a personal, highly meaningful way.

Robert Siodmak, working in tandem with scenarist Bernard Schoenfeld, framed *Phantom Lady* around two key relationships involving Scott Henderson, the designated fall guy for the strangulation murder of his wife. These two associations involved the real murderer, disturbed serial killer and mad genius Jack Marlow (Franchot Tone), presumably his best friend, and his loyal secretary. The vulnerable Henderson, who spends most of the film on Sing Sing Penitentiary's Death Row awaiting execution after being wrongfully convicted of killing his wife, stands between two active forces. One is that of Richman diligently seeking to free him of a false charge while Marlow, on the pretext of sympathizing over his presumed friend's predicament, is instead strategizing to ensure that the death sentence awaiting Henderson is carried out.

A shrewd story irony conveyed brilliantly in *Phantom Lady* is Henderson's exalted view of Marlow. He sees him as the embodiment of what a brilliant international sculptor should be, an artistic genius. He sees himself as someone delighted to be able to walk anywhere near his friend's shadow. Henderson expresses concern that Marlow will be distracted by his plight to divert attention from his creative activities in South America.

Richman's involvement with Henderson constitutes a love story, but one presented under unique circumstances. We see the unique love story evolve from the act of a conscientious secretary who admires her boss's personal traits, holds him in the highest esteem, and is convinced that he is not the type of man who would murder his wife. While this is not spelled out, an understanding of the Richman character as it develops onscreen is of a loyal woman of integrity who would never have allowed herself to fall in love with her boss while he was married, even in the midst of a complicated marriage. What happens is that, as she devotes herself totally to proving his innocence, she falls in love with him. At the same time Henderson, in the midst of his tragic confinement, recognizes his secretary's purposeful commitment and human genuineness and reciprocates.

It is no accident that Richman goes by the nickname of Kansas. It is a reminder of her roots in middle America and less complicated circumstances than those that await her in the big city. She is someone who is naturally drawn to less complicated circumstances such as throwing herself into activities of Henderson's professional career. The storyline draws Richman out as she labors with the zealous intensity of a police detective. This trait is quickly discovered and admired by Inspector Burgess. It is this esteem which prompts him to form an alliance with her.

Searching a Vast City

Siodmak's Berlin film training is evident in the way that the vastness of New York City is conveyed. This emphasis alongside the group shots and close-ups is reminiscent of Fritz Lang's masterpiece *M*. In the earlier film the city of Berlin was overwhelmed by the search for the serial killer of young children and the tensions exhibited by the city's residents, extending to accusations of innocent parties.

The city at night, New York in its vastness, is displayed when Richman seeks out the bartender at the bar where her boss drank with the mystery lady in the hat. She knows that the bartender is aware of more than he is revealing and follows him on his walk home after he closes the establishment.

Mac the bartender is played by Andrew Tombes, who divided his career between comedy and dramatic roles as weak-willed individuals. In *Phantom Lady* Tombes's persona falls into the latter category. He invests the effort with just the right note of edginess to convince the intrepid secretary that his silence has been bought.

Once more "Kansas" Richman is operating out of synch with her true self. She will engage in seductive flirtation with Cliff and leave a bar at closing time to pursue the bartender down darkened, potentially mean streets to help achieve her objective of freeing Henderson from a wrongful death sentence and an execution date at Sing Sing Prison. The drama is further heightened when Richman follows Mac to an otherwise abandoned subway stop. He steals tense glances at his pursuer as they wait for the train to arrive. She follows him all the way to the apartment building where he resides.

This brilliantly cinematic scene harkens back to Siodmak's Berlin training and explains once more why members of that school were so welcome in Hollywood. They repeatedly capsulated tension within large cities, giving those metropolises a sense of realism despite the fact that the exteriors were shot on the studio's back lot. During the same tight-budget World War II period, Fritz Lang turned out the master noir duo starring Edward G. Robinson, Joan Bennett, and Dan Duryea: *The Woman in the Window* (1944) and *Scarlet Street* (1945). Those two films also do a highly credible job of communicating New York by night.

Richman meets with frustration in her effort to extract information from the bartender. When two men standing outside the apartment building where he lives conclude that he might be bothering the lady, they assist her as she applies pressure to obtain information. In the manner of narrative pull cinema mystery, Mac is silenced at that point and another door is shut for Richman. In fearful anxiety the pressured bartender runs into the street, is hit by a car, and dies instantly.

Tone Playing Partially Against Type

Franchot Tone moved from Broadway to film and promptly carved out a career as a matinee idol. In the process he married one of his frequently cast MGM leading ladies, Joan

Crawford, whose luminous presence made her the top female star at the Culver City studio. Franchot was the son of Dr. Frank Jerome Tone, a pioneer in the field of electrochemistry and one-time president of Carborundum Company of America. His brother, Frank Jerome Tone, Jr., went to work for Carborundum, but Franchot's interest lay in drama not business.

Tone graduated Phi Beta Kapa from Cornell University in 1927, and also studied at Rennes University in France. Another impressive honor derived from his days at the prestigious Ivy League university was serving as president of Cornell's drama club during his senior year. Tone and John Garfield were two of the original members of New York's Group Theater formed in 1931 by Lee Strassberg and Harold Clurman. This heralded the introduction of the method school of Russia's Constantin Stanislavski to America.

It took little time for the suave and handsome Tone to create a niche for himself in the Broadway theater world. He made his debut appearing opposite stage legend Katharine Cornell in the 1929 production of *The Age of Innocence*. By 1932 the cinema world beckoned and Tone signed with MGM. He appeared along with Clark Gable and Charles Laughton in the 1935 sea epic *Mutiny on the Bounty*. The result in Academy Award circles prompted a change in future years. All three of the talented stars were nominated for their work in the "Best Actor" category. As could be expected, with a vote divided in three directions the statuette was won by Victor McLaglen for John Ford's *The Informer*. The dilemma prompted a change with the addition thereafter of a "Best Supporting Actor" award.

Actor and film author Robert Kendall worked with Tone in the February 24, 1955 episode of *Ford Television Theater* entitled "Too Old for Dolls." The story involved an effort by Mike Ramsay (Tone) to help find a suitable prom date for his teenaged daughter Polly (Natalie Wood). Laraine Day played Marge, Polly's mother. The comedic spin involved Mr. Ramsay meeting with steady frustration, and daughter Polly making her own decision.

Kendall appeared in the climactic final scene. Mr. and Mrs. Ramsay nervously await the arrival of Wood's prom date, which she keeps a secret. Eventually Kendall, wearing a turban and looking dapper in a suit, arrives with a servant. Polly's date is none other than Arab Prince Aly Muhammad Assis. After Kendall escorts Polly away, Mr. Ramsay turns to his wife and tells her that their worries about their daughter are unfounded and that she is doing very well indeed on her own.

"Franchot Tone was a pleasure to work with," Kendall recalled. "He was the consummate professional and without effort displayed class and delivered his lines in a casual, natural manner. Once the cameras began rolling he assumed completely the character he was portraying."[4]

Tone, regrettably, was involved in a steaming romantic triangle that resulted in tragedy. After divorces from Crawford and Jean Wallace, by whom he had two children, he became enamored with beautiful blonde actress Barbara Payton.

A smitten Franchot Tone was warned by ex-wife Crawford as well as numerous Hollywood friends against pursuing Payton, whose penchant for alcohol and wild living impeded her from shedding her B-actress image. Drunkenness and loud conversation endowed liberally with four letter words badly tarnished her image as well, not to mention associations such as that with self-absorbed sexual athlete Tom Neal.

The triangle that developed over the affections of Barbara Payton and suitors Tone and Neal spilled into excessive bloodshed and stopped just short of homicide on the night of September 15, 1951 in the front patio of Payton's Beverly Hills residence. The fears of Joan Crawford and others concerning Tone's pursuit of Payton were justified when a badly bloodied Tone was rushed by ambulance to California Lutheran Hospital following the altercation with Neal. It took extensive plastic surgery to put Tone's handsome face back together. For one nervous period it was feared that he might die as a result of the savage pummeling.

John O'Dowd wrote a remarkably detailed biography of Payton's tragic but fascinating life, *Kiss Tomorrow Goodbye: The Barbara Payton Story*, which included a foreword by the

A PRINCE ARRIVES—Arab Prince Aly Muhammad Assis (Robert Kendall, second from right) is Polly Ramsay's (Natalie Wood, right) high school prom date in a February 24, 1955 episode of *The Ford Television Theatre*. He is greeted by her father, Mike (Franchot Tone, far left), while her mother, Marge (Laraine Day, second from left), looks on in surprise.

actress's son John Lee Payton. O'Dowd in one chillingly graphic paragraph presents an account of the fisticuffs from Judson O'Donnell, a neighbor of Payton's who related that he had witnessed the bloody incident:

> A next-door neighbor of Barbara's named Judson O'Donnell claimed to have witnessed the fight from his bedroom window, drawn there, he said, "by the sounds of a woman shrieking hysterically." He would later say that Tom pummeled Franchot over thirty times, adding, "It was like watching a butcher slaughter a steer. At first, I thought my refrigerator was on the fritz. It sounded like a prizefighter in a gym beating the bag. It was one of the bloodiest fights I've ever seen, and I've seen plenty — on that very lawn."[5]

O'Dowd revealed in the next paragraph how Tone narrowly escaped death through the intervention of a former roommate of Neal's: "The altercation ended after ten minutes when Jimmy Cross interceded and managed to restrain Tom by tackling him to the ground. As the other party guests dispersed into the night, Cross telephoned for an ambulance and Franchot was rushed to California Lutheran Hospital."

The news flashed over the wires following the brutal beating. It revealed that Franchot Tone lay in his hospital bed in grave condition with a cerebral concussion, a broken nose, a shattered left cheekbone, and a fractured right upper jaw. He would remain unconscious and near death for the next 18 hours.

Both Tone and Neal had imbibed more than their share of alcohol prior to the confrontation and, according to O'Dowd, Tone had "foolishly challenged the younger actor with an outright dare: 'Let's settle this thing outside.'" All the same, this was a situation that Neal could have prudently avoided. Neal was a former football player and amateur boxer at Northwestern University. He was also an avid weight lifter, with physical fitness a continuing element to further his acting career along with his sexual conquests. Indeed, one cited catalyst to the brawl was Tone tripping over a barbell on Payton's patio, a reminder of the closeness of their relationship. The decidedly unathletic-appearing Tone was, as John O'Dowd noted, "Rail thin and bird-like at 155 pounds ... twenty-five pounds lighter than his attacker." O'Dowd stated further that after being attacked Tone "crumpled like a blood-splattered rag doll as Tom inflicted one ham-fisted blow on him after another."[6]

When a distraught Payton sought to intervene by pulling Neal away from Tone, she was given a black eye and knocked unconscious into a rhododendron bush after catching a wayward elbow of Neal's. As someone with boxing experience, Neal could easily have resisted a feeble effort from the drink-plied Tone by grabbing him, taking control by sitting him down and avoiding further violence.

There were those who believed that the brief marriage of Payton to Tone after the beating incident was calculated in that the victim ultimately decided not to press charges through the office of Los Angeles County District Attorney Ernest Roll. This decision led to speculation of a quid pro quo engineered by Payton to protect Neal from criminal prosecution.

The scandal destroyed the career of Neal, whose only remembered credit was the 1945 low-budget noir classic *Detour* directed by Edgar G. Ulmer and co-starring Ann Savage. Neal's violent streak would resurface and land him in the headlines again years after his film career was but a distant memory. In 1965, he killed his third wife, the former Gail Lee Cloke, who at 29 was 22 years his junior. She had been formerly married to Los Angeles main event lightweight boxer Buddy Evatt and was working as a receptionist at the Palm Springs Racquet Club owned by silent film star Charles Farrell. They married three days after they met. While Neal was silent about her death by gunfire, police attributed it to jealousy on his part over an alleged affair. Released from Soledad Prison after serving six years of a one- to 15-year sentence in 1971, a haggard-looking Neal lived in an apartment in the San Fernando Valley community of Studio City until his death in 1972.

Payton plummeted far and fast after the scandal. Her career in subsequent unremarkable B films ended in 1955. When she was arrested on a prostitution charge Tone was dragged into the picture as Payton was referred to as his former wife.

After a brilliant beginning on stage, Tone's Hollywood career had been caught in a vise before and after the 1951 romantic triangle scandal. A superb acting craftsman, Tone endured the brutal reality of numerous talented New York stage performers after moving to Hollywood. Stage efforts involve fewer people and within the intimate settings of New York drama there is a greater focus on the purity of acting basics. This concentration is further enhanced when performing classical drama from works by the likes of Shakespeare or O'Neill.

Despite promptly landing a contract at MGM, the largest Hollywood studio, Tone soon learned the difference between the New York stage and the Hollywood cinema scene, including one additional and bitter ironical note, despite earning an Oscar nomination not long after arriving in Hollywood for his work in *Mutiny on the Bounty*. In 1935, the same year as that film's release, Tone married the queen of the majestic MGM lot, Joan Crawford. Rather than viewed as a positive accomplishment in Tone's favor, her soaring status prompted sniping reference from certain tinsel town quarters to him as "Mr. Joan Crawford."

The career vise in which Tone was trapped during the thirties was the Catch-22 of succeeding on one level but not being able to grab the gold ring occupied by the MGM performer referred to as "The King," Clark Gable. In the more commercial world of Hollywood, which differed notably from New York's stage scene, tickets are sold to theatergoers on a worldwide basis. Roles are therefore accorded to those able to cut a wider swath. A Leslie Howard was much more comfortable playing a role in a George Bernard Shaw drama such as *Pygmalion*, which he did as it was adapted to the screen, or perform on London's West End doing Shakespeare or Ibsen, than Clark Gable. Tone was the kind of fine tuned performer of subtlety who, like Leslie Howard, is more comfortably situated to complex stage drama. He was not the kind of performer who would be cast in the kind of brawling, bravado film roles that would be given to Clark Gable, who had a broader range as a movie leading man.

It was therefore beneficial to Tone that a role such as that of Jack Marlow in *Phantom Lady* emerged. Better than forty years after his 1968 death, at a time when film noir is greatly appreciated, Franchot Tone shines as a towering beacon with a role perfectly tailored to his talents. Robert Siodmak, a director whose career has accelerated in public esteem with his towering noir achievements in works such as *Phantom Lady* along with *The Killers* and *Criss Cross*, possessed the talent and perspective for the broad picture to appreciate what Tone brought to the film.

In that context of a Cornell Woolrich suspense story in which an innocent, thoroughly decent man would die if a psychopathic genius killer, who happened to be the convicted party's best friend, is not brought to justice, the role of Jack Marlow requires a performer of subtle skills. This is a serial killer who is able to rub elbows with the most affluent and powerful members of society. By casting Franchot Tone in that pivotal role, the suave Cornell graduate was required to only partially play against type. The masterful elegance of man-of-the-world architectural genius fell comfortably into Tone's personal bailiwick.

The area where he was traversing new ground onscreen was in playing a murderous psychopath who, beneath a glossy exterior, hates the world and everything in it.

It is fascinating to see the various sides of him surface with different characters with whom he interacts. The role gives Tone the chance to cover shades and gradations from his complex character, enabling him to run the gamut from sympathetic friend to determined, stone-faced murderer.

The viewer possesses insight denied to tragic victim Scott Henderson. He displays pride in knowing such an internationally acclaimed genius sculptor as Jack Marlow and is concerned about him leaving important business behind him in South America to visit him. On one side we see decency and humility; on the other a ruthless hatred for humanity and desire to kill masquerading behind a façade of high intellect combined with decency. The contrast between Henderson and Marlow becomes increasingly observable as the film develops.

The Pivotal Relationship of "Kansas" Richman and Inspector Burgess

A pivotal relationship of the film revolves around the analytical Inspector Burgess and "Kansas" Richman. In a piece of adroit script development, Burgess demonstrates subtle reasoning as he explains to Richman what has convinced him to join her effort to prove Scott Henderson's innocence.

Stubborn insistence on Henderson's part coupled with an important element prompt Burgess to join Richman's team. A guilty defendant with Henderson's intelligence and background would not insist that he had met a woman wearing a unique hat and had been with her during the period when his wife was being murdered. Henderson's inflexibility despite lengthy and futile police efforts to locate the woman convinces Burgess that he is telling the truth and would have invented a more inventive lie had deception been his objective.

The casting of Thomas Gomez as the cool-headed, ever-tenacious police inspector was a case of film noir master director Siodmak instinctively knowing a performer who belonged in the genre. The forties proved to be the key period of Gomez's career. His defining roles came in film noir.

Born and raised in New York City, Gomez fell into an acting career following high school graduation in 1923. He answered a newspaper help wanted ad that led him into the acting group of stage legends Alfred Lunt and Lynn Fontanne. It was but two years following Gomez's 1942 film debut that he appeared in the important role of Inspector Burgess in *Phantom Lady*. His success in that film led to his being cast in *Johnny O'Clock* and *Ride the Pink Horse* (both 1947). The latter film, directed by and starring Robert Montgomery, yielded a "Best Supporting Actor" Oscar nomination.

The following year was also a big one for Gomez. He scored solidly in *Key Largo*, appearing as a subordinate to mob boss Edward G. Robinson in the John Huston-directed adaptation of Maxwell Anderson's play. Future directing great Richard Brooks and Huston collaborated on the script adaptation. While *Key Largo* was a good showcase for Gomez, the other noir film in which he appeared in 1948 provided him with what many believe to be the finest effort of his career. *Force of Evil* was filmed by John Garfield's Enterprise Studios. For many years it lay dormant, initially a victim of the controversies of the period considering Garfield's appearance before the House Un-American Activities Committee along with the

Hollywood blacklisting for some two decades of director-screenwriter Abraham Polonsky. Assisting Polonsky with the script was former Pulitzer Prize-winning war correspondent Ira Wolfert, the author of the novel *Tucker's People*, which was adapted into *Force of Evil*.

Viewing Gomez in *Force of Evil* provides insight into the on camera integrity that made his effort in *Phantom Lady* so compelling. Attorney Joe Morse (John Garfield) makes a compact with New York crime boss Ben Tucker (Roy Roberts) to take control of the city's lucrative numbers racket. Morse hopes to help his ailing older brother Leo (Gomez) from his pedestal as a journeyman numbers operator to the top of the economic pack.

The film's talented actors, each with glossy stage performing records as well as cinema achievements, explode on screen in sharply worded confrontations that result in younger brother Joe displaying the film's character arc. Despite the overall shady nature of his work, Leo feels for the small folk in the numbers field and does not want to see operators like himself destroyed in a master ploy engineered by ruthless boss Tucker and his brother. Leo uses what is left of his quickly ebbing strength to make his case while Joe listens. He turns on Tucker and their association ends with one final gunfight. This occurs after he has spurned a romantic gesture from Tucker's faithless wife, (played by experienced and talented femme fatale Marie Windsor, whose loyalty deficiencies are in full display just as they were in Stanley Kubrick's *The Killing* (1956), when she ruthlessly taunts and abuses her husband, played by Elisha Cook, Jr.)

Whereas Gomez showed more emotion in his *Force of Evil* role, what stands out in his performance in *Phantom Lady* is his cool professionalism. As Inspector Burgess steps into the courtroom and listens to Henderson's testimony, a troubled look surfaces. Here is a police officer who does not believe that his work has concluded because a man he arrested has been tried. His desire to see that justice is done prompts him to join forces with Richman.

One of the most subtly clever scenes in the film occurs when Jack Marlow, pretending to be Henderson's loyal friend, follows Richman around and sits in on meetings. Marlow assumes a troubled look when Burgess refers to killers as uniformly sick. His statement that certain killers are clever fails to change Burgess's mind as he repeats his assertion. Since Marlow is definitely ill he assumes a troubled expression, not wanting to confront the reality of his condition, seeking to place himself on a pedestal of an individual outwitting a diseased, far less intelligent society. This is comparable to the thinking of a serial killer as played by Joseph Cotten in Hitchcock's masterpiece *Shadow of a Doubt*. In one evocative scene Marlow even collapses in front of Burgess after complaining about dizzy spells. Like Cotten's character, Marlow veers between manifestations of cleverness and bizarre behavior reflecting serious illness.

Siodmak's Strong Supportive Woman Contrasted with Femmes Fatales

After his excellent beginning with *Phantom Lady* Robert Siodmak cemented his distinguished imprint as one of the masters of film noir with two aforementioned triumphs, all made on the Universal lot. *The Killers* was released two years later, in 1946, while *Crisscross* debuted onscreen in 1949.

The latter two films were strengthened by the roles of two sharply defined, strong-willed femmes fatales, played by Ava Gardner in *The Killers* and Yvonne De Carlo in *Criss*

Cross, respectively. They torment the male lead (in each case Burt Lancaster) by using their seductive wiles to thrust him into criminal activity to serve their ends along with those of their husbands, portrayed with ruthless effectiveness by Albert Dekker and Dan Duryea, respectively.

In *The Killers*, Kitty Collins (Gardner) and Big Jim Colfax (Decker) shrewdly do not let anyone in his gang, particularly Ole "Sweede" Andreson (Lancaster), know that they are married. The sting they apply is to have Collins show up at Andreson's hotel with a proposal that he rob Colfax and his gang of the proceeds of the recently concluded armed robbery of a hat factory. She promises that they will then be linked in romantic partnership, their relationship enhanced by the robbery proceeds. Andreson does as he is told, then returns to his hotel and takes the money, heading back to Colfax. Andreson never learns that Collins and Colfax are married. He is ultimately killed by two of Colfax's contract killers (played by Charles McGraw and William Conrad).

In *Criss Cross*, Steve Thompson (Lancaster) leaves Los Angeles after his divorce from his wife, Anna (Yvonne De Carlo), hoping to shake her from his burning romantic thoughts. He returns to Los Angeles and learns that he yearns more for her than ever, immediately returning to their nightclub haunt and discovering that she has become the girlfriend of local mob boss Slim Dundee (Dan Duryea).

Anna and Dundee, aware of how deeply the fires burned within Thompson, tempted him into criminal involvement after the shapely brunette shows him bruises and confides how badly her brutish mobster husband has treated her.

At film's end, before they are both shot by a jealous Dundee, who feels he has been double crossed, Thompson tells his ex-wife that he was never interested in the holdup money. She was his sole interest. Anna coolly responds in a manner that befits her role as femme fatale. The sexy brunette informs him that in the cold hard world of reality one must look out for oneself.

The similar plots of the two later film noir triumphs of Siodmak that rely heavily on femmes fatale linked to ruthless husbands can be sharply contrasted with the well-executed plot of *Phantom Lady*, with a totally different structure for the lead female. Ella Raines fell into a category diametrically opposed to the femme fatale image of Gardner, De Carlo, Jane Greer, Barbara Stanwyck, and Claire Trevor. Hers was the character of the strong supportive female willing to surmount all odds to assist the man she loves. In the case of Raines as Richman, her manner of falling in love with her boss is reflective of the depth of her moral being, which is sharply contrasted with the absence thereof with the sociopathic femme fatale. Until Henderson's wife dies tragically she does not begin to fall in love with him until the process of ultimately saving him for a date with the Sing Sing Prison executioner. Kansas Richman, who possesses the bedrock principles of the small-town America in which she was raised, would not wish to inject herself into her boss's marriage. Her implicit faith in him as a decent human being is established with her sturdy confidence that he could never kill his wife or anyone else. This unflagging confidence is further implemented by her resolve to establish his innocence, even if it means undertaking the kinds of danger described earlier.

Raines grew up in Washington state and, like Bruce Bennett and Frances Farmer, performed in student theater at the University of Washington, where she was discovered by Howard Hawks. Her film career was launched in the early forties with two appearances in 1943 releases. The first was a starring role opposite Randolph Scott in *Corvette K-225*. The following year was highly productive as, in addition to starring in *Phantom Lady*, Raines performed with John Wayne in *Tall in the Saddle* and opposite Eddie Bracken in Preston Sturges's madcap comedy *Hail the Conquering Hero*. In real life Ella was married between 1947 and 1976 to flying ace Robin Olds.

Eddie Muller on Ella Raines

Eddie Muller spoke for many enthusiasts of film noir when he said that Ella Raines possessed an impressive talent within the genre. "My biggest regret is that Ella Raines was not better utilized in the noir era," Muller exclaimed. "She was so smart and sexy — a real Hawks dame in the Bacall mode — but she ended up playing mostly opposite leading men with little sex appeal: George Sanders, Charles Laughton, Brian Donlevy, Edmond O'Brien, George Raft. If she'd been trading one-liners with Dennis O'Keefe and Dan Duryea, she'd have a much more memorable screen persona."[7]

Raines's solid effort as a strong supporting woman in *Phantom Lady* led to a similar role with Brian Donlevy in the 1949 film noir release *Impact*, directed by Arthur Lubin. The shrewd script of Dorothy Davenport and Jay Dratler presents Walter Williams (Brian Donlevy) as a man who will fearlessly face down the board of directors of the corporation he runs even when a majority of its members have voted to remove him from power. Soon after this event occurs, with the gritty San Francisco businessman emerging stronger than ever, he calls his wife, Irene (Helen Walker), the film's femme fatale. Immediately his tone and manner change. He affectionately and with relish refers to her as "Duchess." He lets her know that, as tough as he can be in the corporate sphere, he delights in being soft where she is concerned. In fact, he willingly accepts the label as "Softy" where his relationship with her is concerned. He is as smitten and fantasy driven with Walker as he was tough and pragmatic with the board of directors of his company, presenting a sharp contrast for viewers.

Irene successfully operates on her husband's self-acknowledged Achilles heel, dripping counterfeit sincerity as she explains that she has a dreadful headache and could he instead give a ride en route to his Denver destination to her "favorite nephew," Jim (Tony Barrett), seeking to return to his Chicago home. While Donlevy seeks to provide a helping hand, the alleged nephew (actually, his wife's lover) seeks to kill him by slugging him with a lug wrench. In a strange twist, the business executive suffers only a concussion, while his would-be killer, in driving away, is in an accident on a winding mountain road and is himself killed after colliding with a gasoline truck.

Williams ultimately stops in the small Idaho town of Larkspur (population: 4,501). Ella Raines then makes her first appearance 52 minutes into the film as Marsha Peters. The mechanical skills of self-made business tycoon Williams, who began his meteoric career as a sheet metal worker at the company he eventually runs, come in handy. Peters offers him a job working for her as a mechanic at her gas station.

Supporting Woman Guiding a Character Arc

Williams checks by telephone and verifies that the alleged cousin does not exist. This, coupled with the earlier attack, prompt him to conclude that he has been played as a sap by a homicidal wife conspiring to inherit his estate and enjoy the proceeds with her alleged cousin.

In *Impact*, unlike *Phantom Lady*, Raines as the film's strong supporting woman guides a character arc for Walter Williams, making him a better person in the process, one willing to face reality in a way he had not earlier as self-designated "Softy" to an opportunistic wife while blinded in emotional fantasy. Williams's prominence as a business tycoon enables him to follow proceedings in San Francisco through newspaper information. He initially learns that, as a result of knowing nothing about the alleged cousin, and based on the fact that his remains were charred beyond recognition, the national media reports that the tycoon died in an automobile accident.

The freak nature of the killing attempt and death of the perpetrator, highlighted by non-identification of the deceased, cause police to arrest Anna Williams and prepare to try her for her husband's murder. After informing the kindly gas station owner, Peters, of his real identity, he tells her that his wife is receiving her just desserts.

Peters, a war widow whose husband died in Okinawa, has fallen in love with Williams. She can see why he feels such strong anger toward his wife, but earnestly reasons with him that two wrongs do not make a right. Williams is urged to return to San Francisco and explain to police authorities that he is still alive and that it was his wife's paramour who died.

A touching scene where Williams sits by himself in the quiet of night at the Larkspur bus station after he has initially spurned Peters's earnest advice to return to San Francisco and set matters straight causes him to reflect on the goodness of the people in the small town, particularly this understanding woman. In the next scene we see Williams and Peters landing at San Francisco Airport, indicating that her recommendation was heeded.

Coburn and Gomez as Lead Detectives

What is a strong supporting woman but someone who assists a man when his life is at stake? Raines plays two women who are basically reserved and not aggressive. She shifts necessarily into an aggressive mode in both *Phantom Lady* and *Impact*. Two veteran detectives from major city police forces, New York and San Francisco, observe her tenacity coupled with the righteousness of the cause of saving the man she loves. Lt. Quincy (Charles Coburn) in *Impact* steps into the same shoes that Inspector Burgess (Thomas Gomez) wore in *Phantom Lady*.

Another similarity looms after analyzing both films. The detectives are summoned into action after statements made by the men being accused of murder have been literally shoved into a corner based on their improbability. In the case of Scott Henderson, his account of being with the lady with the distinctive hat at the time of his wife's murder is met with scorn by prosecutors and disbelieved by jurors.

Walter Williams is pushed into a comparable fate. The catalyst is none other than his embittered wife, Irene. Rattled by seeing him, she lashes out sharply, accusing him of murdering her lover. An accidental breaking of a vase by her husband in their apartment is depicted by the ruthlessly imaginative Irene as an intentional act occurring during an argument over her affair. She claimed that this was but one example of his towering rage that would ultimately culminate in her lover's murder.

A clever story element is the manifestation of a play-it-by-the-book police captain (Robert Warwick) who is far less imaginative and daring in approach as his experienced chief lieutenant. Capt. Callahan finds the woman's story credible. Soon it is the wife who is free and Williams is standing trial for murder.

Just as Kansas Richman was battling the clock to save her boss from execution, such was the case with Marsha Peters seeking to spare Walter Williams from a first-degree murder conviction and potential death in California's gas chamber. In the latter case, the trial was ongoing, with Williams facing increasingly lengthening odds against acquittal.

Peters's investigative trump card is having Lt. Quincy assist her. Peters literally chases after Williams's former maid, Su Linn (Anna May Wong), to corroborate the fact that he was not at home, sleeping, on the night in question.

The information provides Williams's attorney (Art Baker) with the opportunity to call Irene as a witness. He breaks her down so thoroughly that, after he is finished the deputy district attorney previously intent on convicting her husband announces that it is she who will be held and tried for her conspiratorial activities.

Richman Holding off Marlow as a Killer Attempts to Repeat

While there were numerous similarities between Raines's performance as the strong supporting woman to Brian Donlevy in *Impact* and to Alan Curtis in *Phantom Lady*, in the earlier 1944 release she was afforded additional dramatic latitude in one climactic scene with Franchot Tone, whose role as the sick killer with the superiority complex ranks with the best in Hollywood annals. The buildup to the scene where Jack Marlow intends to kill Richman is niftily handled as she shrewdly picks up on signs indicating his illness. Marlow complains of headaches and contorts his face, almost discombobulating it in the process. He has lured Richman to his home on the pretext that it can serve as an ideal meeting place to discuss the case with Inspector Burgess. This comes after Richman has located the mystery woman and has been given the hat that her boss has been describing. By freeing Henderson, the sinister Marlow will no longer have an innocent victim to face execution for a crime he committed. Furthermore, with the case being solved piece by piece, how long will it be before the wily Burgess connects Marlow to the murders? Time is clearly running out for Marlow, whose advancing illness corresponds with additional information on the homicide front.

As Richman plays for time, hoping that the inspector will arrive and rescue her, Marlow takes off his necktie and begins gruesomely tugging at it. While Richman watches and listens with fear, Marlow adopts a manner of angry superiority. He scoffingly refers to Henderson, the man who admires him so greatly and considers to be his best friend, as a second-rate professional who designs sewer projects. He says that he — not Henderson — deserved to be married to so beautiful a woman. He reaches a roaring crescendo in revealing that the spoiled and vain woman had laughed at him, leading him on for fun, and was never serious about involving herself with him. This clearly became his breaking point.

Alfred Hitchcock successfully utilized the value of extending a scene, of milking every ounce of suspense from it, letting the camera hypnotize audiences awaiting resolution. Siodmak followed that principle skillfully. Siodmak's visual trademark, in this instance, was Marlow's tie. In the scene with Cliff the drummer, it was his scarf. Before he removed it to strangle him, Marlow held out his hands and stared at them continually, conveying the impression that he was about to use them.

Suspense thickens as a wide-eyed Richman, knowing what Marlow has in store for her, does her best to prolong the inevitable, hoping that Burgess will arrive in time to save her. Marlow deems it indispensable to kill Raines before she can implicate him in the murders.

After Burgess arrives Marlow attempts an escape. In that hasty effort he stumbles and falls to his death. Richman has solved a case and her life has been spared by the barest of margins. From there the obvious result occurs of a now-free Henderson returning to work and reuniting professionally and romantically with the woman whose efforts spared him from the electric chair.

A Courtroom Scene from the Lang Berlin Tradition

An inventive courtroom scene done by Siodmak is reminiscent of Fritz Lang and *M*. It reflects strongly on the Berlin tradition and the successful use that can be made of a swiftly moving camera. *M* began with numerous close-ups of Berliners in the midst of a tense period in which a madman is killing children. That same camera later acclimates viewers to the inner torment of the crimes' perpetrator, Hans Beckert (Peter Lorre, in his breakthrough starring role).

In a fascinating story twist, Beckert is ultimately apprehended by the city's criminal element and placed on trial. During the trial a busily moving camera captures the mood of the involved individuals as well as the tormented expression of Beckert, who desperately explains that his homicidal actions are beyond his control.

Siodmak takes an unconventional approach away from traditional cinema trial sequences, which make effective use of the individual being tried as well as the competing attorneys. In *Phantom Lady*, sounds of Henderson testifying as well as the prosecuting attorney ridiculing his account of where he was when his wife was murdered are heard, but this activity is never seen.

Instead viewers are shown how courtroom observers react to Henderson's testimony. Observers scoff and laugh at certain intervals. Richman reveals an understandable reaction of troubled concern. Inspector Burgess's troubled expression also reflects the doubt of a trained police officer who, as he later explains to Richman, finds Henderson's explanation so simplistic that he believes it to be honest.

When the final verdict is announced a unique ploy is used. A woman sitting near Richman coughs so loudly that she is unable to hear the verdict. When she turns and asks the man next to her about the trial result, he looks at her with surprise and bellows "guilty," adding, "What did you expect?" His incredulity that this woman would even bother asking in the wake of what was clear and convincing evidence indicates the difficult road that confronts the loyal secretary in seeking to prove that her boss is innocent.

Curtis as Believable Victim

Phantom Lady not only provided showcase dramatic opportunities for Franchot Tone and Ella Raines but for Chicago-born Alan Curtis as well. His modeling work became his ultimate passport to Hollywood. Curtis played opposite Alice Faye and Don Ameche in the 1939 Fox release *Hollywood Cavalcade*. Two years later he appeared along with Arthur Kennedy as one of the two young sidekicks learning the craft of armed robbery under veteran Roy Earle (Humphrey Bogart) in *High Sierra*. He gained fame playing the romantic lead in the first hit film of Bud Abbott and Lou Costello, *Buck Privates*, also released in 1941.

Curtis received an opportunity to break out of the mold of feature roles in major movies and lead performer in B films when he replaced initial choice John Garfield and was cast opposite Universal's acting and singing star Gloria Jean in *Flesh and Fantasy*, a 1943 release consisting of three occult anthologies with romantic twists. The film, directed with a French artistic flair by Julien Duvivier, starred Charles Boyer, Barbara Stanwyck, Robert Cummings, Thomas Mitchell, Dame May Whitty, C. Aubrey Smith, and Robert Benchley. The segment featuring Curtis and Jean was clipped by Universal. It was expanded and became a full-fledged film, *Destiny*, released in 1944, the same year as *Phantom Lady*. Jean, portraying a blind woman with exsensory powers, has comparable strong supporting woman status opposite Curtis as exemplified by Ella Raines. In *Destiny*, however, a character arc is involved in that Cliff Banks (Curtis), when he meets Jane Broderick (Jean), is a ruthless armed robber on the run. Her positive persona and high ethical standards prompt Banks to undergo a change that results in turning himself in to authorities. The Curtis and Jean team blends superbly. The only sad element is that, whereas the shorter *Flesh and Fantasy* appearance was in a highly publicized A format, *Destiny* was earmarked as a B release. Recently, however, as in the case of other lower budget films of the forties, nostalgia fans of the period have invested the film with greater attention.

Alan Curtis invests his *Phantom Lady* lead role with just the right element of a decent man trapped by a vicious fate. Curtis, in his role as Scott Henderson, is effectively teamed with Ella Raines as the loyal secretary Kansas Richman. That fate is wielded by the individual Henderson believes is his best friend, Jack Marlow, which reveals so much about the film's two male leads. To a mellow optimist a glass is half full. In Marlow's case it is more than the traditional half empty status of the pessimist; it is devoid of water and those expecting any are destined to die of thirst. In the world of deeply sick Marlow, he is the driving force of society and others are no more than pathetic victims, often deadly victims at that.

The combustible interplay of forces involving Tone, Raines, and Curtis marks *Phantom Lady* as a notable film achievement by a master conductor, an Arturo Toscanini of film noir, Robert Siodmak.

Chapter Eleven

Billy Wilder and Alcoholism Noir

> One's too many and a thousand's not enough.— Howard da Silva referring to Ray Milland's thirst for alcohol in *The Lost Weekend*

After a director turns in a film noir effort for the ages with the 1944 blockbuster *Double Indemnity* can one expect another chiller the following year? If Billy Wilder of the Berlin school is the director then the answer is yes. *The Lost Weekend* netted the Austrian émigré director those elusive Academy Awards that *Double Indemnity* deserved but did not receive.

The wartime chiller *Double Indemnity* hit Hollywood in the manner of an unexpected blitz, sending shock waves through the entire film community. The James M. Cain novel that Wilder challenged himself to adapt to the screen presented human relations in a nihilistic manner. The character of Phyllis Dietrichson played with cold and calculating deadliness by Barbara Stanwyck was so brutally unique that the great actress, generally ready to respond to any dramatic challenge, harbored great misgivings. Fred MacMurray expressed similar sentiments about playing Walter Neff, the normally glib talking insurance salesman stunned into ultimate shock after being talked into a murder for insurance money scheme by the ruthless Phyllis.

Neither MacMurray nor Stanwyck had seen anything like the hardboiled story project that Wilder envisioned. Wilder's oozing confidence ultimately convinced MacMurray to assume what became the signature dramatic role of his career. Wilder played up the challenge of the Dietrichson role to Stanwyck, who also assented. It also helped that Stanwyck and MacMurray held each other in high professional esteem.

While theirs was anything but a compatible relationship, Wilder made a stellar move in signing Raymond Chandler to assist him in writing the screenplay. If anyone was capable of matching Wilder in acidic and acerbic line by line dialogue that individual was Raymond Chandler.

Based on Chandler's artistic persona as elucidated in scores of articles, essays, and letters memorialized in numerous anthologies, he considered the writer his friend and the entire Hollywood production network his enemy. While their personalities operated on sharply variant wavelengths, the Chandler who was lionized as an elder statesman by his younger colleagues at Paramount had an important element in common with Wilder. It was Wilder who developed a strong urge toward directing and producing after emigrating to the film colony from Germany to retain the imprint of his own screenplays, dreading the prospect of revision.[1]

When *Double Indemnity* premiered and was quickly projected into the ranks of a new kind of cinematic original, providing a hard hitting form of story presentation that would generate more in the same mold in what would ultimately be termed film noir, prevailing before the Academy at the Oscar level was another matter. The film received seven nominations, but the overall results revealed the disparity between artistic recognition of boardroom reality.

The Hollywood executive community had long been frightened about the Breen Office and censorship problems. Already frightened by the controversial Puck of the community, Alfred Hitchcock, and his brilliant strategy ploys to dance around censors, many executive types were mortified at the prospect of a two-headed hydra of Wilder and Chandler and what the presence and artistic praise of reviewers might portend for the future.

The paradox of *Double Indemnity* is that its raw believability, as exemplified by its two opportunistic lead characters, worked against it within the Breen Office Hollywood of the war period forties. As Eddie Muller asserted, *Double Indemnity* was "the first major Hollywood film of the era in which the protagonists are the criminals. And the audience is made to empathize with them, which to me is an essential facet of noir. That's what I find so bracingly adult about the best noir of that period — it asks the viewer to empathize with flawed characters. Not sympathize, empathize."

The Breen Office examined films within a narrow orbit, exercising a moral compass in which right and wrong are sharply demarcated while ignoring varying gradations of gray. Muller explores a broader range of gray area in asserting relative to film noir, "There are no excuses and no forgiveness. 'I did it for the money, and I did it for a woman,' Walter Neff says. 'And I didn't get the money, and I didn't get the woman. Pretty, isn't it?' He's not asking for forgiveness, just a shred of understanding."

Muller's words harken back to Fritz Lang's supercharged *M*. When Hans Beckert (Peter Lorre) speaks out about himself and his homicidal criminal pattern he does so without seeking forgiveness. In the words of Muller relative to Walter Neff, Beckert seeks a shred of understanding.

Another element worked against *Double Indemnity* in securing Oscars: the fact that the war was in progress. The message emanating from Oscar night was that an upbeat film was favored, and so *Going My Way*, a heartwarming story about a parish priest, was preferred to film noir. While *Double Indemnity* garnered seven nominations for "Best Film" along with Barbara Stanwyck for her brilliant lead role as well as Wilder in the "Best Director" and "Best Screenplay" categories, the latter nomination shared with collaborator Chandler, it was ultimately bypassed for Oscar honors each time.[2]

While Wilder sat and watched the Academy Award proceedings at Grauman's Chinese Theater is was *Going My Way* that received seven Oscars, sending a message that it was a great year for upbeat priests, with Bing Crosby winning for "Best Actor" and the veteran actor who played the older pastor he assisted, Barry Fitzgerald, triumphing in the "Best Supporting" class. The film about the two parish priests and their activities also won "Best Film" honors as well as earning a "Best Director" statuette for Leo McCarey.

For Billy Wilder and the frustration of being shut out for an Oscar in all categories in the wake of presenting one of the most stylish and innovative films in the history of the industry, a pace setter whose fame lived well beyond that of that year's Academy preference, the response was that of the familiar chant of Brooklyn Dodgers baseball fans before the team won its first and only World Series in 1955: "Wait until next year."

With Wilder the challenge would be successfully met with another imaginative entry into what would later be termed film noir. If *Double Indemnity* was an innovative ground breaker in displaying the dark and chilling realm of a woman whose overpowering sexual magnetism and hypnotic manner made a subservient insurance salesman become her prey in collaborative murder for financial greed, *The Lost Weekend* represented a different type of tour de force.

Charles Jackson's first novel, *The Lost Weekend*, debuted at bookstores in 1944 and mesmerized readers with its stunningly accurate portrait of alcoholic excess over a five-day binge. Jackson later became a speaker before Alcoholics Anonymous on the subject of alcoholism and drug addiction. Another work of Jackson's published two years later in 1946, *The Fall of Valor*, was a compelling first-person fictional narrative on the subject of homosexuality. Jackson's life ended with his suicide at New York City's Chelsea Hotel on September 21, 1968. The Chelsea Hotel, located in the colorful section of the old Madison Square Garden on Twenty-third Street, served as residential quarters for such celebrities as Dylan Thomas, Bob Dylan, and Janis Joplin.

Semi-autobiographical novels are often the most graphically compelling given the writer's exceptional closeness to the subject matter. Jackson made a big enough impression to entice Paramount Studios to pay $50,000 for book rights, after which Wilder's vivid imagination went to work on a project seemingly made to order for him. He adapted the script along with frequent collaborator Charles Brackett. The former theater critic for *The New Yorker* collaborated with Wilder on 13 screenplays. Two of them achieved Oscars, *The Lost Weekend* and *Sunset Blvd*. Brackett secured a third statuette for the 1953 film *Titanic*, which he shared with collaborators Walter Reisch and Richard L. Breen.

This time when Academy Awards were presented March 7, 1946, at Grauman's Chinese it would be Wilder walking to the stage to receive "Best Director" honors. *The Lost Weekend* swept the major category Oscars. Along with the aforementioned two categories where Wilder won awards, the film also secured "Best Picture" honors while its star, Ray Milland, was "Best Actor" recipient for his bone-numbing portrayal of Don Birnam, an alcoholic whose ruthless preoccupation for consumption threatens not only to overwhelm him, but the two people who care for him most, his loyal girlfriend, Helen St. James (Jane Wyman), and Don's brother, Wick (Phillip Terry, who was at the time the husband of Joan Crawford).[3]

Chillingly Believable Portrayal

Milland's portrayal is chillingly believable in that he covers two spectrums closely identified with alcoholics, cunning imagination along with deeply rooted desperation to do anything it takes to sustain a habit that, unless corrected, will result in total destruction. Viewers see an illustration of this in the film's opening scene. The camera's eye of cinematographer John F. Seitz shows us an open window of Don Birnam's apartment and a string that he has installed. Attached to it is a bottle of whisky. Accustomed to playing attentive detective to his brother, Wick ultimately snuffs out the plot and pours the contents of the liquor into the kitchen sink. His act is not enough to sink Don's resourcefulness.

Imagination gives way to desperation as Don conceives a way to prevent the intended healthy weekend in the country with his brother, replete with cold drinking well water and buttermilk as substitutes for his raging quest for rye whisky. When he learns that his girlfriend, Helen, has tickets for a Carnegie Hall concert, Don uses his wiles to get her, along with Wick, out of his apartment, suggesting that they attend the concert together. He might be without funds to buy whisky, but this is only a temporary situation.

Fate intervenes on Don's side when his cleaning lady arrives. She asks for the money that Wick had promised. It is there, but Don lies to her that his brother apparently forgot to put it there, but that the situation will be remedied and she will be paid on Monday.

Another Noir Strong Supporting Woman

Don departs from his apartment in a flash, albeit a thirsty one. The resulting "lost weekend" provides the natural title for both Jackson's book and the film. Following Don Birnam on his destructive roller coaster ride makes viewers wonder if he will survive it.

Why was such a sophisticated and elegant young woman as Helen St. James attracted to Cornell University dropout and failed fiction writer Birnam, whose instability and craving for alcohol make him a horrible prospect? For one thing her female nurturing instinct makes her believe that he is not a lost cause, and that ultimately she can help save him from his destructive side. (Wyman fits into the same category of strong supporting woman delineated earlier in the performances of Ella Raines in *Phantom Lady* and *Impact* and Alice Faye as will be seen in the following chapter.) A second reason for her devotion is that Don is such a dapper, witty man. It is observable that after a few drinks he can be charmingly engaging as he discusses Shakespeare and philosophizes.

Howard da Silva provides a solid effort in his role as Nat, the bartender at the local watering hole that Don frequents. Nat is open in his apprehension of a man who, while a regular customer, is so evocative of what can happen to a patron with too great a fondness for the establishment's product. "One's too many and a thousand's not enough," Nat reveals with succinct sadness, summarizing Don's condition along with his refusal to drink with him.

Doris Dowling is memorable in a feature role as Gloria, a dazzling but down-on-her-luck prostitute who uses Nat's bar as a meeting place for salesman types "visiting from Albany." She hopes to change her luck and Don's through romance, an effort destined to fail given his love for Helen. (One year later both da Silva and Dowling would play major

CAUGHT IN THE ACT—Wick Birnam (Philip Terry, left) has caught his alcoholic brother, Don (Ray Milland, right) after the latter unsuccessfully sought to hide a bottle of whiskey in *The Lost Weekend* (1945). Don's girlfriend, Helen St. James (Jane Wyman), looks on with soulful empathy.

LAUNCHING A BENDER—Don Birnam (Ray Milland, right) holds court while bored bar proprietor Nat (Howard da Silva, left) launches a lengthy bender in the aptly titled 1945 Billy Wilder noir masterpiece *The Lost Weekend* (1945).

supporting roles in the Paramount noir release *The Blue Dahlia* starring its dynamic romantic team of Alan Ladd and Veronica Lake. The film is also notable in that, as earlier noted, the screenplay was written by Raymond Chandler.)

At one point during Don's lost weekend, as he grows increasingly desperate for a drink and finds a succession of Upper East Side bars and liquor stores closed, he stops a man and asks him what has happened. The man explains that it is the Jewish holiday of Yom Kippur. When Don asks about Irish establishments he is told that a reciprocal agreement exists whereby Jewish businesses honor St. Patrick's Day by closing down while the opposite also holds true for Yom Kippur.

Haunting Preview of Birnam's Future?

Any such journey into a belly of hell reminiscent of Dante's Inferno such as Don has undertaken is destined to end in some form of calamity. Don's desperation almost lands him in jail when he steals a woman's purse in a nightclub and removes ten dollars. The decision is to physically remove him from the establishment rather than summon police. The scene becomes additionally humiliating for the desperate drink seeker when the sarcastic piano player sings the words "Somebody stole her purse" to the tune of "Somebody Stole My Gal."

Don plunges into even darker depths than purse stealing. After collapsing on the stairwell of Gloria's apartment building, he wakes up on a bed in the alcohol ward of Bellevue Hospital. An expression of torment grips Don as he observes a trembling African American man in the bed next to his. Soon another man cries out and convulses under the influence of delirium tremens.

Male nurse "Bim" Nolan (Frank Faylen, whose career accelerated after a brief but unforgettable interlude in the film) enters the room. Bim makes a deep impression with his well-reasoned sarcasm and foreboding prediction, rendered with confidence, that Don is someone he will see again. The nurse points out other establishment regulars, accelerating the new patient's fear.

Some of Milland's most penetrating acting comes not from the way he delivers his words, as brilliantly rendered as they are, but from his expressions. He runs the gamut from an all too brief on top of the world delusional happiness achieved while in the high state preceding drunkenness, replete with grinning witticisms, to fearful desperation, particularly evidenced when the cynical nurse explains with cool sarcasm the future that awaits him.

Compelling Musical Score

If viewers detect similarity between the chilling orchestral sounds of *The Lost Weekend* and Hitchcock's *Spellbound*, it is understandable: Hungarian émigré Miklos Rozsa wrote both scores. Rozsa was nominated for an Oscar for his *The Lost Weekend* score but did not win, achieving the statuette instead for *Spellbound*. It was a great year for Rozsa since he received yet another nomination for *A Song to Remember*.

The duality of Don Birnam's personality and its impact on Helen St. James are rendered in a flashback sequence revealing how the two met. It underscores the perceptiveness of St. James, an employee at *Time* magazine, of seeing both sides of Birnam and deciding to take a chance on getting acquainted with him.

A cultured former Ivy League Cornell University man, it is no surprise that Don Birnam would attend a performance of *La Traviata*. What marks him as different is that when he stares at the opera singers on stage he is reminded of his coat stored in the cloak room. It contains a bottle of rye whisky. Suddenly any appreciation he might hold for a classical opera work is supplanted by desperate desire for alcoholic consumption.

The shrewdly structured script of Wilder and Brackett dramatizes the key first meeting of struggling writer Don Birnam and elegant *Time* employee Helen St. James by showcasing the Achilles heel that threatens to destroy him, that of alcohol. Due to a mix-up Birnam has St. James's leopard skin coat. He is compelled to wait until the end of the performance before she emerges and is able to swap his coat for hers.

Immediately St. James sees the brittle edge of the Birnam personality displayed. The edginess stems from his hungry urge for a drink and being stymied by the coat mix-up. When she comments on his rudeness as he tosses her umbrella to her and says sarcastically, "Catch!" a wakeup call emerges within him. Suddenly the charming side of him surfaces and she agrees to take him to a party in Washington Square.

Another flashback sequence further delineates the dual side and rocky uncertainty of the couple's relationship. Helen's parents are in town, visiting from Toledo, Ohio, and she wishes for him to meet them. When he arrives ahead of her, Don overhears negative comments from Helen's father. The questioning of Don's stability causes him to make a call to Helen and explain that he will be delayed from coming to the hotel to meet her parents.

It is anything but surprising when Don decides to go home. When Helen arrives at his apartment to inquire about his failure to appear, a critical moment has arrived. Wick Birnam once more shows his unselfish love for his brother when he explains that he has a drinking problem, trying to save his brother embarrassment.

At that point viewers are given additional evidence as to why the shrewd Helen has seen fit to stick with Don despite disappointment. A strong supportive woman can see the good in a man even when others are baffled by her commitment to what they view as a lost cause. Helen seeks to convince Don that it is important to tap into what she is convinced represents a solid creative base, an ability to write, and take the forward step from which he shrinks.

At the film's conclusion Don listens to her and embarks on the challenge of writing his personal experiences in shaking the ravages of alcoholism. Before this occurs he comes perilously close to killing himself. It is Helen who arrives at his apartment in time to encourage him to pursue his writing goal. She wins by convincing Don to look at himself realistically and opt for life and career opportunity rather than death and defeat.

Three years after her triumph in *The Lost Weekend*, Wyman would star in *Johnny Belinda* opposite Lew Ayres. Her captivating performance in the challenging role of a deaf mute subjected to rape in a small town, where numerous additional complications result, brought her a "Best Actress" Oscar in the film directed by Jean Negulesco.

Milland's Film Noir Triple

Milland's Oscar-winning performance in *The Lost Weekend* marked the chronological centerpiece of three film noir triumphs of the suave Welsh actor, all under the Paramount banner. One year before the release of *The Lost Weekend* Milland starred in noir German master Fritz Lang's *Ministry of Fear*, a spy drama based on a novel by former British intelligence operative Graham Greene. Once again Lang, in his best Berlin tradition, delivered suspenseful subject matter depicting a great city with atmospheric credibility without leaving studio sound stages.

Milland plays Stephen Neale, a man who has been released from a British country asylum to which he had been sent for killing his former wife in what we learn was done to spare her unnecessary agony. After winning a cake at a raffle prior to boarding a train for London, he gets caught up in World War II spy intrigue in the city. Carla Hilfe (Marjorie Reynolds) teams up with Neale, helping to save his life from a group of ruthless Nazi intriguers.

The 1948 release *The Big Clock* finds George Stroud (Milland) involved in a game of wits with his boss, Earl Janoth (Charles Laughton). George and his wife, Georgette (Maureen O'Sullivan, at that time wife of the film's director John Farrow), seek a quieter life away from the hub of New York City in their former home of Wheeling, West Virginia. George is so determined to provide his wife their promised honeymoon that his demanding boss prevented earlier, that, in the ensuing discussion, he is fired.

Magazine magnate Earl Janoth has a fixation with clocks and punctuality to the point where he arranges a crucially climactic meeting with current flame Pauline York (Rita Johnson) at exactly 10:55. When he discovers that she has been out on the town he draws the false conclusion that she has a new love interest.

In actuality, Pauline has been drinking and comparing notes with George about Earl. Drinking plays a role in *The Big Clock*, but with a different twist than *The Lost Weekend* and the emphasis on alcoholism. Since Pauline had imbibed with George before her meeting with Earl, the question is whether she would have become angry enough with the magazine empire titan to tell him that he would not be able to find interest from any woman were it not for his money and position.

When Pauline ends her angry commentary, Earl's expression reveals hateful fury. He picks up a sun dial that she had obtained while bar hopping with George and delivers a smashing blow that kills her.

From that point forward a battle of wits occurs between Earl and his faithful executive assistant Steve Hagen (George Macready). The effort is to pin the blame for Pauline's death on the person she had spent her last evening with prior to meeting Earl at her apartment. George recognizes that he is the prime suspect. He vacates his West Virginia honeymoon scene, telling his wife of the necessity of returning to New York to free himself from a potentially grave situation.

George is matched against the ruthlessness of powerful executive Earl and pulls out all stops to vindicate himself. Earl reveals that saving himself from paying the price for his murderous actions prevails over all other considerations. When George's investigation points toward Steve Hagen as the guilty party (based on the tracks he has left seeking to save Earl from being discovered), the faithful troubleshooter is killed by the desperate magazine titan. This is then followed by an unsuccessful escape that ends when Earl falls down an elevator shaft.

As is so often the case in Hollywood drama, the finer points of the legal system are bent and oversimplified in the pursuit of building story drama. From the outset Earl Janoth and Steve Hagen have concluded that it is necessary to find someone to answer to the charge of killing Pauline York to spare the magazine titan from a first-degree murder conviction and the electric chair. While the conclusion reached in the film generates a greater degree of necessity to save Earl, legal reality takes a different turn. In order to secure a first-degree conviction, it must be established that the act was committed in cold blood and with premeditation. Earl was driven to pick up the sun dial and fatally strike Pauline in a towering rage after she had shattered his monumental ego by shouting that no woman would ever be interested in him but for his wealth and social status.

Killings in the midst of rage are devoid of premeditation. Under the circumstances, a criminal lawyer defending Earl in court would be able to present a compelling case for a manslaughter rather than murder one conviction. In addition, a man who runs a magazine empire would be able to afford the very best criminal lawyer and lawyers in that important metropolis of New York City, where numerous attorneys of notable talent practice law.

In order to provide contrast from the weightier aspects of the suspense drama, humor is injected with none other than Charles Laughton's real-life wife, Elsa Lanchester, standing in the forefront of that effort. She plays Louise Patterson, a zany painter who sees George Stroud in an art shop and is outbid by him for one of her own works. Lanchester displays the right measure of kooky gusto without ever going over the top.

Another comedic performer in the film is Lloyd Corrigan, who plays McKinley, a zany radio actor known for numerous personas, and in that befitting connection goes frequently by the name of Colonel Jefferson Randolph. When George adapts the name the sleuthing team of Earl and Steve believe that this is the man for whom they are looking, rather than George Stroud, who is moving in the opposite direction seeking to clear himself of involvement in Pauline's death. The film ends on a hilarious note when it is learned that there is a link between zany personages Louise Patterson and McKinley. Upon seeing him, Patterson announces that McKinley is her long-lost husband for whom she had been searching.

The forties proved to be a productive period for Ray Milland as Paramount provided him with a series of successful starring vehicles. Along with the aforementioned noir efforts, Milland scored big just before his Oscar triumph in *The Lost Weekend* in the 1944 ghost story classic *The Uninvited*. Milland played well opposite his love interest in the film, Gail Russell, who was making her starring debut at Paramount. The film features the frequent playing of the memorable ballad "Stella by Starlight," with Russell cast in the role of Stella Meredith.

From Would Be Killer to Comedy Series Star

While Milland was generally cast in the role of a suave gentleman of refinement, he became a would-be killer for Alfred Hitchcock seeking to eliminate his wealthy wife, Margot (Grace Kelly) in the film adaptation of the Frederick Knott play *Dial M for Murder*. Milland invests the role of former pro tennis player and later marital opportunist Tony Wendice with an outwardly cool, inward hard edge.

An actor of versatility, Milland moved from his role of would be wife killer to that of a college professor, with humor the objective. Milland was polished and intelligent appearing so that the role of an engaging professor suited him. During a period when film stars were moving into the successful arena of television acting Milland assumed the role of Professor Ray McNulty in the series *Meet Mr. McNulty*. The popular comedy series debuted in 1953, with Phyllis Avery cast as his wife, Peggy.

The final year of the series, 1955, found Milland performing in another stellar role, playing a famous man of dignity and accomplishment. Milland assumed the role of prominent New York architect Stanford White in the factually based *The Girl in the Red Velvet Swing*. White, then one of the most regal symbols of New York City success, was gunned down June 25, 1906, in jealous rage by Harry Kendall Thaw, a scion of Pittsburgh wealth, in a triangle with beautiful show girl-model Elizabeth Nesbitt as the object of competition.

The beautifully mounted film captured the Gilded Age faithfully in relation to the fast-stepping aristocratic New York set. It helped launch director Richard Fleischer into the higher budget ranks after his great success with the 1952 film noir low budget thriller *The Narrow Margin* starring Charles McGraw and Marie Windsor. The film was also a springboard in the career of Joan Collins, then in her early twenties. She has referred to the film as her favorite. For Farley Granger, cast as the deeply troubled Harry Kendall Thaw, this was another one of his fifties' memorable roles along with Hitchcock's 1951 release *Strangers on a Train*, which was preceded by the 1948 Hitchcock film *Rope* and Nicholas Ray's 1949 stellar noir effort *They Live by Night*.

Milland's suave manner was used as a man confronted with serious problems in three noir films, in comedy as a professor in a three year television series, and as a heavy seeking to kill his wealthy wife. A more veteran Milland proved a perfect foil in a generation gap context with his appearance in the 1970 blockbuster *Love Story*. The film is highlighted by a generational clash between a strong-willed son played by Ryan O'Neill and his former Rhodes scholar father, portrayed by Milland.

Lang Spawns Duryea as Great American Villain

So much of the Berlin influence exerted on the noir branch of the American film industry during and shortly following World War II stemmed from the efforts of Fritz Lang and his memorable film delineating fear and mass psychology in a great city —*M*. In *M*, as Lang biographer Patrick McGilligan explained, the daring director scaled new heights with his portrayal of a villain.[4]

When he arrived in America and began directing films accenting suspense it was only natural for Lang to transpose the same effective use of villainy in heightening dramatic contrast in his Hollywood vehicles. Two of Lang's most cost-effective and superb noir suspense vehicles involved veteran character star Edward G. Robinson playing a middle-aged man obsessed with a beautiful, much younger woman, in each case played by Joan Bennett. The success of the 1944 release *The Woman in the Window* resulted in a similarly structured film one year later with *Scarlet Street*.

The other skilled performer who filled out the triumvirate of stars who appeared in both Lang films was a man who came from a distinguished family background. He had received an Ivy League education, but on screen conveyed the guise of someone perpetually prepared to snarl in the same way that Richard Widmark in his villainous roles was always prepared to deliver his sadistic and thoroughly sarcastic laugh.

Dan Duryea was someone with whom Lang could work. He let Duryea know that an unforgettable element of any suspense drama involving sharply contrasting characters was the villain. Before Lang began shaping the process that led to Duryea becoming the celebrated heavy of film noir he had launched his film career playing an avaricious nephew in *The Little Foxes*. It was a role he had initially played on Broadway opposite Talullah Bankhead. When casting was done for the film version starring Bette Davis, Duryea was invited to reprise his stage role.

Lang instinctively knew that Duryea possessed the right ingredients to serve as catalyst to the femme fatale of *The Woman in the Window*. Whereas Peter Lorre's homicidal character in Lang's 1931 classic *M* was a creature of disturbance who ultimately cried out that he was not in control of his own actions and did not understand them, Duryea's character, Heidt, was in thorough control of both thought and deed. His sociopath's manner coupled with a snarling, cocky outward bravado made him an object of hate among audience members.

Nothing in Duryea's background indicated that he was headed for fame playing the man with the perpetual snarl. His was a background akin to that of Franchot Tone, who, as noted in the analysis of his career, generally played the smooth-talking aristocrat, consistent with his background as a New York City scion of wealth. Even when Tone played a sick psychopath in his enduring role in *Phantom Lady* he was a creative genius with a superiority complex whose hatred for humanity resided from a smugness that the world was an inferior place and inadequate to accommodate him.

Duryea grew up in the New York City suburb of White Plains as the son of a textile salesman. Like Tone, he attended Cornell University, majoring in English. He followed Tone as president of the Cornell Drama Society. Rather than follow his creative instinct into the acting world after his graduation, Duryea chose what he then deemed to be a safer career route and entered the Madison Avenue advertising orbit.

Duryea found his creative side stifled in the cutthroat competition of the advertising field, which he found repellent. A major career turning point occurred when he suffered a mild heart attack in his late twenties. He decided to then return to his first love of acting and before long he was in Hollywood, etching an unforgettable stamp with his unique style of acting. Who could have been a better teacher than Fritz Lang, the director of *M* with the vivid career establishing portrayal of Peter Lorre into the ranks of international stardom?

In addition to his unforgettable performances in *The Woman in the Window* and *Scarlet Street*, he also delivered commendably for Lang in *Ministry of Fear*. In the first two films, avarice was Duryea's objective. In the 1944 espionage drama, Duryea plays a tailor who serves as a foot soldier in a conspiracy den.

As mentioned at the beginning of this work, Duryea as mob boss Slim Dundee epitomized the true essence of hard-boiled noir of the traditional Dashiell Hammett-Raymond Chandler school in *Criss Cross*. The scene in the dilapidated Angels Flight quarters of alcohol-driven crime genius Alan Napier is so evocative that, if a film instructor wanted to choose one scene capsulizing the essence of noir cinema genre, this would make an intelligent choice.

Duryea's Slim Dundee was not a likely choice to hold anyone in admiring awe. This then makes the scene all the more meaningful when he pays such deference to Napier, someone whose creativity is used to plan armed robberies. Dundee's ego is at work envisioning himself as a pioneer in crime annals capable of pulling off the previously unthinkable, a successful armored truck robbery.

Duryea by a Half

While Duryea emerges as a consummate villainous protégé of Fritz Lang in the three films in which they worked together, *The Woman in the Window*, *Scarlet Street*, and *Ministry of Fear*, as well as in his unforgettable performance under Robert Siodmak in *Criss Cross*, the Universal production *Black Angel* provided a creative casting twist for the Cornell-educated star. This time Duryea's character, rather than someone who uses women for his own selfish ends, proves himself capable of summoning up the sensitivity of falling legitimately in love and, rather than using the woman involved, seeks instead to assist her.

Black Angel was a 1946 Universal release that, like *Phantom Lady*, was adapted from a novel by Cornell Woolrich. Handling the screenplay adaptation was Roy Chanslor, who wrote the novels *Johnny Guitar*, which became a 1954 noir western hit starring Joan Crawford and Sterling Hayden, and *The Ballad of Cat Ballou*, which in the 1965 film adaptation was called *Cat Ballou* and became an Oscar winning "Best Actor" vehicle for Lee Marvin.

Veteran Universal hand Roy William Neill directed *Black Angel*. Neill became notable directing Universal's popular Sherlock Holmes films starring Basil Rathbone and Nigel Bruce.

Black Angel begins with the murder of Mavis Marlowe (Constance Dowling). Marlowe, a glamorous and exceptionally spoiled professional singer, is found murdered in her apartment by strangulation. The immediate suspect is Kirk Bennett (John Phillips), who has engaged in a tempestuous extramarital affair with the grasping, opportunistic Marlowe.

There is sufficient evidence against Phillips along with apparent motive to convict him of the murder. One person steadfastly refuses to believe that Kirk Bennett could kill Marlowe or anyone else, his faithful wife, Catherine (June Vincent), who was willing to overlook his indiscretion with Marlowe in the belief that it was not indicative of the real nature of the man she married.

Catherine realizes that she is battling a time clock as her husband's date for execution in San Quentin Prison looms ever closer. Catherine meets Martin Blair (Duryea) at that crucial juncture. He is a trouble-ridden but talented songwriter and pianist with too strong a liking for alcohol. Martin is Catherine's former husband, understandable in view of them both being in the music field.

This might be film noir, this might be Dan Duryea, but this is one time that he empathizes with a woman for whom he feels genuine love. He indicates a belief that Marko (Peter Lorre), a nightclub owner involved with a local Hollywood criminal syndicate, might be Marlowe's killer. After all, she once sang at his club, and Marko had a known way with the ladies. He was therefore someone that Martin decided that he and Catherine should carefully investigate.

Martin engineers a way to get Catherine inside Marko's club by having her audition as a singer. She had previous experience and he grooms her for the role, liking what he sees and hears. Coaching Catherine while sitting at the piano and accompanying her causes his romantic feelings toward her to skyrocket. His training provides the desired result as Marko hires her, with Martin as her piano accompaniment. Martin is then put in a nervous position in realizing the dangers of Marko as well as his propensities as a nightclub owning lothario he is correctly convinced will develop quick designs on Catherine. At the same time, he knows that, through Marko's romantic designs, the game plan of solving the murder can be enhanced.

A periodic presence in the story's development and effort to prove that Catherine's husband is innocent is Captain Flood (Broderick Crawford). Crawford was then working his way up the ranks. Three years later he would win a "Best Actor" Academy Award for his captivating performance as ruthless and dictatorial Governor Willie Stark in Robert Rossen's 1949 classic *All the King's Men*, a thinly disguised film examination into the incredible life of Governor Huey Long of Louisiana. One year after that he portrayed bullying tough guy Harry Brock opposite Judy Holiday in her "Best Actress" role in director George Cukor's adaptation of Garson Kanin's hit Broadway play, *Born Yesterday*. Crawford's role as a tough, uncompromising policeman in *Black Angel* was a precursor of Chief Dan Mathews in *Highway Patrol*, a popular television series that played for 156 episodes between 1955 and 1959. Captain Flood is initially convinced that Kirk Bennett is definitely guilty. As a fair-minded officer who believes in evidence, however, he listens to Martin and Catherine, and is willing to follow wherever the facts lead him.

Some of film noir's most colorful and fascinating figures have come from the ranks of professional wrestlers and boxers, as evidenced by headline wrestler Mike Mazurki and Boston middleweight boxer Johnny Indrisano, who later became a referee in California as well as an actor and fight scene technical consultant. It is Indrisano who is thrown violently to the ground by Mazurki in *Murder, My Sweet*.

Freddie Steele grew up in Tacoma, Washington, and began his professional career at the incredible age of 13 years, 11 months in November 1926. He became one of the hardest punchers in boxing, winning the world middleweight championship. Sportswriters called him the "Tacoma Assassin." When his career ended, Steele spent some time as a character performer in Hollywood, appearing in Peston Sturges's comedy *Hail the Conquering Hero* (1944) and opposite former boxer Robert Mitchum one year later in *The Story of G.I. Joe*.

In the manner of former boxers and wrestlers in Hollywood, Steele's role in *Black Angel* is that of Lucky, strongman-protector of a mobster. He serves as a Man Friday to Marko at his club. Bad blood surfaces between Lucky and Martin and they fall just short of engaging in a fight at one point. Steele adds just the right touch to his role as a henchman for the underworld, a prevailing reality in the evening entertainment circuits of major cities during that period.

The story structure of *Black Angel* points in the direction of Marko, a suspicious mob figure with ties to Mavis Marlowe, being her killer. The pivotal plot twist shifts dramatically near the film's conclusion.

While earlier activity has revealed that Martin, despite a drinking problem that he seemingly corralled after falling in love with Catherine, is a decent man, viewers learn that he was capable of homicidal violence against his former wife. The film's character arc figure is, in fact, Martin. His love for Catherine, which has seen him put aside the bottle, generates a desire to prevent an innocent man from being executed for a crime he did not commit.

The twist in *Black Angel* concerning criminal accountability stems from Martin's drinking binges, occasioned by the suffocating torch he carries for the beautiful but cold-blooded opportunist Mavis Marlowe. In addition to being a nightclub singer she moonlights as a blackmailer with Kirk Bennett and Marko among her victims. Martin killed her in a drunken stupor, which made it easier for him to blot her strangulation death out of his mind. The symbol that brings the event back in full context is locating a broach that he had given Marlowe for an anniversary gift. When he learns the truth he is hell-bent on doing the decent thing by saving the husband of the woman he loves from the gas chamber, with precious little time to spare. It is up to Captain Flood to awaken the governor early in the morning with the news that a man is slated to die later that day for a murder of which he is innocent.

Black Angel afforded Dan Duryea, bad guy protégé of Fritz Lang, an opportunity to play a different kind of role but still in the film noir realm.

Chapter Twelve

Preminger's Noir Touch with *Fallen Angel* and Alice Faye

> Alice Faye was the girl next door that parents hoped their son would marry, the essence of beauty linked to wholesome sincerity.— Robert Kendall

Otto Preminger, born and raised in Vienna, is another World War II period émigré to leave Europe during the reign of the Third Reich, in the tradition of Fritz Lang, Billy Wilder, and Robert Siodmak. Preminger's pictures were frequently studies of the somber side of existence and, accordingly, it was anything but surprising to see him become involved in film noir.

Preminger's films were noted for dealing with ambiguity. One could call it a form of poetic justice that his life began shrouded in ambiguity. Preminger wrote in his biography that "one set of documents lists Vienna as my birthplace but another set ... places my birth at my great-grandfather's farm some distance away. One records that I was born on the fifth of December, 1906, the other exactly one year earlier."

It is unambiguous that Preminger was born into a distinguished house of privilege. His father, Markus Preminger, was a well-known lawyer who served as chief prosecutor for the Austro Hungarian Empire and then for the imperial army. These were unusually high positions for a Jew in a society immersed in anti–Semitism. Preminger's mother was the daughter of a lumberyard owner.

After World War I and the consolidation of the Austrian Republic, Markus Preminger, a loyal monarchist, left public office and launched a lucrative private practice in Vienna. While his family urged young Otto to pursue the study of law, his interest lay in the creative field and the rich culture of Vienna gave him an outlet for expression. Before long Otto was auditioning for the great Max Reinhardt and was accepted as an apprentice at the Josefstadt Theatre.

By 1931, Preminger had directed two plays in Vienna along with his first film, *Die Grosse Liebe* (*The Great Love*). In 1936, Joseph M. Schenck arrived from Hollywood. As Preminger stated in his biography, "He had just merged a small company— Twentieth Century— with Fox, and he needed young people." Schenck knew of Preminger's reputation and invited him to Hollywood. "It was a very old dream of mine," Preminger wrote, "and it had nothing to do with Hitler, to go to America."[1]

New contractee Preminger was put to work at Fox, but there was an ultimate clash with studio boss Zanuck. Though Preminger was still under contract, Zanuck provided him with no work. Preminger had directed a play in New York before moving on to Hollywood, and it was to Broadway that he returned, notching a success by directing seven plays. One of them was Laurette Taylor's Broadway comeback role, a successful adaptation of Sutton Vane's *Outward Bound.*

Show business annals are replete with successes under the most unpredictable circumstances. Such was the case while Preminger was directing Clare Boothe Luce's drama *Margin for Error.* Due to the defection of a performer, Preminger stepped forward as a last-minute substitute in the role of a bullying Nazi consul. The excellent reviews he received prompted writer-producer Nunnally Johnson to beckon his return to Fox to play a Nazi officer in *The Pied Piper.*

Had Darryl Zanuck been in charge of Fox at the time Preminger would not have received his second chance, but he happened to be performing wartime Army duties, and so he was given that opportunity and more. The irony of the Jewish Preminger impressing in Nazi roles prompted William Goetz, interim studio head during Zanuck's military absence, to offer him the opportunity to reprise his Broadway role in the film version of *Margin for Error.*

Preminger sniffed the bloom of opportunity by offering Goetz a deal. He would enact the Nazi consul role on screen as well as direct for his actor's fee alone. Preminger agreed to relinquish his director's reins if Goetz was not satisfied following his first week of work. A rough patch surfaced in the road when Preminger found the film script adaptation of *Margin for Error* unacceptable, but a young novelist on Army leave successfully doctored it, future film director Samuel Fuller.

A Classic Despite Interlocking Antipathies

When Zanuck returned from service duty and took over from interim studio head William Goetz he was anything but pleased to have Preminger back on the Fox lot. At one point he reportedly told his nemesis that he would never direct a film as long as he was head of the studio, but if such declarations were truly etched in stone we would be bereft of so much of Hollywood history.

In so many instances, such declarations are abandoned when a crisis point looms. A troubled project needs attention and so grudges are abandoned. Two great Hollywood classics began as jinx films seemingly, at best, destined for B labels. One was the Warners classic *Casablanca* and the other was the film in which a teeth-gritting Zanuck worked with Preminger, the 1944 adaptation of the Vera Caspary novel *Laura.*

Rouben Mamoulian was *Laura*'s original director and the circumstances surrounding his departure and producer Preminger's acceptance of Mamoulian's earlier responsibility continues to be a matter of conjecture more than six decades later. Zanuck and Preminger, whose association appeared destined for dispute, clashed on two major casting points regarding the film. Ultimately Zanuck deferred to the film's producer-director, whose judgment was vindicated.[2]

Earlier examples were provided regarding the homophobia pervasive in the Hollywood of the flourishing forties' noir period. Zanuck added his own chapter regarding his stout opposition to Preminger's determination to cast Broadway character performer Clifton Webb in the role of Waldo Lydecker. Zanuck's opposition to Webb was summarized in a two-word comment used as a pejorative against alleged flighty homosexuals, "He flies."

Preminger's creative instincts told him that Webb would be ideal as a highly sophisticated Manhattan columnist and radio commentator with a runaway superiority complex and a domineering Svengali attitude toward svelte and beautiful model Laura (Gene Tierney). When Zanuck refused to see Webb or permit Preminger to test him, the inventive director filmed a performance of the actor, who was then appearing in a production at the Biltmore Theater in downtown Los Angeles. Ultimately Zanuck's opposition was worn down.[3]

Even after filming had commenced, Zanuck, upon viewing production rushes, expressed dissatisfaction with the casting of Dana Andrews. He believed that John Hodiak, a Fox leading man that the studio boss was then assiduously building up, possessed a sturdy masculinity that Zanuck did not believe Andrews was conveying in the rushes. Once more Zanuck deferred to Preminger's judgment.

Twentieth boss Zanuck's comparison between Hodiak and Andrews failed to evaluate Preminger's philosophy of filmmaking. To the Vienna-born director, bred into the German-Vienna school encompassing the likes of Lang, Wilder, and Siodmak, the issue was not embodied by comparative examples of masculinity on the part of leading men. There were those internal complications extending to Preminger's fascination with moral ambiguity.

Andrews was a favorite of Otto Preminger because of the internal complications he could bring to a role. It is one thing to view a leading man on the screen; it is another for audiences to view that individual on the one hand and fill in internal blanks on the other, empathizing with what is happening beneath the surface. In the case of Andrews he so totally empathizes with the painting of Laura he sees seemingly staring down at him from the living room of her apartment. He has become so captivated by her persona at a point when he believes she has been recently murdered that the brilliant Waldo Lydecker tartly informs Andrews that this is the first time he has ever seen anyone "fall in love with a corpse."

One of the major thematic elements that made *Laura* a smashing success and catapulted it into the film noir category was its brooding quality as embodied in the title song written by David Raksin, which became every bit the enduring classic as the film. Andrews as brooding detective Harry McPherson invests the role with complicated internal life in the best Preminger tradition of moral ambiguity. The haunting quality of the song played repeatedly combined with the hypnotically tortured expression of Andrews addresses the element of how captivated and haunted he is by the image.

It is thematically beneficial to those seeking to understand *Fallen Angel* as a unit to closely evaluate the similarities between the roles Andrews played in each film. In each film Andrews is a complicated man who was raised in New York, the nation's largest city and one riddled with complexities. The Great Depression is another element in the tough circumstances in which Detective Mark McPherson and Eric Stanton grew up. Each has a rough-hewn intelligence, a street smartness.

Despite having been filmed entirely on the Twentieth Century–Fox lot, *Laura* offers a splendidly insightful look into the Park Avenue world of power and sophistication. What makes the Jay Dratler, Samuel Hoffenstein, and Elizabeth Reinhardt adaptation of Vera Caspery's novel scale film classic ranks is the manner in which the film's three main characters impinge on one another. Clifton Webb in his most enduring dramatic role is Waldo Lydecker, a columnist and radio commentator intoxicated with his own power in the tenacious Park Avenue power structure. He sees Laura as his personal property, operating as a Svengali and seeking to control her every move. While his interest is not sexual, he uses his power and influence to drive away men with a romantic influence who threaten his control.

Twelve. Preminger's Noir Touch with Fallen Angel *Alice Faye* 183

McPherson falls in love with the image of Laura at a time when it appears she has been murdered. When it is learned that another model was killed instead and that all were operating under a wrong impression, Laura is caught in a tug of war between the domineering Lydecker, by whom she does not wish to be dominated, and McPherson, with whom she falls in love. Meanwhile McPherson begins to realize that the egomaniacal Lydecker sought to kill Laura when he realized he could not control her.

A comparable three-tiered dramatic structure is also at work in *Fallen Angel*. There were numerous elements in common based on design by Zanuck and Preminger. In the 1945 work, however, Eric Stanton (Andrews) stands in the middle as he seeks to use June Mills (Alice Faye) to provide the necessary funds for what Stella (Linda Darnell) deems a proper marital foundation, without which she will not form a romantic attachment to the smooth-talking drifter.

The story element that sends the three-tiered involvement to another level is the murder of Stella. After that Eric, having been seen outside Stella's apartment the evening of her death, becomes the prime suspect of New York City detective transplant Mark Judd (Charles Bickford), who is asked to head the investigation. Eric will ultimately turn the tables on Detective Judd by discovering his checkered past. In fact, Judd has a fixation on Stella just as Lydecker sought to control Laura, but whereas the columnist is interested in psychological

ATTENTIVE ADMIRER— Eric Stanton (Dana Andrews) watches from outside while sultry Stella (Linda Darnell) applies makeup as her boss, Pop (Percy Kilbride, later to achieve fame with Marjorie Main in the Ma and Pa Kettle series), looks on in the 1945 film *Fallen Angel*, directed by Otto Preminger.

control, Judd's interest is of romantic fantasy fixation. He sits by the hour at Pop's Café and drinks coffee, mesmerized at being in Stella's presence.

Judd is not the only older man with strong romantic inclinations toward her. Stella is placed on a pedestal by her employer, Pop (Percy Kilbride), who dotes on her. Meanwhile, tough and beautiful Stella plays the field among the younger men. Dave Atkins (Bruce Cabot), who services the jukebox in the restaurant, has dated her. He is not only questioned by Judd following her death, but subjected to police brutality, being victimized by backroom slapping with the experienced New York police detective transplant wearing the traditional kid gloves designed to produce pain without yielding marks. An airtight alibi clears Atkins, leaving Eric Stanton as Judd's next suspect.

Seeking Another *Laura* and an Odd Couple Teaming

The odd couple element arising from Preminger's 1945 noir film *Fallen Angel* is not that he did a film of that character, but the leading lady who starred in it. Alice Faye was Fox's reigning star in the period from the late thirties until the mid-forties and the release of *Fallen Angel*. It was therefore no surprise that she would be cast in a major film by Darryl F. Zanuck, who always had professional admiration for Alice Faye as well as an appreciation for her popularity at the box office, but what gave this film its tone of uniqueness was Preminger directing her in a noir suspense drama.

SOULFUL LADY—This expressive photograph shows why Alice Faye became filmdom's soulful sweetheart of the thirties and forties.

Alice Faye was the embodiment of wholesomeness. Robert Kendall, a friend of Faye's for many years and someone who interviewed her frequently, captured the essence of the popular blonde star: "Alice Faye was the girl next door that parents hoped their son would marry, the essence of beauty linked to wholesome sincerity."

Kendall's evaluation of Faye makes one think of President Harry Truman's effusive praise of James Stewart amid the national response to Frank Capra's memorable 1946 release *It's a Wonderful Life*. President

Truman exclaimed that he and the nation's First Lady Bess would have been pleased and honored to have Stewart as a son.

The ideal teaming in capturing the spirited essence of wholesomeness among superstars would have been Alice Faye romantically linked to James Stewart. While this never occurred, Faye made her mark registering her brand of steadfast goodness and consolation to leading men in difficulty. Her support and good judgment had steered Tyrone Power, Don Ameche, and John Payne through rough times. As will be revealed, her most challenging effort of all came in *Fallen Angel*.

Cinema critics and historians who evaluated Alice Faye's talent used the word "natural" repeatedly. In the manner of the performer who could be classified as her male counterpart, James Stewart, it was frequently written about both superstars that they never appeared to be acting.

"Having met Alice so many times, I was always struck by how much she resembled in person the character she depicted so convincingly on screen," Robert Kendall observed. "For instance, when she was appearing in the musical *Good News* with John Payne at the Schubert Theatre in Los Angeles I went backstage one night after the show. I had a friend take some pictures of me with Alice. All of a sudden the camera gave us trouble. When you wanted it to work it wouldn't and then suddenly light would begin flashing. My friend and I got disgusted and Alice said calmly, 'It's nothing.' She then called over a technical man versed in cameras and he instantly fixed the problem. It struck me that the way she spoke and acted was just like her actions with her male leads in her Fox roles."

Another element of Alice Faye's screen image was generosity of spirit, and here again Kendall correlated that image with the actual person:

> I recall when I was a struggling college student and did not have much money for entertainment. Alice was starring in the successful radio show with Phil Harris. I would be standing outside the NBC Studio on Sunset Boulevard on Sunday night, when Alice and Phil did their show, and all of a sudden, without fail, an NBC page would appear in his bright uniform and hand me a ticket that had been provided by Alice. It made me feel ten feet tall. She was always doing good turns for people. Alice did volunteer work at Palm Springs Hospital and was always performing with Phil at charity benefits.

BACKSTAGE CONGRATULATIONS — Robert Kendall was backstage to congratulate long time friend Alice Faye at Los Angeles's Schubert Theatre following a 1974 appearance in *Good News*.

Fallen Angel was seen by Darryl F. Zanuck as an opportunity to showcase a new Alice Faye as a transformation to dramatic star from her previous career as Fox's premier leading lady of musicals. Alice Faye's meteoric rise to stardom during the peak of the Great Depression is the stuff from which inspiration is generated. Born Alice Jeanne Leppert, the daughter of a New York City policeman, she used her smooth, mellow voice to become a network singing sensation before Twentieth Century–Fox came calling.

A big assist toward Faye becoming an international superstar goes to the first American crooner, Rudy Vallee, for giving Alice her major show business break. As Robert Kendall revealed, "Alice's career began as a chorus girl in the Broadway production of *George White's Scandals*. At a cast party when the show closed Alice chanced to make a recording of the song 'Mimi' just for fun. Rudy Vallee heard her sing that number."

Vallee was slated for an engagement at a Cleveland hotel. He invited Alice to accompany him. Vallee wanted to see how she would be received by a nightclub audience.

"When Alice sang the audience responded with thunderous applause," Kendall related. "It was then that Vallee knew that Alice Faye was star material."

Vallee was then star of *The Fleischmann's Yeast Hour*, a popular network radio show. It was his practice to introduce talent discoveries. One was Kate Smith. Another, ironically, was Phil Harris, who would eventually become Alice Faye's husband. Vallee introduced Alice resulting in huge audience reaction. When Vallee was called by Fox to Hollywood to perform in the film version of *George White's Scandals* (1935), Faye starred alongside comedian Jimmy Durante. She became a rarity in two respects, starring in her first film and accomplishing that tall feat while still in her teens.

The thirties and forties saw major results for Darryl F. Zanuck at Fox with Alice Faye becoming the studio's leading female star. She starred in such major hits as *In Old Chicago* (1937), *Alexander's Ragtime Band* (1938), *Rose of Washington Square* (1939), *Tin Pan Alley* (1940), *That Night in Rio* (1941), *Week-end in Havana* (1941), and *Hello, Frisco, Hello* (1943).

With Faye films securing solid profits, Zanuck pushed his star into a whirlwind pace. When asked about the surge of activity, Faye delivered her famous friendly laugh and exclaimed, "They didn't call it Twentieth Penitentiary Fox for nothing."

The Song Controversy

At the age of 29, at a time when Faye had introduced more hit songs into films than any female performer before or after her, and was second overall only to Bing Crosby (who appeared in more films than she), Zanuck decided to move Alice into a more concentrated dramatic role. She diligently rehearsed one song, which was to be her lone musical contribution to the film, and therein a controversy surfaced with speculation undiminished better than six decades later.

Arthur Nicholson, who until his recent death was president of the British-based Alice Faye Appreciation Society, revealed that she was supposed to sing the hit tune "Slowly" in a beach scene with leading man Dana Andrews. The inclusion of a song generated a twofold purpose. Thematically there was the heavy studio publicity push toward publicizing *Fallen Angel* as the next *Laura* as Zanuck sought to generate mighty box-office results as the Gene Tierney starrer had one year earlier. The haunting title song was written by David Raksin, who also wrote "Slowly." In the instance of "Slowly," Fox's number-one leading lady and major American film song plugger Faye could be effectively utilized.

Thematic symmetry was sought in the repeated playing of a David Raksin song. In

Laura the repeated playing of the song instrumentally demonstrated the inner psychological turmoil of Mark McPherson as he coped with the reality of being haunted by a presumed dead woman with whom he had fallen passionately in love. Once Laura emerges alive it then becomes a song invoking romantic pangs between the svelte brunette model and a police detective determined to prove her innocence in the death of the real victim, a model who had been romantically linked to Laura's faithless fiancé, Shelby Carpenter (Vincent Price).

The thematic connection in Raksin's song "Slowly" in *Fallen Angel* covered fascinating new ground. It was also slated to be sung by two of the forties' leading balladeers, each of whom was known for mellow delivery: male crooner Dick Haymes and soulful female artist Alice Faye. "The idea was to have Alice sing the song with Andrews and for the popular male vocalist of the forties Dick Haymes to be heard singing it from a jukebox," Nicholson explained. "The reason is that the film's other female star, Linda Darnell, wanted to listen to 'Slowly' on the jukebox and it was her favorite song. This furnished a contrast since Linda and Alice were the two women in Dana Andrews's life."

Nicholson had a close friendship with Alice Faye extending for years. He would send flowers to her hotel suite whenever she came to London, which was one of her favorite cities, a love that Londoners reciprocated. They would go out on shopping excursions together. A trusting relationship emerged and the blonde star confided information about her relations with Zanuck during the filming of *Fallen Angel* that Nicholson was gracious enough to provide to me shortly before his death.

"In the film we see the moonlight beach scene," Nicholson related. "Here Alice and Dana eat hot dogs. She falls asleep . He puts her gently into the car and the scene fades out. What we should have had next but do not is the car arriving at Alice's home with her still asleep. The car radio is on with an orchestra softly playing the film's signature song 'Slowly.' Alice sings along with it."

Nicholson explains what comes next along with the lost dramatic impact from the foregoing material being cut: "As she finishes the song she is all romantic and hopes he feels the same way, too. Unfortunately, he, of course, associates the song with Stella and becomes all bitter and cold toward her and they end up in a very nasty argument with her becoming very hysterical and in tears and rushing into the house, only to have another big row with her sister Anne Revere."

The foregoing segment was cut on Zanuck's orders. "Alice was furious," Nicholson related. "Alice told me, 'It took two whole weeks to shoot those scenes. I was saddle sore sitting in that car for two weeks and completely exhausted after all the hysterical scenes, and all for nothing; two whole weeks on the cutting room floor.'"

Another cut imposed by Zanuck, which arguably is as dramatically significant, occurs on the wedding night of June to Eric where she waits in vain for him to come home while he is out with Stella. By cutting such a key scene a sharp contrast involving the two women and the perfidious manner of Eric at such a critical emotional point was missed. The fact that June being left alone on the wedding night is mentioned later in the film is all the more reason why a successful transitional bridge, as afforded by the cut scene, should have remained.

"Alice heard later that Preminger was furious too over the cuts and had a great row with Zanuck," Nicholson said, "but Zanuck was the boss and his word was law. She also said that she felt she had done her best work and Preminger too had complimented her when the scenes were eventually in the can."

While Otto Preminger had been accused of being exceedingly tough on actresses who starred in his films, and one, Faye Dunnaway, bought herself out of a contract with him after working with him once in one of his biggest flops, *Hurry Sundown* (1967). Alice Faye had a good rapport with the director known in certain Hollywood circles as "Otto the Terrible."

"Alice told me that she found Preminger a very considerate director," Nicholson said. "She hadn't worked for nearly two years and he was very kind and patient with her. Alice said, 'He knew exactly what he wanted and gently coaxed you to get it his way.'"

Alice spent her 30th birthday on the Fox set, on May 5, 1945. Preminger and the crew organized a birthday party, providing a cake and flowers.

Nicholson believed that had the song "Slowly" included a rendition by Faye that it stood a chance of gaining the popularity as an enduring standard as had "Laura." Even if it failed to rise to that rarified level its chances of reaching a higher popularity standard would have increased.

While no reason was given as to why the scenes were cut, Nicholson revealed, "Alice believed he had cut her best scenes for punishment. He wanted her in musicals and was furious with her for not doing *State Fair* as her comeback film. He had brought out Richard Rodgers and Oscar Hammerstein to write the songs to suit her voice. If she had done it, the script would have been different so her character would have sung 'It Might As Well Be Spring.' Zanuck was also full of fury at her taking time out to have two daughters, causing the studio to lose millions at the box office."

Nicholson noted that following the 1940 release of *Lillian Russell* that Zanuck never thereafter personally produced an Alice Faye film. This was the torrid period of non-stop work activity that spawned her aforementioned reference to "Twentieth Penitentiary Fox."

"In my conversations with her, Alice always maintained that she was tired of back stage musicals," Nicholson revealed. "She wanted stronger roles. Alice longed for the type of romantic comedies that Paramount made with Claudette Colbert, with a couple of songs along the way. She asked, 'Why couldn't they have found things like *Meet Me in St. Louis* [1944], that MGM found for Judy Garland, for me?'"

As she rapidly approached the age of 30, Alice Faye sought to expand dramatically. According to Nicholson, "She turned down scripts till *Fallen Angel* came along."[4]

Alice, who grew up in the Depression, had been working from the time she was 14. After the big flap with Zanuck, culminating with her dramatically leaving the keys to her dressing room at the Fox gate, she was happy to stop working and raise her daughters in Palm Springs, some hundred miles from the Hollywood scene. "She wanted her second marriage to work after she had her first to Tony Martin end in divorce," Nicholson said.

Since she remained under contract to Fox, Zanuck refused to allow her to do any other film work. When she embarked on the successful NBC radio show with husband Phil Harris, an always-attentive Zanuck demanded that each episode include a comment that Alice Faye was appearing with permission from Twentieth Century–Fox.

An ironic point revolved around Alice Faye making her return to Twentieth almost two decades later, at a point when Zanuck was no longer running the studio. The film was none other than the remake of the movie that Zanuck wanted her to do the same year that *Fallen Angel* was filmed, *State Fair*. This version starred Tom Ewell, Pat Boone, and Pamela Tiffin. A second irony revolved around the 1945 original version since the male lead was none other than Dick Haymes, who sang the version of "Slowly" that was heard in *Fallen Angel*.

George McGhee and Showing Faye in the U.K.

George McGhee stands in a unique position as an evaluator of what makes a film star succeed in the realm of popular opinion. McGhee was Controller of Program Acquisition for six years at the British Broadcasting Corporation until his retirement last year. He was responsible for all feature films on every BBC channel as well as foreign series' such as *Damages*, *Mad Men*, *Heroes* and others. Previously he had been Director of Carlton Cinema, a basic 24-hour pay television channel showing a diverse range of films.

"I first saw Alice Faye playing Pat Boone's mother in *State Fair* in 1962 when I was six years old," McGhee related. "I then saw her in the first Twentieth Century–Fox film ever shown on U.K. television, *Alexander's Ragtime Band*. It played on BBC 2 at 9 P.M. In 1971, I left school early one afternoon and went to the Classic Cinema in Glasgow to see a reissue of *San Francisco* (1936) and the second feature was Alice starring with Tyrone Power and Al Jolson in *Rose of Washington Square* (1939) and I became absolutely hooked on Alice Faye and her extraordinary talent. I then went out and bought an excellent film book, *The Great Movie Stars: The Golden Years* by David Shipman. I was then able to look up Alice and find all the movies she has made."

Alice Faye, as evidenced earlier through the words of Arthur Nicholson, enjoyed enormous popularity within the United Kingdom. She visited London often as well as Ireland, where she had a chance to touch base with her own Irish roots. George McGhee had the opportunity to meet Alice Faye frequently and got to know her quite well. "Alice was wonderful to meet because she was comfortable with people and was genuinely touched to be remembered," McGhee said. "She was not at all blasé or arrogant. Although offscreen she was not exactly the character she had played onscreen, she was an extension of them and she definitely had the 'vulnerability' factor and was open. What you saw was what you got."

McGhee asserted that Alice Faye was "star struck" and "in awe" of great talents such as Bette Davis, Marlene Dietrich, Peggy Lee, and Frank Sinatra. "It gave me great pleasure to tell Alice that Bette Davis, someone whose talent she admired so greatly, thought Alice's singing was marvelous," McGhee said.

When McGhee's interest in the industry expanded in the 1970s to memorabilia he not only collected a good deal of Faye films and other items; he also noticed how much of a bonanza was generated by Fox in releasing them as well as the number of other collectors involved in securing Faye memorabilia numbering those he classified as "very dedicated" and "manic."

"The BBC showed most of her big films in the 1960s and 1970s as well as into the early 1980s," McGhee noted. "*The Great American Broadcast* (1941)

LONDON APPEARANCE — Alice Faye, a star with a large following in the United Kingdom, is greeted by George McGhee backstage at Shepherds Bush Empire in Southwest London in 1991.

and *Hello, Frisco, Hello* (1943) were the most often shown. Channel Four started showing older matinee movies when they began broadcasting early in the 1980s, including all of Alice's big ones."

While there were many Alice Faye fans who viewed her films and collected memorabilia on the popular star, George McGhee, due to the professional direction his life took, was in a position to do more. His own interest in the entertainment field in general along with the career and public response to Alice Faye, with notable popularity existing within the United Kingdom, gave him an opportunity to showcase her movies.

> When I started at the Carlton Cinema channel in 1998 it gave me great pleasure to premiere there *Sally, Irene and Mary* [1938], *Tail Spin* [1939], and *You're a Sweetheart* [1937] as well as presenting *That Night in Rio* [1941], *Week-end in Havana* [1941], *Lillian Russell* [1940], *Hollywood Cavalcade* [1939], *Rose of Washington Square* [1939], *365 Nights in Hollywood* [1934], *On the Avenue* [1937], *George White's Scandals of 1935*, *King of Burlesque* [1936], *Alexander's Ragtime Band* [1938], *In Old Chicago* [1937], *Tin Pan Alley* [1940], *The Gang's All Here* [1943], *Stowaway* [1936], *Poor Little Rich Girl* [1936], and *Fallen Angel*. We received many complimentary letters from our viewers about the Alice Faye films and the fact that we showed them uncut and with excellent material.

What were the favorite Alice Faye films from the unique twin perspective of a stellar fan and friend along with a professional selecting material to show on major U.K. television networks? "My favorite Alice Faye film is *Alexander's Ragtime Band* and then probably *Hello, Frisco, Hello*, although I love *Weekend in Havana* and *Tin Pan Alley* as well," McGhee said. "I must have seen *Alexander's Ragtime Band* 50 times and it still moves me, especially the scene between John Carradine and Alice in the taxi cab."

What ingredients blended to make Alice Faye an enduring cinema star? "Alice was a great star and what made her so for me were the sincerity and warmth in her acting and, of course, her singing," McGhee explained. "She was the female equivalent of Bing Crosby and, I believe, the first female crooner. Alice was like all the great stars, truly unique and we will never see her like again."[5]

Strong Supporting Woman, Femme Fatale of Sorts

In the tradition of McGhee's comments, Alice Faye as June Mills, the lady of supreme warmth and sincerity, is given a challenge with the arrival in Walton of wandering Depression drifter and con man Eric Stanton. *Fallen Angel* reveals Eric in the first scene being caught by an alert bus driver as he pretends to be asleep so he can ride beyond the price of his ticket to San Francisco.

In the novel by Marty Holland, Eric Stanton is forcibly evicted by the driver. In the film the driver gives him a gesture reminiscent of an umpire tossing a player from a game. Fate, accordingly, connects fast-buck artist Stanton with the small town of Walton, located 130 miles south of San Francisco.

Eric needs fast money. His agile brain connects him to fellow con artist Professor Madley (John Carradine), a circuit traveling charlatan who claims to connect loved ones to the dead. Eric performs with such public-relations gusto that, after he fills the local auditorium for Madley, he is offered a regular job traveling with him. Under other circumstances Eric might have accepted as Madley clearly admires his talents and the prospect of impressive money looms in the future, but by then he has set his sights on a local woman with a contingent of admirers. The object of Eric's fascination is dark-haired, voluptuous, tough-as-nails Stella. She works as a waitress at the local restaurant run by Pop. As noted earlier, Pop has a crush on the younger woman as does another regular patron, former New York City police detective Mark Judd, who has come to California to allegedly improve his health. Meanwhile, Stella is also seen dating traveling jukebox operator Dave Atkins.

Eric experiences Stella's toughness in his first visit to Pop's restaurant. The gentle and accommodating Pop tells new-man-in-town Eric that he does not have to pay for his coffee. Stella tartly demurs, telling her boss that he had supplied coffee for Eric and, hence, he should have to pay for it. Far from being repulsed by Stella's toughness, Eric is, instead, instantly smitten. He feels a camaraderie. She is, like him, someone from the wrong side of the tracks and he can relate to her, which means that Stella has picked up one more male admirer in Walton, and this one is determined to proceed to great lengths to win her over.

June Mills emerges as a designated financial pigeon for Eric. Her deceased father has left his two daughters financially secure, June and older sister Clara (Anne Revere). A skeptical Clara is dubious about Eric's motivation when he begins dating her sister. It seems she has every reason to be skeptical. Tough girl Stella, after telling Eric about her impoverished youth in San Diego, delivers an ultimatum. She wants marriage to a man of means, not a drifter who will move her from town to town. Eric will either obtain sufficient funds to keep her in style, including a house and regular roots, or she will have nothing to do with

A SALESMAN MAKES HIS CASE— Eric Stanton (Dana Andrews) seeks to sell Stella (Linda Darnell) on romance in *Fallen Angel* (1945).

him. She had earlier coldly abandoned Dave Atkins for not measuring up to her expectations.

A dramatic contrast is established between two women, a gentle trusting soul in June not about to give her heart without purposeful sincerity, and a tough opportunist in Stella. June assumes the role of the strong supporting woman, determined to convince him to see a side of him that she is convinced ultimately exists.

June Mills is reminiscent of Helen St. James in another 1945 release, *The Lost Weekend*. Helen is certain that a man of purpose and meaning exists beyond the alcoholic fate into which Don Birnam has plummeted. June sees similar good in the drifting con artist, the self-centered Eric Stanton. They both see different men beyond those that people of lesser vision and patience observe, including, ironically enough, the men themselves.

June fits into the classic definition of the strong supporting woman of film noir, but what about Stella? Can she be classified as a femme fatale? She is definitely tough, uncompromising, and selfish. Stella feels no compassion for June after learning that Eric's game plan revolves around a brief sham marriage to grab her money.

If Stella is a femme fatale then it is one without the deadly sociopath's code of classic noir female characters Phyllis in *Double Indemnity*, Kathie in *Out of the Past*, and Helen Grayle in *Murder, My Sweet*. Murder is an intrinsic part of doing business to Phyllis and Kathie. Embittered, street tough Stella could therefore be called a femme fatale — with qualification. She is a femme fatale of sorts, without any appearance of the deadly rapacity of Phyllis, Kathie, or Helen.

As a film noir author it is anything but surprising that Eddie Muller would conceive of romantic pairings within the genre that might have been but never materialized on camera. One such team that Muller envisioned was Lawrence Tierney and Ann Savage, noting, "That would have been a battle for the ages." He then focused on Linda Darnell, conceiving of her in a key role in one of Robert Siodmak's three film noir classics: "I wish that Linda Darnell had played a few more femme fatale roles, like she did in *Fallen Angel*. She was able to humanize that character completely. She understood the sadness and desperation of a woman who is the object of every man's desire, and the dilemma of whether or not to use that power is ingrained in her performance. No knock on Yvonne De Carlo, but Linda Darnell would have also been great in *Criss Cross*."[6]

Eric Stanton as Prime Suspect and Depression Figure

Eric was seen and heard arguing with Stella the night that she was killed. Hence he is fingered as a murder suspect by Mark Judd, who was called upon by local Walton police authorities to take charge of the investigation.

While in San Francisco with June, Eric is convinced that he needs to continue his traveling ways, telling his wife about his long pattern of scruples deficiency. At that point June's inner strength and persuasiveness rise to the fore. She convinces Eric that just because he has experienced tough times in the past is no reason that he cannot improve his character. June convinces him that continuing to run will only bury him in a deeper mire, asserting that he needs to go back to Walton and clear himself of all suspicion.

At that point Eric's comments to June are reminiscent of what Vincent Parry at one juncture told Irene Jansen in *Dark Passage*. In the latter case Parry is hunted by the San Francisco Police after doing time for a killing he did not commit. Once he escapes and goes to San Francisco in hopes of clearing himself, his best friend, who wanted nothing more out of life than to go to Peru with Parry and play his trumpet, is killed in his apartment. Parry tells Jansen that he brings people bad luck. She is therefore better off without him.

After Eric in his con man phase pursued June to obtain her money and marry the ill-fated Stella, his character arc elevates him to a higher plateau. Just as Parry had told Jansen, Eric, recognizing June's bedrock integrity, asks her during their climactic San Francisco hotel room scene, "Why do you waste your money on a guy like me?"

Eric is very much a creature of the Great Depression, that theme that weaves its way through film noir. June sees decency beyond the con man persona that Eric embodied as he pursued a rootless, traveling existence, seeking enough money to survive. The Depression period was one where men rode the rails or in box cars. Dropping off to sleep or even remaining awake in the wrong company could mean loss of life.

Stella's toughness also stems from an absence of economic security. She tells Eric pointedly that she is through running around and wants the security of marriage and a home. This is a woman who grew up in a meager hotel run by her parents in San Diego. She realizes she can use her dynamic sexuality as a way to achieve a more stable life.

June Mills and Female Intuition

During the early post–World War II period a good deal was written and said about female intuition, the ability of women to analyze psychological phenomena. A case can be made that June Mills was an astute possessor of female intuition and put it to shrewd use in analyzing Eric Stanton.

The first time that Eric visits June's home and talks to her sister, Clara, who perceives him to be an opportunistic con artist, the younger sister holds a different view. She listens from a distance to the conversation during which Clara emphatically tells Eric that she will not attend or cooperate in any way with Professor Madley's scheduled séance. June uses a soft sell approach to alter Clara's position and convinces her sister to attend.

Even though June is intrigued by the new man in town and likes being with him, she is also skeptical. She has intuition but not psychic power. She cannot tell that she is being set up at the time to assist Eric's romantic efforts to woo beautiful brunette tough girl Stella, but does wonder why Eric is showing her attention and questions him on that point. June also shrewdly catches on that Eric, despite his stated zest for having a good time, is not a man who enjoys himself. She picks up on his troubled restlessness.

In a power-packed scene with Mark Judd, who is intent on pinning Stella's murder on Eric, June tells the transplanted New York City detective about Eric's past. June uses dialogue straight out of the Depression period. She tells the detective that, as a child, Eric was beaten for things he did not do, explaining this as the reason why he is always compelled to run.

June Convinces Eric to Stay and Fight

As is the case with certain soft spoken, kindly women like June Mills, there is a rock bottom conviction that has an impact on others. June achieves a breakthrough with Eric during their San Francisco trip. She tells him that running away from Bickford will accomplish nothing. It is time for him to stop running and face up to himself. This is true particularly in the face of adversity. He is innocent and should fight any effort to arrest and prosecute him for a murder he never committed. At that point Eric becomes fulfilled. By then he has advanced to the point where he fully appreciates June's message. He is a shrewd person. It is just that, previously, his intelligence had been put to negative rather than positive use.

When Eric begins his own investigation he discovers that Judd is anything but the former upstanding police officer he purports to be. He learns that he had engaged in the same kind of brutal tactics he employed in Walton on murder suspect Dave Atkins. As a result, he was banished from the force. This is the real reason why he had moved to California, not for health reasons.

Eric demonstrates a clever investigative side in learning the truth about the brutal former New York detective. He ties Judd's past record to his permanent fixture status at Pop's Restaurant and his shared zeal with Stella to play her favorite song, "Slowly," on the jukebox. Judd was done in by his own bitter frustration over rejection from the woman by whom virtually every man in Walton was entranced.

An Angel Face and a Devilish Manner

As Hollywood's master of moral ambiguity, it was natural that Preminger was drawn toward film noir. In a film he directed a little less than a decade later, the 1952 RKO release *Angel Face*, a brunette who looked like an angel behaved as a devil.

Jean Simmons exuded one of the most angelic faces among leading ladies, which made the irony all the more biting by casting her as a sociopath with a penchant for homicidal resolution. As such her role in *Angel Face* is reminiscent of RKO contract player Jane Greer in *Out of the Past*. How appropriate it was, therefore, to have Robert Mitchum cast as Simmons's victim in *Angel Face* as had been his status with Greer in *Out of the Past*.

The sweetness in Simmons's youthful face made her a natural to perform in her hometown for directing giant David Lean in his 1946 screen adaptation of Charles Dickens's *Great Expectations*. This led to a productive screen career that included a starring role opposite Richard Burton in the Henry Koster 1953 biblical epic *The Robe*.

Another major hit in which Simmons appeared was the 1960 release *Elmer Gantry* as a woman infatuated by Burt Lancaster's rousing preacher's demeanor in his Oscar-winning role. The film's director, Richard Brooks, would later become her husband. Starring in the 1969 Brooks directed release, *The Happy Ending*, Simmons received a "Best Actress" Oscar nomination playing the challenging role as a frustrated wife. A hallmark of a talented performer is to extend one's range, and this occurred with Simmons when she undertook the role of the deeply disturbed Diane Tremayne in *Angel Face*. It is a film that was one of Hughes's numerous flops at the time it was made. Unlike most of other Hughes flops, it has recently increased in popularity, buoyed by the recent wave of interest in film noir.

Frank Jessup (Robert Mitchum) enters Diane's tortured world as an ambulance-driving paramedic. He answers an emergency call to the Beverly Hills estate of her father, Charles (Herbert Marshall), a prominent novelist, over an alleged "accident" wherein Diane's stepmother, Catherine (Barbara O'Neil), nearly dies from gas asphyxiation. Frank is suspicious of Diane from the outset, but his failure to act on his better instincts initially costs him his freedom and ultimately his life. (Femmes fatales exercise a pattern of tenaciously digging in their claws and never letting go.)

Simmons is superb in the manner that she pulls off her role of looking sweet, talking softly, but operating as a woman who is all ice water with zero humanity. The only person Diane Tremayne is interested in is herself and her goal is total domination over everyone she encounters. A key scene that shows Diane at her most conniving is a luncheon meeting with Frank's then girlfriend Mary Wilton (Mona Freeman). She coolly informs Mary of her designs on Frank and her determination to take over his life with the nonchalance of asking her to pass the salt.

Whatever asset Diane has she exploits. Her looks and absence of conscience give her advantage enough in dealing with men, but on top of that she has money at her disposal. Not only is her father a prominent author but he married into money as well. Maintaining her unceasing coolness of manner, Diane maneuvers Frank away from his ambulance job and into the family estate. She not only offers him the job of chauffeur but sweetens the offer. He is told that she is willing to sponsor a return to his first love, race car driving, which he pursued before wartime duty intervened.

Diane plays Frank and the situation like a concert virtuoso. One can see the symbolic tooth marks as the femme fatale with the deceiving innocent looks gnaws at Frank, bringing him down, making him her prey, always speaking in a soft voice and her low-key manner that belies her ruthless domination.

Homicidal Action and Courtroom Trickery

Like a restless cat, it is just a question of when Diane would launch a deadly spring. It comes when her father and stepmother are killed in their automobile due to mechanical failure. Frank, destined to experience deep trouble in Diane's company, finds himself on trial for murder with her. Given his automotive expertise as a professional race car driver, he is hard pressed to protest his innocence. It appears that he will suffer the same fate as the guilty Diane.

When the interesting courtroom phase of the drama arrives we see a ploy utilized from the 1946 film noir release *The Postman Always Rings Twice* with one of the dueling attorneys from that earlier film appearing, but in the opposite role. In the earlier drama defense attorney Arthur Keats (Hume Cronyn) uses slick legal tactics to secure the release of Frank Chambers and Cora Smith as they were preparing to stand trial for the murder of Smith's husband.

The district attorney whose prosecution was thwarted by the deftness of Keats was Leon Ames as Kyle Sackett, who told Chambers confidently that he would eventually send him away, and did on the basis of killing Cora in an automobile accident. The irony is that the second time around Chambers was innocent.

This time Ames steps into the shoes of defense attorney Fred Barrett. Barrett's cagey maneuvering results in acquittals for Diane and Frank as he convinces them to marry. Their marital status assists Barrett with his successful legal ploy.

Unflappable sociopath Diane takes events in stride, but innocent party Frank realizes how close he came to San Quentin's gas chamber. He has seen enough of the ruthless killer with the innocent face. After Frank demands a divorce and announces he is through with Diane she reveals that her interest is in control above all else, even if she has to personally suffer. Never has a Preminger moral ambiguity cinema ploy been pushed so far. In Diane's world if you cannot control a man you want then you destroy him, even if you are compelled to suffer the same fate.

BEATING THE RAP—Dazzling defense attorney Fred Barrett (Leon Ames, third from right) succeeds in getting clients Diane Tremayne Jessup (Jean Simmons, second from right) and Frank Jessup (Robert Mitchum, right) acquitted with shrewd legal maneuvering in Otto Preminger's gritty 1952 noir drama *Angel Face*.

Another pivotal moment emerges when Diane visits cagey counselor Fred Barrett in his posh penthouse office suite. She comes armed with a signed confession, asserting that she and Frank were responsible for the deaths of her father and stepmother. Barrett did not reach the penthouse lawyer level by being dumb. He never loses his smooth, smiling demeanor as he casually tears up Diane's confession and explains the common law principle of double jeopardy to his client. Diane and Frank have already been tried. A jury of their peers has found them innocent. Accordingly, they cannot be tried again and there is nothing more to be said. Barrett coolly tells her to go home and forget about it. But forgetting an issue of control is something Diane is incapable of doing. Frank will pay one ultimate lesson due to his ignorance of that basic fact.

Frank has hope that beyond the wreckage of his tumultuous romance with Diane that he can rekindle the flames of passion with former girlfriend Mary Wilton. After Frank leaves Mary to take up with Diane, his former fellow ambulance partner Bill Crompton (Kenneth Tobey) begins dating her. Bill lacks Frank's charisma, but to Mary that is fine since he is reliable. The three-person showdown finds Mary nixing Frank for Bill.

Reminiscent of Greer and Moorehead

With no chance to revive a romance with Mary, Frank decides to leave for Mexico and start a new life. But Frank never reaches Mexico or even the bus station. In fact, he never even leaves Diane's estate after accepting his final ride.

Diane and Frank suffer the same fate as Diane's parents had earlier, death inside an automobile. In this case the calculating brunette backs up her car to a nearby cliff and pushes hard on the gas pedal. They plummet downward from the cliff to their deaths.[7]

The similarity between two beautiful brunette femmes fatale, Jane Greer and Jean Simmons, in how they destroy Robert Mitchum are evident. There is a strong parallel as well to Agnes Moorehead in *Dark Passage*. Moorehead's ruthless determination to destroy any man she cannot control parallels the conduct of the calculating brunettes. As revealed earlier in the analysis of Moorehead's devastating performance as the thoroughly meddlesome Madge Rapf, she was a woman determined to place Humphrey Bogart's character Vincent Parry under her romantic control. If she cannot have him then nobody else would either.

Three main characters all met calamitous deaths. Kathie is gunned down by police after angrily killing Jeff, calling him a "dirty, double-crossing rat." Diane throws her car into reverse, instantly killing herself and Frank. Madge plunges to her death from her apartment after admitting to Vincent Parry that she killed his wife and his closest friend, but declares that she would never sign a confession and preferred seeing him suffer an unjust criminal fate.

Prominent international director Jean-Luc Godard cited *Angel Face* as his number eight choice among his list of the greatest American sound films. This conclusion is far from surprising in that Godard is French. The style of film noir presented by Preminger in accenting the psychologically complex character of Diane Tremayne would be expected to find some artistic community support in the nation of Sartre and Camus.

Jean Simmons and Alice Faye

The two leading stars, one a blonde, the other a brunette, who delivered impressive performances in notable film noir vehicles seven years apart, with each title including the word angel, bear a connection to the world of musical theater.

Alice Faye decided in the early seventies to leave her lovely home at Palm Springs' Thunderbird Country Club and return to live musicals for the first time since her early pre–Hollywood Broadway activity. Interest abounded as she signed to appear with former Fox leading man John Payne in a revival of *Good News*.

Longtime Faye friend and fan Robert Kendall explained what prompted her to accept this challenging assignment in her late fifties: "Alice had always been close to her friend and Fox co-star Betty Grable. When Betty died of cancer [in 1973] this caused Alice to do a lot of thinking. She thought about her many fans and decided that if she was ever going to appear in a major stage musical that this was the time to do it. Her friend Betty Grable's death made her realize how precious a commodity time was."

At the same time that Alice Faye accepted her challenge Jean Simmons did the same thing. She agreed to star in Stephen Sondheim's new musical *A Little Night Music*. The stars appeared one after the other in Los Angeles at the Schubert Theatre in Century City.

Jean Simmons's appearances in Sondheim's show eventually took her back to her native

London. She conceded to a tentativeness when it came to dancing since, unlike Alice Faye, her career had been in the dramatic field. As a result dancing was new to her.

One evening as *A Little Night Music* was nearing the end of its Los Angeles run, and as Simmons was carefully concentrating on a dancing number, the loud sound of an obviously intoxicated patron resounded with the question, "Where's Alice Faye?"

Simmons, a seasoned performer, stayed on message, continuing her number and ignoring the question. When the same question was repeated by the same inebriated fan she halted her dance and responded in a loud, clear tone: "She'll be here next week."

Chapter Notes

Chapter One

1. Series of interviews conducted with Mervyn LeRoy at his West Hollywood office, 1975–1977.
2. Internet interview conducted with Eddie Muller, February 2010.
3. Internet interview with Steve Eifert, February 2010.
4. Oddly, Mervyn LeRoy did not believe in political filmmaking. He explained his idea of story development in his autobiography, *Mervyn LeRoy: Take One*, written with Dick Kleiner: "[I]f you want to send a message, you should go to Western Union.... If you have a fine story that deals with a social issue, that's fine. But the story should come first, not the philosophy" (pp. 132–133).
5. An interesting account of the early Warner Bros. years along with the family that started the studio appears in Clive Hirschhorn, *The Warner Bros. Story*, pp. 8–14.

Chapter Two

1. Julian Symons, *Dashiell Hammett*, pp. 120–121.
2. William Nolan, *Hammett: A Life at the Edge*, pp. 45–46.
3. Ibid., p. 89.
4. Ibid., p. 91.
5. Ibid., p. 90.
6. Ibid., p. 94.
7. Ibid.
8. Ibid., pp. 179–180.
9. Symons, p. 59.
10. Nolan, p. 133.
11. From a series of Internet interviews with Charles Tranberg, April–May 2010.
12. Nolan, p. 227.

Chapter Three

1. *Criss Cross* is comprehensively discussed thematically as well as how it came to be made in my book *L.A. Noir: Nine Dark Visions of the City of Angels*.

Chapter Four

1. Robert F. Moss, ed., *Raymond Chandler: A Literary Reference*, p. 48.
2. William Hare, *Hitchcock and the Methods of Suspense*, p. 13.
3. For a comprehensive discussion of *Strangers on a Train*, see *Hitchcock and the Methods of Suspense*, pp. 149–163.
4. For a comprehensive analysis of *Vertigo*, see *Hitchcock and the Methods of Suspense*, pp. 99–120.
5. For a comprehensive analysis of *Rear Window*, see *Hitchcock and the Methods of Suspense*, pp. 174–187.
6. Internet interviews with Christopher Shaw, February 2009.

Chapter Five

1. Director Sydney Pollack provided insight into crafting a film from Horace McCoy's novel in McCoy, *They Shoot Horses, Don't They?*, pp. 133–136. The novel as well as the screenplay by Robert E. Thompson are also included.
2. This review appeared on January 14, 1960.
3. McCoy, *They Shoot Horses, Don't They?*, pp. 134–135.
4. Ibid., p. 135.
5. Ibid., p. 159.
6. Ibid., p. 161.
7. Ibid., p. 286.
8. Personal interview with Susannah York, London, spring of 1990.
9. Ibid.
10. *They Shoot Horses, Don't They?* script, p. 307.
11. Ibid., p. 312.
12. Ibid., p. 314.
13. Ibid., p. 317.

Chapter Six

1. Raymond Chandler, *The Simple Art of Murder*, p. 16.
2. Ibid.
3. Ibid.
4. Ibid., p. 17.
5. Ibid., p. 21.
6. Robert F. Moss, ed., *Raymond Chandler: A Literary Reference*, p. 184.
7. Ibid.
8. Ibid.
9. Ibid., pp. 184–185.
10. Ibid., p. 185.
11. Ibid., p. 187.
12. Personal interview with Rouben Mamoulian, spring 1975.
13. Ibid.
14. Chandler's meeting with Maugham and Cukor is covered in Judith Freeman, *The Long Embrace: Raymond Chandler and the Woman He Loved*, pp. 254–258.
15. Raymond Chandler, *The Raymond Chandler Omnibus: The Big Sleep, Farewell, My Lovely, The High Window, The Lady in the Lake*, p. 3.
16. See William Hare, *L.A. Noir: Nine Dark Visions of the City of Angels*, pp. 15–17.
17. Raymond Chandler, *The Big Sleep*, pp. 154–155.
18. Comments taken from Charles and Roberta Mitchell, "Audrey Totter: Versatile Queen of Noir," *Classic Images*, 1999.
19. For a reporting of events surrounding the arrests of Lila Leeds and Robert Mitchum, see Lee Server, *Robert Mitchum: "Baby, I Don't Care,"* pp. 158–165.
20. Ibid., p. 204.

Chapter Seven

1. Colin Wilson, *The Outsider*, p. 13.
2. Ibid., p. 16.
3. Ibid., p. 27.
4. Judith Freeman, *The Long Embrace: Raymond Chandler and the Woman He Loved*, p. 129.
5. See Eddie Muller, *Dark City*, pp. 73–75, for a capsulated analysis of Chandler compared to Hammett as well as how Chandler's hard hitting fiction was adapted to film noir.
6. Ibid., pp. 135–136.

Chapter Eight

1. See Lee Server, *Robert Mitchum: "Baby, I Don't Care,"* pp. 118–130 for a comprehensive look at the making and analysis of *Out of the Past*. See William Hare, *Early Film Noir: Greed, Lust and Murder Hollywood Style* for a capsulated viewpoint of the film from the perspective of Jane Greer, the film's leading lady.
2. Charles Tranberg's career insights on Agnes Moorehead's career with a focus on *Dark Passage* stem from Internet interviews with him during March of 2009.
3. Ibid.
4. For a detailed analysis of *Dark Passage*, see J.P. Telotte, *Voices in the Dark*, pp. 120–133.

Chapter Nine

1. For a detailed analysis of *The Blue Gardenia*, see *L.A. Noir: Nine Dark Visions of the City of Angels*, pp. 110–120.
2. For a detailed analysis of all aspects of *The Third Man*, see Charles Drazin, *In Search of the Third Man*.
3. For insight into Carol Reed's films, see Nicholas Wapshott, *The Man Between: A Biography of Carol Reed*.

Chapter Ten

1. A succinct yet detailed biography of Siodmak and his films appears in John Wakeman, ed., *World Film Directors: Volume One 1890–1945*, segment written by Christopher Lambert.
2. See review of *Phantom Lady* on Internet site *Back Alley Noir* written by Steve Eifert and posted February 8, 2008.
3. Ibid.
4. Personal interview with Robert Kendall, June 2009.
5. John O'Dowd, *Kiss Tomorrow Goodbye: The Barbara Payton Story*, p. 161.
6. Ibid., p. 160.
7. Internet interviews with Eddie Muller, February 2009.

Chapter Eleven

1. For an account of the combative but ultimately successful joint effort of Billy Wilder and Raymond Chandler on the script of *Double Indemnity*, see Frank MacShane, *The Life of Raymond Chandler*, pp. 106–109.
2. For additional insight into the crafting of the *Double Indemnity* script, see William Hare, *Early Film Noir: Greed, Lust and Murder Hollywood Style*, pp. 34–36.
3. For a succinct analysis of the career of Billy Wilder, see John Wakeman, ed., *World Film Directors: Volume One, 1890–1945*, pp. 1206–1210.
4. See Patrick McGilligan, *Fritz Lang: The Nature of the Beast*, p. 322.

Chapter Twelve

1. A capsulated biography of Otto Preminger's career can be found in John Wakeman, ed., *World Film Directors: Volume One, 1890–1945*, segment written by Patricia Dowell, pp. 888–897.
2. The production disagreements concerning Preminger and Rouben Mamoulian in the *Laura* project are covered in *Early Film Noir: Greed, Lust and Murder Hollywood Style*, pp. 112–118.
3. Darryl F. Zanuck's impressions of the *Laura* project based on his memos appear in Rudy Behlmer, ed., *Memo from Darryl F. Zanuck: The Golden Years at Twentieth Century–Fox*, pp. 68–71.
4. Arthur Nicholson's comments resulted from a mail interview exchange conducted in the fall of 2009.
5. George McGhee's comments resulted from a series of Internet questions and answers from March 2010.
6. For more of Eddie Muller's analysis of Linda Darnell's performance in *Fallen Angel*, see *Dark City*, pp. 86–87.
7. Lee Server provides a discussion of *Angel Face* in *Robert Mitchum: "Baby, I Don't Care,"* pp. 237–240.

Bibliography

Books

Annakin, Ken. *So You Wanna Be a Director?* Sheffield, England: Tomahawk, 2001.
Armes, Roy. *A Critical History of British Cinema*. New York: Harcourt, 1989.
Auieler, Dan. *The Alfred Hitchcock Notebooks: An Illustrated Look Inside the Creative Mind of Alfred Hitchcock*. New York: HarperCollins, 2001.
Bacall, Lauren. *By Myself*. New York: Knopf, 1979.
Behlmer, Rudy, ed. *Memo from Darryl F. Zanuck*. New York: Grove Press, 1993.
Buford, Kate. *Burt Lancaster: An American Life*. New York: Knopf, 2001.
Cain, James M. *Cain × 3: The Postman Always Rings Twice, Mildred Pierce, Double Indemnity*. New York: Knopf, 1969.
Chandler, Raymond. *The Little Sister*. Boston: Houghton Mifflin, 1949.
_____. *The Long Goodbye*. New York: Vintage, 1992.
_____. *The Notebooks of Raymond Chandler*. New York: Harper Perennial, 2006.
_____. *The Raymond Chandler Omnibus: The Big Sleep, Farewell, My Lovely, The High Window, The Lady in the Lake*. New York: Crown, 1986.
_____. *The Simple Art of Murder*. New York: Ballantine, 1972.
Cotten, Joseph. *Vanity Will Get You Somewhere*. San Francisco: Mercury House, 1987.
Crockett, Art, ed. *Celebrity Murders*. New York: Pinnacle, 1990.
De Carlo, Yvonne, with Doug Warren. *Yvonne: An Autobiography*. New York: St. Martin's, 1987.
DeRosa, Steven. *Writing with Hitchcock: The Collaboration of Alfred Hitchcock and John Michael Hayes*. New York: Faber and Faber, 2001.
DiOrio, Al. *Barbara Stanwyck: A Biography*. New York: Coward-McCann, 1983.
Dmytryk, Edward. *It's a Hell of a Life But Not a Bad Living: A Hollywood Memoir*. New York: Times Books, 1978.
Drazin, Charles. *In Search of The Third Man*. London: Methuen, 1999.
Freeman, Judith. *The Long Embrace: Raymond Chandler and the Woman He Loved*. New York: Pantheon, 2007.
Friedrich, Otto. *City of Nets*. New York: Harper and Row, 1986.
Gardiner, Dorothy, and Kathrine Sorley Walker. *Raymond Chandler Speaking*. Berkeley and Los Angeles: University of California Press, 1997.
Gottlieb, Sidney. *Alfred Hitchcock Interviews*. Jackson: University of Mississippi Press, 2003.
Hanna, Thomas. *The Thought and Art of Albert Camus*. Chicago: Regnery, 1958.
Hare, William. *Early Film Noir: Greed, Lust and Murder Hollywood Style*. Jefferson, NC: McFarland, 2003.
_____. *Hitchcock and the Methods of Suspense*. Jefferson, NC: McFarland, 2007.
_____. *L.A. Noir: Nine Dark Visions of the City of Angels*. Jefferson, NC: McFarland, 2004.
Higham, Charles, and Joel Greenberg. *The Celluloid Muse: Hollywood Directors Speak*. Chicago: Regnery, 1969.
Hiney, Tom. *Raymond Chandler: A Biography*. New York: Atlantic Monthly Press, 1997.
Hirschhorn, Clive. *The Universal Story*. New York: Crown, 1983.
_____. *The Warner Bros. Story*. New York: Crown, 1979.
Hoopes, Roy. *Cain: The Biography of James M. Cain*. New York: Holt, Rinehart and Winston, 1982.
Hughes, Dorothy B. *In a Lonely Place*. New York: Bantam, 1979.

Layman, Richard. *Dashiell Hammett: A Descriptive Biography*. Pittsburgh: University of Pittsburgh Press, 1979.
LeRoy, Mervyn, as told to Dick Kleiner. *Mervyn LeRoy: Take One*. New York: Hawthorn, 1974.
MacFarlane, Brian. *An Autobiography of British Cinema*. London: Methuen, 1997.
MacShane, Frank. *The Life of Raymond Chandler*. New York: Dutton, 1976.
_____, ed. *Selected Letters of Raymond Chandler*. New York: Columbia University Press, 1981).
Maltin, Leonard, ed. *TV Movies and Video Guide*. New York: Signet, 1990.
McCoy, Horace, novel, Robert E. Thompson screenplay. *They Shoot Horses, Don't They?* New York: Avon, 1970.
McGilligan, Patrick. *Fritz Lang: The Nature of the Beast*. New York: Griffin, 1998.
Milne, Tom. *Mamoulian*. Bloomington: Indiana University Press, 1969.
Moss, Robert F., ed. *Raymond Chandler: A Literary Reference*. New York: Carroll & Graf, 2003.
Muller, Eddie. *Dark City: The Lost World of Film Noir*. New York: St. Martin's Griffin, 1998.
_____. *The Wicked Women of Film Noir*. New York: HarperEntertainment, 2002.
Nolan, William F. *Hammett: A Life at the Edge*. New York: Congdon and Weed, 1983.
O'Dowd, John. *Kiss Tomorrow Goodbye: The Barbara Payton Story*. Albany, GA: BearManor Media, 2006.
Perry, George. *The Great British Picture Show*. Boston: Little, Brown, 1985.
Schlessler, Ken. *Ken Schlessler's This is Hollywood: An Unusual Guide*. Redland, CA: Ken Schlessler, 1993.
Sennett, Ted. *Warner Bros. Presents: The Most Exciting Years—from the Jazz Singer to White Heat*. New Rochelle, NY: Castle Books, 1971.
Server, Lee. *Robert Mitchum: "Baby, I Don't Care."* New York, St. Martin's Press, 2001.
_____. *Screenwriter: Words Become Pictures*. Pittstown, NJ: Main Street Press, 1987.
Sperber, A.M. and Lax, Eric. *Bogart*. New York: Morrow, 1997.
Spoto, Donald. *The Dark Side of Genius: The Life of Alfred Hitchcock*. Boston: Little, Brown, 1983.
Symons, Julian. *Dashiell Hammett*. San Diego, New York, London: Harcourt Brace Jovanovich, 1985.
Taylor, John Russell. *Masterworks of the British Cinema*. New York: Harper and Row, 1974.
Telotte, J.P. *Voices in the Dark: The Narrative Patterns of Film Noir*. Urbana: University of Illinois Press, 1989.
Thomson, David. *A Biographical Dictionary of Film*. New York: Morrow, 1976.
Tranberg, Charles. *Fred MacMurray*. Albany, GA: BearManor Media, 2007.
_____. *I Love the Illusion: The Life and Career of Agnes Moorehead*. Albany, GA: BearManor Media, 2007.
_____. *The Thin Man Films Murder Over Cocktails*. Albany, GA: BearManor Media, 2008.
Vaughn, Robert. *Only Victims*. New York: Limelight Editions, 1996.
Wakeman, John, ed. *World Film Directors: Volume One, 1890–1945*. New York: H.W. Wilson, 1987.
Wapshott, Nicholas. *The Man Between: A Biography of Carol Reed*. London: Chatto and Windus, 1990.
Wood, Robin. *Hitchcock's Films Revisited*. New York: Columbia University Press, 1989.
Woolrich, Cornell (writing as William Irish). *Phantom Lady*. New York: J.B. Lipincott, 1942.

Personal Interviews

Ken Annakin
Steve Eifert
Jane Greer
Robert Kendall
Mervyn LeRoy
Ruben Mamoulian
Mike Mazurki
Arthur Nicholson
George McGhee
Eddie Muller
Christopher Shaw
Charles Tranberg
George Ulrich
Susannah York

Newspapers, Magazines, Television

All-Movie Guide, Internet Film Site and Database. www.allmovie.com.
Arts and Entertainment Network. "Murder He Wrote," Biography of Raymond Chandler, 1997.
Crowther, Bosley. *The New York Times*, Review of "Fallen Angel," February 7, 1946.
_____. *The New York Times*, Review of "The Story on Page One," January 14, 1960.
Dirks, Tim. The Greatest Films. Internet site and Database. www.filmsite.org.
Hare, William. "The Ken Annakin Story." *Films of the Golden Age*, Fall 1998.
_____. "Rouben Mamoulian: Impeccable Style." *Films of the Golden Age*. Spring 1999.
_____. "Sir Carol Reed: The Man Behind 'The Third Man.'" *Films of the Golden Age*. Winter 2000–2001.
_____. "Susannah York: Britain's International Star." *Films of the Golden Age*. Winter 1997.
Mitchell, Charles, and Roberta. "Audrey Totter: Versatile Queen of Noir." *Classic Images*. 1999.
The Internet Movie Database. Internet Film Site and Database. www.imbd.com.

Index

Abbott, Bud 165
Abe Lincoln in Illinois 113
The Adventures of Robin Hood 82
Aeschylus 80
After the Thin Man 31
Agar, John 33–34
The Age of Innocence 155
Alda, Robert 132
Alexander's Ragtime Band 186, 189–190
The Alfred Hitchcock Hour 67
Alias Nick Beal 93
All About Eve 114
All the King's Men 98, 178
Allen, Woody 141
Altman, Robert 71
The Amazing Dr. Clitterhouse 10
Ameche, Don 165, 185
An American Tragedy 93, 107
Ames, Leon 93, 95, 100, 195–196
Anderson, Maxwell 159
Andrews, Dana 53, 113–114, 182–183, 186–187, 191
Andrews, Julie 33
Angel Face 100, 194–197
Annakin, Ken 50, 104, 138
Another Thin Man 31
Appointment with Danger 62
Arbuckle, Roscoe "Fatty" 23
Arden, Eve 55
Armendariz, Pedro 129
Arnold, Edward 23, 30
Arnstein, Nicky 23
Around the World in Eighty Days 76
As Good as It Gets 100
The Asphalt Jungle 11
Astor, Mary 21
Atherton, William 58
Auer, John 65

Avery, Phyllis 175
Ayres, Lew 173

Bacall, Lauren 86–87, 108, 116–117, 122–124, 128, 130, 162
Bachman, Sidney 34
Bad Companions 46
Baer, Max 110
Bagdisarian, Ross 55
Baker, Art 164
The Ballad of Cat Ballou 177
Bankhead, Talullah 114, 176
Barbarella 68
Barnum, P.T. 61, 70
Barr, Byron 61–62
Barrett, Tony 162
Barris, Alex 78
Baum, Martin 76, 77
Baxter, Anne 114, 136
Beams Falling: The Art of Dashiell Hammett 30
Beatty, Warren 92
Bedelia, Bonnie 60, 77
Bel Geddes, Barbara 53
A Bell for Adano 108, 114
Belmondo, Jean Paul 130
Benchley, Robert 166
Bendix, William 104, 114–115
Bennett, Bruce (also Herman Brix) 119, 131–132, 136, 161
Bennett, Joan 135, 139–140, 154, 176
Bergman, Ingrid 12, 72, 109
Berkeley, Busby 16–17
The Berlin Stories 133–134
Bernard, James 143
Bernhardt, Curtis 129
Bernie, Ben 70
Bernstein, Walter 141
The Best Years of Our Lives 112–113
Bewitched 77

Bickford, Charles 183
The Big Clock 173–174
The Big Sleep 3, 84–88, 96–97, 108, 115–116, 122, 128, 152
The Big Steal 101–102
Biography 40
Birdman of Alcatraz 144
Black, Karen 58
Black Angel 177–179
Black Legion 9
Blazing Saddles 76
Blood on the Moon 129
Bloom, Claire 140, 142–143, 145
The Blue Angel 133–134
The Blue Dahlia 103–104, 109, 115–117, 151, 171'
The Blue Gardenia 135–136, 151
Blue, White and Perfect 98
Blues in the Night 98
Blyth, Ann 131
Bob Hope's Chrysler Theater 67
Body and Soul 98
Bogart, Humphrey 1, 3, 8–15, 20, 24–28, 31, 64, 81, 86–87, 90, 97, 108–109, 113, 117, 120, 122–124, 128–131, 164, 197
Bonanza 76
Bond, Ward 27
Boone, Pat 188–189
Booth, Charles G. 98
Born Yesterday 178
Boucher, Anthony 80–81
Bowron, Fletcher 106
Boyer, Charles 166
Bracken, Eddie 162
Brackett, Charles 169, 172
Brackett, Leigh 87
The Brasher Doubloon 108
Breen, Joseph 15
Breen, Richard 169
Brice, Fanny 23
Bring Me the Head of Alfredo Garcia 76

Brodine, Norbert 112
Brooks, Geraldine 140
Brooks, Mel 76
Brooks, Richard 76, 194
Brown, Johnny Mack 131
Bruce, Nigel 81–83
Buck Privates 165
The Burglar 130
Burks, Robert 53, 55
Burnett, W.R. 11–12
Burr, Raymond 54, 56, 136
Burroughs, Edgar Rice 131–132
Burton, Richard (also Richard Walter Jenkins, Jr.) 140–148, 194
Buttons, Red 70, 77

Cabaret 134
Cabot, Bruce 184
Cagney, James 27, 63–64
Cain, James M. 2, 7, 88, 106, 167
Campus Honeymoon, 101
Camus, Albert 7, 37, 48, 87, 105, 123, 128, 197
Cannon, Dyan 130
Capone, Al 1, 11, 16
Capra, Frank 31, 65, 184
Carle, Teet 40
Carr, John Dickson 79–81, 84
Carradine, John 190
Carroll, Diahann 100
Carson, Jack 98
Carter, Janis 33–34
Casablanca 12–15, 27, 181
Caspery, Vera 181–182
Cassavettes, John 142
Cassidy's Girl 130
Castle Keep 75
Cat Ballou 177
Cat on a Hot Tin Roof 76
Cat People 38
Chamberlain, Austen 38
Chamberlain, Neville 38
Chandler, Cissy 45–47, 50, 84, 105–106
Chandler, Raymond 2–3, 7–8, 25–26, 29, 37–48, 50–51, 57, 64–65, 78–81, 84–91, 94, 96–98, 103–107, 115–116, 122–123, 130, 151, 167–168, 171, 177
Chanslor, Roy 177
Chaplin, Charlie 67
Chesterton, G.K. 80
The Children's Hour 45–46
Chinatown 91
Chopin, Frédéric 34

Christie, Agatha 49, 78, 83
Christie, Julie 58
Cilento, Diane 72
Citizen Kane 118, 125
City That Never Sleeps 64–65
Clark, Fred 92
Clift, Montgomery 72, 75
Clurman, Harold 155
Coburn, Charles 163
Coburn, James 23
Cohn, Harry 52, 64, 82
Colbert, Claudette 188
Collins, Joan 175
Collins, Wilkie 80
Come Fill the Cup 63
Coming Home 60, 76
Como, Perry 95
Conan Doyle, Arthur 48, 81–83
The Conqueror 129
Conrad, Joseph 80
Conrad, William 161
Conte, Richard 109, 114, 136
Cook, Elisha, Jr. 26–28, 87, 152, 160
Cooper, Gary 10, 125
Coppel, Alec 52
Corey, Wendell 54
Corigan, Lloyd 174
Cornelius, Henry 134
Cornell, Katharine 155
Cortez, Ricardo 20
Corvette K-225 161
Cosby, Bill 110
Costello, Lou 165
Cotten, Joseph 45, 125, 137–138, 160
The Country Girl 63
Cover Girl 63
The Covered Wagon 117
Cowan, Jerome 21
Crawford, Broderick 178
Crawford, Joan 129, 131, 154–155, 158, 169, 177
Crehan, Joseph 151
Criss Cross 37, 39–43, 158, 161, 177, 192
Cromwell, John 64, 97
Cronyn, Hume 195
Crosby, Bing 95, 169, 186, 190
Cross, Jimmy 157
Crowther, Bosley 64
Cukor, George 84
Culp, Robert 110
Cummings, Robert 166
Cummins, Peggy 108
Curtis, Alan 15, 149–151, 164–166
Curtiz, Michael 82, 131

Cusack, Cyril 143
Cushing, Peter 83
Cyrano de Bergerac 65

The Dain Curse 23
Dall, John 108
Damages, Mad Men, Heroes 189
D'Andrea, Tom 119
Darcy, Georgine 55
Dark Passage 108, 111, 115–130, 132, 192–193, 197
Darling 57
Darnell, Linda 183, 187, 191–192
Da Silva, Howard 104, 115, 167, 170–171
Dassin, Jules 89
Davenport, Dorothy 162
Daves, Delmer 116–120, 123, 129–130
Davies, Rupert 146
Davis, Bette 8, 10, 46, 123, 176, 189
Day, Clarence 100
Day, Doris 62–63, 156
Day, Laraine 155–156
The Day of the Locust 58–59
Dead Reckoning 64, 97, 108
The Deadly Affair 143
Dearholt, Ashton 131
De Carlo, Yvonne 37, 39–40, 42–44, 160–161, 192
Dehn, Paul 141, 143–144
Dekker, Albert 42, 153, 161
De Mille, Cecil B. 39
Dern, Bruce 60, 77
Destination Tokyo 97
Destiny 166
Detour 157
Dial M for Murder 175
The Diary of Anne Frank 31
Dickens, Charles 80, 194
Dieterle, William 10
Dietrich, Marlene 133, 189
Disney, Walt 7
Dmytryk, Edward 122
Dockweiler, John 106
A Doll's House 71
Donfeld 75
Donlevy, Brian 23, 162, 164
Double Indemnity 2, 40, 44, 50, 61–62, 88, 104, 106, 115, 122, 125, 128, 167–169, 192
Douglas, Kirk 39, 123
Douglas, Michael 99
Dowling, Constance 177
Dowling, Doris 104, 115, 170
Down There 130
Dozier, William 40

Index

Dratler, Jay 162, 182
Dreiser, Theodore 93, 107
Dunaway, Faye 188
Dunnock, Mildred 64, 109
Duryea, Dan 37, 41–44, 130, 135–136, 149, 154, 161–162, 176–179
Duvivier, Julien 166
Dylan, Bob 169

Eddy, Nelson 31
Edge of the City 142
Eifert, Steve 9–10, 28, 56, 152
Eisenhower, Dwight 18, 32, 35, 92
Elam, Jack 102
Ellroy, James 7
Evans, Vickie 101
Evatt, Buddy 157
Evelyn, Judith 55
Ewell, Tom 188
Eyles, Allen 28
Eythe, William 98

Falk, Peter 83
The Fall of Valor 169
Fallen Angel 3, 182–188, 190–194
Farewell, My Lovely 26, 84, 88, 90, 97
Farmer, Frances 161
Farrell, Charles 157
Farrow, John 76, 173
Farwell, Harriett 56
Father Knows Best 125
Faulkner, William 3, 40, 86–87, 104, 130
Faye, Alice (also Alice Jeanne Leppert) 14, 165, 170, 180, 183–190, 197–198
Ferrer, Jose 65
Fielding, Henry 72
The Fifth Column 46
Finch, Peter 58
Finney, Albert 72
Fisher, Steve 64–65, 97, 99–100
Fisher, Terence 83
Fitts, Buron 106
Fitzgerald, Barry 169
Fitzgerald, F. Scott 40, 58, 130
Fleischer, Richard 175
The Fleischmann's Yeast Hour 186
Fleming, Ian 141
Fleming, Victor 7, 16
Flesh and Fantasy 166
Flynn, Errol 82, 123

Fonda, Henry 76
Fonda, Jane 45, 59–60, 68–69, 75–77
Fontaine, Joan 34
Fontanne, Lynn 159
Force of Evil 159–160
Ford, Glenn 64, 114
Ford, John 27, 155
Ford, Robin 101
Ford Television Theater 155–156
Fosse, Bob 134
Franciosa, Anthony 64
Freeman, Judith 84, 107
Freeman, Mona 195
The French Connection 76
Freud 72
Freud, Sigmund 109
Friedkin, William 76
Friedrich, Otto 109
The Front 141
Fuchs, Daniel 41
Fuller, Samuel 33, 181
Funny Girl 23
Furthman, Jules 87

Gable, Clark 60, 62–63, 155, 158
Gaborieau, Nicolas 48
Galsworthy, John 80
The Gang's All Here 190
Garbo, Greta 109
Gardner, Ava 39–40, 42, 92, 153, 160–161
Gardner, Erle Stanley 30
Garfield, John 92, 97, 100, 142, 155, 159–160, 166
Garland, Judy 1, 5, 139, 188
Garner, James 46
Garnett, Tay 92
The Gay Sisters 61
George, Gladys 38
George White's 1935 Scandals 190
George White's Scandals 186
Gielgud, John 38
Gilbert, Edwin 98
Gilda 64
The Girl on the Red Velvet Swing 175
The Glass Key 23, 30
Godard, Jean-Luc 197
Goetz, William 181
Going My Way 169
Gold Diggers of 1933 17, 19
Golden Boy 63, 142
Goldfinger 144
Goldman, William 10
Goldwyn, Samuel 45, 112

Gomez, Thomas 33, 150, 159, 163
Gone with the Wind 7, 16, 62
Good News 184–185, 197
Goodis, David 130
Goodis, Herbert 130
Goodrich, Frances 31
Gordon, Michael 142
Grable, Betty 97, 197
Granger, Farley 51, 175
Grant, Cary 6, 63, 97, 109
Granville, Bonita 46
The Great American Broadcast 189
Great Expectations 194
The Great Movie Stars: The Golden Years 189
Green, F.L. 139
Green, Johnny 75
Greene, Graham 137, 141, 173
Greenfield, Jeff 85
Greenstreet, Sydney 24–27
Greer, Jane 39–40, 42, 101, 108, 123, 125, 161, 194, 197
Grey, Joel 134
Griffith, Hugh 64
Die Grosse Liebe (The Great Love) 180
Guild, Nancy 108, 115
Guinness, Alec 71
Gun Crazy 108
Gunn, James 130
Gunsmoke 23

Hackett, Albert 31
Hackman, Gene 76, 97
Haight, George 97, 103
Hail the Conquering Hero 162, 178
Hall, Gus 33
The Hamlet 142
Hammerstein, Oscar 188
Hammett, Dashiell 1–2, 7–8, 20–25, 27–32, 34–37, 40, 44–48, 57, 76, 78–79, 81, 85, 87, 89, 122, 123, 177
The Happy Ending 194
Harris, Julie 134
Harris, Phil 185–186, 188
Harrison, Joan 133
Harvey, Lawrence 134
Hasso, Signe 98
Haultain, Phil 24
Hawk of the Wilderness 131
Hawks, Howard 3, 10, 86, 116, 123, 128, 161–162
Hawthorne, Nathaniel 80
Hayden, Sterling 177

Hayes, Joseph Michael 54–56
Hayes, Sam 15–16
Haymes, Dick 95, 187–188
Hayward, Susan 125
Hayworth, Rita 63–64
Heaven Can Wait 92
Hecht, Ben 7, 50, 109
Heisler, Stuart 23, 30
Hellinger, Mark 92
Hellman, Lillian 35, 45–47, 76
Hello, Frisco, Hello 186, 190
Helm, Brigitte 134
Helm, Faye 150
Helmore, Tom 51
Hemingway, Ernest 22, 28, 46, 92, 116
Hendrix, Wanda 92
Henreid, Paul 12
Hepburn, Katharine 72, 76
Here Comes Mr. Jordan 92
Hersey, John 108, 114
Hickson, Joan 83
High Sierra 10–14, 16, 165
The High Wall 94
The High Window 84, 108
Highsmith, Patricia 50–51
Highway Patrol 178
Hill, James 64
Hiller, Wendy 64
His Girl Friday 6
Hitchcock, Alfred 14, 45, 49–56, 75, 89, 103, 109, 114, 133, 139, 160, 164, 168, 175
Hitchcock and the Methods of Suspense 109
Hitler, Adolf 13, 29, 35, 38, 133, 137, 180
Hodiak, John 99, 107–108, 111, 113–114, 182
Hoffenstein, Samuel 182
Hoffman, Dustin 58, 75, 97
Holland, Marty 190
Hollywood Cavalcade 165, 190
Hollywood Nets 109
Hombre 142
The Homecoming 114
Hoover, Herbert 18
Hoover, J. Edgar 98
Hopkins, Miriam 46
Hopper, Edward 125
Hordern, Michael 144
Horner, Harry 75
The Hound of the Baskervilles 83
The House Across the Street 102
House of Horrors 38
The House on 92nd Street 98–99

Houseman, John 103
Howard, Leslie 8, 158
Howard, Trevor 137
Hughes, Howard 33, 129
Humberstone, H. Bruce 97
Humphrey, Hubert 32
Humphrey, Maude 8
Hunt, Helen 64, 100
Hurry Sundown 188
The Hustler 98
Huston, John 1, 10, 12, 15–16, 19–20, 24, 27–28, 31, 72, 116
Huston, Virginia 123
Hutchinson, Josephine 110

I Am a Camera 134
I Am a Fugitive from a Chain Gang 16–17
I Confess 75
I Spy 110
I Wake Up Screaming 97, 152
Ibsen, Henrik 71
Idiot's Delight 113
I'm No Angel 6
Images 71–72
Impact 162–164, 170
In Old Chicago 190
Indrisano, Johnny 178
The Informer 155
Inge, William 142
Isherwood, Christopher 133–134
It Happened One Night 62
It Takes a Thief 66
It's a Wonderful Life 31, 65, 184

Jackson, Charles 2, 169–170
Jackson, Glenda 58
Jane Eyre 34
Jannings, Emil 133
The Jazz Singer 18
Jean, Gloria 166
Jezebel 10
Johnny Angel 97
Johnny Belinda 173
Johnny Guitar 177
Johnny O'Clock 159
Johnson, Nunnally 22, 181
Johnson, Rita 173–174
Jolson, Al 18, 189
Joplin, Janis 169
Juarez 10
Julia 45, 76, 100
Junior Miss 124
Just Off Broadway 98

Kalb, Bernard 32
Kalb, Martin 32

Kanin, Fay 62
Kanin, Michael 62
Kantor, MacKinlay 113
Kazan, Elia 142
Keeler, Ruby 124
Kelly, Grace 53–55, 175
Kendall, Robert 155–156, 180, 184–186, 197
Kennedy, Arthur 15, 165
Kennedy, Douglas 126
Kennedy, John F. 33
Key Largo 10, 128, 159
Khrushchev, Nikita 35
Kilbride, Percy 183–184
Kiley, Richard 33
The Killers (1946) 39, 41–42, 92–93, 158, 160–161
The Killing 160
The Killing of Sister George 71
King, Henry 114
King of Burlesque 190
Kiss of Death 109
Kiss Tomorrow Goodbye: The Barbara Payton Story 155
Klute 75–76
Knott, Frederick 175
Kopay, David 91
Korda, Alexander 137
Kortner, Fritz 110
Koster, Henry 194
Kraft Suspense Theater 67
Kramer, Stanley 18
Krasker, Robert 137, 139
Kruger, Otto 89
Kubrick, Stanley 160
Kurnitz, Harry 140

Ladd, Alan 23, 30, 62, 103–104, 113–116, 171
The Lady from Shanghai 64
Lady in the Lake 64–65, 84, 91–96, 99–100, 103, 120, 130
Lake, Veronica 23, 104, 115, 171
Lamarr, Hedy 39
Lambert, Christopher 133
Lancaster, Burt 37, 39–44, 63–64, 67, 75, 92, 144, 154, 194
Lanchester, Elsa 174
Landis, Carole 97
Lang, Fritz 2, 96, 133–135, 149, 151, 154, 165, 168, 176–177, 179
Lange, Jessica 75
Lasker, Edward 108
The Last Tycoon 57
Laszlo, Ernest 96
Laughton, Charles 155, 162, 173–174

Laura 3, 12, 114, 181–182, 186–187
The Lavender Hill Mob 71
Lawman 23
Lawrence, T.E. 104–106
Lawrence of Arabia 105
The Lawrence Welk Show 2
Lean, David 105–106, 194
Leave Her to Heaven 129
le Carré, John (also David John Moore Cornwell) 141, 143–144
Lee, Christopher 83
Lee, Peggy 189
Leeds, Lila 101–102
Leigh, Vivien 7
Leonard, Sheldon 110
LeRoy, Mervyn 5–6, 11, 16–17, 114
Leslie, Joan 14
The Letter 130
Lewis, Al 66
Lewis, Joseph H. 108
Lewton, Val 38
The Life and Times of Judge Roy Bean 75
Life with Father 100
Lifeboat 114
Lillian Russell 188, 190
Lillies of the Field 76
Lincoln, Abraham 21
The Lineup 99
Little, Jack 101
Little Caesar 11–12, 16–17
The Little Foxes 176
A Little Night Music 197–198
The Little Sister 84
Litvak, Anatole 98
Logan's Run 24
Lombard, Carole 60
The Long Goodbye 84
Look Back in Anger 72, 142–143
Lorre, Peter 26–27, 134–135, 164, 176–178
Losey, Joseph 96
The Lost Weekend 2, 115, 167, 169–175, 192
Love Story 175
Lovers and Other Strangers 76
Lovsky, Celia 136–137
Loy, Myrna 30–31
Lubin, Arthur 162
Luce, Clare Boothe 181
Lukas, Paul 46
Lumet, Sidney 139
Lunt, Alfred 159
Lupino, Ida 15–16, 132
Lupino, Stanley 15

Lyndon, Barre 98
Lyon, Sue 139

M (1931 version) 96, 134–136, 154, 165, 168, 176–177
M (1951 version) 96
MacArthur, Douglas 18, 32
Macbeth 38
MacDonald, Jeanette 31
MacLaine, Shirley 46
MacLane, Barton 14, 27
MacMurray, Fred 40, 44, 124, 128, 167
MacPherson, Aimee Semple 58
Macready, George 174
MacShane, Frank 96
The Magnificent Ambersons 118, 125
Main, Marjorie 183
Mainwaring, Daniel (also Geoffrey Homes) 122–123
Malden, Karl 99
Mallinson, Rory 120
Malone, Dorothy 87
The Maltese Falcon 1, 10, 14, 16, 20–29, 34, 85, 89–90, 152
Mamoulian, Rouben 82, 181
The Man Between 139–140
The Man from U.N.C.L.E. 35
The Man I Love 132
Man of La Mancha 33
The Man Who Wouldn't Die 98
Mankiewicz, Joseph 108, 113–114
Mann, Heinrich 133
Mansfield, Jayne 130
March, Fredric 113
Margin for Error 181
The Mark of Zorro 82
Marlowe, Christopher 38, 71
Marshall, George 104
Marshall, Herbert 194
Martin, Tony 188
Marvin, Lee 177
Marx, Karl 147
Mary Poppins 33
Mason, James 92, 139–141
Mature, Victor 39, 97
Maugham, W. Somerset 50, 84, 104, 130, 141
Mayer, Louis B. 5, 31, 93
Mayo, Archie 8–9
Mays, Willie 91
Mazurki, Mike 88–89, 111, 178
McCarey, Leo 168
McCarthy, Joseph 32, 35
McCoy, Horace 2, 57–60, 67–68, 78, 96

McCrea, Joel 46
McGhee, George 189–190
McGilligan, Patrick 176
McGraw, Charles 161, 175
McKelvy, Frank 75
McLaglen, Victor 155
Meet Mr. McNulty 175
Meisner, Sanford 64, 67
A Memorial of Roger Shaw, 1594–1661 56
Mercer, Johnny 124
Meredith, Burgess 58
Metropolis 2
Midnight Cowboy 58
Mildred Pierce 131
Milland, Ray 115, 169–173, 175
Mills, John 71
Mind at the End of Its Tether 105
Ministry of Fear 173, 177
Minnelli, Vincent 18, 134
Miranda, Aurora 151
Miranda, Carmen 151
Mission: Impossible 76
Mitchell, Thomas 129, 166
Mitchum, Robert 39–40, 42, 100–102, 108–109, 123, 128–129, 178, 194, 197
Monroe, Marilyn 72–73
Montgomery, Elizabeth 76–77
Montgomery, Robert 64, 77, 91–95, 97, 100–101, 103, 120, 159
Moore, Diane 24
Moore, Robin 76
Moorehead, Agnes 116–117, 124–125, 128–129, 197
Morell, Andre 83
Morley, Robert 38
Morris, Oswald 148
Mostel, Zero 141
Muller, Eddie 1, 128–130, 149, 162, 168, 192
Muni, Paul 10, 16, 34, 110
The Munsters 66
Murder, My Sweet 26, 88–90, 111, 115, 122, 178, 192
Murnau, F.W. 133
Mutiny on the Bounty 158

Nabokov, Vladimir 139
Napier, Alan 37–38, 40–41, 177
The Narrow Margin 175
Neal, Tom 155–158
Neame, Ronald 71
Neff, Hildegard 140
Negulesco, Jean 173

Neill, Roy William 177
The New Adventures of Tarzan 131
Newman, Paul 139, 142–143
Newton, Robert 139
Nicholson, Arthur 186–189
Nicholson, Jack 100
Night and the City 89
Nightfall 131
Niven, David 64
Nixon, Richard 32–33, 35
No Down Payment 142
Nobody Loves an Albatross 76
Nolan, Lloyd 65, 96–100, 106, 112–113
Nolan, William 24–25, 30, 46
North by Northwest 139
Notorious 50, 109
Nova, Lou 110–111
Novak, Kim 52–53
Nye, Clement D. 101

Oberon, Merle 34, 46
O'Brien, Edmond 162
Odd Man Out, 139
Odets, Clifford 64, 142
O'Donnell, Judson 157
O'Dowd, John 156–157
O'Hara, John 40
O'Keefe, Dennis 149, 162
Olds, Robin 162
Oliver! 148
On Golden Pond 76
O'Neill, Barbara 194
O'Neill, Eugene 158
O'Neill, Ryan 175
Only Victims 35
Ophuls, Max 139
Ormonda, Czenzi 50
Osborne, John 142
O'Sullivan, Maureen 173
O'Toole, Peter 105
Out of the Past, 39, 101, 109, 122–123, 192
The Outsider 103–105

Pabst, G.W. 133
Page, Geraldine 58
Pal, George 94
Parker, Al 72
Parnassus, George 111
Patton, George 18
Paxton, John 88–89, 122
Payne, John 185
Payton, Barbara 155, 157–158
Payton, John Lee 157
Peck, Gregory 47, 97, 109
Peckinpah, Sam 76

Pedi, Tom 41
Perelman, S.J. 76
Perry Mason 33
Peters, Jean 33
The Petrified Forest 8–9, 20, 117
Phantom Lady 15, 27, 39, 133, 149–154, 158–166, 169, 177
Phillips, John 177
Pickup on South Street 33
Picnic 142
The Pied Piper 181
Pinkerton, Allan 21
Pitfall 62
A Place in the Sun 93, 107
Planer, Fritz 43
Playback 84
Poe, Edgar Allan 48
Poe, James 67, 72, 75–76
Poitier, Sidney 76, 142
Polanski, Roman 91
Pollack, Sydney 2, 59, 67–68, 75
Polonsky, Abraham 160
Possessed 129
The Postman Always Rings Twice 92, 100, 195
Powell, Dick 17, 58, 62, 88, 90, 122, 124, 129
Powell, Dick, Jr. 59
Powell, William 30–31
Power, Tyrone 82, 185, 189
Powers, Mala 65
Powers, Stefanie 66
Preminger, Markus 180
Preminger, Otto 3, 114, 137, 180–184, 187–188, 194–196
Presnell, Robert, Jr. 40–41
Price, Vincent 187
Pursued 129
Pygmalion 158

Raft, George 11, 23, 27, 30, 162
Raines, Ella 149, 152, 161–166, 169–170
Rains, Claude 92, 109
Raksin, David 182, 186
Rappe, Virginia 23
Rathbone, Basil 81–83, 177
Rawhide 23
Ray, Nicholas 175
Raymond, Paula 65
The Razor's Edge 114
Ready, Willing and Able 124
Reagan, Ronald 9, 92
Rear Window 49, 53–55, 153
The Reckless Moment 139–140
Red Harvest 23
Redford, Robert 75

Reed, Carol 137–140
Reefer Madness 102
The Reincarnation of Peter Proud 75
Reiner, Rob 85
Reinhardt, Elizabeth 182
Reinhardt, Max 180
Reisch, Walter 169
Revere, Anne 187, 191
Reynolds, Marjorie 173
Richardson, Tony 72, 142–143
Ride the Pink Horse 64, 92, 159
Ridgely, John 87
Ritt, Martin 141–142, 145
Ritter, Thelma 54
Rivkin, Allen 28
Robards, Jason, Jr. 45, 76
The Robe 194
Roberts, Roy 160
Robinson, Edward G. 10–11, 27, 135, 154, 159, 176
Robson, Mark 114
Rockefeller, John D. 16
Rodgers, Richard 188
Rooney, Mickey 1, 5
Roosevelt, Franklin Delano 1, 16–18, 46, 113
Roosevelt and Hopkins 113
Rope 175
Rose of Washington Square 186, 189–190
Rosenberg, Ethel 34
Rosenberg, Julius 34
Rosenberg, Meta 40
Rossen, Robert 98
Roughead, William 46
Rozsa, Miklos 172
Russell, Gail 175
Russell, John L. 65
Russell, Rosalind 6
Ryan, Kathleen 139
Ryan, Robert 33
Ryan, Sylvester 34
Saint, Eva Marie 139

Sally, Irene and Mary 190
Salt, Waldo 58
Sandburg, Carl 65
Sanders, George 162
San Francisco 189
San Francisco Beat 99
Sarrazin, Michael 59, 68–69, 75
Sartre, Jean-Paul 7, 48, 87, 128, 197
Satan Met a Lady 20
Savage, Ann 157, 192
Sawyer, Diane 68

Sayers, Dorothy 80
Scarlet Street 135, 154, 176–177
Schenck, Joseph 180
Schlesinger, John 58
Schmidt, Kim 76
Schoenfeld, Bernard 149, 151
Schwarzenegger, Arnold 85
Scott, Adrian 122
Scott, Lizabeth 62, 97, 101, 108
Scott, Randolph 161
Scott, Zachary 131
Seaton, George 62
Seitz, John F. 169
Sellers, Peter 139
Selznick, David 109, 137
Separate Tables 64
Sergeant York 10
The Setup 93
Seven Days to Noon 143
Seven Pillars of Wisdom 105
Shadow of a Doubt 45, 49, 160
Shakespeare, William 38, 71, 80, 158, 170
Shariff, Omar 23, 130
Shaw, Chris 56
Shaw, George Bernard 71, 105–106, 158
Shaw, Capt. Joseph 2, 7, 29, 47–50, 53, 56, 57, 84–85
Shaw, Robert 56
She Done Him Wrong 6
Sheridan, Ann 130
Sherriff, R.C. 139
Sherwood, Robert 8, 20, 46, 113, 117
Shipman, David 189
Shirley, Anne 122
Shoot the Piano Player 130
Short, Elizabeth 64
Siegel, Bugsy 106
Siegel, Don, 101
Simmons, Dick 65, 95
Simmons, Jean 100, 194, 196–198
The Simple Art of Murder 78–81
Sinatra, Frank 189
Siodmak, Robert 27, 38, 43, 133, 149, 151, 153–154, 158, 160, 164, 166, 177, 180, 192
Sister Carrie 107
Smith, C. Aubrey 166
Smith, Kate 186
Sometimes a Great Notion 75
Somewhere in the Night 99, 108–109, 111, 113–115, 121
Sondheim, Stephen 197
A Song to Remember 34, 172

Spade, John 25
Sparks, Ned 17
Spellbound 50, 172
Spoto, Donald 49
The Spy Who Came In from the Cold 141–148
Stafford, Jo 124
Stalin, Joseph 35, 140
Stander, Lionel 66
Stanislavski, Constantin 142, 155
Stanwyck, Barbara 40, 128, 161, 166–168
State Fair 188–189
Steele, Bob 87
Steele, Freddie 178–179
Steinbeck, John 114
Steinkamp, Fredric 75
Sternberg, Joseph von 133–134
Stevenson, Adlai 33
Stevenson, Houseley 111, 121
Stevenson, Robert 33
Stevenson, Robert Louis 80
Stewart, James 53, 63, 125, 144, 184–185
Stone, Lewis 1, 5
The Story of G.I. Joe 178
Story of Louis Pasteur 110
Story on Page One 63–64
Stowaway 190
The Stranger 105
Strangers on a Train 49–51, 103, 175
Strassberg, Lee 155
The Stratton Story 144
Street of No Return 131
Street with No Name 99
A Streetcar Named Desire 68
The Streets of San Francisco 99
Streisand, Barbra 23, 75
Sturges, Preston 178
Suchet, David 83
The Summing Up 84
Sunday Bloody Sunday 58
Sunday Dinner for a Soldier 114
Sunset Blvd. 169
Sutherland, Donald 58
The Sweet Ride 75
Swerling, Jo 114
Symons, Julian 29, 35

Tail Spin 190
Tall in the Saddle 162
Talman, William 33
Tarzan the Ape Man 131
Taylor, Laurette 181
Taylor, Robert 94, 97
Taylor, Rod 94

Taylor, Samuel 52
Teacher's Pet 62–63
Temple, Shirley 1, 5
Tension 93
Terry, Phillip 169–170
Thalberg, Irving 7, 57
That Night in Rio 186, 190
That Touch of Mink, 63
Thaw, Harry Kendall 175
Thaw, John 83
There Shall Be No Night 46, 113
These Three 45–46
They Drive by Night 11, 16
They Live by Night 175
They Shoot Horses, Don't They? 2, 57, 59–61, 66–76, 96
The Thin Man 23, 30–31, 78
The Thin Man Films: Murder Over Cocktails 31
The Third Man 137–139
This Gun for Hire 23, 30
Thomas, Dylan 168
Thompson, George 30
Thompson, Robert E. 67–68, 72, 75–76
Three Days of the Condor 75
365 Days in Hollywood 190
Tidyman, Ernest 76
Tierney, Gene 53, 114, 129, 182, 186, 192
Tiffin, Pamela 188
The Time Machine 94
Time to Kill 98
Tin Pan Alley 186
Titanic (1953) 169
To Have and Have Not 116
Tobey, Kenneth 196
Tombes, Andrew 154
Tone, Franchot 153–158, 164, 166, 176
Tonight and Every Night 63
Toomey, Regis 150
Toone, Geoffrey 140
Tootsie 75
Toscanini, Arturo 166
Toth, Andre de 62
Totter, Audrey 65, 92–94, 100–101
Touchdown 131
Tourneur, Jacques 39, 122
Towne, Robert 91
Tranberg, Charles 31, 124–126, 128
The Treasure of Sierra Madre 131
Trent's Last Case 79
Trevor, Claire 97, 122

Trial 114
Trosper, Guy 141, 144
Truffaut, François 130
Truman, Harry 32, 184–185
Tully, Tom 99–100
Tunes of Glory 71
Turner, Lana 92, 114
Tuttle, Frank 23, 30
Twain, Mark 80
20-20 69
The Two Mrs. Carrolls 81

Ulmer, Edgar G. 157
The Unfaithful 130
The Uninvited 38, 175
Ure, Mary 142
Ustinov, Peter 138

Vallee, Rudy 186
Valli, Alida 137
Van Dine, S.S. 30
Van Dyke, W.S. 31
Vane, Sutton 181
Van Eyck, Peter 143
Vaughn, Robert 35
The Verdict 139
Vertigo 49, 51–54
Vickers, Martha 86, 130
Vincent, June 177
The Virginian 23
Vogel, Paul 93–95
Voight, John 58

Wagner, Robert 66
Waiting for Lefty 63
Wald, Jerry 116
Walker, Helen 162
Walker, Robert 51
Wallace, Jean 155
Wallis, Hal 101
Walsh, Raoul 11–13

Walton, Douglas 89
Wanamaker, Sam 145
Warden, Jack 142
Warner, Jack 2, 9–11, 16, 18–19, 46, 116, 123–124, 128
Warren, Dale 79–80
Warren, Earl 22, 27
Watch on the Rhine 46
Watson, Lucile 46
The Way We Were 75
Wayne, John 25, 27, 129, 162
Webb, Clifton 181–182
Week-end in Havana 186
Welch, Raquel 47
Welk, Lawrence 67
Welles, Orson 34, 38, 64, 118, 137
Wellman, William 66
Wells, H.G. 94, 105
Wendkos, Paul 130
Werner, Oskar 146, 148
West, Mae 6
West, Nathanael 57–59
Whately, Kevin 83
White, Stanford 175
Whiting, Barbara 124
Whiting, Richard 124
Whitty, Dame May 166
Widmark, Richard 89, 99, 176
Wild Weed 102
Wilde, Cornell 34
Wilde, Oscar 38, 71
Wilder, Billy 2, 44, 50, 88, 115–116, 122, 137, 149, 167–169, 171–172, 180
Wilder, Gene 76
William, Warren 20
Williams, Ted 41
Wills, Chill 65
Wilson, Colin 103–105
Wilson, Dooley 13

Windsor, Marie 160, 175
Winters, Shelley 134
The Wiz 148
The Wizard of Oz 5–7, 16
Wolfe, Peter 30
Wolfert, Ira 160
The Woman in the Window 154, 176–177
Woman on Pier 13 (also known as *I Married a Communist*) 33–34
Wong, Anna May 164
Wood, Natalie 155–156
Woodbury, Albert 75
Woode, Margo 110
Woodward, Joanne 142
Woolrich, Cornell 7–8, 149, 158, 177
The Wounded and the Slain 131
Wright, Frank Lloyd 43, 114
Wright, Teresa 14
Wyatt, Jane 62
Wyler, William 10, 46, 112–113, 130
Wyman, Jane 115, 169–170

York, Dick 125
York, Susannah 71–73, 75, 77
Young, Alan 94
Young, Clifton 117, 129
Young, Elaine 77
Young, Gig 57, 61–67, 69–70, 75–77
Young, Perry Dean 91
Young, Robert 125
You're a Sweetheart 190
You're in the Army Now 61

Zanuck, Darryl F. 3, 114, 180–182, 184–188
Zinneman, Fred 45

www.ingramcontent.com/pod-product-compliance
Lightning Source LLC
Chambersburg PA
CBHW081555300426
44116CB00015B/2889